TYPOLOGICAL STUDIES IN NEGATION

Edited by

PETER KAHREL

RENÉ VAN DEN BERG

JOHN BENJAMINS PUBLISHING COMPANY
Amsterdam/Philadelphia

1994

Library of Congress Cataloging-in-Publication Data

Typological studies in negation / edited by Peter Kahrel, René van den Berg.
   p.   cm. -- (Typological studies in language, ISSN 0167-7373; v. 29)
  Contributions on aspects of negation of sixteen languages.
  Includes bibliographical references and index.
  1. Grammar, Comparative and general--Negatives. 2. Typology (Linguistics) I. Kahrel,
Peter. II. Berg, René van den. III. Series.
P299.N4T97   1993
415--dc20   93-5763
ISBN 90 272 2919 8 (hb.) / 90 272 2920 1 (pb.) (European; alk. paper)   CIP
ISBN 1-55619-422-6 (hb.) / 1-55619-423-4 (pb.) (U.S.; alk. paper)

John Benjamins Publishing Co. · P.O. Box 75577 · 1070 AN Amsterdam · The Netherlands
John Benjamins North America · 821 Bethlehem Pike · Philadelphia, PA 19118 · USA

Contents

Contents

Introduction

Peter Kahrel

This book is a collection of studies of negation in sixteen languages. It offers detailed descriptions of aspects of negation and relates the encountered features and properties of negative utterances to previous cross-linguistic characterizations of this phenomenon.

To date, the five most important typological treatments of aspects of negation are Dahl (1979), Payne (1985), Dryer (1989), Croft (1991) and Bernini and Ramat (1992). Dahl gives a statistical analysis of the expression of sentential negation on the basis of a sample of 240 languages. Payne (1985) presents an overview of the various forms used to express negation across languages. Although his study is not based on an explicit sample of languages, he manages to cover an impressive array of negative constructions. Dryer's (1989) study of negation is in many ways comparable with Dahl's in that it investigates the position of the verbal negative element with respect to major syntactic constituents in the clause (verb, subject, direct and indirect object). Croft, provides an interesting analysis of a process by which negative elements in a language appear to cycle from verbal negators to existential negative constructions. (Croft's study appeared when this book was in its final stages of completion. Therefore his observations are not reviewed by any of the authors.) Finally, Bernini and Ramat (1992) present a detailed overview of various aspects of negation in the languages of Europe.

This book adds to our knowledge of negation in two significant ways. Firstly, it broadens our knowledge of syntactic and semantic aspects of negation by providing data on some languages that were hitherto undescribed or hardly described. Secondly, it deepens our understanding of a number of semantic and pragmatic characterizations of negation. The typological studies mentioned above all deal with syntactic aspects of negation. Dahl and Dryer for example, discuss the categorical status and the position of negative morphemes. By contrast, the articles in this book treat issues such as the expression of negative indefinites; the interaction of negation and quantifiers; matters pertaining to scope of negation; and the pragmatic or semantic factors that play a role in the use of one form of negation as opposed to another if a language has several forms of negation at its disposal.

The articles in this book were prepared on the basis of a questionnaire that was by the editors. While working with the questionnaire, the authors were of course at liberty – and have taken that liberty – to dismiss questions that were not relevant for their language, or conversely to elaborate on points of special interest. Some of the questions, especially those pertainong to complex semantic issues, have been dealt with by only a subset of the authors. For example, the questions concerning the interaction of negation and specific/non-specific indefinites remained unanswered in a number of cases. The issue can be illustrated with the aid of the following English examples:

(1)   a. He did not buy a book.
       b. He did not buy any book.

Many native speakers of English or languages that show similar phenomena (such as Dutch and German) find it difficult to interpret sentences like (1a). And indeed in the literature there is no consensus about the status of such sentences, nor about their interpretation; see for example the discussions in Givón (1984) and Horn (1989, Chapter 6). When dealing with issues such as these, field workers will often be confronted by speakers who flatly deny that sentences like (1a) occur in their language, or by conflicting judgements.

Most of the languages included in this volume have not featured prominently in the linguistic literature: Waorani, Nadëb, Tuyuca, Wayampi, Lewo, Zazaki, Sentani, Berbice Dutch and Babole. The four languages that are better known are Hungarian, Mandarin Chinese, Turkish and Evenki. We feel justified in including these languages in the present collection since only the standard forms of negation that they manifest, of the type *John is not ill*, are well-known, while more complicated issues such as the interaction of negation and quantifiers are treated in much less detail. In fact, in the case of Hungarian and Turkish, the negation system has never been adeqautely described. Though the same cannot be said of Mandarin Chinese, Wiedehof offers a number of new insights; what is of special interest is that all his examples are taken from live recordings. And finally, Evenki, though well known in the former Soviet Union, is almost entirely unknown outside of it.

The languages included in this volume cover a large part of the globe and represent nine language phyla. A full list of languages with genetic affiliations is included in the appendix. As can be seen, some phyla are not represented at all, while other phyla, most notably the Amerindian languages, are represented by more than one language. This situation is mainly due to the response we received to calls for a paper. While the original set of manuscripts included a wider variety of languages, the current list is the result of cancellations and a selection procedure.

The editors wish to thank the series editor, T. Givón, and Barbara Wiese-mann for reading the manuscript and making suggestions that led to improvements in the final text.

References

Bernini, G. and P. Ramat (1992). *La frase negativa nelle lingue d'Europa*. Bologna: Il Mulino.

Croft, W. (1991). 'The evolution of negation.' *Journal of Linguistics* 27, 1-27.

Dahl, Ö. (1979). 'Typology of sentence negation.' *Linguistics* 17, 1/2, 79-106.

Dryer, M. S. (1989). *Universals of negative position*. In: E. Moravcsik, J. Wirth and M. Hammond (eds), *Studies in syntactic typology*. Amsterdam: John Benjamins. 93-124.

Givón, T. (1984). *Syntax. A functional typological introduction*. Amsterdam: Benjamins.

Horn, L. (1989). *A natural history of negation*. Chicago and London: The University of Chicago Press.

Payne, J. R. (1985). 'Negation.' In: T. Shopen ed., *Language typology and syntactic description*, Vol. I (*Clause structure*), 197-242. Cambridge: Cambridge University Press.

Evenki

Igor Nedyalkov

1 Introduction

Evenki is one of the ten Manchu-Tungusic languages (the other languages in this group being Even, Negidal, Solon, Nanai, Uil'ta, Ulcha, Orochi, Udeghe and Manchu); together with the Turkic and the Mongolian languages, these languages belong to the Altaic phylum. Evenki is spoken in a vast area in Siberia, ranging from the Ob and Yenisey regions in the West to the shores and the Okhotskoye Sea and Sakhalin in the East; and from the Arctic area in the North to the Amur river in the South. There are also Evenks in China. There are about 29,000 Evenks, most of whom live in the Far East of the Soviet Union and in Yakutia – it may be fair to say that Evenki has the fewest speakers per square kilometer. The so-called Southern dialects are spoken in the Evenki National District in the Krasnoyarsk region (an area approximately one and a half times the size of France), and these dialects are considered to be 'standard' Evenki.

In total there are about fifty dialects, most of which are mutually intelligible: syntactically the dialects are the same, while there are some lexical and phonological differences. The majority of the Evenks are at least bi-lingual, Russian being the second language, while many also speak Yakut, Even, Dolgan, or Nanai. Young Evenks as a rule learn Russian as their first language – Evenki is generally not learnt until the age of four, when children start going to school.

Since the Evenki dialects resemble each other so closely syntactically, the description of Evenki negation in this paper is valid for all dialects. I will use the spelling conventions prevalent in the Southern dialects.

2 General typological information

Word order in Evenki in neutral indicative clauses is SOV (see 4 and 5), though other word order variants are also possible under certain contextual conditions. An attribute almost always precedes the head noun. There are almost no complex sentences with two finite verb forms. In such cases, different non-finite (converbal or participial) verb forms are used.

In question word questions, the question word is generally placed at the beginning of the clause, as in (1). In yes-no questions, the question particle is placed after the questioned word, see (2).

(1)   Okin nuŋan eme-che-n?
       when 3Sg   come-Past-3Sg
       'When did s/he come?'

(2)   Nuŋan eme-che-n-ŋu,   e-che-n-ŋu?
       3Sg   come-Past-3Sg-Q   Neg-Past-3Sg-Q
       'Did s/he come, or not?'

In noun phrases adjectives, demonstratives, and numerals precede the head noun. Relative clauses formed by means of participles may precede or follow the head noun. This depends on the length of the relative clause: if it is long – more than two words – it almost always follows the head noun. Comparative constructions are formed by means of the suffix *tmar/dimar*, which is added to the adjective, while the standard of comparison is marked by the ablative case; see (3):

(3)   Tar purta minŋi-duk aya-tmar.
       that knife my-Abl   good-Comp
       'That knife is better than mine.'

2.1 Preview of negation in Evenki

There are two major ways of expressing negation in Evenki: (a) by means of the conjugated negative auxiliary verb -*e* 'not to ...' (see 4b), and (b) with the negative noun *āchin* 'no' (see 5b).

(4)   a. Nuŋan min-du purta-va bū-che-n.
          he   I-Dat knife-Acc give-past-3Sg
          'He gave me the knife.'

       b. Nuŋan min-du purta-va e-che-n   bū-re.
          he   I-Dat knife-Acc Neg-Past-3Sg give-Ffnlv
          'He did not give me the knife.'

(5)   a. Min-du purta   bi-si-n.
          I-Dat knife-Nom   be-Pres-3Sg
          'I have a knife.' (Lit: to-me knife is)

       b. Min-du purta   āchin.
          I-Dat knife-Nom   Neg
          'I have no knife/I have not got the knife.'

Peripheral means of expressing negation include negative modal verbs with the meaning 'not to be able', 'not to want', 'not to dare', etc. (see section 9). In Evenki there are no inherently negative particles, negative prefixes or suffixes, nor negative quantifiers or negative adverbs. There are no negative forms of either quantifiers or adverbs, such as *nothing* or *not always*. In all such cases ordinary negative constructions are employed including the negative verb *e-* and either an indefinite pronoun or an adverb with a positive meaning:

(6) a. Nuŋan okin-da ele eme-vki.
        he   always here come-HabPart
        'He always comes here.'

     b. Nuŋan okin-da ele e-vki   eme-re.
        he   always here Neg-HabPart come-Ffnlv
        'He never comes here.'

2.2 Note on morphology

In order to understand the language material quoted in the paper, the reader may need the following information, which is presented in a rather simplified way.

2.2.1 Noun morphology

The nominal parts of speech, including participles, can take the case endings listed in table 1 on the next page.

The plural marker is *l/r* (the latter variant is used only after stem final *n*; in this case the stem final *n* is omitted); in participles only *l* is used. Relative possessive suffixes are *vi/mi* (singular) and *var/mar* (plural). Suffixes of personal possession – which are homophonous with person-number endings of verbal tense forms in *cha* (past tense), *ŋki* (past habitual) and *d'aŋa* (future) – are shown in table 2.

Table 1. Case forms and functions.

Case	Form	Function
nominative	ø	Subject and possessor in possessive NP
accusative	*va/ve/vo* *ma/me/mo* (after stem final *n*)	direct object

Table 1. Case forms and functions.

Case	Form	Function
dative	du/tu	indirect object adverbial modifiers of place agent in passive
locative	la/dula/tula	final point of motion or action
directive	tki/tiki	object to which the action or motion is aimed
ablative	duk/tuk	point of departure from which an action proceeds
comitative	nun	person with whom or the object with which an action is performed
instrumental	t/di	instrument of an action
prolative	li/duli	place through which the motion goes on object which is spoken about
indefinite ac- cusative	a/ya/o/yo/ye	indefinite object part of an object nouns used with āchin 'no'
elative	git	the place from which an action proceeds

Table 2. Nominal suffixes of personal possession

	Singular	Plural
1st person	-v 'my'	-vun (exclusive) -t/-p (incusive)
2nd person	-s 'thy'	-sun 'your'
3rd person	-n 'his/her/its'	-tin 'their'

2.2.2 Verb morphology

There are seven simple tenses, which fall into two groups. In the first group the marker of each tense recurs in all the seven personal forms without change (the 1st person plural has an inclusive and an exclusive form); here belong three tenses with the following markers: *chV* (the value of V is determined by vowel harmony) in the past tense; *ŋki* in the past habitual; *d'VŋV* in the future. Finite verb forms with the listed tense suffixes take person-number endings of subject agreement which coincide with those in table 7. Example:

(7) Loko-cho-s.
hung-thou
'You hung.'

In the second type, which consists of four tenses, the tense marker is either omitted or loses the component *ra/re/ro* in the 1st and the 2nd person singular; the markers here are *d'VrV* in the present tense, *rV* (also *la/ta/na/a* plus vowel harmony variants – consonant variants are determined by the preceding consonants) in the non-future tense, *d'V* in the near future tense or *d'VllV* in the future inchoative tense. Person-number endings of subject agreement for these four tense forms are shown in table 3.

Table 3. Subject agreement suffixes for tense forms in *ra*, *d'a* and *d'alla*

Person	Singular	Plural
1	*-m*	*-v* (exclusive)
		-p (inclusive)
2	*-nni*	*-s*
3	*-n*	*ø* (singular)
		-l (plural)

Table 4. Aspect markers

-l	inchoative
kta	distributive
-d'a	imperfective
-t/chi	durative
ŋna	habitual
van/vat	iterative
sin/sn/s	semelfactive
cha/che	stative
malcha	instantaneous

Table 5. Valency/voice markers

vkan, -v	causative
v/p/mu, rga	decausative
v/p/mu	passive
ldi	sociative
mat/mach	reciprocal

Table 6. Modality markers

mu	want
ssa	try
na	go

Table 7. Evaluation markers

kakun/kakut	'very much'
gachin/gechin	'as if', 'resembling' (may be added both to nominal and verbal forms)
mati/meti	'not even' (used as a rule in negative sentences)

The suffixes of non-indicative moods and of non-finite forms are given in sections 3.3.2.3 and 3.3.2.4.

3 Expression of standard negation

The expression of standard negation, i.e. negation in a simple clause containing a verb, is formed according to the following model:

(8)   conjugated form of the negative verb *e-* 'not to' +
       fixed form of the negated lexical verb (FFNLV) with the suffix *-ra* (or its variants)

Variants of the suffix *ra* forming FFNLV are determined by vowel harmony and/or the final consonant of a verbal stem. Taking into consideration these factors the suffix *ra* has fifteen variants:

ra/re/ro	when the stem ends in a vowel;
ta/te/to	when the stem ends in *k,s,t* or *p*;
la/le/lo	when the stem ends in *l*;
na/ne/no	when the stem ends in *ŋ* or *m*;
a/e/o	when the stem ends in *n*

The variant of the FFNLV marker always coincides with the variant of the non-future tense suffix of the 3rd person plural of the same verb; compare the following examples:

(9) a. Nuŋartin   d'u-va   is-ta-ø.
         they   house-Acc reach-NonFut-3Pl
         'They reached the house.'

     b. Nuŋartin   d'u-va   e-che-tin   is-ta.
         they   house-Acc Neg-reach-3Pl reach-Ffnlv
         'They did not reach the house.'

The negated lexical verb is not inflected as to (a) person-number distinctions
of the subject, and (b) mood, tense and finite-non-finite distinctions of the
verb. It may, however, take different markers of valence, voice, aspect,
modality and/or evaluation, but after any possible combination of the above
mentioned categories only the suffix *ra* (or one of its variants) may follow.
Thus, the FFNLV is homonymous with the non-future tense form 3rd person
plural of the same verb. This form is not used in any other contexts.

The only verb which has two negated forms is the verb *bi-* 'be'. If it is used
with the lexical meaning 'be situated', 'live', then its FFNLV is formed
canonically, i.e. by means of the suffix *re*; compare the following example:

(10) a. Er   beye tadu   bi-d'e-re-n.
         this man there be-Imp-NonFut-3Sg
         'This man lives there.'

     b. Er   beye tadu   e-si-n   bi-re   // bi-d'e-re
         this man there Neg-Pres-3Sg be-Ffnlv // be-Imp-Ffnlv
         'This man does not live there.'

If the verb *bi-* 'be' is used in the function of a copula, then its fixed form is
formed by means of the suffix *si*, homonymous with the present tense
marker of the negative verb *e-*:

(11) a. Bi beyumimni   bi-si-m.
         I hunter   be-Pres-1Sg
         'I am a hunter.'

     b. Bi e-si-m   beyumimni bi-si (*bi-d'e-si)
         I Neg-Pres-1Sg   hunter   be-FFNCopula
         'I am not a hunter.'

If an NP is used in the function of a predicate, then the Evenki sentence
always has the copula *bi-*:

(12) a. Tar   mō   d'agda   bi-si-n.
         that tree pine-tree be-Pres-3Sg
         'That tree is a pine tree.'

b. Tar mō e-che   d'agda   bi-si.
   that tree Neg-Past pine-tree be-FFNCopula
   'That tree is not a pine tree.'

The copula in the present tense form 3rd person singular (as in sentences like 12a), may be deleted, but only in positive clauses, and never in negative clauses.

3.1 The position of the negative verb *e-* and a FFNLV in a sentence

The predominant position of the components of the analytical negative form is presented in examples (4b), (6b) and (9b), where the negative verb immediately precedes the FFNLV. The former may also be separated from the latter by either objects or adverbials, as in (13) and (14):

(13) Eveŋki-l e-ŋki-tin   utele   gule-l-ve   ō-ra.
      Evenk-Pl Neg-HabPast-3Pl formerly house-Pl-Acc make-Ffnlv
      'The Evenks did not build houses previously.'

(14) E-kel   bu eme-ne-ve-vun   d'u-la-vi
      Neg-Imper:2Sg   we come-part-Acc-1PlPoss house-Loc-RelPoss
      ulguchen-e.
      tell-Ffnlv
      'Don't tell that we came home.'

In emotive sentences a FFNLV may precede the conjugated form of the negative *e-*:

(15) Nuŋan dukuvun-ma duku-mati-re   e-che-n.
      he   letter-Acc write-Eval-Ffnlv Neg-Past-3Sg
      'He did not even write a letter (as he was supposed to).'

(16) Nuŋan soŋo-ro   e-che-n   – ekun bi-d'e-n   soŋo-n?
      he   weep-Ffnlv Neg-Past-3Sg   what be-Fut-3Sg weep-Nmr
      'He did not cry – what's the use of crying?'

3.2 Functions of the negative verb *e-*

The negative verb *e-* has only one function: the expression of negation. It can negate actions, states, qualities and properties, but not possession which, when negated, is expressed by means of the negative noun *āchin* (see section 4). The negative verb *e-* is predominantly used as an auxiliary verb, i.e. with the lexical element expressed by either a verb or a nominal. Only rarely will the verb *e-* be used independently: either in the meanings 'not to be', 'not to take place' (see 3.7), or in one-word negative answers (see section 5).

Depending on the part of speech of the lexical element involved, the following types of negative forms may be distinguished:

- Verbal negative forms (section 3.3).
- Nominal negative forms, including negation of nouns, adjectives and pronouns (section 3.4).
- Adverbial negative forms (sections 3.5 and 3.6).

3.3 Negative forms of the verb

Conjugated forms of the negative verb *e-* may be either finite or non-finite. The finite forms include indicative and non-indicative mood forms, the non-finite ones participial and converbal forms. The indicative mood forms include personal (tense) and impersonal (modal) verb forms. The non-indicative mood forms of the verb *e-* include its imperative, subjunctive, debitive and suppositional forms. The majority of finite and non-finite forms of the verb *e-* take person-number endings which mark the person and number of either the subject of the clause or the agent/possessor of the possessive construction. The negated form of the lexical verb may take the suffixes of valence, voice, aspect, modality, and evaluation. Thus, the negative complex consisting of the conjugated verb *e-* plus negated lexical verb may involve almost any morphological marker of Evenki verbal morphology. The distribution of grammatical categories over the negative verb and the negated lexical verb is shown in table 8. The table shows that all the derivational categories (valence, voice, aspect, evaluation), with the exception of the aspectual iterative suffix *ŋne*, are marked in the negated lexical verb, while inflectional categories, e.g. tense, mood, and agreement, are marked on the conjugated form of *e-*. We will start with the analysis of inflectional possibilities of the negated lexical verb, since its form is the same for all forms of *e-*, both finite and non-finite, indicative and non-indicative, etc.

3.3.1 Inflectional possibilities of the FFNLV.

The inflectional possibilities are shown in table 8 above, according to which the FFNLV may have the markers of valence, voice, aspect, modality, and evaluation (generally not more than two in one verb form of either one and the same or different categories). In fact, the majority of FFNLVs do not have any additional suffixes except for the suffix -*ra* (or one of its variants) added to the verb root (see examples 4b, 6b, 9b, 13, 14). Nevertheless, both the folklore texts and the oral speech records contain FFNLVs with one, two, and even three suffixes belonging to the above mentioned categories. We will analyse them in the order given in table 8.

Table 8. Distribution of grammatical categories over the negative verb *e*- and the FFNLV in *ra* (or its variant)

The negative verb *e*-			The negated lexical verb
Finite forms			1. Valence (causative, decausative)
Indicative	Non-indicative	Non-finite	2. Voice (passive, sociative, reciprocal)
Personal (tense) vs Impersonal (modal)	(imperative, subjunctive, debitive, suppositional)	(participles and con- verbs)	3. Aspect (imperfective, inchoative, iterative, habitual, semelfactive, distrib- utive, etc.)
			4. Modality (volitive, conative, departure)
Aspectual iterative suffix *ŋne* Marker of resemblance *gechin* Person-number or possession endings			5. Evaluation (high versus low degree of action; pejorative)

3.3.1.1 Valence markers in the FFNLV

These include the productive causative marker *vkan* (there is also the non-productive *v*), and the decausative markers *v*, *rga*. Causative markers in the FFNLV may express both factitive ('to make someone do something') and permissive ('to let/permit someone do something') meaning; the following examples illustrate, respectively:

(17) Nuŋan tar beye-ve e-vki havali-vkan-e.
      he that man-Acc Neg-HabPart work-Caus-Ffnlv
      'He did not make that man work.'

(18) Horoki Pute-ve e-ŋki-n degili-vkan-e.
      heath:cock Pute-Acc Neg-HabPast-3Sg fly-Caus-Ffnlv
      'The heath-cock did not let Pute fly away.'

Reflexive permissive meaning is expressed if the clause contains reflexive pronouns *mēnmi* 'oneself' or *mērver* 'oneselves'; see (19). While the causative suffix *vkan* is productive, the causative suffix *v* (which is homonymous with the passive and decausative markers) is not productive: it forms about fifty causatives mainly from intransitive verbs of motion and other minor semantic groups. Negative forms of causatives with the suffix *v* can express only contact-factitives, but not permissive, causation, as in (20c).

(19) Nuŋan e-ŋki-n   mēnmi kokchu-la-vi   ugdu-sini-
     he   Neg-HabPast-3Sg oneself sl:bag-Loc-RelPoss get:into-
     vkan-e.
     Sem-Caus-Ffnlv
     'He did not let himself get into the sleeping bag.' or:
     'He made himself not get into the sleeping bag.'

(20) a. Nuŋan suru-che-n.
        he   go:away-past-3Sg
        'He went away.'

     b. Nuŋan nekun-mi   suru-v-che-n.
        he   younger:brother-RelPoss go:away-Caus-Past-3Sg
        'He led away his younger brother.'

     c. Nuŋan nekun-mi   e-che-n   suru-v-re.
        he   younger:brother-RelPoss Neg-Past-3Sg go:away-Caus-Ffnlv
        'He did not lead away his younger brother.'

Decausative markers include the suffix *-v*, which forms about forty decausatives and the suffix *-rga*, which forms not more than twenty decausatives. Both suffixes are thus not at all productive and the decausative forms include such examples as 'break', 'get soaked', etc. The following examples illustrate:

(21) a. Beyetken mokan-me   sukcha-ra-n.
        boy   branch-Acc break-NonFut-3Sg
        'The boy broke the branch.'

     b. Mokan sukcha-v-ra-n.
        branch break-Decaus-NonFut-3Sg
        'The branch broke.'

     c. Mokan e-che-n   sukcha-v-ra.
        branch Neg-Past-3Sg break-Decaus-Ffnlv
        'The branch did not break.'

3.3.1.2 Voice markers in the FFNLV

These include the suffixes of passive *(v/p/mu)*, sociative *(ldi)* and reciprocal voice *(mat/mach)*. The category of voice differs from the category of valence in the following way: the valency marker is obligatory with a given verb whenever there is a need to express a certain meaning/function, whereas the voice marker is optional with a given verb, i.e. there is always a choice between voice forms; for example, a passive clause may be substituted for the corresponding active one with the same meaning, and sociative and reciprocal markers as a rule may be absent, though the sociative or reciprocal meaning may be expressed lexically or emerge from the context.

3.3.1.2.1 Negation of the passive forms

Passive verb forms, both positive and negative, are used in case of object promotion to the syntactic subject position, as in (22b):

(22) a. D'apka   iche-v-d'ere-n.
        shore   see-Pass-Pres-3Sg
        'The shore is seen/The shore can be seen.'

     b. D'apka   e-che-n   iche-v-d'e-re.
        shore   Neg-Past-3Sg   see-Pass-Imp-Ffnlv
        'The shore is/was not seen.'

The agent in passive constructions can be expressed by a noun in the dative case, as in the following example:

(23) Mun-du ulivu-r e-che-l   ō-v-ra.
     we-Dat oar-Pl   Neg-Past-Pl make-Pass-Ffnlv
     'The oars are not (yet) made by us.'

If an object denotes an animate entity, the negative passive construction may acquire a permissive reading, as in the following example:

(24) Chipkan avdun-du-vi   bi-d'e-vki,   avadi-du:da
     sable   burrow-Dat-RelPoss be-Imp-HabPart   any-Dat:Encl

     bulen:du   e-vki   baka-v-ra
     enemy-Dat   Neg-HabPart   find-Pass-Ffnlv

     'A sable lives in his burrow, (and it) does not let any enemy find itself.'
     Lit: 'by any enemy is not usually found'

Passive forms are also used in impersonal negative clauses with negations *e-d'eŋe* 'one musn't', *e-vki* 'one shoun't' and *e-ŋi* 'it is not possible' (see 3.3.2.5).

3.3.1.2.2 Negation of sociative forms

The sociative marker denotes the existence of at least two agents with one and the same role; the syntactic subject may be expressed by a nominal either in the singular, as in the following:

(25) Nuŋan   e-che-n   sun-nun   girku-ldi-d'a-ra.
     he   Neg-Past-3Sg   you-Comit   walk-Soc-Imperf-Ffnlv
     'He did not walk/go with you.'

The sociative marker may express the reciprocal function, i.e. it may denote that two participants have both two semantic roles: agent and object of action:

(26) Bi girki-vi   e-si-m   baka-ldi-ra.
     I   friend-RelPoss   Neg-Pres-1Sg   find-Soc-Ffnlv
     'I did not meet with my friend.'

(27) D'ur beye-l   mēn mēnmer   e-si   iche-ldi-re.
     two   man-Pl   one another Neg-Pres   see-Soc-Ffnlv
     'Two men do not see each other.'

3.3.1.2.3 Negation of reciprocal forms
The reciprocal marker denotes that at least two participants have two symmetrically intersecting semantic roles: those of agent and at the same time of object of the action:

(28) Tar   nekune-sel e-vki-l   ayav-mat-te bi-che-l.
     that   brother-Pl NegHabPart-Pl   love-rec-Ffnlv be-Past-Pl
     'Those brothers did not love each other.'

(29) E-kellu   iche-t-met-te.
     Neg-2PlImper   see-Dur-Rec-Ffnlv
     'Don't look at each other.'

3.3.1.3 Aspect markers in the FFNLV

All aspectual suffixes listed in table 2 may be added to the FFNLV: see (6b) and (25), in which the FFNLV has the imperfective aspect marker *d'a/d'e*, and (29), in which the FFNLV has the durative marker *t*. The habitual marker *ŋna/ŋne* is more often added to the negative verb *e-*, though it may also be added to the FFNLV. Only the iterative marker *van/ven* seems not to fit very well with the majority of the negative forms. Below we will give some examples of negative forms with aspectual suffixes:

(30) Nuŋan   e-che-n   isi-l-la,   suru-l-le-n.
     he   Neg-Past-3Sg   reach-Inch-Ffnlv   go:away-Inch-NonFut-3Sg
     'He did not begin to approach, he began to go away.'

(31) Beyumimni e-che-n   pektirevun-mi   ga-malcha-ra.
     hunter   Neg-Past-3Sg   gun-RelPoss   take-quickly-Ffnlv
     'The hunter did not seize the gun.' (i.e. he did not have the time to do so).

(32) Beyetken e-che-n   purta-va   d'avu-cha-d'a-ra.
      boy   Neg-Past-3Sg knife-Acc   take-Stat-Imp-Ffnlv
      'The boy did not hold/was not holding the knife.'

3.3.1.4 Modality markers in the FFNLV

Only Three suffixes expressing modal meanings – *mu* 'want', *ssa* 'try', and *na* 'go (in order to do something)' – may be added to the FFNLV. These three suffixes express a certain degree of inclination to do something. The most frequent is the volitional suffix *mu*, both in positive and in negative forms:

(33) Evenki e-si-n   suru-mu-l-d'e-re.
      Evenk   Neg-Pres-3Sg go:away-Vol-Inch-Imp-Ffnlv
      'The Evenk did not want to go away.'

Quite usual are negative imperatives addressed to the second person with the aim to cause him not to want something:

(34) E-kel   nekni-l-ve-v   va-mu-ra.
      Neg-2SgImper   brother-Pl-Acc-1SgPoss   want-Vol-Ffnlv
      Lit: 'Don't want to kill my brothers!'

(35) E-kel   kusi-mu-re.
      Neg-2SgImper   fight-Vol-Ffnlv
      Lit: 'Don't want to fight.'

As is the case with the volitional suffix *mu*, the scope of negation with suffixes *na* 'go' and *ssa* 'try' involves only the corresponding modal meanings:

(36) Nuŋan e-vki   e-ya-val   va-na-d'e-re.
      he   Neg-HabPart   anything-IndefAcc-Encl   kill-go-Imp-Ffnlv
      'He does not go to kill anything.'

(37) Sēŋan e-che   buktu-sse-meti-re.
      burbot Neg-Past   rush:forward-try-Eval-Ffnlv
      'The burbot [a kind of eel] did not even try to rush forward.'

3.3.1.5 Evaluation markers in the FFNLV

There are at least three suffixes expressing evaluation of the action by the speaker: *kakut* 'very', *mati* 'not even', and *gachin* 'like, as if'. The first two suffixes are added to the stem of the FFNLV, the last suffix, however, is added to the conjugated form of the negative verb *e-* as its final morpheme (see 39). Here is an example of the negative verb with the suffix *kakut*:

(38) Asatkan:nun e-che-n   soŋo-kokut-te.
      girl:Encl   Neg-Past-3Sg cry-Eval-Ffnlv
      'But the girl did not cry very bitterly.'

3.3.2 Inflectional possibilities of the negative verb e-
3.3.2.1 Aspectual and evaluation markers

The negative verb *e-* may take only one evaluation marker – *gachin*, which expresses resemblance, see (39) – and one aspectual marker – *ŋne*, which expresses habitual meaning (see 40 and 41):

(39) Nuŋan e-che-gechin mede-re bi-d'e-vki.
      he Neg-Past-Resem feel-Ffnlv be-Imp-HabPart
      'He lives as if he does not feel (anything).'

(40) Bi tari-l-di e-ŋne-m ŋele-t-te.
      I that-Pl-Inst Neg-Hab-1SgPres be:afraid-Dur-Ffnlv
      'I am never/not afraid of them.'

(41) E-ŋne-kel tadu ŋene-re.
      Neg-Hab-2SgImper there go-Ffnlv
      'Don't ever go there.'

The habitual suffix *ŋne* is used with the negative verb *e-* rather often in imperative utterances (see 41) for the purpose of emphasizing the request. Sometimes the iterative suffix *ŋne* is used not in its literal meaning, but instead of the present tense marker *si*, as in:

(42) Esitken bi samā-sel-du e-ŋne-m ted'e-re.
      now I shaman-Pl-Dat Neg-Hab-1Sg believe-Ffnlv
      'Now I do not believe the shamans.'

3.3.2.2 Indicative forms

The negative verb *e-* has four tense forms which are formed by means of the suffixes in table 9. Verbal expressions based on the first two suffixes (*e-si* and *e-te*) take predicative endings of the second type (see table 2). The last two forms take predicative endings of the first type. Person-number forms of these tense forms are shown in table 10.

Table 9. Tense suffixes

Suffix	Meaning
si	non-future
te	future
che	past (sometimes also present)
ŋki	past habitual

Table 10. Tense forms of the negative verb *e-*

	Non-future	future	Past	Past habitual
1 singular	e-si-m	e-te-m	e-che-v	e-ŋki-v
2 singular	e-si-nni	e-te-nni	e-che-s	e-ŋki-s
3 singular	e-si(-n)	e-te-n	e-che-n	e-ŋki-n
1 plural excl.	e-si-v	e-te-re-v	e-che-vun	e-ŋki-vun
1 plural incl.	e-si-p	e-te-p	e-che-t	e-ŋki-t
2 plural	e-si-s	e-te(-re)-s	e-che-sun	e-ŋki-sun
3 plural	e-si(-l)	e-te-re	e-che-tin	e-ŋki-tin

The future marker *d'ara*, which is included in the system of positive tense forms, is not a temporal but rather a modal form with the negative verb. In fact, the form *e-d'eŋe*, which would denote impossibility of a certain action, is devoid of any temporal meaning. Impossibility can be expressed by affixing the tense suffix on the auxiliary verb *bi*:

(43) Tar   tirgani   nuŋan-dun   e-d'eŋe   omŋo-v-ro   bi-che-n.
      that   day   he-Dat   Neg-FutPart   forget-Pass-Ffnlv be-Past-3Sg
      'That day was unforgettable for him.'

Below we will analyse tense meanings of the four tense forms of the negative imperative verb shown in table 11.

3.3.2.2.1 Past tense forms
In narration, past tense forms are the most frequent of the four tense forms. The form *e-ŋki-* always denotes the negation of an action in the past, whereas the form *e-che-* may be used both in the past and in the present context. The following examples illustrate.

(44) Nuŋan   e-ŋki-n   purta-va   bū-re.
      she   Neg-HabPast-3Sg   knife-Acc give-Ffnlv
      'As a rule, she did not give the knife.'

(45) Si   min-e   e-che-s   doldi-ra.
      you   I-Acc   Neg-Past-2Sg   hear-Ffnlv
      'You did not hear me.'

(46) Bi   nuŋan-man   e-che-v   ŋele-t-che-re.
      I   he-Acc   Neg-Past-1Sg   be:afraid-Dur-Imp-Ffnlv
      'I am not afraid of him.'

The past habitual suffix *ŋki* may also be used in the meaning of concrete past (imperfect), as in:

(47) Hindir e-ŋki-n   suru-mu-re.
      Hindir Neg-HabPast-3Sg go:away-Vol-Ffnlv
      'Hindir did not want to go away.'

The negative verb form may be placed either in sentence initial position (before the subject) or in sentence final position, in case the speaker wants to stress some part of the utterance, say an adverbial component:

(48) Ōkin:da e-ŋki-n   er   beye nuŋan-man tugi archa-ra.
      always Neg-HabPast-3Sg that man he-Acc   so   meet-Ffnlv
      'That man never met him in such a way.'

3.3.2.2.2 Non-future
Traditionally considered as the present tense form, the non-future may express the negation of both the present action/state and recent past situations as is demonstrated in the following examples:

(49) Bi er guleseg-tu   e-si-m   bi-d'e-re.
      I this village-Dut Neg-NonFut-1Sg   be-Imp-Ffnlv
      'I do not live in this village.'

(50) Si ē-va:da   e-si-nni   duku-ra.
      you anything-Acc:Encl   Neg-NonFut-2Sg write-Ffnlv
      'You have not written anything (just now).'

The last example may also be interpreted in the progressive: 'you are not writing anything', said for example by a teacher who addresses one or more pupils. Nowadays there is a tendency to use the negative form *e-vki* of the habitual participle of the negative verb to express the negation of the present:

(51) Nekun-in   e-vki   suru-mu-re.
      younger:brother-3SgPoss Neg-HabPart   go:away-Vol-Ffnlv
      tar   hokto-li.
      that   road-Prol
      'His younger brother does not want to go along that road.'

(52) Asatkan agi-la   e-vki   ŋene-d'e-re.
      girl   taiga-Loc   Neg-HabPart   go-Imp-Ffnlv
      'The girl does not go to the forest.'

3.3.2.2.3 Future
The future forms are used in the negation of future situations which do not contain the modal component of impossibility or prohibition to perform a

certain action. If such a component is present, the negative form *e-d'eŋe* is used (see 3.3.2.4.1 and 3.3.2.5.1). Here are two examples with the future form *e-te*:

(53) Bi   nuŋan-nun   agi-tki   e-te-m   suru-re.
      I   he-Comit   taiga-Dir   Neg-Fut-1Sg   go:away-Ffnlv
      'I will not go to the taiga with him.'

(54) Akin-mi   sin-dule   e-te-n   duku-ra.
      elder:brother-1SgPoss   you-Loc   Neg-Fut-3Sg   write-Ffnlv
      'My elder brother will not write to you.'

Compare the last example with the next one, in which the modal form is used:

(55) Akin-mi sin-dule e-d'eŋe-n duku-ra.
      'My elder brother will not be able to write to you.'

3.3.2.3 Non-indicative forms

These include negative forms of the verb *e-* with imperative, subjunctive, debitative, and suppositional forms.

3.3.2.3.1 Negative imperative

All non-indicative forms of the negative verb are formed by the same suffixal means employed by the other verbs. The formation of negative imperative forms of the verb *e-* is shown in table 11 (the FFNLV are omitted in this table).

Table 11. Negative imperative

Peron-number	Imperative 1	Imperative 2	Meaning
1 singular	*e-kte (vā-re)*	*e-ŋne-m (vā-re)*	Let me not
2 singular	*e-kel*	*e-dē-vi/e-ne*	Don't
3 singular	*e-gin*	*e-ŋne-n*	Let him not
1 plural excl	*e-kte-vun*	*e-ŋne-vun*	Let us not
1 plural incl.	*e-get*	*e-ŋne-t*	Let us not
2 plural	*e-kellu*	*e-dē-ver/e-ne-l*	Don't
3 plural	*e-ktin*	*e-ŋne-tin*	Let them not

Imperative 1 conveys the necessity to perform a certain action immediately, whereas imperative 2 expresses the wish of the speaker that a certain action should (not) occur in future, not necessarily at the moment of speech or in the near future. Below are some examples of negative imperatives.

(56) E-ŋne-kellu   tala   girku-ra.
      Neg-Hab-2PlImper there   go
      'Don't go there.'

(57) Togo-vo e-ne   ila-ra.
      fire-Acc Neg-Imper light:fire-Ffnlv
      'Mind you, don't light a fire.'

3.3.2.3.2 *Negative subjunctive*
Negative subjunctive forms are formed by means of the suffix *mche*; the subject
agreement suffixes are the same as the possessive type shown in table 2. An
example:

(58) Bi tara-ve   e-mche-v   sā-re   si   min-tik'i
      I   that-Acc   Neg-Subj-1Sg know-Ffnlv you I-Dir
      e-siki-s   ulguchen-e.
      Neg-CondConv-2Sg tell-Ffnlv

      'I would not have known that if you had not told me.'

3.3.2.3.3 *Negative debitive*
Negative debitive forms are formed by means of the suffix *mechin* 'must',
plus variants of possessive suffixes occurring after final *n: mi* (1Sg), *ni* (2Sg),
in (3Sg), *mun* (1Pl exclusive), *ti* (1Pl exclusive), *nun* (2Pl), and *tin* (3Pl). The
following example illustrates:

(59) Nuŋan   tara-ve   e-mechin-in   gun-e.
      he   that-Acc   Neg-Deb-3SgPoss   say-Ffnlv
      'He should not have said that.'

3.3.2.3.4 *Negative suppositional*
These forms express certain degrees of uncertainty or possibility that the
action did not take place. There are three suffixes expressing this function:
rke, *ne*, and *rgu*. The form *e-rke* takes subject agreement suffixes of the possessive type (see table 2) with only one exception: the third person singular
takes no ending, instead of the ending *n* (see example 59). The forms *e-ne*
and *e-rgu*, which mean 'it is possible that the action did not take place', take
subject agreement suffixes of the verbal predicate type (see table 3), with the
addition of the suffix *re* in the plural:

(60) Sinŋi amin-ni   e-rke   haval-la   d'evkit-tu.
      your father-2SgPoss Neg-Sup work-Ffnlv canteen-Dat
      'I suppose that your father did not work at the canteen.'
      (i.e. 'I am not sure that he worked there.')

(61) Si   er   tatkit-tu   e-rgu-nni   alagu-v-ra.
      you this school-Dat   Neg-Sup-2Sg   teach-Pass-Ffnlv
      'I believe you did not teach at that school.'

(62) Nuŋartin   unta-l-va   e-ne-re-ø   ga-ra.
      they   boot-Pl-Acc Neg-Sup-3Pl take-Ffnlv
      'I think/suppose that they did not take their fur boots.'

3.3.2.4 Non-finite forms

Non-finite forms of the negative verb *e-* include participial forms (i.e. forms which may be used attributively) and converbal forms (i.e. forms which are mainly used as adverbial clauses and are never used attributively).

3.3.2.4.1 Participial forms

There are five participial forms:
- participle of simultaneous situation *e-si (vā-ra beye)*. E.g. 'the man *who is not* killing', 'the man *who has not* killed'.
- participle of prior situation *e-che (vā-ra beye)*. E.g. 'the man *who did not* kill'.
- participle of possible action *e-d'eŋe (vā-ra beye)*. E.g. 'the man *who will not be able* to kill'.
- habitual participle *e-vki (vā-ra beye)*. E.g. 'the man *who is not in the habit* of killing'.
- participle of not yet occurring situation *e-chin (vā-ra beye)*. For example 'the man *who has not yet* killed'.

All the negative participial forms may take the plural endings *l* and *r* for the participle *e-chin* (Pl *e-chi-r*); they may also be declined together with the head noun. Below are some examples:

(63) E-si   ē-va:da   gun-d'e-re   beyetken   yū-che-n.
      Neg-Pres   anything-Acc:Encl   say-Imp-Ffnlv   boy   enter-Past-3Sg
      'A boy entered without saying anything.'

(64) D'av-va bi   e-chin   ō-ra   bi-si-m.
      boat-Acc I   Neg-Part   make-Ffnlv   be-NonFut-1Sg
      'I have not yet made a boat.'

3.3.2.4.2 Converbal forms

Converbal forms include four non-conjugated forms used only in cases of subject-coreference and five conjugated forms which may be used in cases of non-coreferential subjects (in fact, one conjugated converb, the conditional-temporal form with the suffix *siki*, is used only when the subjects are non-coreferential). Non-conjugated converbs used only with coreferential subjects include the forms with the suffixes *ne* (simultaneous action), *kse/keim* (prior action), and *mi* (conditional/temporal converb). Non-conjugated converbs may have the plural ending *-l*. Below are some examples.

(65) E-mi   suru-re   min-dule   eme-kel.
      Neg-CondConv go:away-Ffnlv   I-Loc   come-2SgImper
      'If you do not go away come to me.'

(66) E-keim   taŋ-na   hurkeken amaski suru-re-n.
      Neg-PriorConv read-Ffnlv   boy   back   go:away-NonFut-3Sg
      'The boy went away without having read (something).'

Conjugated converbs include forms with the suffixes *ŋesi* (remote past), *dē* (purpose), *d'eli* (posterior action), *knen* (action as the ultimate aim), and *siki* (condition or prior action). In case of non-coreferentiality of subjects, the converbal forms take possessive suffixes shown in table 1, in case of co-referentiality of subjects the markers of relative possession are used instead: *vi* for singular and *ver* for plural subjects. Examples:

(67) Min-e   e-siki-s   edile-re
      I-Acc   Neg-CondConv-2SgPoss   marry-Ffnlv

      nekni-l-ve-s   vā-d'eŋa-v.
      brother-Pl-Acc-2SgPoss   kill-Fut-1Sg

      'If you do not marry me I will kill your younger brother.'

(68) Tulile   e-d'eli-n   haktira-ra   bi ŋene-d'e-m.
      outside Neg-PostConv-3SgPoss   get:dark-Ffnlv I go-Fut-1Sg
      'I will go before it gets dark outside.'

(69) Beye-l   oro-r-vor   dyaya-ra   e-dē-n
      man-Pl   deer-Pl-RelPoss hide-NonFut-3Pl Neg-PurpConv-3SgPoss
      d'ava-ra.
      take-Ffnlv
      'The men hid their deer so that he could not take them.'

The most frequent converbs are the forms *mi* and *siki*, which express condition or prior action, and the forms *ne* and *de*, which denote simultaneous action and purpose. Ordinary verbs cannot take the suffix *siki*; they take the converbal suffix *raki* instead, which expresses either condition or prior situation with non-coreferential subjects. Sometimes the negative verb *e-* takes the suffix *raki* instead of *siki*; example:

(70) E-reki-n   edin-e   bi d'avi-t
      Neg-CondConv-3SgPoss   wind-Ffnlv   I boat-Instr
      motima-sini-mcha-v.
      elk:hunt-Sem-Subj-1SgPoss
      'If it were not windy, I would have gone hunting elks by boat.'

There are four converbal forms that cannot be formed from the negative verb *e-*. These include converbs of prior situation in *chala* and *ktava*, the converb of simultaneous action *d'anma* and the converb of purpose *vuna*. The converbal forms in *ktava*, *d'anma* and *vuna* are very rare in general, both in written texts and in speech. In most dialects these forms have almost gone out of use, since their functions are performed in all the dialects by the following corresponding converbal forms: *ksa/kaim* for prior situation, *(d'a)na/(d'e)ne* for simultaneous situation, and *da/de/do* for the converb of purpose.

3.3.2.5 Impersonal forms

Impersonal forms of the verb *e-* include forms with the following suffixes: (a) *d'eŋe* (homonymous with the participle of possible action); (b) *vke* 'must not', 'should not'; (c) *ŋi* 'impossible'. All the forms of the negative verb *e-* – *e-d'eŋe/e-vke/e-ŋi* – express rather close meanings of either negative possibility or negative necessity with certain nuances of potential inability to perform an action (forms with *e-d'eŋe*), or prohibition (*e-vke* and *e-ŋi*). It is necessary to stress that the Ffnlv with all these negative forms as a rule carries the marker of the passive voice. Forms with *e-d'eŋe* in impersonal constructions denote the meaning of impossibility connected with potential impossibility of a person to fulfil a certain action, as in:

(71) Chaski e-d'eŋe   ŋene-v-re.
      further Neg-Impers go-Pass-Ffnlv
      'It is impossible to go further.'

Forms with *e-vke* denote either impossibility to perform an action, or the prescription not to perform an action in accordance with accepted rules of life or behaviour. Examples:

(72) Mu   achin-di-n   e-vke   in-e.
      water Neg-Instr-3SgPoss Neg-Impers live-Ffnlv
      'It is impossible to live without water.'

(73) Komnata-du   e-vke   damgati-v-ra.
      room-Dat   Neg-Impers smoke-Pass-Ffnlv
      'Smoking is not allowed in this room.'
      'One should not smoke in this room.'

Forms with *e-ŋi* denote a person's inability to perform an action:

(74) Tar   bira-va   e-ŋi   elbeskechi-v-re.
     that river-Acc Neg-Impers   swim:across-Pass-Ffnlv
     'It is impossible to swim across that river.'

(75) Er   oron-mo   e-ŋi   d'ava-v-ra.
     this deer-Acc Neg-Impers   take-Pass-Ffnlv
     'It is impossible to catch this deer.'

3.4 Negative forms of nominals

3.4.1 Negation of nouns

Negation of nominal phrases by means of the negative noun *e-* occurs rather seldom, since negation of existence or possession is as a rule expressed by the negative noun *āchin* (see section 4). Clauses consisting of two nominal phrases linked by a copula, however, are negated by means of the negative verb. Example (see also 11b and 12b):

(76) Nuŋan e-che   alagumni bi-si.
     he   Neg-Past teacher   be-Ffnlv
     'He is not a teacher.'

Quite seldom, negation with the negative noun *āchin* can compete with the negative verb *e-* in cases of negation of existence; example:

(77) a. Min-du sin-ŋi   purta-s   āchin.
        I-Dat   you-Poss knife-2SgPoss   Neg
        'I have not got your knife.'
        'Your knife is not at my place.'

     b. Mindu   sin-ŋi   purta-s   e-si   bi-re.
        I-Dat   you-Poss knife-2SgPoss   Neg-Pres   be-Ffnlv
        'There is no knife belonging to you at my place.'

3.4.2 Negation of adjectives

This phenomenon is very rare in Evenki. There are two types of forming negative attributive phrases: (a) verbal, i.e. by means of the negative verb *e-* and the auxiliary *bi-*, and (b) nominal, by means of the negative noun *āchin*. The first type of negative attribute may be illustrated by the following examples:

(78) a. *ted'e* 'correct'
     b. e-che   ted'e bi-si
        Neg-Past Adj   be-Ffnlv
        'not correct, just, right'

(79)   a. *aya* 'good'

      b. *e-che aya bi-si* 'not good', i.e. 'bad'

The second, nominal type of negative attributes involves indefinite accusatives forms of the nouns plus the negative nominal *āchin*. Examples: *mudan* 'end', *mudan-a āchin* 'continuous'; *kutu* 'happiness', *kutu-ya āchin* 'unhappy' (see also section 2.2).

3.4.3 Negative indefinites

Negation of indefinite pronouns involves always negation of the verbal predicate only, while the pronoun itself never forms a negative. Indefinite pronouns include the following:

ē-da/ē-val	'anything'
ēkun-da/ēkun-mal	'anything, anybody'
ŋi-de/ŋi-vel	'anybody'
ī-de/ī-vel	'anywhere'
avadi-da/avadi-val	'any, whatever'
ekuma-da	'any'

These indefinite pronouns as a rule take case suffixes, as in the following examples:

(80)   Bi   ē-ya-val   e-che-v   iche-re.
      I   anything-Acc-Encl   Neg-Past-1Sg   see-Ffnlv
      'I did not see anything/ I saw nothing.'

(81)   Nuŋan   ere   ī-du:de   e-che-n   iche-re.
      he   this   anywhere-Dat:Encl   Neg-Past-3Sg   see-Ffnlv
      'He did not see this anywhere.'

The indefinite pronouns *ē-da/ē-val* and *ēkun-da/ēkun-mal*, which denote inanimate entities, may be used interchangeably:

(82)   Nuŋan   ēkun-ma:da   e-vki   sā-re.
      he   anything-Acc:Encl   Neg-HabPart   know-Ffnlv
      'He does not know anything.'

(83)   Nuŋan   e-va-da   e-che   sā-mu-d'e-re.
      he   anything-Acc:Encl   Neg-Past   know-Vol-Imp-Ffnlv
      'He wants to know nothing.'

3.4.4 Negation and indefinite subjects

Indefinite subjects expressed both by the indefinite pronouns (see the previous section) and by the indefinite nominal phrases may be used in negative clauses, for example in situations when the speaker discovers that not all people came, but he does not know exactly who has not come, as in (84b):

(84) a. ŋi-vel   eme-che-n.
          who-Encl   come-Past-3Sg
          'Somebody came.'

      b. ŋi-vel   e-che-n   eme-re.
          who-encl   Neg-Past-3Sg   come-Ffnlv
          'Someone did not come/There is is someone who did not come.'

(84b) is synonymous with the following sentence containing the indefinite nominal phrase:

(85) Avadi-val   beye e-che-n   eme-re.
      any-encl   man Neg-Past-3Sg   come-Ffnlv
      'There is a person who has not come.'

The last sentence would be appropriate if a speaker finds out that one person of the group is missing. Indefinite pronouns quite freely occur as subjects in positive sentences, as in the following examples:

(86) a. Ēkun:da   e-che   ō-ra.
          anything:Encl Neg-Past   become-Ffnlv
          'Nothing happened.'

      b. Ēkun:da   ō-ra-n.
          anything-Encl become-NonFut-3Sg
          'Something happened.'

(87) D'u-la   ēkun:mal   ile   ī-re-n.
      house-Loc   anybody-Encl person   enter-NonFut-3Sg
      'Someone entered the house.'

(88) Ēkun:mal   stol-du   bi-d'ere-n.
      anything:Encl table-Dat   be-Pres-3Sg
      'There is something on the table.'

3.4.5 Negative partitive expression

Negation of clauses of the type 'none of them came' or 'I took none of it' is expressed by means of the negative forms of the verb and the indefinite pronouns *ŋi-de* 'anybody' or *ēkun-da* 'anything'. Examples:

(89)   ŋi:de   tari-l-duk   beye-l-duk   e-che-n   eme-re.
        anybody   that-Pl-Abl man-Pl-Abl   Neg-Past-3Sg   come-Ffnlv
        'Nobody of those people came.'

(90)   Bi ēkun:ma-da   tari-l-duk   d'eptile-l-duk   e-che-v   ga-ra.
        I   anything-Acc that-Pl-Abl food-Pl-Abl   Neg-Past-1Sg   take-Ffnlv
        'I took nothing of that food.'

3.5 Negative forms of adverbs

It has been mentioned above that there are no inherently negative adverbs
in Evenki. Some adverbs express negation semantically, such as *erut* 'bad'.
Negation of adverbials is usually achieved by negating the predicate, as in
the example below:

(91)   a.   Bi umne:de   Moskva-du   bi-che-v.
             I once:Encl Moscow-Dat be-Past-1Sg
             'I was in Moscow once (one time only).'

        b.   Bi umne:de   Moskva-du   e-che-v   bi-si.
             I once:Encl Moscow-Dat Neg-Past-1Sg   be-Ffnlv
             'I have never been in Moscow.'

3.6 Negation of quantifiers

Negation of quantifiers like *all, many, much* and *every* is expressed by means
of the negative verb *e-* and the auxiliary *bi-* 'be'. This negative frame *e-che
... bi-si* appeared in the last decade, perhaps under the influence of Russian,
in which negation of nouns, adjectives, and adverbs is very frequent. Examples:

(92)   E-che-l   upkat   eme-re.
        Neg-Past-Pl   all   come-NonFut-3Pl
        'Not all (the people) came.'

(93)   E-che   tirgani-tik'in   bi-si.
        Neg-Past   day-every   be-Ffnlv
        'Not every day.'

This negative frame occurs freely in the speech of younger people who also
speak Russian:

(94)   Ere   e-che   tin'ive   bi-si.
        this Neg-Past   yesterday   be-Ffnlv
        'That was not yesterday.'

Negation of quantifiers such as *much/many* was outlined in section 3.5 above. In addition we must say that negation of clauses with *kete* 'much/many' is achieved by means of predicate negation:

(95)   Kete   ile-l   e-che-l   eme-re.
        many   person-Pl   Neg-Past-Pl   come-Ffnlv
        'Not many people came.'

3.7 Independent use of the negative verb

The negative verb *e-* is seldom used independently, i.e. without the FFNLV. One type of independent use includes negative one word answers (see section 5), the other one includes rare cases when the negative verb means 'not to become', 'not to go away', as in the following examples:

(96)   esile   e-d'eli-m   tadu-gla,   mēvan-mi   e-si-n   elekte-re   ...
        now   Neg-Fut-1Sg   there-Encl   heart-1SgPoss   Neg-Pres-3Sg   endure-Ffnlv
        '...now I will not be (live) there, [because] my heart does not endure.'

4 Negation of nouns with *āchin*

The negative noun *āchin* is used to express negative existential and negative possession (see example 5b). In this section we will discuss the position of the negative noun, its inflectional possibilities, and the expression of number, case and the possessive forms.

4.1 The position of *āchin*

As a rule, the negative noun is used predicatively, which is why it is usually placed at the end of the clause:

(97)   Nuŋan-dun   oro-r   āchi-r.
        he-Dat   deer-Pl   Neg-Pl
        'He has no deer.'

(98)   Esitirga   n'aŋn'a-du   tuksu-l   āchi-r.
        today   sky-Dat   cloud-Pl   Neg-Pl
        'There are no clouds in the sky today.'

Āchin may be followed by the auxiliary *bi-* 'be':

(99) Amin-du   pektirevun āchin   bi-che-n.
      father-Dat gun   Neg   be-Past-3Sg
      'My father had no gun.'

When used in other syntactic functions, *āchin* always follows the word which is negated, as in:

(100) D'ikte-ye   āchin   aŋnan'i.
       berry-IndefAcc   Neg   year
       'A year without berries.'

When stressed, *āchin* can also be placed clause initially:

(101) Āchin   ēkun:da   depi-v-d'eŋe.
       Neg   anything:Encl eat-Pass-FutPart
       'There is nothing to eat.'

(102) Āchin   ŋi:de   ile-du   bele-d'eŋe.
       Neg   anybody:Encl   man-Dat   help-FutPart
       'There is nobody to help the man.'

4.2 Inflectional characteristics of *āchin*

Āchin may be inflected for number, case and possession (both personal and relative). When used predicatively or as a negative element in an attributive group, *āchin* has no case or possession suffixes. Examples:

(103) a. Kutu-ya   āchin   beye.
          luck-Obj   Neg   man
          'Unlucky man.'

       b. Madan-a   āchin   tigde.
          end-Obj   Neg   rain
          'Ceaseless rain.'

       c. ŋāle-ye āchin   amāka.
          eye-Obj Neg   old man
          'An old man without an arm.'

4.2.1 Number

The plural of *āchin* is formed like all other nouns ending in *n*: the final *n* is replaced by *r*, as in *oron* 'reindeer' – *oror* 'reindeer' (Plural). Both forms may be used in all functions.

4.2.2 Possessive forms

Āchin may have relative possession suffixes, as in *āchin-mi* 'one's absence' and *āchin-mar* 'one's (plural) absence', and the personal possession suffixes shown in table 2:

(104) Hokto   āchin-in.
road   neg-3SgPersPoss
'The lack of the road.'

(105) Meŋu-r āchin-in
money
'Lack of money.'

4.2.3 Case forms

Case forms of the *āchin* may be used either in the function of an object or as an adverbial modifier. Isolated case forms of *āchin* may also be used as syntactic objects or adverbial modifiers, as in:

(106) a. Āchin-du-v.
Neg-Dat-1SgPersPoss
'In my absence/ without me.'

b. Āchi-r-du-tin.
Neg-Pl-Dat-3PlPersPoss
'In their absence/ without them.'

Below we will give some examples of complex negative phrases with case marked *āchin*:

(107) Bi mede-che-v   purta   āchin-ma-n.
I   feel-Past-1Sg knife   Neg-Acc-3SgPersPoss
'I realized I had no knife.'

(108) Det-tu nuŋartin mo-l   āchi-r-va-tin   iche-re.
bog-Dat they   tree-Pl   neg-Pl-Acc-3PlPersPoss   see-Past-3Pl
'They saw that there were no trees on the bog (swamp).'

Adverbial modifiers with *āchin* may denote location or cause:

(109) Bu nulgi-che-vun   moti-l   āchi-r-tik'i-tin.
we wander-Past-1Pl elk-Pl   Neg-Pl-Dir-3PlPersPoss
'We wandered to the place where there were no elks.'

(110) Siŋilgen āchin-du-n   beyumimni-l girkumat   beyukte-che-tin.
snow   Neg-Dat-3SgPoss   hunter-Pl   on:foot   hunt-Past-3Pl
'Since there was no snow, the hunters hunted on foot.'

5 Negative one-word answers

There are three possible one-word answers to a question: *eche (e-che)* if a present or past situation or its property is negated; *e-te* (plus a person-number marker) if a future situation is negated; or *āchin* if existence or possession is negated. Compare the following examples (phrases in parentheses are optional):

(111) Nuŋan eme-che-n?   E-che   (e-che-n   eme-re).
      he   come-Past-3Sg no   (Neg-Past-3Sg come-Ffnlv
      'Did he come? No (he did not)'

(112) Sin-du   oro-r   bi-si?   āchi-r.
      you-Dat deer-Pl be-Pres-Pl Neg-Pl
      'Do you have deer? No.'

There is a tendency to use the one word negative answer *eche* to negate situations of all tenses and even possession, as in:

(113) A: Er minŋi   murikan-mi.
         this my   horse-1SgPoss
         'This is my little horse.'

      B: Eche, eche. Eche tar   sinŋi bi-si.
         no   no   Neg that   your be-Ffnlv
         'No, no – this is not yours.'

6 Negation in complex clauses and negative transport

In Evenki there are numerous types of participial and converbal constructions used in the function of Indo-European subordinate clauses (see for example 58, 62, 65, 66, 67, 69 and other examples). Recently, under the influence of Russian, a mechanism of subordination has developed which makes use of finite verbs rather than non-finite verbs. Example:

(114) Su   e-che-n   sā-re   bi oron-mo baka-m.
      you Neg-Past-2Pl   know-Ffnlv   I deer-Acc find-NonFut-1Sg
      'You did not know that I found the deer.'

(115) Beyetken   sā-cha-n   eni-n:da   e-che
      boy   know-Pst-3Sg   mother-3SgPersPoss:Encl   Neg-Past

      esitken   ā-d'e-re.
      now   sleep-Imp-Ffnlv
      'The boy knew that his mother was not sleeping at that time.'

In the last two examples, rather than the finite forms *baka-m* 'I found' and *e-che ād'e-re* 'did not sleep', participial forms with the definite accusative case or the relative possessive marker would usually be used, as in the following example:

(116) Nuŋan guncha-d'e-che-n goroyodu e-che-vi
he think-Imp-Past-3Sg long:ago Neg-Past-RelPossSg
ile-l-nun ulguche-met-te.
person-Pl-Comit speak-Rec-Ffnlv
'He was thinking that he had not spoken with people for a long time.'

With verbs of thinking, sense perception, volition and obligation, negative transport is impossible in Evenki. This means that literal equivalents of English constructions in Evenki like *I do not think he will come* and *I do not hope that he will come* are ungrammatical. There are nevertheless two verbs – *ted'e* 'believe' and *gele-* 'want' – which do permit negative transport:

(117) Bi e-che-v ted'e-d'e-re nuŋan
I Neg-Past-1Sg believe-Imp-Ffnlv he
eme-d'eŋe-ve-n d'u-la-vi.
come-FutPart-Acc-3SgPersPoss house-Loc-RelPossSg
'I do not believe that he will come home.'

(118) Bi e-che-v gele-d'e-re nuŋan tadu
I Neg-Past-1Sg want-Imp-Ffnlv he there
haval-d'a-da-n.
work-Imp-PurpConv-3SgPersPoss
'I do not want him to work there.'

The usual constructions without negative transport do not contain negation in the matrix clause, as in:

(119) a. Bi d'aldā-d'e-m nuŋan ele e-d'eŋe-ve-n eme-re.
I think-Pres-1Sg he here Neg-FutPart-Acc-3SgPoss come-Ffnlv
'I think that he will not come here.'

  b. *Bi e-che-v d'aldā-re nuŋan ele eme-d'eŋe-ve-n.

Of the two semantically different constructions corresponding to English *I knew that he would not come* and *I did not know that he would come* only the former is possible in Evenki:

(120) Bi sā-cha-v nuŋan ele e-d'eŋe-ve-n eme-re.
I know-Past-1Sg he here Neg-FutPart-Acc-3SgPersPoss come-Ffnlv
'I knew that he would not come.'

7 Double negation

Restrictions on the co-occurrence of two negations in one sentence are conditioned only by semantic considerations. If there is no such semantic block, more than one negation can be applied in a sentence. There are three types of double negation: two negative verbs, two negative nouns, and a negative verb plus a negative noun. Below are examples of each of these types.

(121) Nime-sel   e-che-l   iche-re   mulekit-ve
neighbour-Pl   Neg-Past-Pl   see-Ffnlv   ice:hole-Acc
e-si-n-me   doŋoto-v-ro.
Neg-Pres-3Sg-Acc freeze-Pass-Ffnlv
'The neighbours did not notice that the ice hole was not frozen over.'

(122) Meŋu-r   āchi-r   –   kutu āchin.
money-Pl   Neg-Pl   luck Neg
'If one has no money, one has no luck.'

(123) Bi e-che-v   sā-re   nuŋan-du-n   purta   āchin
I Neg-Past-1Sg know-Ffnlv he-Dat-3SgPoss knife   Neg
bi-che-ve-n.
be-Past-Acc-3SgPoss
'I did not know that he had no knife.'

Coordination of two negated noun phrases or two or more predicates is achieved by means of one negative element, either verbal *(e-)* or nominal *(āchin)*. As a rule the coordinating enclitic *da/de* 'and' is used in this case:

(124) Bi:de nuŋan:da e-che-vun   suru-re.
I:Encl he:Encl   Neg-Past-2Pl go:away-Ffnlv
'Neither I nor he went away.'

Coordination of adverbials in a negative sentence is expressed by means of the same coordinating clitics:

(125) Nuŋan bira-du:da   d'u-du:da   āchin   bi-che-n.
he   river-Dat:Encl   house-Dat:Encl Neg   be-Past-3Sg
'He was neither near the river nor at home.'

8 Stress, intonation, and scope

The influence of stress/intonation in negated sentences on the scope of negation is minimal. In Evenki it is quite possible to say literally *He will not leave tomorrow* or *He **did not come** yesterday*; but it is not possible to say *He will leave **but not** tomorrow* or *He came (**but**) **not** yesterday*. In the latter case it is obligatory to negate the verb predicate, as in:

(126) Nuŋan tegemi e-te-n suru-re, tegemi
　　　he tomorrow Neg-Fut-3Sg go:away-Ffnlv tomorrow
　　　chagudu suru-d'e-n.
　　　after go:away-Fut-3Sg
　　　'He will not leave tomorrow, he will leave the day after tomorrow.'

Stress on a Subject does not imply in Evenki that someone else came, as in *John did not come, but Peter*. Quite rarely, intonation together with word order seems to opt for different readings of the sentence; compare the neutral (146a) with the stressed adverbial combined with falling intonation in (146b):

(127) Nuŋan tin'ive e-che-n eme-re, tin'ive
　　　he yesterday Neg-Past-3Sg come-Ffnlv yesterday
　　　chagudu eme-che-n.
　　　after come-Past-3Sg
　　　'He did not come yesterday, he came the day before yesterday.'

(128) Nuŋan e-che-n ⤸ tin'ive eme-re, tin'ive chagudu eme-che-n.
　　　'He did not come yesterday, he came the day before yesterday.'

The stress on *tin'ive* 'yesterday' in the last example does not necessarily imply the given development of narration, but it makes it easier to achieve the needed interpretation.

9 Negative modal verbs

There are five modal verbs in Evenki, and all five of them have a negative equivalent: *alba-* 'not want, not be able, cannot', *dup-* 'not be able, cannot', *bā-* 'not want', 'refuse', *mulli-* 'not be able', *heche-* 'not dare'. These verbs require a second verb in the form of the conditional-temporal converb with the suffix *mi* (this converbal form may function as the infinitival verb form), but sometimes (in certain dialects and contexts) the form of the converb of purpose *(da/de)* may be used instead. Below we give some examples with these negative modal verbs.

(129) Bi alba-m ichet-che-mi.
　　　I ModNonFut-1Sg watch-Imp-CondConv
　　　'I could not watch it (because my eyes ached).'

(130) Hunat   dup-te-n   baka-d'a-mi   oro-r-vi.
       girl   ModNonFut-3Sg   find-Imp-CondConv   deer-Pl-RelPoss
       'The girl could not find her reindeer.'

(131) Asatkan ba-l-le-n   mun-du   bū-de-vi
       girl   Mod-Inch-NonFut-3Sg   we-Dat   give-PurpConv-RelPoss
       kachikan-me.
       puppy-Acc
       'The little girl did not want to give us the puppy.'

As a rule constructions with the verbs *alba-* and *dup-* imply the existence of a real attempt to perform an action; this property differentiates these verbs from the verb *mulli-*, which denotes the potential inability to perform an action:

(132) Bi   mulli-m   duku-d'a-mi.
       I   Mod-NonFut-1Sg   write-Imp-CondConv
       'I cannot write.'

None of the negative modal verbs can be used in combination with the negative verb *e-*. Probably their co-occurrence is blocked by their negative component and the impossibility of combinations such as *not + not want, not + not be able.*

Abbreviations

Abl	ablative	Fut	future	Pers	personal
Acc	accusative	Hab	habitual	Pl	plural
Caus	causative	Imp	imperfective	Poss	possession
Comit	comitative	Imper	imperative	Post	posterior
Con	conative	Impers	impersonal	Pres	present
Cond	conditional	inch	inchoative	Prior	priority
Conv	converbal	Indef	indefinite	Prol	prolative
Dat	dative	Indic	indicative	Purp	purposive
Deb	debitive	Instr	instrumental	Q	quest. particle
Decaus	decausative	Iter	iterative	Rec	reciprocal
Def	definite	Loc	locative	Rel	relative
Dir	directive	Mod	modal verb	Resem	resemblance
Dist	distributive	Mon	monitory	Sem	semelfactive
Dur	durative	Mot	motion	Sg	singular
El	elative	Nmlzr	nominaliser	Simult	simultaneity
Emot	emotive	Nom	nominative	Soc	sociative
Encl	enclitic	NonFut	non-future	Stat	stative
Eval	evaluative	Opt	optative	Subj	subjunctive
Ffnlv	fixed form of	Part	participial form	Supp	suppositional
	the lexical	Pass	passive	VBLZR	verbalizer
	verb	Past	past tense	Vol	volition

P299.N4 TYP

TYPOLOGICAL STUDIES I

TYPOLOGICAL STUDIES IN LANGUAGE (TSL)

A companion series to the journal "STUDIES IN LANGUAGE"

Honorary Editor: Joseph H. Greenberg
General Editor: T. Givón

Editorial Board:

Volumes in this series will be functionally and typologically oriented, covering specific topics in language by collecting together data from a wide variety of languages and language typologies. The orientation of the volumes will be substantive rather than formal, with the aim of investigating universals of human language via as broadly defined a data base as possible, leaning toward cross-linguistic, diachronic, developmental and live-discourse data. The series is, in spirit as well as in fact, a continuation of the tradition initiated by C. Li *(Word Order and Word Order Change, Subject and Topic, Mechanisms for Syntactic Change)* and continued by T. Givón *(Discourse and Syntax)* and P. Hopper *(Tense-Aspect: Between Semantics and Pragmatics).*

Volume 29

Peter Kahrel & René van den Berg (eds)

TYPOLOGICAL STUDIES IN NEGATION

Turkish

Gerjan van Schaaik

0 The language

Turkish is the official language of *Türkiye Cumhuriyeti* 'Republic of Turkey' and of *Kuzey Kıbrıs Türk Cumhuriyeti* 'Turkish Republic of Northern Cyprus'. Apart from at least 50 million inhabitants of these countries, the language is spoken by several millions of people living outside of these countries. First of all, since the fall of the Ottoman Empire it is still in use by its descendants scattered over vast territories in Southeast Europe. Secondly, since the nineteen sixties, Turkish is widely spoken in Western-Europe by immigrants and their children.

According to Ruhlen (1987), Turkish is classified as Altaic\Altaic Proper\ Turkic\Common Turkic\Southern. Sister languages of Turkish are Azeri or Azerbaijani (Soviet Azerbaijan and northwest Persia), Khalaj and Qashqai (south Persia) and Turkmen (Soviet Turkmenistan). In the remainder of this section, I will sketch the major characteristics of the language.

Turkish shares with other languages of the Turkic family, as well as with languages of the Uralic family, the interesting phonological feature of vowel harmony. Vowel harmony means that the vowel quality of a suffix depends on the quality of its preceding vowel. This can be exemplified by the following, where a possessive marker precedes the locative marker: *ev-imiz-de* 'in our house'; *at-ımız-da* 'near our horse'; *ot-umuz-da* 'in our grass'; *göl-ümüz-de* 'in our lake'. Compare: *ev-de; at-ta; ot-ta; gül-de*. We will return to this in section 1.

From a morphological point of view, Turkish is an agglutinative language *par excellence*. Both the derivational and the inflectional systems apply the principle of adding suffix to suffix. This may result in huge words which may be the equivalent of a whole phrase, clause, or sentence in nonagglutinative languages. Clear examples are (1) and the well known specimen (2):

(1)   Ev-de-ki-ler-in-miş.
       house-Loc-Rel-Plur-Gen-Rep
       'It seems to be of those who are in the house.'

(2)   Avrupa-lı-laş-tır-ıl-ama-yacak-lar-dan-mı-sınız.
       europe-Der-Der-Caus-Pass-NegPot-Fut-Plur-Abl-QM-Cop=2p[1]
       'Are you one of those who will not be able to be Europeanized?'

Further, apart from case markers for nominal inflection, Turkish has a series of postpositions at its disposal, some of which govern one or more case markers. Prepositions do not occur in Turkish.

The syntax of Turkish is, at first glance, very straightforward. With respect to constituent ordering in a sentence, the general tendency is to place the verb at the end of the sentence, all verbal complements preceding it. Thus, in what is traditionally called an 'unmarked sentence', the Subject comes first and is followed by the Indirect and Direct Object, e.g.

(3)   Ali,   kardeş-i-ne   bir   kitap ver-di.
       Ali brother-his-Dat   a   book give-Past
       'Ali gave a book to his brother.'

Therefore, in a typical typological sense, Turkish is an SOV language[2]. This pattern, however, is related to what Lewis (1967:240) calls a *literary* sentence. As the typical order of constituents, he gives: (1) Subject, (2) expression of time, (3) expression of place, (4) Indirect Object, (5) Direct Object, (6) modifier of the verb, and (7) Verb. Sentences based on a noun have a similar ordering pattern, the nominal or adjectival predicate is sentence final. This can be exemplified by:

(4)   Ndisi-nin meşhur oluş-u   devlet-in kuruluş-u-ndan   sonra-dır.
       itself-En famous becoming-Agr   state-Gen foundation-Agr-Abl   after-Cop
       Lit: 'its-becoming-famous state's-foundation after-is.'
       'It is after the foundation of the state that it became famous.'

In this example, the predicate *sonra* 'after' is placed in sentence-final position. In colloquial Turkish, however, much of the constituent ordering is primarily determined by pragmatic factors instead of by syntactic notions. Taking this into account, orderings such as (5) seem to be the rule rather than the exception.

(5)   a.   Kardeşine kitap verdi, Ali   (IO-DO-V-S)
       b.   Ali kitap verdi, kardeşine   (S-DO-V-IO)
       c.   Kardeşine verdi, kitabı   (IO-V-DO)

In terms of 'informational value' of the several constituents that make up a sentence, one could say that a sencence develops according to the principle of increasing information value. Thus, it starts with 'low-grade' information ('Topic', 'Given') and it ends in 'high-grade' information ('Focus', 'New'), directly followed by the verb. Finally, constituents that do not belong to the predication proper are placed in post-verbal position. Note that this is compatible with the observation that questioned constituents are placed in pre-verbal position:

(6) a. Ali, kardeşine kitap mı verdi?
        'Did Ali give a *book* to his brother?'

    b. Ali, kitabı kardeşine mi verdi?
        'Did Ali give the book *to his brother?*'

    c. Kitabı Ali mi verdi, kardeşine?
        'Did *Ali* give the book, to his brother?'

    d. Ali, kardeşine mi verdi, kitabı?
        'Did Ali give (it) *to his brother*, the book?'

Of course, when the proposition as such is questioned, the question particle follows the predicate, as in for instance:

(7) Ali, kardeşine kitabı verdi mi?
    '*Did* Ali give the book to his brother (or didn't he)?'

A similar placement of the question particle is found in sentences based on a nominal predicate. Compare (8a) with (8b):

(8) a. Hasan hasta mı?
        'Is Hasan ill?'

    b. Hasan mı hasta?
        'Is it Hasan who is ill?'

Within the domain of the noun phrase, however, the ordering principles are far less complicated. As a rule, the modifier precedes the modified, e.g.

(9) Güzel bir   bahçe.
    nice   a   garden
    'A nice garden.'

Compare (9) with (10), where *bir* functions as the numeral *one*:

(10) Bir güzel bahçe.
     'One beautiful garden.'

Also (11 a-e) show that the modifier precedes the modified:

(11) a. Bu güzel bahçe.
         'This beautiful garden'

     b. Bu üç güzel bahçe.
         'These three beautiful gardens.'

c. Sokak-ta   gid-en   kadın.
   street-loc go-part woman
   'The woman walking in the street.'

d. Fransa kralı kadar kabak kafa-lı   bir adam.
   France king as   bold   head-Adj   a   man
   'A man as bold as the king of France.'

e. Merkez-i   ol-duğ-u   devlet-e ism-i-ni   ver-en Gazne şehr-i.
   centre-3Sg be-PP-Agr   state-Dat name-3Sg-Acc give-PP G.   city-CM
   'The city of Gazne that gave its name to the state because it was its centre.'

As for the lexicon, during centuries of contact with the Islamic world, the
lexicon has been enriched by several thousands of words from Arabic.
Another source for thousands of borrowings in the fields of administration
and literary culture was Persian, since, under the Seljuk dynasty, Persia was
overrun by the Turks in the eleventh century.

1 Verbal negation

Standard negation in Turkish verbs is expressed with a suffix that comes
immediately after the verb stem, e.g.

(12) a. Gel-me-yecek.
         come-Neg-Fut
         '(S)he will not come.'

      b. Çalış-ma-yacak.
         work-Neg-Fut
         '(S)he will not work.'

All other verb stems of Turkish are negated likewise. The suffix contains a
vowel that is subject to the rules of vowel harmony. Hence, the suffix is
often represented as -mE, where the E stands for a two-fold vowel: e or a.
Vowels of Turkish can be classified in three groups according to their
articulatory properties. A first distinction is between *front* and *back*, according to the position of the tongue during pronunciation: front vowels belong
to the set (e, i, ö, ü) and back vowels are (a, ı, o, u). The second criterion is
the position of the lips. Vowels are *rounded* (o, ö, u, ü) or *unrounded* (a, e, ı,
i). The third factor that determines the quality of a vowel is the amount of
space left between palate and tongue. Accordingly, vowels are *open* ('low')
or *close* ('high'), e.g. the sets (a, e, o, ö) and (ı, i, u, ü) respectively. The para-

meter front versus back determines the form of the negation suffix. If the
last vowel in a verb stem is a front vowel the suffix is -*me*, otherwise it is -*ma*.

1.1 Peculiarities

As a rule all verb stems and expressions based on verbal roots are negated by
the suffix -*mE*. Apart from the examples given above, we can illustrate this by:

(13)   a.   Gel-me-di.
            come-Neg-Past
            '(S)he didn-t come.'

       b.   Çalış-ma-yacak-tı.
            work-Neg-Fut-Past
            '(S)he wouldn't work.'

       c.   Inan-ıl-ma-z.
            believe-Pass-Neg-Aor
            'Unbelievable.'

       d.   Türk-leş-tir-il-me-miş-ler-den-siniz.
            turk-become-Caus-Pass-Neg-Partpast-Plur-Abl-Cop=2p
            'You are of those who didn't have themselves been Turkified.'

Although the orthography of Turkish is very straightforward, in some cases
it deviates from the pronunciation. The vowel of the negation suffix shifts
from open to close (high to low) when followed by the suffix fut(ure), as in
çalış-ma-yacak /*çalış-mı-yacak*/ and *gel-me-yecek* /*gel-mi-yecek*/.

A similar phenomenon occurs in the negative of the Present Continuous
where it is reflected in the spelling. Since we primarily deal with orthographic representations of the Turkish negator, we will go into this matter
in a special section, see 1.1.1.

1.1.1 Negation of the Present Continuous

As has been indicated in 1, the choice between *e* and *a* is determined by the
opposition front-back. However, this doesn't hold for the negation of the
Present Continuous. Instead, we find the vowels *ı, i, u, ü*, as a part of the
negational suffix[3]. In abstracto, the Present Continuous is negated by a suffix
that has a four-fold (-*mI*) vowel, whereas the 'standard' negation suffix (-*mE*)
contains a two-fold vowel. The vowel of -*mI* is determined by two parameters: front-back and rounded-unrounded.

A stem ending in a back unrounded vowel (*a, ı*) triggers -*mı*; after a front
unrounded stem vowel (*e, i*) we get -*mi*; after back rounded (*o, u*) comes -*mu*;

and finally, the suffix *-mü* occurs after a front rounded stem vowel *(ö, ü)*. This can be illustrated by the following forms:

(14)   *Back unrounded*   *Front unrounded*

    a. al-mı-yor   gel-mi-yor
          'isn't taking'   'isn't coming'

    b. çık-mı-yor   iç-mi-yor
          'isn't going out'   'isn't drinking'

          Back rounded   *Front rounded*

    c. koş-mu-yor   dön-mü-yor
          'isn't running'   'isn't returning'

    d. dur-mu-yor   gül-mü-yor
          'isn't stopping'   'isn't laughing'

1.1.2 Negation of Possibility

Possibility or potential[4] is expressed in Turkish by the suffix *-(y)Ebil*, as in the following examples:

(15)   a. Gel-ebil-di-m.
          come-Pot-Past-3Sg
          'I was able (could) to come.'

      b. Anla-yabil-ecek.
          understand-Pot-Fut
          '(S)he will be able to understand (it).'

For the negative potential, the suffix *-(y)EmE* is attached to the stem:

(16)   a. Gel-eme-di-m.
          come-NegPot-Past-3Sg
          'I was not able (couldn't) come.'

      b. Anla-yama-yacak.
          understand-NegPot-Fut
          '(S)he will not be able to understand (it).'

The suffix *-(y)Ebil* may be combined with both the 'regular' negation suffix *-mE* as with the 'impotential' suffix *-(y)EmE*. Negation is always expressed first. Compare (17a) with (17b):

(17)   a. Ev-de   ol-ma-yabil-ir.
          house-Loc be-Neg-Pot-Aor
          '(S)he may not be home.'

    b. Ev-de   ol-ama-z.
       house-Loc 'be'-NegPot-Aor
       '(S)he can't be home.'

(18) a. Adres-in-i   bildir-me-yebil-ir.
       adres-Poss3Sg-Acc know-Caus-Neg-Pot-Aor
       '(S)he may not need to give his/her address.'

    b. Adres-in-i   bildir-eme-z.
       adres-Poss3Sg-Acc know-Caus-Negpot-Aor
       '(S)he is not able to give his/her address.'

(19) a. Toplanti-ya   gel-me-yebil-ir.
       meeting-Dat come-Neg-Pot-Aor
       '(S)he may be able not to come to the meeting.'

    b. Toplantı-ya   gel-eme-yebil-ir.
       meeting-Dat come-NegPot-Pot-Aor
       '(S)he may not be able to come to the meeting.'

    c. Toplantı-ya   gel-eme-z.
       meeting-Dat come-NegPot-Pot-Aor
       '(S)he is not able to come to the meeting.'

2 Nominal negation

The (invariant) particle *değil* '(is) not' is the negator for non-verbal predicative expressions. It functions as an auxiliary: various suffixes for tense and
mood, and personal endings can be attached, as is exemplified by:

(20) a. Hasta-yım.   Hasta değil-im.
       ill-1Sg   ill   Not-1Sg
       'I am ill.'   'I am not ill.'

    b. Ev-de-ydi-k.   Ev-de   değil-di-k.
       house-Loc-past-2Sg house-Loc Not-past-2Sg
       'We were at home.' 'We were not at home.'

Compare these also with the following examples:

(21) a. Bu kalem Hasan-ın   değil-miş.
       this pen   Hasan-Gen   Not-Rep
       'This pen seems not to be Hasan's.'

    b. Bu kalem Hasan-ın-mış.
       'This pen seems to be Hasan's.'

(22) a. Ali zengin değil-se.
       'If Ali is not rich.'

> b. Postacı değil-dir.
>   'He certainly is not a postman.'
>
> c. Ayşe İzmir-de   değil mi-ydi?
>   Ayşe Izmir-Loc Not QM-Past
>   'Was Ayşe not in Izmir?'

The particle *değil* cannot be used whenever 'future' is to be expressed. The negative is then formed by means of the auxiliary verb *ol* (compare 'be'). To say that *Ali bir öğretmen değil* 'Ali is not a teacher' pertains to the future, one must say: *Ali bir öğretmen ol-ma-yacak* (*ol*-Neg-fut).

2.1 Contrastive negation

The scope of *değil* can be a predication, but also a noun phrase. It thus allows for contrastive negation. This can be exemplified by the following:

(23) a. Ali   değil, Hasan geldi.
        A.   NOT   H.   come-Past
        'Not Ali, (but) Hasan came.'

     b. Ankara'ya değil, İzmir'e   gittik.
        Ankara-Dat NOT   Izmir-Dat go-Past-2Sg
        'We didn't go to Ankara, but to Izmir.'

     c. A: –Türkiye'de mi doğ-du-nuz?
           Turkey-Loc   Q   born-Past-2Sg
        A: 'Were you born in Turkey?'

        B: –Türkiye'de değil, Kıbrıs'ta.
           Turkey-Loc   NOT   Cyprus-Loc
        B: 'Not in Turkey, but on Cyprus'

Contrastive negation of this type is of course not restricted to third person subjects:

(24) a. Ben değil, sen bunu   yaptın.
        1Sg NOT   1Sg arrange-Aor-1Sg this-Acc
        'Not I, but you did it.'

     b. Sen değil, ben hallederim   bunu.
        2Sg NOT   1Sg arrange-Aor-1Sg this-Acc
        'It is not you, but me who is going to arrange that.'

2.2 Negation of nominalized verbs by *değil*

As was outlined above, the primary function of the particle *değil* is that of a negation marker, having a predicate or a noun phrase in its scope. This particle is further used in so-called periphrastic constructions (cf. Mixajlov, 1965). This type of construction consists of a nominalized verb form (that may contain a negational suffix itself) plus the negative particle, e.g.

(25) a. Ben de on-u pek anla-mış değil-im.
      1Sg too 3Sg-Acc very understand-PartPast Not-1Sg
      'I *really* didn't understand him either.'

    b. Oraya git-me-yecek değil-sin.
       there go-Neg-Fut Not-2Sg
       'You *certainly* will go there.'

As Tura (1981:320) states, these constructions 'may occur in discourse as contradiction, rejection or refutations of prior utterances, assumptions or beliefs'. As opposed to (normal) verbal negation, they thus express epistemic modality: it reflects the attitude of the speaker with respect to the truth value of the proposition. This can be exemplified by contrasting the neutral negative sentence of (26a) with the modal sentence of (26b):

(26) a. Ali gel-me-miş.
      Ali come-Neg-Rep
      'It seems/appears that Ali didn't come.'

    b. Ali gel-miş değil.
       Ali come-PartPast Not
       'Ali really didn't come.'

In Van Schaaik (1986) it was argued that the verb forms in periphrastic constructions of this type are based on nominalized verbs rather than participles. Hence, *gel-miş* and *git-me-yecek* in the examples (25b) and (26b) are to be interpreted as 'someone who has come' and 'someone who will not go' respectively.

2.3 Tag questions

Together with the question marker mi the negative particle *değil* forms yet a new particle *değil mi?* 'isn't it'. It functions as a trigger for confirmation or refutation of the previous utterance, as for instance in:

(27)   a.   Hasan Ankara'da çalışır, değil mi?
· 'Hasan works in Ankara, isn't it?'

b.   Ali hasta, değil mi?
'Ali is ill, isn't he.'

Compare these constructions with:

(28)   Ali hasta değil mi?
'Isn't Ali ill?'

As follows from the last examples, in written form it sometimes is hard to distinguish both types, especially when a comma lacks. Whereas *Ali hasta, değil mi?* is an assertion ('Ali is ill') for which a reaction is requested ('Say so, if not true') by means of *değil mi?*, the particle *değil* in *Ali hasta değil mi?* is the negator over *Ali hasta* 'Ali (is) ill'. The proposition *Ali hasta değil* 'Ali NOT ill', then, is finally questioned by the marker *mi*. The ambiguity 'negator plus question marker' versus 'the particle *değil mi*' may arise only when a third person singular is involved, since the category grammatical person (other than the one mentioned here) is overtly expressed on various chunks of grammatical material. Compare (29a) with (29b), which clearly show the difference in placement of the personal suffix *-sIn* 'you':

(29)   a.   Sen hasta-sın, değil mi?
'You are ill, isn't it?'

b.   Sen hasta değil mi-sin?
'Aren't you ill?'

In speech, however, there is no chance for ambiguity at all, since the particle *değil mi* is pronounced as /demi/, with stress on the first syllable.

3   Existential negation

Existence in Turkish is expressed by the particle *var* and non-existence by *yok*. Compare the positive existentials in the left hand column with the negative existentials of the right hand column:

(30)   a.   Su   var.   Su   yok.
water   EX   water   NegEX
'There is water'   'There's no water.'

b.   Su   var   mı?   Su   yok   mu?
· water   EX   QM   water   NegEX QM
'Is there water?'   'Is there no water?'

Apart from the question marker *mI*, the particles for existence and nonexistence may take a suffix for past (31a), conditional (31b), and reportative (31c):

(31) a. Su   var-dı.   Su   yok-tu.
        water   EX-past   water   NegEX-past
        'There was water.'   'There was no water.'

     b. Su   var-sa.   Su   yok-sa.
        water   EX-cond   water   NegEX-cond
        'If there is water.'   'If there is no water.'

     c. Su   var-mış.   Su   yok-muş.
        water   EX-rep   water   NegEX-rep
        'There seems to be water.'   'There seems to be no water.'

In special cases the particles may carry a personal (copula) marker. For instance, when talking about some holiday pictures one might use (32a), and when talking about a party or so (32b) may be used:

(32) a. Ama sen   yok-sun.
        but you   NegEX-2Sg
        'But you are absent.'

     b. O   zaman ben yok-tu-m.
        then   I   NegEX-1Sg
        'Then I wasn't (there).'

Turkish has no equivalent of 'to have'. Its functions are performed by the existential particles *var* and *yok* applied to a possessive noun phrase:

(33) Güzel bir araba-m   var-dı   ama, şimdi yok   artık.
     nice a   car-1Sg   EX-Past but   now   NegEX   anymore
     'I had a nice car, but now I don't have (it/one) anymore.'

3.1 The use of *yok* in prohibitions

When combined with an infinitive verb form (and complements), the particle *yok* expresses prohibitions, as often found in official inscriptions and the like. This usage can be exemplified by:

(34) a. Avuç aç-mak   yok.
        hand open-Inf   'yok'
        'Begging prohibited.'

     b. Orta   salla-mak   yok.
        fishing-rod   swing-Inf   'yok'
        'No fishing.'

c. Burada şapka   çıkar-mak yok.
   here   hat   take-off   'yok'
   'It is not allowed here to take your hat off.'

3.2 Negation of nominalized verbs by *yok*

As was indicated in 2.2, the negative particle *değil* can be combined with a nominalized verb, denoting the agent of the action. *Yok* can occur in similar constructions:

(35) a. Bu-nu   bil-me-yen   yok.
         this-Acc   know-Neg-PartPres NegEX
         'There is nobody who doesn't know this.'

      b. Bu-na   kabul ed-ecek   yok.
         this-Dat   accept-PartFut   NegEX
         'There is no one who will agree with that.'

The scope of the negator in these constructions is typical: in *ben de on-u pek anlamış değil-im* 'I really didn't understand him either' the fragment *on-u pek anlamış*, which functions as a complex predicate, is negated, and in *bu-nu bil-me-yen yok* 'there is nobody who doesn't know this' it is the entity *bu-nu bil-me-yen* which is not existant. In the latter example the entity referred to is based on a nominalized verb, as is the case in the *değil*-constructions, discussed in 2.2. The particle *yok*, however, may be used as a negator of an entire state of affairs expressed by a verbal complex. Again, a kind of epistemic modality is reflected. Compare the neutral (36a) with the modal (36b):

(36) a. Kadın   Ali-ye   bak-ma-dı.
         woman   Ali-Dat   look-Neg-Past
         'The woman didn't look at Ali.'

      b. Kadın-ın   Aliye   bak-tığ-ı   yok-tu.
         woman-Gen   Ali-Dat look-PartPast-Agr   'yok'-Past
         'The woman didn't look at Ali at all.'

Such a construction can be paraphrased by 'There was no "woman's-to-Ali-looking"', compare the Dutch equivalent *Het bestaat niet dat de vrouw naar Ali keek*, literally 'It doesn't exist that the woman looked at Ali'.

4 Other negative elements

4.1 Emphatic negation

In contemporary Turkish, the originally Persian noun *hiç* 'nothing' has several functions. First, in negative sentences (with a verb containing the Neg-suffix) it is used as an intensifier of the negation in the sense of *none whatever, none at all; never, never at all, not the least*. Examples are:

(37) a. Hiç bira bul-ama-dı-m.
          hiç beer find-NegPot-Past-1Sg
          'I couldn't find any beer at all.'

      b. Oraya hiç git-me-di-k.
          there hiç go-Neg-Past-1Pl
          'We have never gone there.'

      c. Ankara-ya git-ti-n mi? —Hiç.
          Ankara-Dat go-Past-2Sg QM hiç
          'Did you go to Ankara? —Not at all.'

Secondly, in interrogative sentences *hiç* can be translated as 'ever', in responses as 'never':

(38) Türkiye'ye hiç gittin mi? —Hiç.
      'Did you ever go to Turkey?' —'Never.'

Thirdly, the Turkish equivalent of an indefinite pronoun is often synthetic. In principle, it is based on a noun: *bir kim-se* = a who (ever it is), 'someone'; *bir yer-de* = a place-loc, 'somewhere'; *bir vakit* = a time, 'sometime'; *bir şey* = a thing, 'something'. The negative counterparts are formed with *hiç*, as in: *hiç bir kim-se* 'no one, nobody'; *hiç bir yer-de* 'nowhere'; *hiç bir vakit* 'never'; *hiç bir şey* 'nothing'. Further, we find such negations in a partitive sense: *bir-i* means 'one of them', and hence, *hiç biri* is 'none of them, not one of them'. The word *hiç* frequently implies a negative answer, as is shown with (39b) as a response to (39a):

(39) a. Bugün ne yap-tı-n?
          today what do-Past-2Sg
          'What did you do today?'

      b. 'Hiç.' (omitting yap-ma-dı-m 'do-Neg-Past-1Sg)
          'Nothing'.

4.2 Negational intensifiers

Apart from the synthetic *hiç bir vakit* and *hiç bir zaman*, both meaning 'never', there are two borrowings from Arabic with a related meaning: *asla* 'never' and *katiyen* 'by no means, never; categorically, absolutely, definitely'. As is the case with *hiç* in negative sentences, these words function as an intensifier. They too are used in combination with a negative verb as can be shown by the following examples:

(40) a. Asla   yap-ma-z-dı-m.
          never   do-Neg-Aor-Past-1Sg
          'I never would do (so).'

      b. Katiyen   yanıl-ma-dı-m.
          absolutely Err-Neg-Past-1Sg
          'I am absolutely not mistaken.'

4.3 The negative suffix *-sIz*

Besides negative particles and the negation suffix for verbs, Turkish has a privative suffix, *-sIz*, that is attached to nouns thereby yielding an adjective[5]. Hence, *su-suz (bir memleket)* is '(a region) without water'; *süt-süz (bir kahve)* is '(a coffee) without milk'; *et-siz (bir yemek)* '(a meal) without meat'; *tat-sız* 'tasteless'; *merhamet-siz* 'merciless'.

5 Negators in speech

Finally, now that we have seen how the various negators of Turkish are to be classified morphologically and how their syntactic properties can be described, it seems useful to pay at least some attention to the way they are used in conversation. In well educated speech, generally speaking, the answer to a so-called yes-no question contains mostly (if not always) a fragment of the question. Thus, if someone asks *Hasan geldi mi?* 'Did Hasan come', the appropriate answers are *Geldi* 'yes' and *Gelmedi* 'no'; for *Hasan hasta mı?* 'Is Hasan ill' both *Hasta* 'yes' and *Hasta değil* 'no' are 'good' answers; and on a question pertaining to existence, e.g. *Bira var mı?* 'Is there beer' both *var* 'yes' and *yok* 'no' can be expected. In colloquial speech, however, much of the work is done by *yok* in a negative reply, often pronounced with a long vowel. So one may hear *yoook* as an answer to *üalış-tı mı?* 'Did he work?'; *Zengin mi?* 'Is (s)he rich?'; and *Para-nız var mı?* 'Do you have (some) money?'. Apart from the devices described here there are the words *evet* 'yes; indeed' and *hayır* 'no; on the contrary' as the means for influencing the course of a conversation.

Notes

1. The derivative ('der') suffix *-lI* denotes here 'inhabitant of x', for instance, *avrupa-lı* 'a european'. The derivative suffix *-lEş* means 'to become x', and combined with *avrupa-lı* it yields 'to become (as) a european': 'europeanize'.

2. For an extensive treatment of Turkish word order, see Erguvanlı (1979).

3. The Present Continuous is formed by *-yor* when a verb stem ends in a vowel and by *-Iyor* after a consonant stem. Thus, *gel-me-yor* underlies *gel-mi-yor*. For a full account of this problem, see Van Schaaik (1988:52-55).

4. Cf. Kerslake (1990).

5. The 'positive' counterpart of such adjectives is formed by the noun plus the four-fold suffix *-lI*, as in *süt-lü (bir çay)* 'a tea with milk'; *et-li yemek* 'meal(s) with meat (in it)'; *tat-lı* 'tasteful; nice'; *merhamet-li* 'merciful, kind'.

Abbreviations

Abl	ablative	Loc	locative
Acc	accusative	Neg	verbal negator
Agr	agreement	NegEX	non-existential particle
Aor	aorist	Negpot	impotential
Caus	causative	NOT	nominal negator
CM	compound marker	PartFut	future participle
Cond	conditional	PartPres	present participle
Cop	copula	Pass	passive
Dat	dative	Plur	plural
Der	derivative (nominal).	Pot	potential
EX	existential particle	Pp, PartPast	past participle
Fut	future	QM	question marker
Gen	genitive	Rel	relativizer
Inf	infinitive	Rep	reportative

References

Erguvanlı, E. (1979). *The function of word order in Turkish grammar.* (UCLA dissertation), University of California Publications in Linguistics, vol 106. Berkeley and Los Angeles, UCP 1984.
Kerslake, C. (1990). 'The semantics of possibility', Paper read at the Fifth International Conference on Turkish Linguistics, 15-17 August 1990, London.

50   *Gerjan van Schaaik*

Lewis, G.L. (1967). *Turkish Grammar*. Oxford, Clarendon Press.
Mixajlov, M.S. (1965). *Issledovanija po grammatike Tureckogo jazyka (perifrastieskie formy Tureckogo glagola)*. Moskva, Izdatel'stvo Nauka.
Ruhlen, M. (1987. *A guide to the world's languages*. Vol. I. Stanford, Stanford University Press.
Schaaik, G.J. van, (1986). 'Verb based terms and modality in Turkish', Paper, Institute for General Linguistics, University of Amsterdam.
Schaaik, G.J. van, (1988). *Basiscursus Turks (A basic course in Turkish)*. Muiderberg, Coutinho.
Tura, S.S. (1981). '"Yes, he hasn't" and a few other not's in Turkish'. *Proceedings of the 7th annual meeting of the Berkeley Linguistic Society*, (317-327), Berkeley, BLS.

Sentani

Margaret Hartzler

0 Introduction

The Sentani language is one of the many Papuan (non-Austronesian) languages spoken on the island of New Guinea. According to Wurm (1982:18,94), the three dialects of Sentani, together with Tabla and Nafri, comprise the Sentani language family, and are part of the Trans-New Guinea phylum. Speakers number approximately 25,000. For further details of the phonological relationships existing in this family, see Gregerson and Hartzler (1987:1-29). This paper is based on the Central Sentani dialect.[1]

As is typical of the Papuan languages of New Guinea, Sentani is characterized by a SOV ordering in the clause, and postpositionals. In the noun phrase, adjectives and numerals follow the noun head, while demonstratives, possessives, noun modifiers, and relative clauses precede it.

In the following examples, the parenthetical forms show the pronunciation of the word after morphophonemic changes have taken place.

(1) Nebei yo   neke-ø-ai-le (nekate) yun ran na   anuwau
     that village stay-pres-3psR-VE   head top its place

     mbai na   kani hasai.
     one its ground red

     'Above the head of the village is a place with red dirt.'

(2) Nebei anuwau emæho-le   Koi   Yau wæ
     that place kangaroo-with Dancing Land manner

     e-ele-wo-ai-le (eyelewate).
     Nt-say-PIpf-3psR-VE

     'That place was called the Kangaroo Dancing Land.'

There are no special markers for yes-no questions, apart from sentence final rising intonation. Content questions are handled with interrogative words, which are found immediately after the initial Subject word. In reality, as the subject can be omitted, the interrogative is often found sentence initial. The focus of the question will also alter the word ordering, as items in focus will be fronted.

(3)   Weyæ   makei-se   e-e-le-re?   (elere)
       you   where-to   go-2ssI-VE-to
       'Where are you going?'

(4)   Næendæ   yæ   moko-ø-a-bo-en-le? (mokabonde)
       how   manner make-Pres-1dsI-hit-3ssI-VE
       'How are we going to do this?'

Comparatives are relatively rare, but can be accomplished:

(5)   Ka   na   koko   w(a)-oro   hului?
       fish   its   length   your-foot   possible
       'Was the fish as long as your foot?'

This paper, however, is concerned with the ways that negation, in all its facets, operates in the Sentani language. The Sentani speaker can choose to negate verbs, nominal, pronominal, adjectival and adverbial elements, and clauses. Each of these three categories employs a different method of negation.

1 Negation of verbs

1.1 Simple non-imperative verbs

The simple Sentani verb comprises an initial verb root, followed by a series of affixes marking the person and number of the clause subject and object, and aspect. As the subject markers for past and present 'tense' differ from those for future, they set up a natural dichotomy between realis and irrealis, with aspectual markers providing further distinctions in the realis status only. These markers are: -*ke*- 'past perfect,' -*wo*- 'past imperfect,' and -*ø*- 'present.' The optional verb ending (ve) morpheme -*le* appears to have no function beside separating the basic verb string from certain modals (certainty, uncertainty, desire), clause level conjunctions which may attach to the string, and any new verb which follows. This latter, in a heavily serialized verb environment, makes this morpheme useful to the analyst. The usual configuration is as follows: root ± Aspect + Subject Marker ± Object Marker ± Verb ending

(6)   Neyæ   u-eu-ne.   (weunge)
       he   say-3ssR-3so
       'He is saying to him.'

(7)   Neyæ   u-ke-eu-mi-le.   (ukeumile)
       he   say-PPerf-3ssR-3po-VE
       'He said to them.'

(8) Neyæ u-en-ne-le. (wennele)
he say-3ssI-3so-VE
'He will say to him.'

When the verb is negated, all affixation is dropped, and replaced by non-temporal (Nt) marker -*iy*.[2] This means that the negative verb is not differentiated for subject or object person and number, realis, irrealis, or aspect.

Negation is achieved by prefixing a vowel homogeneous to the vowel in the first syllable of the verb root to the root, and suffixing -*i* to the root. When the verb begins with a vowel, the prefixed vowel is elided. Verbs whose first vowel is *a*, *æ* or *u* will be prefixed with *e*, rather than the homogeneous vowel.

(9) O-boro-i.
Neg-hear-Nt
'I/you/we/he/she/they didn't/aren't/will not hear.'

(10) E-me-i.
Neg-come-Nt
'I/you/we/he/she/they didn't/aren't/will not come.'

(11) I-kile-i.
Neg-catch-Nt
'I/you/we/he/she/they didn't/aren't/will not catch.'

(12) E-buke-i.
Neg-turn back-Nt
'I/you/we/he/she/they didn't/aren't/will not turn back.'

(13) E-yaro-i.
Neg-take-Nt
'I/you/we/he/she/they didn't/aren't/will not take.'

1.2 Complex non-imperative verbs

Verb units in Sentani can involve more than one verb root. Serialization of verb roots in this manner has several purposes in Papuan languages: (1) to compress a complex series of actions into one verbal expression; (2) to create new verbs; and (3) to modify, by adding a second verb root, the action of the first verb root (Foley 1986:113-128). In many cases, then, the second root is regarded as an aspectual marker, and to achieve the correct meaning, the serial construction is obligatory. This second aspectual root, moreover, may become ritualized, so that the whole meaning of the verb is not the sum of its parts.

(14)   Raisimbe   yomo-re   au-ei-ho-ke.
       Raisimbe   point-to   row-3dsR-kill-PPerf
       'Those two rowed straight to Raisimbe Point.'

The verb *ho-* 'kill', in the serial position, gives the meaning 'directly, with no deviance' to the main verb.

(15)   Nane anuwau ere-i-me-i-en-le   eyæ kena okoikoi...
       that place see-Nt-come-Nt-3dsR-VE   we want do not
       'We don't want any of the places we have seen so far.'

The verb *me-* 'come', in the serial position, insinuates that the main action has occurred up to the present point for some length of time.

In the positive construction, the order of morphemes in a complex verb is as follows: Root + Subject Marker ± Object Marker + Verb Root ± Aspect ± Subject Marker ± Object Marker ± Verb ending. Up to four roots may be found in these serial constructions. Not all are fully conjugated. The extent of the conjugation in Central Sentani depends on the subject of the verb, and whether the verb is realis or irrealis.

(16)   Reyæ ijoko ere-re-ne-ko-en-le   mo.
       I   eye   see-1ssI-3so-do-3ssI-VE   just
       'I will just look all around...'

(17)   Kamendake   bu   ran-ne i-eu-fako-eu-bo-ke.
       crocodile   water   top-on go up-3ssR-float-3ssR-hit-PPerf
       'The crocodile suddenly appeared, floating on top of the water.'

When serial verbs are negated, all affixation is again dropped. The negative marker is prefixed to the first root, and non-temporal markers as outlined above suffixed to all roots in the string.

(18)   Nda   ro:miyæ   ma:hi   e-ye-i-bo-i.
       these people   condition   Neg-happen-Nt-hit-Nt
       'The condition of these people is not going to change quickly.'

(19)   Ney   uwa   e-huba-i-hi-i.
       he   body   Neg-feel-Nt-enter-Nt
       'He didn't feel it.'

The concepts 'always' and 'never' are handled through this process of verb serialization:

(20)   Weyæ   o-bo-i-e-i.
       you   Neg-pray-Nt-go-Nt
       'You never pray.'

(21)   Allah Hubale Mando, i   u   boye u   yæ   mangko u   rai
        God   highest one   fire   body wind body with cloud   body fog

        na u   yæ æi   yobe   næi kamahe   næi-re he-ra
        its body with our   ancestors   their ancestors   their-to time-from

        kele-eu-e-ke-eu-mi   me-ke   nda   he-ne.
        show-3ssR-go-PPerf-3ssR-3po   come-PPerf   this   time-in

        'Almighty God, from our ancestors' time until now, has always shown himself
        to people, through fire, wind, clouds, and fog.'

Logical connectors can be attached to the negative verb complex when
applicable. No verb ending particle is attached; this morpheme does not
appear in negative verbs.

1.3 Negative imperative

There are two distinct negative imperatives, one which includes subject and
object markers and one which does not. These are handled separately below.

1.3.1 Negative imperatives without Subject or Object markers

This type of negative imperative resembles the normal negative verb complex, in that it comprises a verb root prefixed by a vowel (as outlined in the
previous section), and suffixed by -*i*. This construction is then followed by
portmanteau focus marker *yæ*, which, because it usually follows a glide
ending in /i/, is manifested as *jæ* (see Hartzler, M.: 1976). This focus marker
is not obligatory, and has been found, in fact, on non-imperative verbs when
a special emphasis is required. The imperative nature of the negative can be
determined from the grammatical structure of the sentence or tone of the
exclamation. However, it is normally used, and the command loses much
of its power if it is omitted.

(23)   O-ko-i   jæ!
        Neg-do-Nt   focus
        'Don't do it!'

(24)   Fe   e-fæ-i   jæ!
        fear   Neg-fear-Nt   focus
        'Don't be afraid.'

Again, when -*e*- 'go' is added, the meaning of the unit is changed from a one-
time prohibition, to an instruction to avoid certain actions as a way of life,
i.e. it adds an 'always' or 'never' dimension to the imperative.

(25) Be   ho   yen   raba   moko-nai-mi-e-en-le
      betel nut   coconuts   leaf   fence   make-3psI-3po-go-3ssI-VE

      behau-uhau   wæ   e-yaro-i-e-i   jæ!
      bravely   with   Neg-take-Nt-go-Nt   focus
      'When people make, [as they] always [do], fences around their gardens, never
      have the gall to go and take [their produce].'

(26) Mai   miyæ   na-re   me   u   na:jen   ban   mæ
      your   wife   her-to   hand   body properly   not   manner

      o-moko-i-e-i   jæ!
      Neg-do-Nt-go-Nt   focus
      'Never behave improperly toward your wife.'

1.3.2 Negative imperatives with Subject and Object markers
When subject and object markers are included in the negative imperative
complex, the initial consonant of the focus marker *yae* changes from *y/j* to *m*.
This phonological change occurs normally when this portmanteau focus/in-
strument/manner marker occurs after a nasal consonant. This is not always the
case in this construction. However, the regular occurrence of *m* rather than *y/j*
here may originally have been influenced by the fact that most object markers
involve nasal consonants, and it is customary in Sentani to elide vowels, under
specific conditions, between nasals and nasals, and between nasals and voiced
stops. Again, the focus marker is not obligatory, but normally used.

The subject markers are irrealis. They and the object markers occur postpositional in the verb. The non-temporal marker is omitted.

(27) Fe   e-fæ-em-me   mæ!
      fear   Neg-fear-2psI-1po   focus
      'Don't you all be afraid of us.'

(28) Ra-re   wæi fa   yæ   me   e-bæ-ei-se   mæ.
      me-to   your child manner hand   Neg-count-2ssI-1so   Focus
      'Don't you (singular) count me as one of your children.'

(29) Wa   rambun wæi-sa   nuke-en-ha-en-le-na,   benen
      your   things you-from   seize-3sfs-put-3sfs-VE-if   again

      i-riye-ei-ne   mæ.
      Neg-collect-2ssI-3so   Focus
      'If your possession is seized, don't collect it again.'

(30) Ra-re   i-rime-em-re   mæ. (rimense)
      me-to   Neg-cry-2psI-1so   Focus
      'Don't you all cry for me.'

(31) Na-re   e-ahe-em-mi   mæ.
      them-to   Neg-forbid-2psI-3po   Focus
      'Don't you all forbid them.'

1.4 Negative qualifiers to the verb complex

Aside from the outright negative as outlined above, qualifiers such as 'not yet' and 'still' can be added. Both of these expressions use the word *naman*; however, 'not yet' requires a negative verb, while 'still' combines *naman* with a positive verb. Examples are:

(32) Reyæ naman kalia   e-bæ-i-so-i.
      I   not:yet work   Neg-finish-Nt-kill-Nt
      'I haven't finished work yet.'

(33) Reyæ naman kalia moko-a-le. (mokale)
      I   still   work make-1ssR-VE
      'I am still working.'

When *naman* 'not yet/still' is used as an answer to a question, the positive verb is repeated, to avoid ambiguity:

(34) Weyæ   naman kalia moko-æ? Naman mok(o)-a-le.
      you   still   work make-2ssR still   make-1ssR-VE
      'Are you still working? I am still working.'

(35) Weyæ   naman kalia moko-æ? Naman.
      you   still   work make-2ssR not:yet
      'Are you still working? I haven't started yet.'

2 Negation of nominal, pronominal, adjectival, and adverbial elements

Non-verbal elements in Sentani are negated by adding *ban* after the item to be negated.

(36) A   hele ban.
      word   true not
      'It's not true, untrue word.'

(37) Reyæ ban!
      I   not
      'Not me!'

(38) Neyæ na   malo ban orayeke.
      they their clothes not they:always:walked
      'They used to walk around with no clothes all the time.'

Regular quantifiers, such as 'all,' 'many,' and 'few' can be negated by *ban*:

(39) Nebei nanemene ban ma,   na   name keli me-ke-ai-le.
      that all   not shape its   three four come-PPerf-3psR-VE
      'Not everyone came, only a few.'

3 Negative relationships on the clause level

Negative logical relationships between clauses can be achieved through the use of negative conjunctions and conjunctive compounds. Apart from the adversative 'but' sentence structure, the formation of these types of constructions is very rare in this language. The two which have so far come to light are *bele-ne* 'so that...not,' and *mo...ban, nebeibe* 'not only...but.' These are handled below.

3.1 *Nebeibe* 'but'

The commonly used adversative or contra-expectation sentence is formed by using *nebeibe* between the opposing clauses:

(40) Ebale Yakali iwoine   nebeibe neyæ a   hi
      Ebale Yakali 2:were:giving:him   but   he   word   other
      y   ukeumi.
      with he:said:to:them
      'Those two were trying to give it to him, but he didn't want it.'

3.2 *Bele-ne* 'so that....not'

This type of clause negation is formed by adding *bele-ne*[3] 'not-reason' to a clause with a positive verb complex. See the following examples:

(41) Nane merau hiwa yo   wa-re   me   nonaiyewonde bele-ne
      that also other people you-to hand they:put:down not-reason
      nebeinye a   na   ijen   mæ   mo   keleumile.
      therefore word its straight manner just you:will:show:them.
      'So that they will not condemn (put down hand) you, show them honesty in your speech.'

(42) Ako   næi   holo-na   mæi fafa-re   a   lækei
     fathers their group-poss   your children-to   word   strong

     helen sele eweyei   jæ,   na   hibi-hibi   kena   beko
     much very   don't   say   pos immediately   desire bad

     konaiyende   bele-ne.
     they:will:do:it   not-because

     'Fathers, don't speak strongly to your children, so that they will not want to do bad things.'

3.3 *Mo (...) ban, nebeibe* 'not only... but'

This type of clause negation is achieved by adding *mo (...) ban, nebeibe* 'not only, but...' between the two clauses involved. An example is:

(43) Kalia foi   ræi   ijoko be-ne   ererete   he   mo   ban
     work good my   eye   face-in I:see:you   time just not

     nebeibe reyæ erele   he   nebei   sului mbai mokole.
     but   I   I:will:go time that   the   same it:does

     'Work well, not only when I am looking, but when I go away.'

(44) Nda kiyæ   rare   mo   be   ei   haweufe   ban
     that person me-to just face he   welcomes:me   not

     nebeibe nane merau r:i   miy be   ei   haweunge.
     but   that like   my   wife face he   welcomes

     'That person welcomes not only me, but my wife also.'

3.4 Psychological negation

Occasionally the Sentani add their noun and adverbial negator *ban* to clauses to create a negative psychological effect. In this first example below, the speaker is leading into a request for services from his audience. The sentence literally means, 'I want to ask you for something, no.' When this is said, however, the audience then expects the follow-through: 'but...I do have this one problem...' In other words, the addition of *ban* is a surface-structure politeness which is meant to be ignored.

(45) Rabuhi-re   mokonsele-re   ban.
     something-to   you:will:do:for:me-purpose   not
     'I don't intend for you to do anything for me [but there is just this one small thing....]

In the following two examples, we see again the speaker's use of *ban* to acknowledge the sensibilities of his audience, without in any way ambiguating his message.

(46) Nændæ yæ   mokabonde ban?
      how   manner we:will:do:it not
      'How will we do this [considering that we've already done everything already]?'

(47) Mekele ijen-de yæ   ale   ban?
      where   place-to manner we:will:go not
      'Where will we go [considering we have gone everywhere already].'

In this case, then, it is seen that *ban* does not change the underlying meaning of the clause to which it is attached.

4 Negation of the indefinite

Words exist in Sentani for specific denotation of inherently negative situations. The use of each word depends on whether the reference item is human or non-human, and on whether the reference point does in fact exist, even if unable to be found at that particular point in time. *Olo* is used for people, while *an* is used for animals or objects, which do exist somewhere. *U* is used for objects which do not exist at all. Non-existent humans usually take *ban*. Examples of usage are as follows:

(48) Eli imæ-na?   Olo.
      Eli house-his No (person)
      'Is Eli at home? No, he's not.'

(49) Rey ekale be   nebei ro   miyæ   olo.
      I   went   but   that   man woman none
      'I went, but there was nobody [there].'

(50) Nebei aye ekale   bæle   an   ma.
      that bird I:went I:hunt none shape
      'I went and looked for that bird, but there was nothing there.'

(51) Reyæ isi   an.
      I   know nothing
      'I don't know.'

(52) Weyæ fi   bele? U.
      you   sago with   none
      'Do you have any sago? No, I don't.'

(53) Weyæ   fa   bele? Fa   ban.
     you   child with child none
     'Do you have any children? No, I don't.'

The concept of 'nobody' or 'nothing' can be handled with verbal inflection as well:

(54) Ro:miyæ   nanemene me-ke-ai-le?   Ro:miyæ   e-me-i   mo
     people   all   come-PPerf-3psR-VE   people   Neg-come-Nt   just
     'Did everyone come? No, nobody came.'

As can be seen from the above examples, the answer 'No' can take many different forms, using verbal negative inflection, negativizer *ban* and other inherently negative words. Further examples are:

(55) Nahului bulu ahune-eu-ne-ko-en-le?   Nahului   ban.
     possible hole fix-2sfs-3so-do-3ssI-VE   possible not
     'Can you fix this hole? No, I can't.'

(56) Weyæ   Jayapura-re   e-ke-æ?   E-e-i.
     you   Jayapura-to   go-PPerf-2ss   Neg-go-Nt
     'Did you go to Jayapura? No, I didn't go.'

5 Negative combinations and scope

All of the negatives outlined above can be combined in one clause. Each negated item requires its own negative. A negative applied to one item does not extend its range of meaning to other sentence elements, as often occurs in English. Examples are:

(57) Nebei reyæ ubene   nekaise   neyæ   e-me-i.
     that I   thoughts I:think:them he   neg-come-Nt
     'I think he will not come.'

Note here that 'I don't think he will come' is not possible in Sentani. The negative in one clause will not transfer to the next. Similarly, if the adverbial element of ability is added to the verb, both the verb and the ability adverb must be negated.

(58) Reyæ nahului   ban e-e-i.
     I   possible   not Neg-go-Nt
     'I cannot possibly go.'

In the following example, there is no girl, and there is no girl present:

(59) Nane mængke   ban-ne an.
      that girl   not-in no one
      'There's no girl, not here.'

When the adverbial is a complex of two or more words, each word receives its own negation:

(60) Neyæ nebei anuwau-ra rei   ban mai ban mæ
      he   that   place-from happy not happy not manner

      aloungekoke ewole.
      he:departed he:went
      'He left that place sadly.'

The following example combines negatives to give a more forceful effect:

(61) Nda miyæ   yaweisoi-re   nahului   ban nibi u.
      this woman leading-to   possible   not road none
      'Getting this woman finally back is impossible, there's no way.'

6 Negative in focus

There are occasions when Sentani speakers wish to focus on the item being negated, i.e. 'It wasn't me who did it,' vs. 'I didn't do it.' In this situation, the item in focus is fronted in the clause, and bracketed with *nebei... yæ*. See the examples below:

(62) Nebei reyæ e-ere-i-bo-i   jæ,   neyæ ere-eu-ko-ke.
      that I   Neg-see-Nt-hit-Nt focus   he   see-3ss-do-PPerf
      'It wasn't me who saw it, it was him.'

When the negated item in focus is not a verbal element, it is again fronted, but bracketed instead with *nebei... ban*.

(63) Nebei na   name   keli ban ma,   nanemene me-ke-ai-le.
      that its three four not shape all   come-PPerf-3psR-VE
      'Not just a few came, but everyone.'

Negation in Sentani, then, is achieved in various ways, depending on the grammatical item being negated or the purpose of the speaker. These different methods can be used in conjunction with each other, to create special nuances of meaning and greater negative emphasis. Table 1 summarizes these various negators.

Table 1. Summary of Sentani negators

Verbs	
Simple Non-Imperative	V + root + *i*
Complex Non-Imperative	V + root + *i* + root + *i*
Referenced Imperative	V + root + subject +/- object +*mæ*
Non-referenced Imperative	V + root + *i* + *jæ*
Nominals, Pronominals, adjectives, adverbs	
	ban
Other	
Not yet/still	*naman*
So that...not	*bele-ne*
Not only...but	*mo (...) ban, nebeibe*
But	*nebeibe*
No (person)	*olo*
No (bird or animal)	*an*
No (non-existent inanimate)	*u*
No (non-existent animate)	*ban*
Psychological	*ban*

Notes

1. This analysis was based on texts from native Sentani speakers collected and translated by Dwight Hartzler, who gave his insights into the Sentani verb as a basis for the analysis in this paper. Sentani speakers include Usiel Pallo, Chris Mehue, Beris Monim, Gad Monim, and Yu Felle, all of the Central Dialect.

2. The suffix *-i* can be used not only in negative constructions as outlined in this paper, but in imperatives, present participles, and to mark customary actions. When *-i* appears, all references to time are removed; hence the label 'non-temporal.' Examples are:

(i)   a.   Imperative: *Boro-i!* 'Listen!'

      b.   Present Participle: See example (61)

         Nda miyæ yawe-i-ho-i = this woman lead-Nt-kill-Nt
         'Finally bringing back this woman....'

c. Customary actions (from the text *Emaeho Kili Bahele Yoku Kili Bahele Ahuba*) in which kangaroos would every day come and dance, while the Kili Bahe dog would come every day and watch):

(ii)   Yoku ene-ra   e-i-nuwe-i-bo-i-o-le.
        dog   edge-from go-Nt-sit-Nt-hit-Nt-go down-VE
        'The dog would go and sit down on the edge of the hill...'

3. *Bele* is a negative on the clause level only. On the phrase level, *bele* means 'with' or 'accompanied by', or indicates possession, i.e.

(iii)   Ya   mbai mo,   Hele na   ro   *bele* miyæ *bele* kaisa haweiboke.
        day   one   just Sere its man with   woman with   by:boat they:came
        'One day a man from Sere *and* his wife rowed over *with* their boat...'

Abbreviations

Neg	negative marker	2psI	2nd person plural subject, ir-realis
Nt	non-temporal marker		
PIpf	past imperfect	3ssR	3rd person singular subject, realis
PPerf	past perfect		
Pres	Present	3psR	3rd person plural subject, realis
VE	verb ending	3ssI	3rd person singular subject, irrealis
V	vowel		
1ssR	1st singular subject, realis	3psI	3rd person plural subject, ir-realis
1ssI	1st singular subject, irrealis		
2ssR	2nd person singular subject, realis	1so	1st person singular object
		1po	1st person plural object
2ssI	2nd person singular subject, irrealis	3po	3rd person plural object

References

Foley, William A. (1986). *The Papuan Languages of New Guinea.* Cambridge: Cambridge University Press.
Gregerson, Kenneth, and Margaret Hartzler (1987). 'Towards a reconstruction of Proto-Tabla-Sentani phonology.' *Oceanic Linguistics*, Vol. XXVI, No. 1-2, 1-29. Honolulu: University of Hawaii Press.
Hartzler, Margaret (1976). 'Central Sentani phonology.' *Irian bulletin of Irian Jaya development* 5, 1:66-81. Abepura: Universitas Cenderawasih.
Wurm, Stephen A. (1982). *Papuan languages of Oceania.* Tübingen: Gunter Narr Verlag.

Lewo

Robert Early

1 Introduction

The Lewo language[1] is spoken by around 1000 people on the island of Epi, right at the geographical centre of the small Pacific Island micro-state of Vanuatu, for which over one hundred other vernacular languages are reported (Tryon 1976).

Following the classification adopted by Ruhlen (1987:167), all of the languages of Vanuatu will be classified as Austronesian\Malayo-Polynesian\ Central-Eastern Malayo-Polynesian\Eastern Malayo-Polynesian\Oceanic. One of the higher order subgroups of Oceanic is Southern New Hebrides (Vanuatu) (sv), another is Remote Oceanic. Within Remote Oceanic can be found the Central and Northern New Hebrides (Vanuatu) subgroup (NCV), to which Lewo belongs.[2] The only other languages in Vanuatu outside of sv and NCV are three Polynesian Outlier languages.

Lewo is a prepositional svo language, without a formal or morphological comparative construction. In content questions, question words are found in pattern-position, while yes-no questions are marked by intonation. While some individual modifiers may occur preposed to the head noun, the normal order of constituent classes in the nominal phrase is head-adjective-plural marker-numeral-demonstrative-relative clause:[3]

Sira	kokan	la telu	nene	naρa suρe la a-pisi	pani-la.
female	small	Pl three	these	Rel chief Pl 3Pl-spoke	to-3Pl

'These three girls that the chiefs reprimanded.'

As is the case for the large majority of Vanuatu languages, no modern description of Lewo grammar has yet been published. However, this data paper on negation is a good place to start for Lewo, because one of the more interesting features of the language is the morphological complexity of the standard clausal negation strategy. Most of the paper is devoted to describing this (section 2), and then placing it in typological (section 3) and comparative (section 4) perspective. Some other aspects of negation in Lewo are also mentioned in 2.9.

2 Description of Lewo negation

2.1 Negative particles

There are three distinct morphological forms which may be used to construct negative expressions in Lewo. For now, these forms will be called 'elements' or 'particles', and they will be written with word breaks in all the examples that follow, with their morphological and word-class status to be discussed later. The three forms are as follows:

- The particle *ve*, which occurs before the item being negated. This particle is marked for the only morphological tense or aspect distinction that is made in Lewo: the realis/irrealis aspect. The formal marking of the distinction is carried by an alternation in the initial consonant of the verb stem.[4] The irrealis form *ve* is used as the citation form, while the realis form is *pe*. It should be noted at this point that this element is identical in form to that of the copula verb.

- The particle *re*, which occurs following the item being negated. We will see that under certain conditions, the other two negative particles (*ve/pe* and *poli*, below) may be absent from a negative construction, but *re* always occurs. As with the first particle, this form is also homophonous with another element in Lewo structure, in this case, the partitive particle.

- The particle *poli*, which normally occurs right at the end of the clause in which an item is negated. A major restriction on the occurrence of *poli* is that it only marks negative in expressions which are in realis aspect, where *pe* rather than *ve* occurs as the first negative particle. *poli* is often reduced to *po*.

In the morpheme transcriptions in examples, and in the text, *ve* and *pe* will normally be glossed or referred to as NEG1 (negative particle 1). If it seems advantageous to distinguish them at any point, *ve* will be glossed as I.NEG1 (negative particle 1 portmanteaued with irrealis marking) and the realis form *pe* will be glossed as R.NEG1 (negative particle 1 portmanteaued with realis marking). *Re* will be glossed as NEG2, and *poli/po* as NEG3. These designations will also be used for similar particles from other languages. The negative particles will be underlined in examples.

2.2 Negation in standard verbal predicate clauses

We will now see how these three forms occur in standard clauses. With Lewo being an svo language, *ve/pe* and *re* cluster very tightly with the verb phrase material, actually enclosing it fore and aft, and helping to define it, while *poli* may not occur until after any object or oblique argument has been stated, which often sets it off quite a distance from the first two particles. Therefore, we can characterise the standard negated sv(o) clause in Lewo as being of the form:

> S NEG1 V NEG2 (O) (X) (NEG3)
> i.e. realis: S *pe* V *re* (O) (X) *poli*
> or irrealis: S *ve* V *re* (O) (X)

These patterns are exemplified in (1-2) for a simple intransitive clause, and in (3-4) for a simple transitive clause. (Note that *vano/pano* in (a) and *va/pa* in (b) are simply utterance final and non-final variants.)

(1) Irrealis Affirmative Irrealis Negative
    Naga ø-vano.   Naga ve   ø-va   re.
    he   3Sg-I.go   he   I.Neg1   3Sg-I.go Neg2
    'He will go.'   'He won't go.'

(2) Realis Affirmative   Irrealis Negative
    Naga ø-pano.   Naga pe   ø-pa   re   poli.
    he   3Sg-R.go   he   R.Neg1   3Sg-R.go Neg2   Neg3
    'He has gone.'   'He hasn't gone.'

(3) Irrealis Affirmative
    Naga ø-visa   suniena tai.
    he   3Sg-I.say   story   Art
    'He will tell a story.'

    Irrealis Negative
    Naga ve   ø-visa   re   suniena tai.
    he   I.Neg1   3Sg-I.say Neg2   story   Art
    'He will not tell a story.'

(4) Realis Affirmative
    Naga ø-pisa   suniena tai.
    he   3Sg-R.say   story   Art
    'He told a story.'

    Realis Negative
    Naga pe   ø-pisa   re   suniena tai poli.
    he   R.Neg1   3Sg-R.say Neg2   story   Art Neg3
    'He didn't tell a story.'

In (4b) we can see how the object *suniena tai* 'a story' is placed between *re* NEG2 and *poli* NEG3.

Both (2b) and (4b) show that the realis aspect is used when indicating an event that did not take place in the past. This is also the case for anticipated events, which have not yet taken place, which are constructed with a particle *wa* after *poli* (see (7)). From some perspectives, it might be thought that irrealis is more appropriate to express the notion of an event that did not occur, or of an event that has not yet taken place. However, Lewo assigns realis marking to both these situations, which is not unreasonable, as the negative is indicating the non-occurrence of events which if they had taken place, would have been completed events in past time. However, the use of realis in these contexts requires that the semantic specification of realis as referring to already completed or commenced events needs some expansion, and in fact challenges the claim that Lewo marks aspect, arguing perhaps for a future/non-future tense distinction.

Before looking at how these negative elements also function in negating non-verbal constituents and predicates (2.3.), further sets of examples of the pattern negating verbal predicates are given.

In (5), another example with the irrealis pattern, just *ve* and *re*, is given, while in (6), all three negative elements can be found with realis aspect. The clause being negated in each is enclosed in square brackets.

(5)   ...sape nua [inna   ve   ne-visuar   re   sisi kokan la naᵽa]
         ...say that I   Neg1 1Sg-look.after Neg2 child small   Pl that
         '(A message reached me) saying that I wouldn't look after those children.'

(6)   Yaru na yo   pe   nene, [pe te-kilia   re   yaru nene poli]
         man of   place where this   Neg1 1Pl-know Neg2 man this Neg3
         'This man from where, we don't know this man.'

Continuing with further examples, some clauses with additional components or more complex constituents are given. In (7), we see two members of a very small class of particles that may follow *poli* at the end of the clause. These particles give aspectual and truth-value assessments of the whole clause, and may be regarded as clause periphery, with *poli* still marking the boundary of the clause nucleus. (7) also shows that not just direct objects, but also oblique arguments occur before *poli*.

(7)   Naga pe   pisawal re   pani ko   poli   yo   wa.
         he   Neg1 tell   Neg2   Prep you Neg3 maybe yet
         'Maybe he hasn't told you yet.'

Next, we see that other constituents of more complex verb phrases can be included in the core that is surrounded by *pe* and *re*. Two examples of this are object person suffixes (8), post-verbal modifiers (which are relics of an earlier serial verb construction) (9), and various other modifiers closely knit to the verb (10-11). (9) shows how Lewo forms a 'never' construction: the regular negative elements, plus post-verbal modifier *-li*.

(8) Pe   ne-mi-loge-miu   re   a-patomi   poli.
     Neg1 1Sg-R-hear-2Pl   Neg2   2Pl-R.come   Neg3
     'I didn't hear you come.'

(9) Pe   ne-pisu-li re   Santo   poli.
     Neg1 1Sg-see-try Neg2   ...   Neg3
     'I've never seen Santo.'

(10) Pe   su   manene   re   koperin po.
     Neg1 exist greatly   Neg2   distant Neg3
     'It's not too far away.'

(11) President pe   poru   mesmesu re   sane naga pisa poli.
     ...   Neg1 arrive straight Neg2   like he   say Neg3
     'The President didn't arrive as (at the time) he had said he would.'

This last example is a good place to note that the Lewo negative construction does allow for a certain amount of focussing of semantic scope of the negation. The meaning of (11) is that the President did not come at the time he had said he would, but it is possible for *pe* and *re* to embrace just the verbal adjunct, rather than the combination of verb plus adjunct (i.e. giving *...poru pe mesmesu re...*), in which case the meaning is that the President came, but not at the expected time. A third arrangement is also possible, where *pe* and *re* embrace just the main verb. When this happens, *mesmesu* ceases to be a closely knit verbal adjunct, and is more closely associated with the following adverbial phrase, and the sentence comes to mean that the President did not come, just as he had said he would not come. *poli* has no role in these various specifications of negative scope.

Some verbal predicates in Lewo use a periphrastic construction with the verb 'to be' and an adjective. This is also the vehicle by which most borrowed verbs are imported into the language, and in each case ((12) and (13) respectively), the negative construction retains its usual form. (*lanem* in (13) is borrowed from Vanuatu's English-based pidgin, Bislama.)

(12) Pe   ø-pe   piavi re   poli.
     Neg1 3Sg-R.be long Neg2   Neg3
     'It was not (a) long (time), then...'

(13) Pe   a-pe   lanem-in-riru-la   re   poli.
      Neg1 3Pl-R.be   learn-TR-well-3Pl   Neg2   Neg3
      'They didn't teach them properly.'

All the above examples show negated matrix clauses, but we can note that there is no change in the pattern of negative marking for clauses that are embedded in some way, such as for speech complements (14), perception complements (15), and various kinds of nominal adjuncts (16).

(14) Yaru tai   ø-sape   ve   a-ure   re   la-u.
      man   Art   3Sg-say   Neg1   3Pl-pull Neg2   leg-1Sg
      'A man said they shouldn't pull on my leg (dislocated knee).'

(15) Ne-pisu   sane pe   ne-sitomali   re   suri   poli   narui.
      1Sg-R.see   like Neg1   1Sg-remember Neg2   thing   Neg3   now
      'Then I felt like I couldn't remember anything.'

(16) Ø-pisa   suri   tai   pe   mesmesu   re   nena   poli.
      2Sg-R.say   thing   Art   Neg1   right   Neg2   Emph   Neg3
      'You said something (that) wasn't right at all.'

Finally in this section, it should be noted that in Lewo, some body part idioms, delimited with square brackets below, are constructed with a grammatical clause in the predicate nucleus slot (17). When this is negated, *pe* and *re* surround the whole idiom clause (18).

(17) Naga [sine-na po-n-la].
      he   gut-3Sg forget-Tr-3Pl
      'He forgot them.'

(18) Naga pe   [sine-na po-n-la]   re   yam   tai   poli.
      he   Neg1   gut-3Sg forget-Tr-3Pl Neg2   times   Art   Neg3
      'He didn't forget them once.'

2.3 Negation of nominal constituents

The three negative elements that have been exemplified above can also be found negating nominal constituents in sentences. This can be seen where the noun phrase occurs as a non-verbal predicate (19-23), and in verbal clauses where the scope of negation is focussed around the subject nominal (25). Nominal predicates can be found in equational clause structures:

(19) Yaru nene na   pe   yaru   re   nene poli   yo.
      man   this 3Sg   Neg1   man   Neg2   this Neg3   maybe
      'This man is maybe not a man after all.'

(20) Naga pe   nakoneva re   naɓa yaru nene pimi   po.
     it   Neg1 yesterday Neg2   REL man this R.come Neg3
     'It wasn't yesterday that this man came.'

This last example indicates that the location of NEG3 is fixed within the construction, and does not vary according to the scope of negation. Here, the man has indeed come, and the semantic scope of the negation is the constituent 'yesterday', but the syntactic span of the total negative construction still takes in the non-negated constituent. Other nominal predicates are found in negative existential clauses:

(21) Pe   wii   re   poli.
     Neg1 water Neg2   Neg3
     'There's no water.'

(22) Sa-na   puruvi lala pe   ka-la   kinanena re   si   poli.
     Poss-3Sg brother Pl   Neg1 Poss-3Pl   food   Neg2 again Neg3
     'His brothers didn't have any more food.'

(23) Pe   suɓe re   tai   naɓa kilia suɱo-ni-la   e   yuɱaena poli.
     Neg1 chief Neg2 Art   Rel can go.ahead-TR-3Pl Prep work   Neg3
     'There's no chief who can lead them in their work.'

Where the subject of a negated clause is marked for indefinite with the normal indefinite article *tai* 'a/one', the nominal subject itself becomes the constituent that is negated, not the verbal predicate. These negative indefinite expressions are the closest Lewo comes to having something like a negative quantifier. (24) gives the affirmative sentence that is negated in (25).

(24) Yaru   tai   teke e   nene.
     person Art   stay Prep here
     'There's somebody here.' / 'Somebody is here.'

(25) Pe   yaru   re   tai   teke e   nene poli.
     Neg1 person Neg2 Art   stay Prep here Neg3
     'There's no-one here.' / 'Nobody's here.'

2.4 Negating prepositional phrases

We have seen that the Lewo negative construction retains its basic form in many different syntactic contexts. This is also the case where the scope of negation is focussed around a prepositional phrase. In these cases, we see a finely specified and semantically precise constituent negation, where the preposition itself, as the head of the phrase, is alone negated by being enclosed by *pe* and *re*, with *poli* occurring later. However, an added complication in Lewo is that when the preposition occurs with adjuncts (including negatives), it is then doubly specified, once with the adjunct, and again immediately following it. This pattern can be observed in (26-27), where the preposition *e* occurs twice in the negated prepositional phrase, and (in 27) twice again in the following phrase where the adjunct *ena* 'too' modifies the preposition.

(26) Ana   pe   e   re-ga   e   pogosi nene poli,
      Conj   Neg1   Prep   Neg2-just Prep time   this Neg3
      'And not only at this time,...'

(27) A-kila   yuaena piowa tai, pe   e   re-ga   e   sa-la
      3Pl-do   work   bad   Art   Neg1 Prep   Neg2-just Prep Poss-3Pl

      visena   la poli, ana   e   ena-ga   e   sa-la   elaga la.
      talk   Pl Neg3   Conj Prep too-just Prep Poss-3Pl style Pl
      'They did a bad deed, not only in their words, but also in their behaviour.'

2.5 More complex clauses

2.5.1 With Complex Subjects

When a clause subject itself incorporates a negated relative clause, the contiguity of the lower negative construction remains intact, and is not broken up by the higher clause. *Poli* still occurs at the end of the clause at the syntactic level in which it is operative.

(28) Teras   la nap̃a pe   a-pe   praktis   re   poli
      youth   Pl Rel Neg1   3Pl-be   practise Neg2   Neg3

      ve   a-te   re   pol   e   Sarer.
      Neg1   3Pl-kick   Neg2   ball Prep Saturday
      'The young guys who haven't practised will not play (kick ball) on Saturday.'

The heads of some nominal phrases (bracketed below) are nouns derived from verbs, and these constituents may be negated, using just NEG2 and NEG3, independent of the negation of the clause as a whole.

(29) [Kie-na   na-imi-ena   re po] pe   po   re   po.
      Poss-3Sg Nom-come-Nom   Neg2 Neg3 Neg1   R.good   Neg2   Neg3
      'His not coming was not good.'

2.5.2 With complex objects

The more complex or expanded the object is, the further NEG3 is potentially separated from the other negative elements, with which it combines to express a single semantic category. This is further discussed in 2.6.5., but for now it is noted that instances can be found where mature speakers do equivocate on whether the NEG3 element is required, or where it should be located in relation to complex object noun phrases. Such cases have been encountered as I have worked with speakers editing their own written and translated texts. For example, in (30), the writer went through two changes of mind in deciding if the NEG3 element was needed, and if so, where it should be placed.

(30) Ana   naga pe   sinena p̃esani re   kiom̃a p̃elaga
      and   he Neg1   gut   forget Neg2   your behaviour

      wo   la (poli) nap̃a ko   o-kila   ke   pa la
      good   Pl (Neg3) Rel you 2Sg-make Ta   Prep them

      nap̃a lima-la   korena (poli).
      Rel   hand-3Pl   empty   (Neg3)

'And he has not forgotten your good behaviour which you have shown to those who are poor.'

In the first drafting of this complex clause (note the double embedding of relative clauses in the object), the NEG1 and NEG2 elements were inserted as in the first line, but there was no NEG3 included at the end. However, on a later second look, the writer commented that "there needs to be a *poli* here somewhere to finish the sentence properly", and inserted *poli* right at the end of the full clause (*poli* in parentheses in last line above). But on a subsequent third reading, the *poli* was felt to be too distant, and was moved up nearer the head of the object noun phrase, before the first relative clause, thus interspersed within the confines of the object phrase. In so far that both of these positions are to the right of the object head, it does not seem possible to regard the movement of *poli* here as evidencing a difference in the scope of negation. This fine-tuning of the position of *poli* in complex clauses is taken to reflect stylistic evaluations of the amount of material that it is appropriate to span before it appears.

2.5.3 Complex clause with double negation
In (14-15) it was shown that complements of verbs of speaking and perception can be negated, and we will now see that this is independently of the main verb, which may itself also be negated. In these clauses with double negation, each verb will require NEG1 and NEG2, while the occurrence of realis aspect in either the main verb or the complement verb will require the presence of *poli* at the end of the clause.

(31) Ne-sitom   save yoko naga vimi.
      1Sg-think   that Fut he   come
      'I think he will come.'

(32) Ne-sitom   save yoko naga ve   vimi   re.
      1Sg-think   that Fut he   Neg1   come   Neg2
      'I think he won't come.'

(33) Ne-sitom   save naga pe   pimi   re   poli.
      1Sg-think   that he   Neg1   come   Neg2   Neg3
      'I thought he didn't come.'

(34) Pe   ne-sitom   re   save yoko naga vimi   poli.
      Neg1 1Sg-think   Neg2   that Fut he   come   Neg3
      'I didn't think he will come.'

(35) Pe   ne-sitom   re   save yoko naga ve   vimi   re   poli.
      Neg1 1Sg-think   Neg2   that Fut he   Neg1   come   Neg2   Neg3
      'I didn't think that he will not come.'

(36) Pe   ne-sitom   re   save naga pe   pimi   re   poli.
      Neg1 1Sg-think   Neg2   that he   Neg1   come   Neg2   Neg3
      'I didn't think that he did not come.'

This sequence of examples is clearly elicited, and natural text equivalents of all the possibilities have not been found. However, they do appear to indicate that the system has been applied quite rigourously, with both main and complement clause verbs always taking the full negative specification as usual. The only slight modification, not unexpected, is that the theoretical double NEG3 at the end of the clause in (36) has been reduced to just one instance of *poli*.

A similar configuration of examples could be presented for clauses with negated main verbs and negated embedded relative clauses, such as (37). Note that the object here is a headless relative clause, and that the final vowel of *poli* becomes *u* before *wa*.

(37) Ve   a-kan   re   naṗa kana kuruta pe
      I.Neg1 3Pl-eat   Neg2   Rel its blood R.Neg1

      m-lau-riru   re   polu   wa.
      R-flow-well   Neg2   Neg3   yet

      'Don't eat (the meat) whose blood hasn't properly run out yet.'

2.6 Variations

The typological rarity of the Lewo negative construction (discussed in 3.4.), and its relative complexity, could be taken to suggest that this way of expressing negatives does not sit well with the way human languages operate. If so, we should expect that the configuration may be highly susceptible to change (probably reduction of some sort), and that some variants in the basic pattern might occur as the language experiments with possible changes. Some ways in which the Lewo pattern has been observed to vary are noted. Some of these variations can be associated with minor pragmatic nuances, but not yet for every case.[5]

2.6.1 Loss of NEG1

Particularly in the speech of younger speakers, loss of the NEG1 element can occur. The bracketed *pe* below is what we would expect.

(38) Yuwa (pe)   kove re   po.
      rain Neg1   fall Neg2   Neg3
      'It didn't rain.'

2.6.2 NEG1 occurring with verbal prefixes

The NEG1 element will sometimes occur with the same subject person and number prefix as required on the main verb. Speakers generally respond to this form as entailing additional negative force, but its use appears restricted to some older speakers, and to 2nd person (imperative) forms.

(39) Ø-ve   o-ure   re   vetani imimi.
      2Sg-Neg1   2Sg-flee Neg2   Prep   us
      'Don't leave us.'

2.6.3 NEG1 occurring as *pere*

For just a few older speakers, NEG1 occurs as *pere*, which appears to combine both NEG1 and NEG2. However, NEG2 still occurs again in its usual position.

(40) Pe-re   a-pimi   re   poli.
      Neg1-Neg2   3Pl-come   Neg2   Neg3
      'They didn't come.'

2.6.4 NEG1 before subject

The normal position of NEG1 is immediately before the verb. Examples can be found where it occurs before a subject pronoun (41) or subject noun phrase (42):

(41) Pe   naga   p̃asup̃e   re   si   poli.
      Neg1   he   return   Neg2   again Neg3
      'He didn't come back again.'

(42) Pe   yaru   tai   teke re   e   nene poli.
      Neg1 person Art   stay Neg2   Prep   here Neg3
      'There isn't any person staying here.'

2.6.5 Loss of NEG3

Poli is sometimes not required where the emphatic particle *nena* occurs. This particle means 'completely' in affirmative expressions, and '(not) at all' in negative ones. Its presence presumably signals enough negative force that *poli* can be omitted.

(43) Ana   ko   pe   sino-m̃a-n-li re   nena-ga.
      Conj you   Neg1   'want'   try   Neg2:at:all-only
      'But you never wanted (it) at all.'

There are some other occasions too when *poli* does not occur as expected. In all these cases, the material intervening between the negated verb and the end of the clause is heavy both in quantity and structural depth (an example from a written text was given in 2.5.2.). These are taken to be performance errors, resulting from some kind of information processing overload under the constraints of short-term memory.[6]

2.7 Prohibition

When a verb in the irrealis aspect is negated, and the subject of the verb is in the second person, this conceptually, and formally in Lewo, constitutes the negative imperative.

(44) Ve   a-kan   re.
      Neg1 2Sg-eat Neg2
      'Don't eat it!'

Lewo can also convey this by expressing the prohibited activity as a nominalisation, as the subject of the verb *toko* 'desist'.

(45) Na-kan-ena   toko.
      Nom-eat-Nom   desist
      'Don't eat it!'

A very recent modification has been to substitute the negative verb phrase in (44) for the nominalised form in (45). This gives (46):

(46) Ve   a-kan   re   toko.
      Neg1 2Sg-eat Neg2   desist
      'Don't eat it!'

This latter form, frowned upon but also increasingly used by mature speakers, is clearly a single phonological phrase, and can be distinguished from the double clause sequence, which has juncture between *re* and *toko*, and which can be glossed as 'Don't eat it; don't!'

2.8 Independent negative

The independent negative in Lewo is essentially the maximally under-specified negative construction, that is, the remnant of the negated clause after everything except the negative elements have been removed from it. These independent negatives combine the negative construction elements into single phonological words, which are written as single grammatical words. The four forms that are used are *peraga*, *pere*, *perepo*, and *perepoli*. Apart from noting that the first of these includes the limiter *-ga* 'just', which changes the vowel in *re* from *e* to *a*, the internal structure of these forms will be obvious by now. The differences between them seem to be a matter of degree, with the first of them being neutral (and the most common), the second somewhat more abrupt, and the third and fourth entailing heavier emphasis, the latter being quite uncommon. Two of these forms will also commonly occur with *wa* to give 'not yet' answers: *perewa* and *perepoluwa*.

(47)   Pe-re-(poli)-wa.
       Neg1-Neg2-(Neg3)-yet
       'Not yet.'

All of these independent forms so far have NEG1 as *pe*. The independent negative formed with NEG1 as *ve* is not common, and functions to express conditionality, mostly along with the conjunction *visae* 'if':

(48)   Visae ve-re,   ...
       if   Neg1-Neg2
       'If not, ...'

There are some dialects of Lewo for which just the NEG3 element *poli* alone stands as the independent negative.

2.9 Other negative words

2.9.1 Inherently negative verbs
Two Lewo verbs can be analysed semantically as containing NEGATIVE as a component of their meaning. The two verbs are *ninuwe* 'to not know' and

mon 'to not want'. More often than not, both verbs will occur with the delimiting post-clitic *-ga*, and both nearly always occur in the realis aspect (not marked on *mon* in (50)).

(49)   Imim me-mi-ninuwe sape   naga ne   komin naga mai.
        we   1Pl-R-not.know Comp   it   this because he   sick
        'We didn't know whether it was because he was sick.'

(50)   A-mon   na-kan-ena.
        3Pl-not.want   Nom-eat-Nom
        'They don't want to eat it.'

It is possible to negate these verbs using the normal clausal negation strategy, giving affirmative effect, although this is a contrived usage.

Besides *mon*, Lewo can also express the anti-desiderative using a body part construction: *yepe=na mavi* 'body not.want'.

(51)   Yepe-la   mavi-n   imi-ena.
        body-3Pl   not.want-Tr   come-Nom
        'They didn't want to come.'

2.9.2 Expressing incompetence

Lewo has an extended set of verbal modifying suffixes, relics of an earlier system of verb serialisation, which can be employed to amplify and modify in various ways the meaning of the verb. Two of these suffixes, *-tete* and *-ele* express incompetence, in the sense of the subject not being able for some reason to perform the action. The two are near synonyms, but in some cases are collocationally restricted to certain verbs.

(52)   Ne-kan-tete   kinanena marera lala.
        1Sg-eat-can't   food   hard   Pl
        'I can't eat strong foods.'

(53)   A-pisa-yu-ɓele-ga.
        they-say-expand-can't-just
        'They just can't talk about it.'

A combination of *-tete* with the verb *taa* 'do/make' can be made into a higher verb, to give incompetence clauses that may function as a prohibition:

(54)   Taɓa-tete   a-vano.
        make-can't   3Pl-go
        'They can't go.' / 'They are not to go.'

3 Typological perspective

Lewo negative constructions, entailing a higher degree of redundancy than is usual, are of obvious typological interest, particularly with respect to the etymology of the particular forms, and the provenance of the system as a whole.

Two very useful surveys of negation typology are Dahl 1979 and Payne 1985. Dahl surveyed 240 languages, as widely representative as was possible, and establishes the types of clausal negation strategies that they employ, as well as providing counts of the relative frequencies of each type. He first distinguishes syntactic and morphological negation, and then subcategorises these according to the linear ordering of elements, particularly in relation to the negated verb, and relates this to word order typology. Payne gives a wider treatment of negation in general, including how the category appears in many different word class and syntactic contexts. Standard clausal negation is fully covered, and Payne says that it "may take a variety of forms, ranging from fully inflected 'negative verbs' to fully bound derivational morphemes" (p. 207). The actual gradation of types that he presents begins with higher negative verbs, then auxiliary negative verbs, then negative particles, morphological negatives, and finally negative nouns (pp. 207-228). Overall, the conclusions of the two typologies in this area are very similar. They have been assessed more recently by Horn (1989:447-462), again without significant expansion or modification. These surveys are used here as a basis for discussing the status of the Lewo negative elements, in terms of their syntactic origins and their synchronic function.

3.1 What is *ve* 'Neg1'?

There seems little reason to analyse the Lewo *ve* NEG1 as a higher negative verb, mainly because there is no formal indication that the negated verb (phrase) is a full sentential complement to it.[7]

We should ask next then, is it a negative auxiliary verb? Typologically, we should be very open to this possibility, because we have seen that Lewo *ve* is also the verb 'to be', and as Payne again comments (for both higher and auxiliary negative verbs), "evidence ... exists that in at least some cases the negative verb is simply a negative form of the verb 'be'" (p. 222). In the prototypical cases, well-exemplified in the highly inflectional languages Payne cites, the auxiliary verb can be seen to accrue the normal verbal markings for various categories, while the verb being negated is reduced to an 'invariant, participial form' (p. 212). This does not seem to characterise completely what happens in Lewo, where the negated verb still retains all its usual markings, and where *ve*, besides being marked for aspect as *ve* or *pe*, shows little evidence of attracting other verbal inflections or adjuncts.

However, Payne allows that the way in which the verbal inflectional categories are divided between, or shared by, the negative verb and the negated verb can vary in many ways. The range of possibilities that can result from this 'complex distribution' (p. 221) is such that as long as the negative verb can be shown to retain its 'independent word status' (p. 214), having not yet become a derivational morpheme on the negated verb, then it is best described as an 'auxiliary negative verb'.

Various criteria suggest firstly, that Lewo *ve* does have independent word status (no phonological binding, and possibility of other words intervening between it and the main verb), and secondly, that it is a verb (marked for aspect, and rarely, for subject person and number). Trying to discover from native speakers of the language whether they felt *ve* NEG1 to be the same as *ve* 'to be' was somewhat confirmatory, and it was certainly not felt to be the same as some of the other homophones of *ve* (verbs meaning 'to weave' and a commonly reduced form of one of the verbs 'to say').

It therefore seems best to conclude that the NEG1 element in Lewo negatives is a negative auxiliary or support verb, probably deriving originally from the verb 'to be'.

3.2 What is *re* 'Neg2'?

re shows some degree of mobility, and should be accorded independent grammatical word status, rather than being considered a bound morpheme. However, many people do not recognise an orthographic word break before it; and it is probably a post-clitic. It does not display inflectional marking of any kind, so is certainly not a negative verb or auxiliary. We can continue to regard it as an invariant negative particle.

Dahl (pp.103-104) has 115 of his 240 languages using a particle like this, found pre-verbally twice as often as post-verbally in SVO languages, with English *not* and French *pas* (without preceding *ne* as is common in modern colloquial French) both in the minority case here. However, Payne (p.224) shows that the historical negative in both these languages was in fact originally a single pre-verbal negative particle. We have seen that Lewo can sometimes also show loss of NEG1, and just retain NEG2 and NEG3.

Payne's description of the mechanism by which post-verbal French *pas* and English *not* have developed is actually instructive for the Lewo situation. He states that there is a "strong tendency for particle negatives to be emphasised and reinforced ... more frequently by the addition of a further particle elsewhere in the sentence, forming a pair of linked negatives" (p.224).[8] For French and English, the precursors of the now generalised negative particles were full objects, meaning 'a step' and 'nothing' respectively, so they clearly had the function of emphasising the negative by limiting the extent of the effect of the negated action, along the lines of modern English forms like 'I didn't eat the least little bit,' and '(?)I didn't eat nothing'. For Lewo, it is also possible to find a similar kind of source for the NEG2 particle *re*. However, we do not find it in the object position of the clause as in French and English, and fortunately, neither do we have to look into the (unrecorded) history of the language to discover it. The source of *re* NEG2 would seem to be the current partitive particle of the same form, that has a limiting function in affirmative clauses, and that is one of several post-verbal modifying particles in Lewo:[9]

(55) Ne-suma   na   sineun   sape   na-kan   re   kumpui.
     1Sg-stayed   now   'I.wanted'   Comp   1Sg-eat   Part   pork
     'After a while I wanted to eat a bit of pork/try eating some pork.'

This *re* is found as either NEG1, or as the partitive particle with the limiting function in affirmative statements, but not both, suggesting it is the same form occurring in two mutually exclusive environments. However, the fact that it is an obligatory component in negative clauses means that it functions as a syntactic marker of negation, and in this context, has lost the semantic content it seems to have in the limiting function. For this reason, the forms will probably be regarded as distinct particles in Lewo grammar.

Payne also describes linked negative pairs in several African (Chadic) SVO languages where the second negative element occurs after the object, giving negative constructions of the form S-NEG1-V-O-NEG2. Some of these languages have then lost the NEG1 form, so that a single final negative marker remains: S-V-O-NEG; this pattern is also found in German (p.226). These patterns move us on to the Lewo NEG3 element *poli*.

3.3 What is *poli* 'Neg3'?

In the previous section, we have already seen Payne's statement about particle negatives being strengthened by the addition of a further particle elsewhere in the sentence. This process is taken to be the mechanism by which linked negative pairs are formed. In the absence of any clear reason as to why this process could not be recursive,[10] it stands as the best way of explaining how Lewo has come to have yet a third element in its negative construction.

Although there is no claim being made here about the relative ordering of accrual of the negative elements, we are still very interested to know where this third element in the linear ordering comes from. It appears from Payne's discussion, reinforced by the origins of Lewo *re* NEG2, that languages prefer to draw additional negative particles from existing resources, rather than create new ones. Is this so for *poli*?

While there are no other morphemes with this form in Lewo, it was noted above that *poli* is indeed found as the independent negative in some dialects. It is not possible to say immediately that this must be the source of the NEG3 element, because the independent negative itself seems to be formed from a maximal reduction of the clausal negative construction.

However, there is a construction type in the language that does hint at how the NEG3 element may have come to occur right at the end of the clause. This is where, for both affirmative and negative clauses, the independent negative can be attached as a kind of tag to the whole clause, indicating either that the intended action was not accomplished in some way (for affirmative clauses), or, for clauses already in the negative, as an additional emphasis of the negative force of the statement.

(56) A-kila-yoni m̃a   pano-o, peraga.
      3Pl-do-try Cont go-Dur no
      They tried hard on and on, to no avail.

(57) Pe   sa-na   mama   re   poli,   peraga.
      Neg1 Poss-3Sg mother Neg2   Neg3   no
      (That) was not his mother, indeed no.

The other interesting detail about *poli* is the restriction of its occurrence to realis aspect clauses. It is hard to know what kind of functional or typological explanation will satisfactorily relate the presence or absence of *poli* to the contextually-determined aspectual distinction made in the clause.[11] Possibly it reflects the relative degrees of intensity of expression of negativity that are appropriate for events that incontrovertibly did not take place, as against those that it is asserted are not to take place.

From the start, the three negative elements have been regarded as distinct entities, all independent words. The discussion above on their morphological status indicates that the only modification that might be required is to analyse *re* as a clitic, with no strong motivation for trying to regard them as components of a single tripartite discontinuous negative morpheme. A third approach would be to accommodate *poli* dangling at the end of the clause by regarding the negative construction as made up of two words, one of them being *poli*, the other a discontinuous morpheme comprising a prefix *ve/pe* and a suffix *re*. Again, the separate word status of these elements argues against this.

3.4 Typological status

The three elements that constitute the Lewo negative as just discussed do not display individually any particular typological peculiarities, with their formal equivalents occurring in negative constructions in other languages. In Dahl's survey (1979), 40 out of the 240 languages have negative auxiliaries, 28 of them pre-verbal, and we have seen that the occurrence of the verb 'to be' with this function is known elsewhere. Secondly, about half the languages show some kind of post-verbal affix or particle, and we have also seen that 'negative polarity minimizers' (Horn 1989:453) are often found in this position as negative intensifier particles or clitics in double particle constructions. And thirdly, there are eight other svo languages in the sample which have a negative particle in sentence-final position. Finally, we can note that using more than one negative element is uncommon, but not rare: Dahl (1979:102) lists 12 out of his 240 languages which have double particle negative constructions. What is interesting about the Lewo pattern of course, is that it most frequently uses all three of its negative elements at once in a tripartite linked negative construction. This construction type is obviously extremely rare in the languages of the world, possibly uniquely attested in Lewo.[12]

In the literature on negation, reference is often made to two early typological claims made by Jespersen. One of these is labeled by Horn (1989:293) as NEG FIRST, and represents "the general tendency for negation to be attracted leftward, and generally to precede the material over which it has scope" (p.292). Horn restates it as the tendency that "negation tends to be signalled as early as possible in the sentence, for ease in processing" (p.311). The other claim, Horn notes (p.452), has come to be known as JESPERSEN'S CYCLE, and he describes this as the frequently observed "cyclical pattern wherein the negative marker is gradually weakened [...] then reinforced by the accretion of [...] minimizers or indefinites, and ultimately replaced by its reinforcement". We can observe that Lewo relates to these tendencies somewhat non-typically. Firstly, the highly rightwards position of *poli* would not be predicted by NEG FIRST, and secondly, while some additional elements have been incorporated into the Lewo negative construction, the earlier negative form, whichever it was, has not been lost as JESPERSEN'S CYCLE would lead us to expect.

4 Comparative perspective

The above typological claim immediately creates interest in the negative construction types that might be found in related and neighbouring Oceanic languages in island Melanesia. There is increasing interest in the comparative syntax of these languages, and the existence of a phenomenon like this complex negative marking could have some potential as a diagnostic construction-type for subgrouping. However, there is no intention here to attempt to reconstruct the historical development of these negative forms or construction types, but to review the range of forms and types that are found. We will look briefly at negative constructions firstly in other Epi languages, and then note some details from some other more and less closely related languages. Although it makes the many gaps in the data more obvious, it seemed useful to summarise the information given below in Table 1.

4.1 Other Epi languages

None of the other Epi languages (Lamen, Paki, Bieria, Bierebo,[13] Mae-Morae) display this three-fold marking. They do show various combinations of NEG1 and/or NEG2 elements, which themselves occur as various different forms, but none of the languages have NEG3 elements of any phonological shape.

The language which by all measures is most closely related to Lewo is Lamen. Lamen has the form *maa* (clearly not the verb 'to be') for NEG1, and *re* (which is also the partitive) for NEG2. For the negative imperative, NEG1 is *sipa*, with *re* still as NEG2. Like Lewo, the independent negative is formed of a composite of NEG1 and NEG2: *maare*.

Paki has a similar form to Lamen for the NEG1 element, *maka*. There is no partitive *re* in Paki, but this form is retained as NEG2. The main independent negative in Paki is derived just from NEG1: *makan(io)*; but *mbueli* and *markanio* have also been found. Tryon's sketch (n.d.) of Mae-Morae indicates that only one element is ever used in negative constructions. The future negative takes the particle *avei*, in the pre-verbal NEG1 position, and this is also used for the prohibitive. Non-future negatives take *vei/voi* in NEG2 position, following the verb. There is also an example of a negative existential expression, which uses the negative form *mbuel*.

This pattern of negative marking is also paralleled in Bieria, where the same form *se* occurs pre-verbally for future, and post-verbally for non-future clauses. The independent negative, also used in negative existential clauses, is *buoli*.

4.2 Other NCV languages

None of the three Central Vanuatu languages, which by Tryon's (1976) internal classification are most closely related to the Epi languages, are known to exhibit tripartite linked negatives. Of these, Namakir has NEG1 *te* and NEG3 *-ih*, but no NEG2 (Wolfgang Sperlich, p.c.). At first, Nguna looks like having just a single pre-verbal negative particle *taa* (Schütz 1969:28), but Schütz also describes a post-verbal particle *mau* 'at all', which is described as a limiter, and all the instances of this form that I could find were in negative constructions. Example (58), from Schütz (1969:40), shows this element clause finally rather than explicitly post-verbal, making it look very much like a NEG3 element. Another example (p.69) has both *taa* and *mau* in a future tense negative.

(58) E   taa   pei   sikai maau   mau.
      it   not   be   one   only   at-all
      'It wasn't just one at all.'

However, Paamese, geographically closer but in the next most closely related group (East Vanuatu), has a very clear linked negative pair, which Crowley (1982:140-2) describes as a 'disjunctive morpheme', in that the two parts form part of the internal morphology of the verb. Paamese uses the form *ro-* for NEG1, which is not related to the verb 'to be', and *-tei* for NEG2, which is also the Paamese partitive (p.171).

The other language most closely related to Paamese, again in East Vanuatu, is South-East Ambrym. This has *naa-/taa-* (depending on tense) for NEG1, and *ti*, also the partitive, for NEG2 (Parker 1970:vi,33). Again, closely related to both of these, is another Ambrym language, Lonwolwol. Summarising some other variations, its negative occurs only preverbally, with the present tense form *tolo*, the past *tolohon*, and the future involving both the particle *sinca* and the prefix *n-* (Paton 1971:53).

Further afield within NCV, data is available for some of the Malakula Coastal languages. Atchin has NEG1 *se(re)* and NEG2 *te*, the latter also being the form of the partitive (Capell and Layard 1980:84,136,144).

Close to Atchin is Uripiv (McKerras 1988), where the primary pattern seems to be a single pre-verbal particle *se(te)*. However, the dictionary also contains a form *te* which is simply cross-referenced to the NEG1 element mentioned, under which the following example is found (it is not clear why *ete* occurs rather than *sete*):

(59)   Ete   nu-majing te   lelingen.
       neg   I-work   'emphasis' today
       'I'm not working today.'

Thus, while NEG2 does not seem obligatory in Uripiv, there are hints of a linked-pair construction present in the language. The partitive in Uripiv is *ta*.

In his atlas of 19 languages in south Malakula, Charpentier (1982) includes data on the verbal negative construction, although the relationship of the forms he gives to other grammatical particles like a partitive is not clear. However, 10 of the languages clearly show a linked negative pair, with a verbal prefix of the form *sa-* or *se-*, and a post-verbal particle of varying shapes for the different languages: *vaj, vej, ve, re, ndeh, sege*. The other nine languages only have verbal prefixes *sa-, su-, se-, s^mba-, semba-*.

Two other NCV languages that have been described, regarded as more innovative (Clark 1983:220), are Big Nambas and Sakao. Both of these show single non-discontinuous verbal prefixes in their negative constructions. The former has *a(h)-* (Fox 1979:65), and the latter *ja(h)-* (Guy 1974:48).

Some of these negative markings, along with those from several other NCV languages, are noted in Tryon 1973:330. The combined data leaves the impression that discontinuous marking is frequent in NCV, and that the most stable item across the languages is a particle of the form *se/re/te*, mostly found as either NEG2 of a linked pair, or NEG1 where there is no NEG2. Pawley has already reconstructed a Proto North Hebridean-CentralPacific form *teqe* as a pre-verbal negative particle (Pawley 1972:56).

Clark (1983:209) reports finding 'biposed negative constructions' in a number of other NCV locations as well (Banks Islands, Aoba-Maewo, and Rerep – actual language names not given). He also reconstructs ProtoNCV *(st)a(vb)V* for NEG1, and *tea* for NEG2, and considers the linkage of them in the negative construction to be an innovation in NCV. The first form is considered to be related to other Oceanic preverbal negative markers of the form *ta-, and the second is considered to recall PNCV *tea 'one', which has come to function as an additional negative emphasiser.

4.3 Outside NCV within Vanuatu

The other Vanuatu languages outside NCV are mainly the Southern Vanuatu languages. As noted at the start of this paper, Ruhlen places these as a different first-order subgrouping of Oceanic than Remote Oceanic, of which the NCV languages are a subgroup. However, it is interesting that at least a bipartite negative construction is attested among these SV languages as well. The data from Lynch (1978:47,64) on Lenakel of Tanna indicates that there is a negative verbal prefix *s-*, and what he calls a 'negative post-clitic' of the form *-aan*, which occurs either verb finally, or following some other post-verbal adjuncts.

(60)   R-ɨs-va-aan   apwa   Ifila.
        3Sg-NEG-come-NEG   Loc   Vila
        'He didn't come to Vila.' (from Lynch 1978:64)

What is fascinating about this morpheme is that it is the same form as the 'suffixal part of the discontinuous general nominalizing morpheme' in the language, *n-...-aan* (Lynch 1977:26), which has cognate forms with the same function in most if not all the NCV languages as well (e.g. Lewo *na-...-ena*). So here we have another example of a language drawing on its already existing resources to extend its negative construction.

   The use of the nominalising strategy is found in two other languages on Tanna as well, but these use firstly a full negative verb, which takes all the verbal affixes, and then the nominalised form of the negated verb. This is found in Kwamera (reported in Crowley 1982:148) and South West Tanna, for which an example from Lynch (1982a:52, slightly modified) is given:

(61)   Kuli   aan   l-ø-am-apwah   n-aan-ien   nauga   tɨksɨn.
        dog   that   3Sg-Ta-Ta-not   Nom-eat-Nom   meat   some
        'That dog is not eating any meat.'

Lynch also provides information for the other SV languages. For the two languages now spoken on Erromango (Sie and Ura) he reconstructs an original negative construction with the single verbal prefix *edu-* (Lynch 1983:204). For Anejom, there is a single preverbal negative particle *itiyi* (Lynch 1982b:121).

4.4 Oceanic outside Vanuatu

Are there languages outside of NCV and SV with negative constructions which entail more than one constituent (sub-morphemic or morphemic)? Many of these languages are still undescribed, and only a few sources have been consulted. However, a quick survey of Fijian (declarative semi-auxiliary *sega*; Dixon 1988:281); Nakanai (preverbal particles *kama* for declarative/interrogative and *umala* for imperative; Johnston 1980:62); Manam (preverbal particle *tago*; Lichtenberk 1985:384ff.), and ProtoEasternOceanic (*t[a,i]ka(i)*; Pawley 1972: 56) shows that they all have just single modal adverbs, auxiliaries, or higher verbs for negatives, with the same form also often functioning as the independent negative. Separate negative imperative forms can be found for some of these languages, but linked negative constructions are not evident.

Dahl's survey included three Oceanic languages (Sakau (=Sakao, above), Luangiua and Maori (both Polynesian)), and five other Austronesian languages. Many of these have different negative forms for different clause types, but all of them form their basic indicative clausal negatives with single elements: preverbal affixes or particles (Sakau, Malagasy, Tagalog, Indonesian, Malay); preverbal auxiliaries (Maori, Yapese); or a post-verbal particle or affix (Luangiua).

However, just a single case is needed to show that linked or discontinuous negatives are not solely confined to Vanuatu, and for this we can turn to Takia, a Western Oceanic language spoken off the north coast of Papua New Guinea. Ross (1991:9) includes the following example (slightly modified):

(62)   Bom   tita   i-puk-di-na-do-go   ...
       bomb NEG   S:3Sg-break-already-NEG-TA-TA
       'The bomb still hadn't exploded ...'

Takia typically negates clauses with the pre-verbal particle *tita* (or *ta* in some dialects), and the post-verbal suffix *-na* (not always, in some dialects).

4.5 Conclusion

This review indicates a wide range of negative forms and types for these languages, perhaps wider than might have been expected, even among the more closely related NCV and Epi languages in particular.

There is a high incidence of discontinuous negative marking within NCV, and this pattern is only sporadically attested elsewhere in Oceanic. For NCV, there is also an equally high degree of apparent non-cognacy in the forms that appear, which will render any attempts to reconstruct negative marking within NCV particularly difficult. Patterns involving NEG1 and NEG2 elements are found on Epi and to the north, while patterns involving NEG1 and NEG3 are found on Epi and to the south. It appears to be a unique innovation of Lewo to have adopted all three elements into its negative construction. Table 1 gives an overview of form of the negative elements cited in this paper.

Table 1. Negative elements in the languages cited.

	Neg1	Neg2	Neg3	*to be*	partitive	independent negative	prohibitive
Lewo	ve/pe	re	po(li)	ve/pe	re	pere(ga/po(li))	ve ... re
Lamen	ma	re		ve/pe	re	maare	sipa ... re
Paki	maka	re		ve/be	kija	makan(io)	
Mae-Morae	avei	vei/voi		ve/mbe	ndai?	mbuəl	avei
Bierebo						marare	
Bieria	se	se				buoli	
Namakir	te					mbu(a/e)l	
Nguna	taa		mau	vei		ee	
Paama	ro-	(-tei)		ve	-tei	tovueli	-tei
SE Ambrym	naa-/taa-	ti		he	ti		
Lonwolwol	tolo(hon); sinka n-						
Atchin	se(re)	te		we	te	etsiga/tse	
Uripiv	se(te)	te?		ivi	ta	e-jki	
S Malakula	sa-,se-,s-,.. sa,su,se,..	vaj,vej, ve,re,...					
Big Nambas	a(h)-						
Sakao	(j)a(s)						
Lenakel	is-	-aan				kapwa	
SW Tanna	apwah	n-..-ien					
Erromango	*edu-						
Takia	(ti)ta	(-na)					

Abbreviations

Art	article	Part	partitive
Comp	complementizer	PL	plural
Dem	demonstrative	Poss	possessive
Emph	emphatic	R	realis
Fut	future	Rel	relative pronoun
I	Irrealis	TA	tense/aspect particle
Loc	location	TR	transitive marker
Nom	nominalizer		

Notes

1. This paper was written as part of my PhD studies, and some of the material will be included in the dissertation. Helpful comments were received when the paper was presented at a seminar in the Linguistics Department of the Research School of Pacific Studies at the Australian National University. My thanks go to the editors of this volume as well for their comments on an early draft of the paper.

2. A more recent classification of the whole Austronesian family (Grimes, et al., in press) supercedes this, and advances beyond it with respect to Lewo's position in Oceanic at two points. Firstly, Lewo is assigned in the first place to an Epi subgroup of NCV, and secondly, an additional node (Central Eastern Oceanic) is inserted above Remote Oceanic, before Oceanic.

3. In examples, some morpheme breaks and glosses are omitted where they are not directly related to the discussion. The zero subject person prefix for third person singular (as in (1-4)), along with realis and irrealis glosses for verb stems, are also only given where necessary. In Lewo orthography, most letters have expected values, but note that *g* is voiced velar nasal, *m̃* and *p̃* are labiovelars, *r* is trilled, and *v* is bilabial.

4. This parallels how verb stems operate generally, and is a feature of all the Epi languages, and some other Vanuatu languages, as well as other Oceanic languages. Fuller descriptions of this system, as well as the history of the analysis and interpretation of it, have most recently been made by Tryon (1986) and Crowley (1991). Note that depending on the first consonant of the stem, some verbs are not marked at all for realis/irrealis mode, e.g. *sape* in (14).

5. Instances of some of these variant forms can be found in Ray's (1926) early description of Lewo (known then as Tasiko), as well as a variant not now seen, the omission of Neg2. Ray knows of the three negative particles, but only has them in two pairs: *re* and *poli* are associated with realis negative, and *pe* (not *ve*) and *re* with irrealis. Further study of his sources will indicate whether the negative with all three forms does occur in the early missionary Bible translations.

6. Others, e.g. Mallinson and Blake (1981:434ff.), also allow at many points that the limited capacity of our short-term memory is a "physiological limitation that [...] affects syntax".

7. Note too that Payne, referring to another source, indicates that higher negative verbs are not found in verb-medial languages (1985:207) .

8. This is actually a restatement of Jespersen's cycle (see 3.4.). An extensive discussion of this same mechanism is given in Horn 1989:452ff.

9. Crowley has already pointed out almost exactly the same situation for the Paamese partitive *-tei*, cognate with Lewo *re* (Crowley 1982:140-2). He also discusses the historical development of the function of this particle more fully (pp.146-148), and relates it to the wider Oceanic context, including Lenakel data from Lynch similar to that given later here in 4.3.

10. Although there will be constraints relating to the cognitive processing of language, as well as the extent to which languages permit the encoding of redundancy: we should surprised be very probably to find a language which allows four or more elements in a linked negative construction – although Lewo could be regarded as having four elements in its 'never' construction; see (9). Dahl considers that NEGATIVE is a 'simple, un-decomposable concept' and so finds the occurence of even double particle constructions 'baffling' (Dahl 1979:89). Horn (1989:456ff.) asks "why does negation need to be strengthened or reinforced in the first place (and) what triggers each round of postverbal reescalation?"

11. Horn (1989:448-451) describes differences in negative marking in one language depending on mood (various Indo-European languages); identity vs. existence (Classical Chinese); tense (Arabic); and on other syntactic category and semantic distinctions.

12. The data Payne (p.231) gives from Nanai (in the Soviet Far East) come close to matching the Lewo situation. While Lewo has three distinct negative particles or elements, Nanai shows a negative verb form which occurs before the negated verb, and following the verb, the verb 'to be' occurs as an inflected auxiliary. What gives the third element here is the fact that the negated verb takes an invariant participial-like form. This construction occurs with just one form of the Nanai verb, and does not constitute the normal clausal negation strategy.

13. Confirmatory data for this language is still lacking.

References

Capell, A. and J. Layard. (1980). *Materials in Atchin, Malekula: grammar, vocabulary, and texts*. *Pacific Linguistics* D-20.

Charpentier, Jean-Michel. (1982). *Linguistic atlas of south Malakula*. Langues et Cultures du Pacifique, No. 2.

Clark, R. (1983). Languages of north and central Vanuatu: groups, chains, clusters and waves. In A. Pawley and L. Carrington (eds.), *Austronesian linguistics at the 15th Pacific Science Congress*, *Pacific Linguistics* C-88, 199-236

Crowley, Terry. (1982). *The Paamese language of Vanuatu*. *Pacific Linguistics* B-87.

—— (1991). Parallel development and shared innovation: a case study from Central Vanuatu. Paper presented at ICAL, Honolulu, May 1991.

Dahl, Östen. (1979). Typology of sentence negation. *Linguistics* 17:79-106.

Dixon, R.M.W. (1988). *A grammar of Boumaa Fijian.* University of Chicago Press.

Fox, G.J. (1979). *Big Nambas grammar. Pacific Linguistics* B-60.

Grimes, B.F., et al. In press. Listing of Austronesian languages. In D.T. Tryon (ed.), *Comparative Austronesian dictionary.* Berlin: Mouton de Gruyter.

Guy, J.B.M. (1974). *A grammar of the northern dialect of Sakao. Pacific Linguistics* B-33.

Horn, Laurence R. (1989). *A natural history of negation.* University of Chicago Press.

Lichtenberk, F. (1985). *A grammar of Manam. Oceanic Linguistics Special Publications* 18.

Lynch, John. (1977). *Lenakel dictionary. Pacific Linguistics* C-55.

—— (1978). *A grammar of Lenakel. Pacific Linguistics* B-55.

—— (1982a). South-West Tanna grammar outline and vocabulary. *Pacific Linguistics* A-64.

—— (1982b). Anejom grammar sketch. *Pacific Linguistics* A-64.

Mallinson, Graham, and Barry J. Blake. (1981). *Language typology.* North-Holland Linguistic Series, 46. North-Holland Publishing Company.

McKerras, Ross. (1988). Uripiv sketch grammar. Typescript.

Parker, G.J. (1970). *Southeast Ambrym dictionary. Pacific Linguistics* C-17.

Paton, W.F. (1971). *Ambrym (Lonwolwol) grammar. Pacific Linguistics* B-19.

Pawley, Andrew. (1972). On the internal relationships of Eastern Oceanic languages. *Studies in Oceanic culture history,* vol 3. R.C. Green and M. Kelly, eds., Pacific Anthropological Records, No 13:1-142. Honolulu: Bernice Pauahi Bishop Museum.

Payne, John. (1985). Negation. In Timothy Shopen, ed., *Language typology and syntactic description: Vol 1, clause structure,* 197-242. Cambridge: Cambridge University Press.

Ray, S.H. (1926). *A comparative study of the Melanesian island languages.* Cambridge: Cambridge University Press.

Ross, Malcolm D. (1991). Describing inter-clausal relations in Takia. Paper presented at the International Seminar on Descriptive Austronesian and Papuan Linguistics, Leiden, September 1991.

Ruhlen, M. (1987). *A guide to the world's languages.* Volume 1. Stanford: Stanford University Press.

Schütz, Albert. (1969). *Nguna grammar. Oceanic Linguistics Special Publications* 5. Honolulu: University of Hawaii.

Tryon, Darrell. (nd.) Notes on Mae-Morae. Typescript.

—— (1973). Linguistic subgrouping in the New Hebrides: a preliminary approach. *Oceanic Linguistics* 12:303-351.

—— (1976). *New Hebrides languages: an internal classification. Pacific Linguistics* C-50.

—— (1986). Stem-initial consonant alternation in the languages of Epi, Vanuatu: a case of assimilation? In Paul Geraghty, Lois Carrington and S.A. Wurm, eds. *Focal II:* papers from the Fourth International Conference on Austronesian Linguistics. *Pacific Linguistics* C-94:239-258.

Standard Mandarin

Jeroen Wiedenhof

因其所無而無之
則萬物莫不無　莊子·秋水

If regarded as defective for being deficient in
something, among the ten thousand things
there will be none not defective.
— *Zhuāng Zǐ* 'Autumn Floods'

0 Introduction

Standard Mandarin is the present-day dialect of Peking promulgated as a
standard language in the People's Republic of China, in the Republic of
China (Taiwan), and in Singapore. Social, political and regional differences
have produced lexical, phonological and syntactic variations, in decreasing
order of significance. Mandarin dialects are distributed continuously over
the area stretching from the Amur River in northeast China to Yúnnán
Province in the southwest. Mandarin belongs to the Sinitic branch of the
Sino-Tibetan family. The other languages of this branch are Wú, Gàn, Xiāng,
Mǐn, Hakka and Yuè, spoken in the central and southern parts of China.

Standard Mandarin is perhaps best known for its lack of inflectional
morphology. Remnants of an inflectional system survive in the lexicon.
Synchronically, morphological phenomena are largely restricted to derivation. Word classes can be defined on syntactic grounds. Morphemes are
overwhelmingly monosyllabic, and the majority of words consist of two or
more morphemes.

In sentence patterns, the prevalent word order is SVO. Content question
words (e.g. *shéi* 'who', *zěme* 'how') conform to this order. In yes-or-no
questions, either the interrogative particle *ma* is appended to the sentence,
or the affirmative verb is followed by a negation of the same verb, as will be
explained below (section 4.1). None of the interrogative patterns call for
changes in the SVO order.

Modifying elements precede modified elements. Cardinal numbers and (in
formal speech) demonstratives must be followed by a measure word when
they modify nominal expressions. A number of verbs have developed into
grammatical function words. As such, they may perform aspectual, prepositional, comparative and other grammatical functions.

Phonologically, the Mandarin dialects have been extremely innovative
compared to other Chinese languages. Standard Mandarin combines a

simple syllable structure with a simple tonal system. Five phonemic tones can be distinguished synchronically.[1] The orthography used here is the Hànyǔ Pīnyīn system. Four tones out of five are indicated by diacritic signs over the main vowel of a syllable. These four tones can be described by means of a five-point scale of pitch defined by Yuen Ren Chao (1930): low, half-low, medium, half-high and high, assuming equal intervals. On this scale, the four tones have the following values:

first tone	level, high, e.g. *xiāng* 'fragrance';
second tone	rising, medium to high, e.g. *xiáng* 'hover';
third tone	falling and rising, half-low to low to half-high, e.g. *xiǎng* 'think';
fourth tone	falling, high to low, e.g. *xiàng* 'towards'.

The fifth tone is called the neutral tone. A syllable with a neutral tone is short, unstressed, and its pitch is usually determined by the tone of the preceding syllable. Syllables with a neutral tone are transcribed without a tone symbol. There are a number of phonetic tone sandhi phenomena within and between words. Most of the sandhi phenomena involve allophones, but three types of sandhi have wider consequences:

- before a third tone, the contrast between a second tone and a third tone is neutralized. Both are realized as a second tone and transcribed as such in the example sentences;
- following a first or second tone, and preceding a non-neutral tone, the contrast between a first tone and a second tone is neutralized. Both are realized as a first tone and transcribed accordingly;
- a non-neutral tone may be realized as a neutral tone, correlating with varying semantic effects.

Beyond the lexicon, the occurrence of tone sandhi interacts with syntactic structure as well as speech style, including tempo. The majority of example sentences presented here were collected from speakers of Standard Mandarin talking amongst themselves. Within the confines of the Hànyǔ Pīnyīn system, they have been transcribed as actually pronounced. Transcribed forms in example sentences may therefore be different from the quotation forms used in the text. For example, in section 3 I describe resultative verb compounds as being 'negated by placing *méi* or *méi yǒu* before the compound', but in example (31), *hái méi yǒu tīng dào* 'have not yet heard' has *méi yǒu* in accordance with the second tone sandhi rule.

Each example taken from the corpus carries a four-digit number indicating its place in the corpus of data. At this moment, the corpus consists of 5,000 sentences. The transcriptions and recordings are part of a larger project carried out at the Sinological Institute of Leiden University. Most of the informants were native speakers. A minority spoke Standard Mandarin as a second language. The native speakers came from Chéngdū, Peking, Taipei, Tiānjīn and Qíqíhǎěr. The data of non-native speakers, from Shanghai and Hong Kong, were used only after verifying them with native speakers.

1 Negation with *bù*, *bú* and *bu*

1.1 Negation of verbs and adverbs

The most widely applicable marker of negation in Standard Mandarin is *bù* 'not'. All verbs except the existential verb *yǒu* 'be in a place, exist' (see section 2.1) can be negated by *bù*. Phonologically, *bù* conforms to the following tone sandhi rules:

- it occurs as *bú* before fourth-tone syllables and as *bù* in all other positions;
- an additional tone sandhi rule producing a neutral tone in *bu* is obligatory for a number of syntactic positions;
- at normal conversational speed *bu* is very common in positions where careful enunciation would restore *bù* or *bú*.

Bù is an adverb, which in Standard Mandarin means that it can precede and modify predicates. Examples of other adverbs are *yě* 'also' and *hái* 'still'. Adverbs typically, though not exclusively, precede verbs or other adverbs. Between *bù* and a verb, only other adverbs may be inserted, as in the third sentence below. Mandarin adjectives such as *duō* 'many' and *qīngchu* 'clear' in the first two examples may constitute predicates without the use of a copula.

(1) Wǒ   zìjǐ   cónglái   jiu   bu   xǐhuān zhèi ge fāngshì.
     1S   self   all.along just   not   like   this M style
     'I myself have never liked this style.' (1780)

(2) Zhèi yàng lù   shang   kàn de dōngxi bu duō   <nà
     this kind way   above   look Sub thing not many   that
     (dào   shi)>
     indeed   be
     'Then there wouldn't be many things to see on the way <(yes indeed)>.' (0248)

(3) A, wǒmen bú   tài   qīngchu.
     ah 1P   not too   clear
     'Ah, we don't know much about it.' (0962)

Unlike many adverbs, *bù* may occur as the only word in a sentence or precede a pause separating it from the rest of the sentence. Hence *Bù.* 'No.' is acceptable, but there is no isolated **Hái!* corresponding to 'Still!'. The isolated use of *bù* is however not as common as the type of negative reply shown in (4), which repeats and negates the verb used in the question. Correspondingly, a typical formula for an affirmative reply simply repeats the verb used in the question, as shown in (5).

(4) A: Pàng ma?
     fat   Q
     'Were they fat?' (4826)

     B: Bú   pàng a.
        not fat   Cnf
        'Well, no.' (4827)

(5) A: Nà   nǐmen zài   nèi ge dàxué   lǐbiar xué
        that 2P   be.in   that M university inside learn

        Yīngyǔ   ma?
        English.language Q

        'Well, did you study English at, eh, university?' (2874)

     B: Xué.
        learn
        'Yes.' (2875)

1.2 Negation with *bú*

The form *bú* does not only appear as the morphophonemic alternant of *bù* 'not' before fourth-tone syllables mentioned in the previous section. *Bú* is also an independent form meaning 'not to be' used to negate one type of raised nexus. As far as I am aware, this function of *bú* has not been described in the literature.

Nexus is the phenomenon that two meanings (a) refer to the same entity in the real world, or *referent*, and (b) are explicitly presented as referring to the same referent. The meaning of *the dog barks* contains a nexus because (a) the meanings of *the dog* and *barks* point to the same referent, viz., typically and appropriately a barking dog, and because (b) part of the meaning of *the dog barks* is a notification that (a) is the case. The functional division between the first and second nexus members, often characterized as nominal and verbal, respectively, can be described as reflecting the order in which the meanings are conceptualized by the speaker in constructing his message. Examples such as *the dog barks* are usually contrasted with expressions of the type *the barking dog* which conform to (a) but not to (b), and hence do not constitute a nexus.[2]

As noted above, Mandarin adjectives such as *gāo* 'high' can form predicates without a copula:

(6) Fèiyòng   gāo.
     expenses   high
     'The expenses are high.'

Here the meaning of *fèiyòng* and the meaning of *gāo* have the same referent, viz., something in the world constituting expenses and being high. Moreover, (6) states the identification explicitly. Hence the meaning of the sentence illustrates nexus in Mandarin.

Nexus always combines two meanings, but these two nexus members are not necessarily represented by separate morphemes. In the following example, nexus is expressed by a single morpheme:

(7) Gāo.
     high
     'It's high.'

In the semantic description of sentence (7) it can be supposed that the speaker has a definite entity in the real world in mind, i.e. an entity which he assumes can be identified by the hearer. This entity is the referent of a meaning in (7) which may be provisionally symbolized as 'IT', and which plays the same part as the meaning of *fèiyòng* in (6). Hence the meaning of (7) contains a nexus, but 'IT' is not represented by a separate form.

By *raised nexus*, I mean a nexus one of whose members is in turn a nexus. One common type of raised nexus in Mandarin is constructed by means of *shi* 'be'. This construction is duly described in other terms in most grammars of Mandarin, e.g. those by Chao (1968: 721) and by Charles N. Li and Sandra A. Thompson (1981: 151-154). In this usage, *shi* precedes the expression denoting the embedded nexus and corresponds roughly to translations such as 'it is the case that', 'it is a matter of', and 'the point is that'. The embedded nexus is the second nexus member of the raised nexus. Compare examples (6) and (8):

(8) Shi   fèiyòng   gāo.
     be   expenses   high
     'It's that the expenses are high.'

In the nexus of (6), it is stated that the expenses are high. The same nexus is present in sentence (8), but the additional raised nexus presents the expenses being high as the matter at hand. In other words, (6) is about the expenses being high, but (8) is about something being identifiable with the fact that the expenses are high.

With respect to the presence of a supposed something, the raised nexus in (8) parallels the single nexus in (7). For both sentences, (a) the speaker has an entity in mind which he assumes can be identified by the hearer, (b) this entity is the referent of a meaning 'IT' and (c) this meaning lacks a separate form. In (8), 'IT' is the first member of the raised nexus, the second member being the nexus of *fèiyòng gāo*: 'the expenses are high'. If sentence (8) is used, for example, to explain a lack of funds, the lack of funds can serve as the referent of 'IT', and (8) can be translated as *It's because the expenses are high*.

With raised nexus as with ordinary nexus, the two nexus members may have separate formal correlates, as illustrated in the following example. Here, the speaker had just been pointing out how much money is usually spent on wedding parties in Taiwan.

(9) Suóyi   fèiyòng   shi   hěn gāo, <duì,   duì, duì> fēicháng
     therefore expenses be   very high right   right right extraordinary
     gāo.
     high
     'So the expenses are very high <right, right, right>, are huge.' (1771)

The two members of the raised nexus in example (9) are, on the one hand, the meaning of *fèiyòng* 'expenses', and on the other hand, the nexus formed with *hěn gāo* 'very high'. The meaning 'expenses' does not partake of the embedded nexus. Hence, this time a meaning 'IT' can be assumed for the first member of the embedded nexus: *hěn gāo* means 'IT is very high'. Note that the meaning 'IT' need not be coreferential with the meaning 'expenses'. In other words, *fèiyòng shi hěn gāo* in (9) states that with regard to the expenses something is the case, viz., that something, not necessarily the expenses, is very high. The speaker might, for example, have been talking about tax deductions for expenses being higher than tax deductions on medical grounds. With these deductions in mind, *fèiyòng shi hěn gāo* can be translated as 'for expenses, the point is that they are very high'. In the translations of example sentences it is not possible to differentiate between contrasting types of raised nexus, or even to represent each case of raised nexus consistently. A semantic description will however be attempted in each case.

Before turning to the negation of raised nexus, some phonological details of the verb *shi* 'be' must be considered. Most grammars recognize two realizations of this verb, viz. with a neutral tone: *shi*, and with a fourth tone: *shì*. The neutral tone frequently occurs in the negative form *bú shi*, as noted by Chao (1968: 716): '*sh* is negated by the use of *bu*, in which case *sh* is usually in the neutral tone except when specially stressed'. The incompatibility of the neutral tone and stress is a matter of definition, applying regardless of negation (*cf.* section 0). Outside of negative contexts, Chao describes '*sh*' as optionally carrying a neutral tone (p. xxxi). Mandarin syllables with an optional neutral tone are usually described in terms of a neutralizing tone sandhi rule following after any other tone sandhi rules. In this case, a rule *shì > shi* must follow the rule *bù > bú* which applies when *bù* 'not' precedes fourth-tone syllables, as explained in section 1.1. The resulting derivation is *bù shì > bú shì > bú shi* 'not to be' instead of **bù shì > bù shi*.

Returning now to example (9), negations may occur on both nexus levels. First, consider two negations occurring on the level of the nexus which is formed with *hěn gāo* 'very high'.

(10) Fèiyòng shi   hěn bù   gāo.
     expenses be   very not high
     'The expenses are very low.'

(11) Fèiyòng shi   bù   hěn gāo.
     expenses be   not very high
     'The expenses are not very high.'

In (10) it is stated that regarding the expenses something is the case, namely that something (not necessarily the expenses) is, literally, 'very un-high'. Example (11) likewise states that something is the case with regard to the expenses, viz. that something is not very high.

The negation of the raised nexus in (9) is shown in (12). This sentence states that regarding the expenses it is not the case that something is very high.

(12) Fèiyòng bú   shi hěn gāo.
     expenses not be   very high
     'The expenses are not very high.'

In the following example, taken from the lyrics of a pop song, negations occur on both nexus levels.

(13) Bú   shi wǒ bù   míngbai/   Zhèi shìjiè   biànhuà kuài
     not be   1S not understand this world   change   fast
     'It's not that I don't see/ This world's too fast for me' (Cuī 1989)

The frequency of the neutral tone in *shi* following *bú* has the effect that *bú shi* is often realized as *búr*, where -*r* represents a voiced retroflex approximant [ɹ]:

(14) Fèiyòng   búr   hěn gāo.
     expenses   not.be   very high
     'The expenses are not very high.'

This kind of reduction has been described in general terms by Chao (1968: 37)[3]: 'In rapid speech, weakened initials tend to become voiced continuants; *zh*, *ch*, *sh* all becoming *r*, and *j*, *q*, *x* all becoming *y*, as in *Wáng Xiansheng → Wáng yanreng* "Mr. Wang"'. In my experience, the phenomenon also occurs at normal conversational speed. The data I have collected also show that when negated by *bú*,

• *shi* may weaken further, e.g. to nasalized schwa: *bú* [ə̃];
• *shi* may disappear altogether, leaving the second tone in *bú* as the only reflex of *shi*.

When *shi* is absent, the negation of the raised nexus of sentence (9) takes the following form:

(15) Fèiyòng   bú   hěn gāo.
     expenses   not.be   very high
     'The expenses are not very high.'

Changing the second tone of *bú* to a fourth tone produces a minimal contrast between (15) and (16):

(16) Fèiyòng   bù   hěn gāo.
     expenses   not   very high
     'The expenses are not very high.'

In (16), the nexus formed with *hěn gāo* 'very high' is negated, i.e., the statement is about the expenses not being high. Example (15), like (12) and (14), states with regard to the expenses that something being high is not the case. As far as I am aware at this moment, the semantic difference between (12), (14) and (15) is largely one of increasingly informal style. But the occurrence of *bú* 'not to be' does seem to be restricted to cases of raised nexus, whereas *bú shi* and *búr* are not so restricted.

In the following example of *bú* 'not to be', speaker B had been giving a tongue-in-cheek lecture on the art of contemplating the dancing leaves in a glass of tea, and speaker A had replied that she preferred drinking tea to looking at it. She appeared to be taking speaker B's remarks at face value:

(17) B: Nà   zhèi ge chá.dào   shi   duō   zhǒng duō   yàng de
          that this M art.of.tea be   many   sort   many   kind Sub
          suóyi nǐ   dàgài   shi-hahaha guāng hui hē,   nà n–
          therefore 2S general be-hahaha bare   can drink that [2S]
          'Well, the art of tea comes in many different kinds, so probably you
          merely can drink, so y–' (4931)

      A: Bú   shi   wǒ   guāng hui   hē,   nà   nǐ– wó   ye   bú
          not   be   1S   bare   can   drink   that 2S   1S   also not.be
          guāng hui   hē
          bare can   drink
          'It's not as though I merely can drink, so you– it's not as though I merely
          can drink though.' (4932)

Bú 'not to be' is apparently a recent innovation in Peking Mandarin. If it
had existed half a century ago, it is highly improbable that Chao (1968)
would have overlooked it. In addition, Chao introduces a 'morphophonemic
notation' in his Gwoyeu Romatzyh spelling, viz., *bu* for '*bu, bwu, buh*'
(p. xxx, *cf.* p. 568), i.e. for Hànyǔ Pīnyīn *bu, bú* and *bù*. This spelling convention presupposes the mechanic substitution of *bù* by *bú* before fourth-tone
syllables, the occurrence of the neutral tone in *bu* being subject to further
criteria (e.g. on p. 39). The same principle is adopted by Li (1981: xviii).
Chao's spelling *bu* would not have been feasible if a minimal contrast
between *bú* and *bù* had existed at the time. However, as indicated above, the
existence of *búr* in Chao's time is likely in view of his general rule deriving
r from weakened initial *sh–*. To sum up, the negated copula may have under-
gone a development *bú shi > búr > bú*. Synchronically, all three of these forms
occur along with intermediate realizations.

Different factors may have contributed to the lack of linguistic attention
for *bú* 'not to be'. First, the Chinese character script lacks a character for *bú*
'not to be'. Moreover, *bú* is largely restricted to free conversational styles,
which tend to receive less attention than written sources. In spite of these
factors, written examples can be found in which the character 不 for *bù* 'not'
is apparently borrowed to write *bú* 'not to be'. The following example is
taken from one of Wáng Shuò's (1990) dialogues, which reflect spoken
Mandarin to an unusually realistic degree.

(18) ... wó   zhǐ   zhīdao fán   shì   dōu yǒu ge lǐr,   dǎ ge
           1S   only know   every affair   all exist M   principle hit M
           pēnti bú   yě   yǒu rén xiě jǐ   shí   wàn
           sneeze not.be also exist person write how.many ten 10,000

zì	de	lùnwen,	dé	le	bóshì.
character	Sub	thesis	obtain	Pfv	doctor

'... all I know is everything has something to it. Didn't someone write a thesis several hundreds of thousands of characters long about a sneeze, getting him a Ph.D.?' (p. 9, transcribed as read by my informant)

As can be predicted from the first tone sandhi rule for *bù* given in section 1.1, the position before a fourth tone neutralizes the distinction between *bù* > *bú* 'not' and *bú* 'not to be'. Still, the difference is evident in most cases:

(19) B: Nǐ   kéyi géi wǒ   zhèr dǎ   diànhuà, èr   sān   liù   jiǔ
          2S   may   give 1S   here hit telephone two three six   nine
          'You can call me up here, two-three-six-nine' (4518)

      A: Shì   ma,   èr   sān–?
          be   Q   two three–
          'Really? Two-three–' (4519)

      B: Wǒ   bú   gàosu nǐ   le   ma?
          1S   not.be   tell   2S   Pfv Q
          'Didn't I tell you?' (4520)

      A: Nǐ   méi   gàosong wǒ   guo!
          2S   not.exist tell   1S   Exp
          'You didn't tell me' (4521)

If *bú* meant 'not' in this example, *Wǒ bú gàosu nǐ le ma?* would mean 'Am I not telling you anymore?', which doesn't tally with the context. Hence *bú* here means 'not to be'. The use of the perfective particle *le* will be discussed in section 2.2.

2 Negation with *méi*

2.1 The existential verb *yǒu*

The verb *yǒu* means 'be in a place, exist'. If its subject is animate and possession is implied, *yǒu* can be translated as 'have', as in the second example below. *Yǒu* cannot be negated with *bù* 'not', but is negated with *méi* instead.

(20) Dàn   shi   zhěng ge   fángzi dōu méi   yǒu   shéme dōngxi.
      but   be   whole M   house   all not.exist exist what   thing
      'But there wasn't anything worthwhile in the whole house.' (0891)

(21) W[ǒ]–   wǒ shuō– wǒ shuō: 'Tóngzhì, wǒ duì.bu.qǐ wǒ
     [1S]   1S   say   1S   say   comrade   1S   sorry   1S
     méi   yǒu yóupiào   yě   méi   yǒu liángpiào.'
     not.exist exist oil.coupon also not.exist exist grain.coupon
     '[I]– I said– I said: "Comrade, I'm sorry, I have neither oil coupons nor grain coupons".' (0905)

Like *bù*, *méi* is an adverb when it precedes and modifies a verb. But *méi* also functions as a negative verb 'not to exist', being a close synonym of *méi yǒu* in all but sentence-final and clause-final positions. Synchronically, the coexistence of *méi yǒu* 'not to exist' and *méi* 'not to exist' may suggest a description in terms of a "deletion" of *yǒu* in the latter form. Diachronically, however, *yǒu* apparently has left its trace in the negation marker *méi*. Jerry Norman (1988: 126) derives *méi* from an earlier *mǝ*, the modern offglide *-i* being a reflex of *yǒu*. An example is given in (22). In order to bring out its dual character, *méi* is glossed as 'not.exist'.

(22) Wǒ shuō: 'Wǒ méi   liángpiào.'
     1S   say   1S   not.exist   grain.coupon
     'I said: "I don't have grain coupons".' (0847)

A yes-or-no question such as *Ní yǒu liángpiào ma?* 'Do you have grain coupons?' cannot be answered with **Méi.* or with **Wǒ méi.* I am not aware of diachronic reasons for the non-acceptability of *méi* in sentence-final position. Acceptable utterances can be formed by the addition of a single morpheme:

(23) Méi.   yǒu.
     not.exist   exist
     'No.'

(24) Méi   ne.
     not.exist Rlv
     'Well, no.'

2.2 Other verbs

Méi and *méi yǒu* occur before verbs other than *yǒu* 'exist' to form the negative perfective aspect. What is usually described as the Mandarin perfective aspect combines notions of completion, anteriority, and for some authors a change to a new situation. For Peking Mandarin, it is primarily a semantic notion because affirmative and negative perfective are expressed by disparate forms without common elements. In the affirmative, the article *le* follows the verb.

In the corresponding negative form, *méi* or *méi yǒu* precedes the verb. In the example below, both the affirmative form and the negative form occur.

(25) Fǎnzhèng xué le Hélān.yǔ gēn méi xué shi bù
    anyway learn Pfv Dutch with not.exist learn be not
    yiyàng.
    the.same

    'Anyway, having learned Dutch is different from not having learned it.' (0469)

The addition of *le* to a verb negated by *méi* or *méi yǒu*, as shown in (26)/1704, is less common. The verb used here is a compound verb of the resultative type, *jiǎng dào* 'get to talk about'. More details about such compounds will be given in section 3. The informant was talking about the written notes she had brought to the recording studio.

(26) B: A, wo d– pà yílòu, suóyi wó méi xiàng wó
    ah 1S [?] afraid omit therefore 1S each item 1S

    xiǎng dào dōngxi wǒ dōu yōu xiě <he!>.
    think arrive thing 1S all exist write wow

    'Ah, I– was afraid I'd leave something out, so whenever I thought of something I wrote it down <wow!>.' (1703)

    B: Rúguo méi yōu jiǎng dào le, kéyi <m> shuō.
    if not.exist exist talk arrive Pfv may mm say
    'If I haven't yet talked about it, I can <mm> say it.' (1704)

When the verb is negated by *bù* instead of *méi*, the use of the particle *le* is very common. The perfective meaning is then associated with the negated predicate: 'it has come about that it does not happen', i.e. something is 'no longer' or 'not anymore' the case:

(27) Oh, di yí di èr nián xué <ê>, ránhòu jiu
    oh Ord one Ord two year learn uh-huh afterwards just
    bù xué le?
    not learn Pfv

    'Oh, you study it in the first and second year <uh-huh>, and then you don't study it anymore?' (2878)

With the verb *yǒu* 'exist', the meaning 'no longer, not anymore' is expressed by *méi ... le* instead of *bù ... le* because of the incompatibility of *bù* and *yǒu*:

(28) Kěshi nǐ   kāi dào   nǐ   gōngsī   fùjìn   de   shíhou
      but   2S   drive arrive 2S   company vicinity Sub   time

      fāxiàn   méi   yǒu tíng chē wèi   le   <m>.
      discover not.exist exist stop car position Pfv   mm

      'But when you drive to a place near your office, you discover there are no parking places left <mm>.' (2161)

The example given in (26) also demonstrates a usage of *yǒu* which is not attested in Peking Mandarin: *yǒu xiě* 'have written' in sentence 1703. This usage supplies a formal analogue to the semantic notion of a perfective: the affirmative is formed with *yǒu*, the corresponding negative with *méi (yǒu)*. Note that even without *yǒu* in the negative, a degree of formal correspondence remains because of the status of the offglide *-i* discussed earlier. The affirmative perfective *yǒu* is common in Taiwan Mandarin, where it is reinforced by the corresponding constructions in the Mǐn dialects. Affirmative perfectives with *yǒu* and *le* coexist in Taiwan Mandarin and are semantically distinct. Details of these semantic differences will not be dealt with here. Instead I will give just one example of the perfective auxiliary verb *yǒu*, which does not correspond with Peking Mandarin *le*. In the context of the following sentence the speaker was describing several types of bread:

(29) Birú   shuō zhèi ge miànbāo   shàng   yǒu fàng yi   xiē
      for.instance say this M   bread   above   exist put one few

      em,   eh,   cōnghuā   <m>... zhīlèi   de   <m>.
      em   eh   chopped.green.onions mm   or.something Sub   mm

      'Say for instance the bread would be topped with, em, eh, some chopped green onions <mm> or something <mm>.' (1293)

The Peking Mandarin equivalent of *yǒu fàng* 'be placed on' in (29) is *fàng zhe*, the aspect particle *zhe* denoting a state which ensues from the action of *fàng* 'placing'.

The experiential aspect expressed by the particle *guo* denotes the completion of an action and the passing of a certain amount of time between the completion and the time of reference. In the affirmative, *guo* closely follows the verb. The corresponding negative is *méi (yǒu)* VERB *guo*.

(30) B: Nèi ge fúwù   bāokuò hǎo–   m,   yǒu yì   zhǒng
         that M service include good–   mm   exist one sort

         sèqíng de,   yǒu yì   zhǒng jiù   shì... zhuānmén
         sex   Sub   exist one sort   just be   special

jiù shi péi   nǐ dú shū de.
just be accompany 2S read book Sub
'The service includes quite– m, one kind is with sex, and another kind is...
is especially just to help you with your studies.' (2494)

A: Oh, méi   yǒu tīng   guo!
   oh not.exist exist listen Exp
   'Oh, I have never heard about it!' (2495)

B: Méi   tīng   guo?
   not.exist listen Exp
   'Never heard about it?' (2496)

Normative grammars have *guo* immediately follow the verb, but a complement may sometimes be found to be inserted in between. In (19)/4521 the complement is a pronoun, but common nouns can be inserted in the same position.

3 Resultative verbs

Resultative verbs are compound verbs in which the second element denotes the result of the meaning of the first element. *Tīng* 'listen' and *qīngchu* 'clear' together form a resultative verb *tīng qīngchu* 'hear clearly'. Lexicalized compounds may satisfy the description, e.g. *cùjìn* 'promote' from the bound forms *cù* 'urge' and *jìn* 'progress'. However, the availability of so-called potential forms is often regarded as an additional characteristic of resultative verbs. These potential forms are formed by means of infixed elements and are not available for lexicalized compounds. An exhaustive treatment of varying degrees of internal cohesion of resultative verbs is given by Chao (1968: 435-438). Some characteristics of potential forms will be discussed below.

Resultative verbs can be negated by placing *méi* or *méi yǒu* before the compound.

(31) Kěshi jiù wǒ zhīdào de, yīnwei wǒ– wǒ zìjǐ hái měi
      but as.to 1S know Sub because 1S 1S self still not.exist
      yǒu   tīng   dào   Kēi Shū Zhōngxīn li yǒu sèqíng de <m>.
      exist listen arrive cram book center in exist sex Sub mm
      'But as far as I know, because I– I myself have never heard that there was any sex in Reading Room Centers <mm>.' (2537)

In section 2.2, the perfective semantics of *méi* and *méi yǒu* were noted. The compatibility of *méi (yǒu)* with resultative verbs is hardly surprising in view of the fact that the meaning of the second element of a resultative verb serves as a type of perfective extension of the meaning of the first element. Apart from denoting completion or achievement, the second element specifies the nature of the consequences. *Bù* instead of *méi (yǒu)* can be used before a resultative verb only if it is highly lexicalized. E.g. for *cùjìn* 'promote' mentioned above, *méi cùjìn* 'not to have promoted' can be contrasted with *bú cùjìn* 'not to promote'. But for *tīng dào* 'hear', *méi yǒu tīng dào* 'not to have heard' in (31) is not normally contrasted with **bù tīng dào*. *Bù* can however be inserted before the second element of a resultative compound:

(32) A: Oh, hm, yào wǒ– <wó xiǎng> wǒ hahaha-yí jù
     oh hm will 1S   1S think 1S hahaha-one phrase
     dōu tīng bu dǒng.
     all listen not understand
     'Oh, hm, if I– <I think> I wouldn't understand a thing.' (3130)

   A: Wǒ dào nèi xiē dìfāng qù wó zhǐ néng xiào <oh>.
      1S arrive that few place go 1S only can laugh oh
      'When I go to those places I can only smile <oh>.' (3131)

Forms such as *tīng bu dǒng* 'not to understand (aurally)' are usually described as potential forms of resultative verbs. *Tīng bu dǒng* can be translated as 'cannot understand', but it also corresponds to English 'not to understand'. I will discuss some semantic aspects of potentiality below. In terms of form, when *bù* is inserted into a resultative verb it is invariably toneless. If the second element of the resultative verb is toneless, the insertion of *bu* restores the original tone. E.g. *kàn jian* 'see', literally 'look perceive', corresponds to the negative potential form *kàn bu jiàn* 'cannot see' or 'not to see'.

The 'negative potential' with infixed *bu* is usually[4] paired off with an 'affirmative potential' formed by the infixation of *de*, as follows:

(33) Resultative verb forms:

base form	affirmative potential		negative potential	
shuō hǎo	*shuō de hǎo*		*shuō bu hǎo*	
say good	say so.that good		say not good	
'say right'	'can say right'		'cannot say right'	

The particle *de* fulfils a large number of functions in Mandarin. I have provisionally glossed the particle *de* in (33) as 'so that' because it is often assumed to derive from the Classical Chinese verb *dé* 'obtain'. One of the problems with the alignment shown in (33) is that the position after *de* can also be filled with verbal expressions denoting an extent or manner to be associated with the meaning of the expression preceding *de*. Hence *shuō de hǎo* can also mean 'say well', and *shuō de bù hǎo* 'say poorly' exhibits the same pattern. Moreover, *shuō de hǎo* can mean 'what is said is good' and *shuō de bù hǎo* can mean 'what is said is not good'. For the latter two meanings, *de* is usually regarded as a subordinative particle rendering *shuō* 'say' into a nominal phrase *shuō de* 'that which is said'. The distinction between the two *de*'s is reinforced by the Chinese script, which has separate characters for the 'extent' and 'subordinative' usages, and more characters for still other functions of *de*. Some of these distinctions make diachronic sense, but a synchronic lack of a formal difference keeps the possibility of a unifying treatment open. This problem of 'affirmative' semantics falls outside the scope of the present work however.

The forms considered so far can tentatively be aligned as follows:

(34) | *shuō* | *hǎo* | | *shuō* | *bu* | *hǎo* | | *shuō* | *de* | | *hǎo* |
say good | | | say not good | | | say so.that/Sub good
'say right' | | | 'cannot say right' | | | 'say well / can say right / what is said is good'

| | | | | | | *shuō* | *de* | | *bù* | *hǎo* |
say so.that/Sub not good
'say poorly / what is said is not good'

To sum up, the complexity of forms with *de* precludes the establishment of a simple contrast between 'affirmative potential forms' with -*de*- and 'negative potential forms' with -*bu*- because the latter are semantically more straightforward.

Potentiality in other verbs is expressed periphrastically by the auxiliary verb *néng* 'be able'. For resultative verbs, these forms coexist with the infixed forms. Compare e.g. *tīng bu dǒng* 'cannot understand (aurally)' in (32) with *néng tīng dǒng* 'can understand (aurally)' in the following example:

(35) A: Wǒ tīng hái xíng.
1S listen still go
'My comprehension is quite all right.' (2949)

A: Jiù tāmen shuō de wǒ dōu néng tīng dǒng.
just 3P say Sub 1S all can listen understand
'I mean I can understand everything they say.' (2950)

The semantic difference between the potential forms with *néng* and *bù néng* on the one hand, and with infixed *de* and *bu* on the other hand, is a well-known problem in the description of resultative verbs. Li (1981) considers the following example for a context in which the subject has a broken ankle:

(36) 'tā   bu   néng tiào   – guò –   qù
     3sg   not   can   jump   – cross –   go
     S/He can't jump across (because s/he can't jump).' (Li 1981: 57)

According to Li, the negative potential form *tiào bu guò qù*, literally 'jump not cross go', cannot be used in this context because it would 'explicitly mean that the subject initiates the action of jumping', while 'in spite of this, s/he is not able to get across' (*ibid.*). I do not doubt that this is a possible interpretation of *tiào bu guò qù*. The expression, however, does not seem too farfetched even in the event of a broken ankle. I cannot substantiate this claim beyond reporting that two native speakers of Mandarin considered the broken ankle context quite compatible with the use of *tiào bu guò qù*.

Perhaps the matter is worth looking at in more detail. Li (1981) bases the infelicity of *tiào bu guò qù* in this context on a description by Timothy Light (1977: 35): 'The agent of a resultative compound must have initiated the primary action referred to by the compound, or he must have sincerely imagined himself to have initiated the action'. I think this description is too restrictive. The agent's broken ankle need not stop a speaker from having sincerely imagined him to have initiated the action, but the idea is precisely to exclude such cases. Consider the following definition of *lóng* 'deaf' given in the dictionary *Xiàndài Hànyǔ Cídiǎn* (Cídiǎn 1983:732; my transcription):

(37) **lóng**   ěrduo   tīng   bu   jiàn   shēngyīn
     deaf   ear   listen   not   perceive   sound
     'deaf the inability to hear sounds with the ears'

Compare a similar example which is quite acceptable:

(38) Tā   shi   ge   lóngzi,   tīng   bu   jiàn   nǐ   de   huà
     3   be   M   deaf.person   listen   not   perceive   2S   Sub   word
     'He's deaf, he can't hear what you say.'

I think talking of deafness or deaf persons cannot prevent the speaker from sincerely imagining the initiation of *tīng* 'listening'. Light is right in pointing out the importance of the imagination in these matters. The consideration in the speaker's mind of meanings to be encoded necessarily precedes the choice of linguistic forms. The order of the three elements of *tīng bu jiàn* in

(38) is a fair reflection of the way in which the three associated meanings may be assumed to be organized in the speaker's mind. First, 'listening' is presented, and this meaning is subsequently portrayed as something characterized by the 'absence of perception'. From a logical point of view, one might argue that 'listening' should not enter into the picture when talking about the deaf, but in language the notion of deafness can be inextricably bound up with the concepts of listening and hearing.

To return to example (36), logical arguments cannot prevent the human mind from associating someone with a broken ankle with the act of *tiào* 'jumping', and to subsequently present this jumping in terms of *bu guò qù* 'not getting across'.

A small number of resultative verbs occur only in the potential form, notably those ending in *liǎo* 'finish' or *lái* 'come' which, according to a description by Chao (1968: 453), 'have, as complements, very little specific meaning and serve as a kind of dummy complement, thus making the potential form available'. Chao does not distinguish between forms with *liǎo* and those with *lái*, but at present the former are far more frequent than the latter. The following two sentences illustrate the use of *bu liǎo*:

(39) Nème ne, yě kéyi zhèi ge, dì yí cì huídá bu liǎo
    so Rlv also may this M Ord one time answer not finish
    tóngxué de wèntí ni ye kéyi dì èr cì huídá.
    fellow.student Sub question 2S also may Ord two time answer
    'So you may, eh, if you cannot answer the students' questions the first time, you may also answer them the second time.' (0128)

(40) Késhi wŏ xiǎng tāmen de xuéshēng a, rúguo yào yí
    but 1S think 3P Sub student Cnf if will one
    èr niánjī de kěnéng hāi jiāo tamen bu liǎo ba.
    two school.year Sub possible still teach 3P not finish Sug
    'But I think that their students, if they are in first or second year, maybe you cannot teach them [in Chinese] yet.' (3317)

There is no *huídá liǎo* corresponding to *huídá bu liǎo* 'cannot answer' in (39). Example (40), which was spoken by a native of Peking, is remarkable in that *jiāo* 'teach' is separated from the remainder of the negative potential form *bu liǎo* by an object pronoun *tāmen* 'they'. According to standard grammar books, the object follows the resultative verb: *jiāo bu liǎo tāmen* 'cannot teach them'.

Potential forms of resultative verbs also allow the limited insertion of adverbials. The following example contains the resultative verb *kàn jian* 'see' mentioned before:

(41) Xībānyá de *sinology* kǒngpà kàn yě kàn bu dà jiàn.
      Spain Sub sinology fear look also look not big perceive
      'Spanish sinology, I'm afraid when you look for it you won't see much either.'
      (9000)

Longer phrases generally cannot be inserted adverbially. Consider the following example:

(42) Wǒ– wǒ– xiàng wǒmen zhe yàngzi tá[n]– jiāotán
      1S 1S like 1P this appearance [talk] converse
      <m> wó xiǎng tā bù néng bǎi fēnzhī.bǎi tīng dǒng
      mm 1S think 3 not can hundred percent listen understand
      'W– w– like when we t– talk together in this way <mm>, I think they wouldn't be able to grasp 100% of it.' (3320)

With the negative potential form, *bǎi fēnzhī bǎi* '100%' could hardly have been infixed: *?tīng bu bǎi fēnzhī bái dǒng* is at best marginally acceptable. *Bǎi fēnzhī bǎi tīng bu dǒng*, on the other hand, means 'be 100% incapable of understanding'.

4 Interrogatives

4.1 The use of negation in the formation of questions

Declarative sentences may be turned into yes-or-no questions by means of the sentence-final interrogative particle *ma*. Examples of *ma* were given in (4) and (5). Another way of forming yes-or-no questions combines affirmative and negative forms of the same verb:

(43) Huì bu huì shēng bìng ne, tài jǐnzhāng, hahaha?
      can not can come.forth illness Rlv too strained hahaha
      'So were you prone to illnesses, being under too much stress, hahaha?' (0617)

Both the affirmative and the negative part of the question may assume different forms. Variations on the question in (43) are:

(44) (a) *Huì shēng bìng bú huì shēng bìng?*
      (b) *Huì shēng bìng bú huì shēng?*
      (c) *Huì shēng bìng bú huì?*
      (d) *Huì shēng bú huì shēng bìng?*
      (e) *Huì bu huì shēng bìng?*

In (43), the predicate contains an auxiliary verb *huì* 'can, be likely to', a main verb *shēng* 'come forth' and a complement noun *bìng* 'illness'. The number of possibilities grows with the complexity of the predicate, but either the affirmative or the negative part of the question must appear in full. Also note that *bu* is toneless when it is preceded and followed by the same verb, as in (44)(e). Amongst the various possibilities, this latter pattern is probably the one most frequently used.

With *méi* instead of *bù*, the same patterns are possible, but there are two corresponding affirmatives, VERB *le* and *yǒu* VERB, as mentioned in section 2.2. Both affirmative forms were recorded in yes-or-no questions from the same Taiwanese informant:

(45)   Jiéguǒ   nǐ   cānjiā   le   méi   yǒu ne?
       after.all 2S   participate Pfv not.exist exist Rlv
       'So did you join in after all?' (0718)

(46)   Yǒu méi   yǒu zāoyù   zěme   yàng de   cuòzhé.gǎn?
       exist not.exist exist encounter how   kind Sub   frustration
       'Did you suffer any kind of frustrations?' (0600)

For the question in (46), the two sets of possible combinations have been listed in (47). As noted before, *méi yǒu* alternates with *méi* unless it is sentence-final.

(47)   A.   questions formed with affirmative 'VERB + *le*'
       (a)   *zāoyù le cuòzhé gǎn méi (yǒu) zāoyù cuòzhé gǎn?*
       (b)   *zāoyù le cuòzhé gǎn méi (yǒu) zāoyù?*
       (c)   *zāoyù le cuòzhé gǎn méi yǒu?*
       (d)   *zāoyù le*   *méi (yǒu) zāoyù cuòzhé gǎn?*

       B.   questions formed with affirmative '*yǒu* + VERB'
       (a)   *yǒu zāoyù cuòzhé gǎn méi (yǒu) zāoyù cuòzhé gǎn?*
       (b)   *yǒu zāoyù cuòzhé gǎn méi (yǒu) zāoyù?*
       (c)   *yǒu zāoyù cuòzhé gǎn méi yǒu?*
       (d)   *yǒu zāoyù*   *méi (yǒu) zāoyù cuòzhé gǎn?*
       (e)   *yǒu*   *méi (yǒu) zāoyù cuòzhé gǎn?*

The most frequently used patterns are (c) in (47)/A and (e) in (47)/B.

As noted in section 2.2, the patterns in (47)/B are common in Taiwan Mandarin. Outside Taiwan, the status of the perfective auxiliary verb *yǒu* may be on the increase. Chao (1968: 748) describes the interrogative form with *yǒu* as 'getting to be fairly acceptable Mandarin among those in contact with

Southerners', whereas the affirmative, 'sometimes heard in Taiwan' (p. 669), 'still grates on Northern ears' (p. 748). As far as I have been able to observe, the affirmative form is still absent in present-day mainland usage. As to the interrogative forms, I have no clear examples from mainland speakers in my corpus. But Dīng Shēngshù (1980) provides the following sentence amongst similar examples which he describes as recent developments:

(48) Tā yǒu méi   yǒu qǐ.lái?
     3   exist not.exist   exist rise
     'Has he risen?' (p. 206, my transcription)

If this interrogative pattern is gaining acceptance in mainland Standard Mandarin, it is noteworthy that of all the possibilities in (47)/B, type (e) is spreading. This is the only pattern in which *yǒu* does not directly precede the verb, so that the unacceptable (in mainland terms) **yǒu zāoyù* 'have encountered' is avoided.

It is not easy to pin down the semantic difference between questions formed with *ma* and their counterparts formed by means of the VERB-not-VERB pattern. According to Chao (1968: 800), the latter are 'completely noncommittal as to the answer', whereas the corresponding sentences with *ma* express 'a slight or considerable doubt about an affirmative answer'. Li (1981: 548-554), however, describes *ma* as a form which can be used in noncommittal contexts as well. Lǚ Shūxiāng likewise ascribes noncommittal as well as rhetorical meanings to *ma* (1980: 336-337). Chao's description of *ma* seems to be confirmed by my own data, as suggested by the contexts of the following two questions:

(49) A: Nǐ   jué   Fǎwén   hǎo tīng   ma?
       2S   feel   French.language good listen   Q
       'Do you find French nice to listen to?' (3528)

       A: Tāmen dōu jué   Fǎwén   tèbié   hǎo tīng   <duì>.
       3P   all   feel   French.language special   good listen   right
       'They all find French especially nice to listen to <right>.' (3529)

       A: Wǒ méi   you juéde   zeme   hǎo tīng.
       1S   not.exist   exist feel   so   good listen
       'I didn't find it so nice to listen to.' (3530)

(50) A: Kěshi   Cháoxiǎn wén   méi   yǒu
       but   Korea   language not.exist exist

Zhōngwén,   méi   yǒu ba?
Chinese.language not.exist   exist Sug
'But there is no Chinese in Korea, there is none, is there?' (3271)

B: Ei,   dà   liàng de   Zhōngwén!
     well big degree Sub Chinese.language
     'Well, large amounts of Chinese!' (3272)

A: Shì ma?
     be   Q
     'Really?' (3273)

4.2 The development of sentence-final question particles

The etymology of Mandarin sentence-final question particles is largely unrecorded. No cognates of these particles seem to occur in Classical Chinese, which until the beginning of the 20th century was the only form of Chinese deemed worthy of linguistic attention and documentation. Even the reconstruction of *bù* is problematic. At first glance, *bù* is identical to the most common Classical Chinese marker of negation, but this is an illusion created by the Chinese script:

'The pronunciation *bù* [...] does not correspond to the Middle Chinese readings found in the *Guǎngyùn*. The reading [pjəu] [...] would regularly yield *fōu* or *fū* rather than *bù*; but since the character [不] is the most common negative in classical texts, it has been borrowed to write the corresponding common negative in the modern language. Modern *bù* should go back to a Middle Chinese *puət*, which is not attested in the early lexical sources.' (Norman 1988: 76)

Diachronically, it seems likely that sentence-final question particles developed from negative forms at or near the end of a sentence. E.g. the particle *ma* discussed in the previous section is regarded by Chao (1968: 801, 807-808) as a fusion of an older negative beginning with *m-* and the particle *a*, which in modern Mandarin has a number of modal functions. He supports this view with a modern example from the Mandarin dialect of Bǎodìng, Héběi Province. In this dialect *bù* can be tagged to a sentence either with or without *a*. When *bù* is followed by *a*, the two forms are fused into *ba*:[5]

(51) (a) Nǐ   qù   bù?   (b) Nǐ   qù   ba?
          2S   go   not   2S   go   not.Cnf
          'Are you going?'   'Are you going?' (pp. 807-808)

In a similar vein, Chao (p. 807) suggests that *ba* derives from *bù* and *a*. *Ba* is used in questions soliciting confirmation, as in (50). Chao (p. 808) also describes *ba* as being used in noncommittal questions such as *Nǐ zhīdao ba* 'do you know?'. As far as I know, this noncommittal usage has all but disappeared nowadays. *Ba* can also be used in an adhortative sense:

(52) Xiànzài shi   bu   shi   qíng   nǐ   xiān jièshao
      now   be   not   be   invite   2S   first introduce

      yi.xià– jiù   nǐ   n–   jièshao   yi.xià nǐ   zìjǐ ba.
      once   just 2S   [2S] introduce once   2S   self Sug
      'Now let me just invite you to first introduce yourself a little– I mean just i– introduce yourself a little.' (0012)

For a charming parallel consider the adhortative use of *non* 'no' in Zaïrese French appearing on the painting *Les enfants malhonnêtes* 'The naughty children' by Cheri Samba. The text is spoken by a little boy awaiting his turn before the crack in the wall of the women's bathhouse:

(53) Grand   frère,   fais   vite   non! Moi aussi je veux regarder.
      big   brother do   quick   no   me   also I want look
      'Big brother, be quick about it! Me too I want to have a look' (NRC 1992)

Even though the adhortative sense of *ba* is sometimes regarded as diachronically distinct and deriving from the verb *bà* 'finish', the modern usages of the particle *ba* can be described in terms of polysemy. In (50) as well as (52), the basic notion is one of making a suggestion. In (50), the suggestion amounts to a claim to be confirmed, viz., that there are no Chinese loanwords in Korean. In (52) the suggestion is a proposition or mild exhortation that the hearer introduce himself.

Bei is a sentence-final modal particle denoting that from the speaker's point of view something is evident or obvious. According to Lǚ (1980: 57), 'the modality is basically similar to that of *ba*, with slightly more emotional coloring'. Lǚ distinguishes between different collocations, but in his most general description, *bei* 'expresses that an argument is plain and that there is no need to elaborate'. The particle occurs only once in my corpus. In this example, the speakers were discussing the phenomenon of graffiti in inner cities:

(54)   B: Xiǎo   hár   nèng de?
           small   child do   Sub
           'Is it done by kids?' (3939)

       A: Wó xiǎng kěnéng shi, wó xiǎng kěnéng shi <hahaha>
           1S think possible be   1S think possible be   hahaha
           'I guess so, I guess so <hahaha>.' (3940)

       B: Hǎowár   bei.
           amusing Evd
           'Must be fun.' (3941)

The context of this conversation showed the speaker's unfavorable attitude towards graffiti, so there is a sense of irony in the sentence with *bei*: it must be fun – for them, but not for us.

I have found no sources or even educated guesses regarding the history of the particle *bei*, but the formal and semantic similarities with the other particles mentioned here are obvious: *bei* has an initial *b-*, is used sentence-finally, and denotes a modal meaning.

Finally, the sentence-final particle *me* conveys that the hearer had better comply with the suggestion made by the speaker. An example will be given in (61)/3047.

4.3 Interrogative forms of negated sentences

In negated sentences followed by the question particle *ma* the negative statement is literally called into question and its affirmative counterpart is suggested as an answer to the question. In the following example, the speaker conveys that rather than being *bù gāoxìng* 'unhappy', he would in fact be happy under the circumstances described:

(55)   Wǒ   de   Yīngyǔ   fāyīn   yào   yǒu
       1S   Sub English.language pronunciation will exist

       tāmen zhèi ge Zhōngwén   de   fāyīn   de
       3P   this M Chinese.language Sub pronunciation Sub

       shuǐpíng nà   bu   gāoxìng ma?
       level   that not happy   Q
       'If my English pronunciation were on a par with their, eh, Chinese pronunci-ation, wouldn't I be glad?' (3378)

A similar effect can be produced by questions formed from a negative sentence by means of intonation only, as in (56) below. Another example occurs in (30)/2496.

(56) Kěshi nǐ   zài, eh, xuéxiào huòzhe shi yīyuàn   méi   yǒu
     but   2S   be.in eh   school perhaps be hospital not.exist exist

     yi   ge cāntīng?
     one   M dining.hall
     'But didn't you, eh, have a dining hall at [medical] school or at the hospital?'
     (0967)

The set phrase *kě bu shì ma* is no longer a question. Instead of suggesting the affirmative counterpart of *bú shi* 'not to be' as an answer, it denotes the affirmative notion explicitly:

(57) Kě   bu shì ma
     may not be   Q
     'Exactly!'

4.4 The negation of content question words

Content questions are questions which cannot be answered with 'yes' or 'no'. They are formed with interrogative pronouns and adverbs such as *shéme* 'what', *nǎr* 'where' and *zěme* 'how'. These content question words request information of a specified kind, e.g. a thing, a place or a means. Most content question words in Standard Mandarin can be used as indefinite pronouns. Compare the interrogative function of *shéme* 'what' in (58) with the indefinite usage in (59):

(58) B: Wǒ chī guo yi ci   shi diǎnxíng de   Hélán   fàn.
        1S eat Exp one time be typical Sub   Holland food
        'I once ate what was typically Dutch food.' (3179)

     A: Shi shéme dōngxi a,   hahaha?
        be what thing Cnf   hahaha
        'What was it, hahaha?' (3180)

     B: A! Tǔdòu!   <duì, hahaha>
        ah potatoes right hahaha
        'Ah! Potatoes! <right, hahaha>' (3181)

(59) Jiù shi niánjī bíjiao   dà de   ya, lǎo jiào-
     just be age   relatively big Sub Cnf old pro-

    shòu a,   yǒu shéme wèntí   yě kéyi suíshī   qǐngjiāo.
    fessor Cnf exist what   question also may anytime   consult
    'I mean those advanced in years, you know, old professors, if you have any
    questions you can always ask them.' (0082)

In (59), *shéme* means 'something, some ... or other'. Another example of this usage is given in (61)/3045. Similarly, *nǎr* 'where' can be used in the sense of 'somewhere' and *zěme* 'how' can be used to express 'somehow'.

    In negated sentences, a content question word with indefinite reference can be used in two ways. When it follows the negated verb, the sentence conveys that the meaning denoted by the content question word is to be regarded as something of little consequence:

(60) B: Zhèi ge fán   zǒng.de.lái shuō ba, zhè ge wǒ gèrén
          this M anyway generally   say Sug this M 1S individual

          de   zhèi ge jīnglì   ne   shì bǐjiao   jiǎndān de.
          Sub this M experience Rlv be relatively simple Sub
          'Eh, anyway, generally speaking, eh, my personal, eh, experiences are
          rather simple.' (0067)

      B: Yě   méi   yǒu shéme fùzá   de.
          also not.exist exist what complicated Sub
          'And there isn't anything particularly complicated.' (0068)

Here the speaker admits that *fùzá de* 'something complicated' did exist, but downplays its importance. There was, in other words, 'nothing complicated to speak of'. Similarly in (61)/3047, there may be 'something' that is different, but speaker A asserts that it is of no consequence:

(61) A: Kěshi   nà   ta jiào lìng   yi   zhóng yǔyán   kěshi
          but   that 3 call other one sort   language but

          dàn yúfǎ   shéme dōu yíyàng.
          but grammar what   all   the.same
          'But, well, they call it a different language, but the grammar and things
          are all the same.' (3045)

      B: Ei,   zhèi ge–
          well this M
          'Well, there–' (3046)

      A: Zhèi méi   yǒu shéme me!
          this not.exist exist what Sup
          'There is nothing much there, right?' (3047)

B: Zhèi ge yé yǒu xiē bu yiyàng.
  this M also exist few not the.same
  'There are some differences there also.' (3048)

Note that in terms of position it is impossible to tell the difference between the interrogative and the indefinite use of content question words. In (58), (59) and (60), a content question word *shéme* 'what' modifying a noun, like any other modifying expression, precedes the noun. The two usages are optionally distinguished by stress. A content question word cannot be stressed in the indefinite sense, while in the interrogative sense it can. Thus, stressing *shéme* in the sentence *Yě méi yǒu shéme fǔzá de* 'And there isn't anything particularly complicated' of example (60) yields a question: *Yě méi yǒu shéme fǔzá de?* 'What kind of complicated things [did you say] are not there either?'.

Alternatively in negative contexts, content question words can be used to express absolute, categorical negation. There are no negative content words in Standard Mandarin corresponding to English 'nothing' or 'nowhere'. The notional equivalents are expressed by placing a content question word, usually stressed, before a negated verb. In this pattern, the verb is usually preceded by *yě* 'also' or *dōu* 'all, at all'.

(62) B: Búguo zhèi ge shéme hahaha-zhǔnbèi yě méi yǒu.
      but this M what preparation also not.exist exist
      'But, eh, I haven't made any hahaha-preparations at all.' (0016)

A: M– m– bú xuyào zhǔnbèi, nǐ jiu suíbiàn shuō le.
      mm mm not need preparation 2S just freely say Pfv
      'Mm, mm, you don't need any preparation, just say whatever you like.'
      (0017)

5 Other phenomena

5.1 Special forms of negated auxiliary verbs

Auxiliary verbs are verbs which take other verbs as complements. The auxiliary verb *yào* 'want, will, have to' has two frequently occurring negative counterparts: *bú yào* 'don't' and *bú yòng* 'need not'. Apart from its use as an auxiliary verb, *yòng* is a transitive verb meaning 'use'. The interrogative form of *yào* is *yào [...] bú yào* 'do ... have/need to?'.

In the following fragment about a Taiwanese wedding ceremony, *bu yào* is apparently used in a meaning very similar to that of *bú yòng* 'need not'.

Note that Speaker B does not finish his question in (63)/1378, and that speaker A uses *bú yòng* instead of *bu yào* or *bú yào*:

(63) B: Yào bú yào, eh, bài– bài mǔqīn bài
         will not will eh salute salute mother salute

         fùqīn jìng– birú shuō–
         father pay.respect for.instance say

         'Do you have to, eh, salute– salute your mother and salute your father and
         pay respect to– say for instance– ' (1376)

      A: A, yào júgōng <yào júgōng>, duì.
         ah will bow will bow right
         'Ah, you must bow <you must bow>, right.' (1377)

      B: Bu yào guì (dào)–?
         not will kneel [arrive]
         'You don't have to kneel down–?' (1378)

      A: Bú yòng, bú yòng.
         not need not need
         'No, you don't need to.' (1379)

I think *bu yào* in (63)/1378 can be interpreted in at least the following two ways. It may be a less common way of saying 'need not', *bú yòng* being the more common form. It is also possible that *bu < bú < bú shi* negates a raised nexus (see section 1.2), in which case *bu yào* means 'it is not the case that you have to'.

For both negative forms corresponding to *yào* 'have to', shorter forms exist: *béng* 'need not' for *bú yòng* and *bié* 'don't' for *bú yào*. *Béng* is apparently a contracted form of *bú yòng*. *Bié* may be a comparable contraction of *bú yào*, but Ōta Tatsuo (1958: 303; *cf.* Norman 1988: 127 and Ōta 1987: 282) proposes a development from *bié* 'different' to an originally mild prohibitive 'do something other than'. Perhaps both developments have reinforced each other.

A special pattern exists for some auxiliary verbs denoting potentiality: *bù* Aux *bù* VERB. This combination of two negatives denotes necessity: 'cannot but VERB'. Some of the auxiliaries concerned are bound forms derived from Classical Chinese: *kě* 'be permissible', *dé* 'obtain'. But *néng* 'be able' and *kéyi* 'may, can' occur as free auxiliaries.

(64)   Zhèi yàng dehuà, xuéshēng ta jiu   bù.de.bu   hǎohāor
        this   kind if   student   3 just   not.can.not   proper

        xuéxí le,   hahaha <nà dào   shi, hahaha>.
        study Pfv   hahaha that indeed be   hahaha

        'That way, the students, they are now forced to study properly, hahaha <yes
        indeed, hahaha>.' (0163)

5.3 Negative forms with non-negative meaning

In the previous section, a double negative was shown to result in strong assertion. A special case must be noted for the negative verb *fēi* in Classical Chinese, meaning 'not to be, not to be the case that'. In Standard Mandarin, it has developed into an adverb meaning 'definitely'. The example is taken from Lǚ (1980):

(65)   Tā bù   lái   jiu   suàn.le,   wèi.shéme fēi   jiào ta lái?
        3 not   come   just forget.it   why   definitely call 3 come
        'If he won't come, forget it! Why should we by all means ask him to come?'
        (pp. 179-180, my transcription)

The development is due to the deletion of a second negative expression, *bùkě*, optionally tagged onto the end of the predicate. In Classical Chinese, *bù kě* means 'not to be permissible'. *Fēi* VERB *bùkě* is therefore literally '[if it] is not [the case that] VERB, [it will] not be permissible' – hence 'necessarily VERB'. Forms with and without the tag still coexist, the latter being only slightly less formal.

Another instance of non-negative meaning carried by a negative form concerns the temporal expressions *yǐqián* 'earlier', *zhīqián* 'previously' and *qián* 'before'. When expressions preceding these forms are negated with *méi* (*yǒu*) 'not to exist', the resulting meaning remains affirmative:

(66)   Dāngrán   ni   kéyi záo yi   diǎn dào   gōngsī,   hái   mēi
        of.course   2S   may early one bit   arrive   company still not.exist

        yǒu kāishǐ   shàng   bān yǐqián <m, m, m>   xiān chī.
        exist begin   above   duty earlier   mm mm mm first eat

        'Of course you can go to the office a little early and eat it first <mm, mm,
        mm>, before you even start working.' (1283)

The idea is that before something is done, it is not being done. *Méi yǒu* and *yǐqián* co-occur without yielding the logical sum of their meanings, i.e. 'before something is not done'. The combination of a form meaning 'before' with a negative form into one expression meaning 'before' has parallels in many languages. Compare e.g. French *Ne parlez pas avant qu'il n'ait fini* 'Don't talk before he has finished'.

Abbreviations

The following codes are used to specify personal pronouns:

1, 2, 3	1st, 2rd, 3rd person
S	singular
P	plural

Tā has been glossed as '3', not as '3S' because the examples represent informal speech styles, in which *tā* is unmarked for number. In more formal usages, *tā* usually denotes the singular.

(...)	transcription uncertain
[...]	words possibly intended by the speaker
<...>	interjection by the hearer
–	interruption or hesitation
>	development: A > B 'A develops into B'
/	1. 'or'
	2. specifies a subnumber, e.g. (61)/3047
Aux	auxiliary verb
Cnf	request for or declaration of confirmation as expressed by the final partical *a* and its morphophonemic variants, e.g. *ya*

Evd	final particle *bei*, indicating that a statement should be evident
Exp	experiential aspect expressed by the particle *guo*
hahaha	laughter
hahaha-	laughing onset
M	measure word (or 'classifier'), preceding nouns modified by demonstratives and/or cardinal numerals
Ord	ordinal numeral prefix *dì*
Pfv	perfective aspect expressed by the particle *le*
Q	question
Rlv	final particle *ne*, indicating strong relevance of an expression in the context
Sub	subordination, expressed by the final particle *de*
Sug	suggestion as denoted by the final particle *ba* (see section 4.2)
Sup	supposition, assumption as expressed by the final particle *me*

Notes

1. Standard Mandarin is traditionally described as having four tones, each neutral tone deriving from one of the four 'full' tones. Minimal pairs do however exist between each of these four tones and the neutral tone. For details see e.g. Chin-Chuan Cheng (1973: 54ff).

2. For the notion of *nexus* the *locus classicus* is Otto Jespersen (1924: 97, 114ff.). I have greatly benefited from Carl Ebeling's (1978: 231-248, 323-329) penetrating treatment.

3. I have converted Chao's Gwoyeu Romatzyh transcription to Hànyǔ Pīnyīn and omitted Chinese characters.

4. For example, in Chao (1968: 452), Li (1981: 56), and Light (1977: 34).

5. Chao transcribes his characters for the Bǎodìng dialect sentences according to their Standard Mandarin readings. The translations given here are Chao's, the glosses are mine, and Chao's Gwoyeu Romatzyh transcription has been converted to Hànyǔ Pīnyīn.

References

Chao, Y.R. (1930). 'A System of Tone Letters.' *Le maître phonétique*, troisième série, No. 30, 24-27. Reprinted in: *Fāngyán* [Dialects] 2, 1980, 81-83.
―― (1970). *A Grammar of Spoken Chinese*. Berkeley: University of California Press, 1968. 2nd printing.
Cheng, C.C. (1973). *A Synchronic Phonology of Mandarin Chinese*. The Hague: Mouton & Co.
Cídiǎn (1983). Zhōngguó Shèhuì Kēxué Yuàn Yǔyán Yánjiū Suǒ Cídiǎn Biānjí Shì [Dictionary Editing Office, Institute of Linguistic Research, Academia Sinica], ed., *Xiàndài Hànyǔ Cídiǎn* [Dictionary of Modern Chinese]. Peking: 1978¹, 1983².
Cuī Jiàn (1989). 'Bú shi wǒ bù míngbai' [It's not that I don't see]. In: *Xīn Chángzhēng lù shàng de yáogǔn* [Rock'n'roll on the road of a new Long March]. Peking: Zhōngguó lǚyóu shēngxiàng chūbǎn shè.
Dīng Shēngshù a.o. (1980). *Xiàndài Hànyǔ yúfǎ jiǎnghuà* [Talks on the grammar of Modern Chinese]. Peking: Shāngwù yìnshū guǎn.
Ebeling, C.L. (1978). *Syntax and Semantics: A Taxonomic Approach*. Leiden: E.J. Brill.
Jespersen, O. (1924). *The Philosophy of Grammar*. London: George Allen & Unwin.
Li, C. N. and S.A. Thompson (1981). *Mandarin Chinese, A Functional Reference Grammar*. Berkeley: University of California Press.
Light (1977), T. 'Some Potential for the Resultative: The Need for Analytical Redundancy'. *Journal of the Chinese Language Teachers Association*, Volume 12:1, 1977, 27-41.
Lǚ Shūxiāng ed. (1980). *Xiàndài Hànyǔ bābǎi cí* [800 words in Modern Chinese]. Peking: Shāngwù yìnshū guǎn.
Norman, J. (1988). *Chinese*. Cambridge: Cambridge University Press.
NRC (1992). 'Samba: groot en klein leed uit Kinshasa' [Samba: big and small sorrows from Kinshasa]. In: *NRC Handelsblad*, 11 December 1992, 6.

Ōta Tatsuo (1958). *Chūgokugo rekishi bunpō* [Chinese historical grammar]. Tōkyō: Kōnan Shoten.

—— (1987). *Zhōngguó lìshǐ wénfǎ* [Chinese historical grammar]. Jiǎng Shàoyú, Xú Chānghuá, tr., Peking: Běijīng Dàxué Chūbǎnshè. Translation of Ōta (1958).

Wáng Shuò (1990). 'Wánzhǔ' [Hipster]. In: *Wáng Shuò xiéqù xiǎoshuō xuǎn* [Selected amusing stories by Wáng Shuò]. Peking: Zuòjiā Chūbǎnshè, 1-74.

Zazaki

Marie Sandonato

1 Introduction

Zaza is the name of a language (or network of dialects) spoken in the region of the head waters of the Euphrates River in east-central Anatolia. It is classified as an Indo-European language belonging specifically to the north-western sub-group of Iranian languages (cf. Todd 1985 and Payne 1987). Zaza is also referred to as 'Zazaki,' 'Dimilki,' or 'Dimili.' The variety of Zaza described in this paper is spoken in villages around the city of Tunceli. It is northern Zaza or 'Dersim' Zaza, referred to here as 'Zazaki.' Estimates for the number of Zaza speakers worldwide range from one million *(Institut für Entwicklungsforschung* 1985) to three million (Pamukcu 1988).

1.1 Word order

Word order in Zazaki is SOV, but not strictly verb final. It is possible to find the subject pronoun placed after the verb for emphasis, or as a reaction to an imperative.

(1)   Ẏz $\widehat{ts^h}$aj   sɪmon.
      I-Dir tea   drink
      'I am drinking tea.'

(2)   T^{h}ɛlɛfon k^{h}on ɛz.
      telephone do I-Dir
      '*I* will phone (you)!'

(3)   a. P^{h}ijaz mɛ-wiɛ.
           onion Neg-eat:Imp
           'Don't eat onions!'

      b. Won ɛz.
           eat I-Dir
           'I am *going to eat* (them)!'

1.2 Direct and Oblique pronouns

There are two sets of pronouns in Zazaki: direct and oblique. The subject of any verb (transitive or intransitive) in the present tense is always in the direct case form and the object in the oblique case form. In the past tense, however, one must differentiate between transitive and intransitive verbs. The subject of an intransitive verb in the past tense is in the direct case form and the object is in the oblique case form. The subject of a transitive verb in the past tense, on the other hand, is in the oblique case form and the object is in the direct case form. The distinction between direct and oblique case pronouns is not made in the first and second persons plural. The sets are shown in table 1.

Table 1. Direct and Oblique pronouns.

	Direct	Oblique
I	εz	mi
You	t^hi (t^hu)	t^ho (t^hu)
He	o (u)	εj
She	a	aε
We	ma	ma
You	sima	sima
They	i	yino

(4) a. O   ga-i   vinεno.
          he-Dir ox-Obl   sees (Trans)
          'He sees the ox.'

     b. εj   ga   di.
          he-Obl ox   saw (Trans)
          'He saw the ox.'

(5) a. O   mi   vinεno.
          he-Dir I-Obl   sees (Trans)
          'He sees me.'

     b. εj   εz   dinε.
          he-Obl I-Dir saw (Trans)
          'He saw me.'

(6) a. I   nisεne   ro.
          they-Dir   sit   down (Intr)
          'They sit down.'

     b. I   nisthe   ro.
          they-Dir   sat   down (Intr)
          'They sat down.'

(7) a. A sona mɛkʰtʰɛv.
   she-Dir goes school (Intr)
   'She goes to school.'

  b. A sia mɛkʰtʰɛv.
   she-Dir went school (Intr)
   'She went to school.'

1.3 Questions

In content questions, the question word keeps the position of the word it replaces.

(8) a. Tʰɨ $\widehat{\text{ts}}$ʰɨkʰ sɨmɛna.
   you-Dir what drink
   'What are you drinking?'

  b. ɛz $\widehat{\text{ts}}$ʰaj sɨmon.
   I-Dir tea drink
   'I am drinking tea.'

(9) a. A kʰɛj sona.
   she-Dir when goes
   'When is she going?'

  b. A mɛsdɛ sona.
   she-Dir tomorrow goes
   'She is going tomorrow.'

Yes-no questions contain no question particle, but are instead signalled by a sharp rise in intonation.

(10) Tʰo dɛwɛ diɛ.
   you-Obl village saw
   'Did you see the village?'

(11) Tʰɨ sia wotʰɛl sultʰan.
   you-Dir went hotel Sultan
   'Did you go to Hotel Sultan?'

The intonation of a content question differs from that of a yes-no question in that in the former there is no sharp rise in intonation at the end of the utterance. The intonation marked below is similar to that of statements as well.

(12) A kʰɛj sona.
   she-Dir when goes
   'When is she going?'

128	*Marie Sandonato*

1.4 The nominal phrase

Word order within a nominal phrase is as follows:

demonstrative + numeral + head + ezafe + modifier.

'Ezafe' morphemes are an important element of the noun phrase in Zazaki: they are vowels that connect post-nominal modifiers (adjectives, nouns, possessive pronouns, and other noun phrases) to the head of the nominal phrase. Ezafe morphemes agree in gender and number with the head noun and vary depending on whether they are linking an adjective, noun or pronoun, or another phrase to the head noun. Numerals and demonstratives occur before the head of a nominal phrase and are consequently not linked by means of an ezafe.

(13) Dem Num Head   -Ez Adj   -Ez Adj   -NO
      (Ni dɨ portʰaqal-e tsʰɛqɛr-e rɨndɛkʰ-i) je   mɨn   e.
      these 2   orange-Ez   yellow-Ez nice-NO   Part mine   are
      'These two nice, yellow oranges are mine.'

(14) (Ni dɨ hɛr-e   sia-e   girs-i-e
      these 2 donkey-Ez   black-Ez   big-NO-Ez
      kʰɛ   hega dɛ   tsʰrɛne) je   mɨn   e.
      that field in   graze   Part mine   are
      'These two big, black donkeys that are grazing in the field are mine.'

1.5 Comparative constructions

Comparisons of equality are formed with the word *hondɛ* as in the following examples:

(15) ɛz   hondɛ tʰo   baqɨl   o.
      I-Dir as/same you-Obl   intelligent am
      'I am as intelligent as you.'

(16) Sɛr-e   mɨ   hondɛ   sɛr-e   tʰuj e.
      year-Ez I-Obl as/same year-Ez   your are
      'I am as old as you.'

(17) Alamanja hondɛ   itʰalia rɨndɛkʰ a.
      Germany   as/same Italy   nice   is
      'Germany is as nice as Italy.'

The postposition /ra/ (homophonous with the Ablative postposition) marks the standard in comparisons of inequality.

(18)   A   mɨ   ra   pʰil   a.
       she-Dir I-Obl than big   is
       'She is older than I am.'

(19)   Hega-e mɨ   hega-e tʰo   ra   hewl   o.
       field-Ez I-Obl field-Ez you-Obl than valuable is
       'My field is more valuable than your field'

(20)   T͡sʰe-e   mɨ   t͡sʰe-e   tʰo   ra   pʰak   o.
       house-Ez I-Obl house-Ez you-Obl than clean is
       'My house is cleaner than your house.'

1.6 Prepositions and postpositions

Zazaki employs both prepositions and postpositions, the latter being more numerous. Some examples of prepositions are:

    sɛvɛtʰa 'because of'
    ɛvɛ~ pʰe 'with' (manner, instrument)

(21)   Mo-a   tʰo   sɛvɛtʰa   tʰo   bɛrvena.
       mother-Ez you-Obl because-of you-Obl cries
       'Your mother cries because of you.'

(22)   ɛz   ɛvɛ   pʰisikʰiletʰ   amo (amunɛ)
       I-Dir with bicycle   came
       'I came by bicycle.'

(23)   Aɛ   na   fistʰan pʰe dɛstʰ dɛstʰo.
       she-Obl this dress   by   hand   sewed
       'She sewed this dress by hand.'

Some examples of postpositions are:

    ra   'from', 'than'
    ro   'along'
    dɛ   'with' (comitative)
    sɛr 'on', 'about'

(24)   Ma   kʰar ra jɛmɛ.
       we-Dir work from come
       'We come from work.'

(25)   ɛz   dɛrɛ   ro   son.
       I-Dir river:valley along go
       'I go along the river valley.'

(26) A   ma   dɛ   ama.
     she-Dir   we-Obl   with   came
     'She came with us.'

(27) Xavɨkɛ   jena   sɨtʰ   sɛr.
     cream   comes   milk   on
     'Cream forms on top of the milk.'

The postposition *dɛ(r)* meaning 'in' or 'at' is usually used in conjunction with a noun having a locative semantic element.

(28) Tʰo   dɛstʰ-e   mɨ   pʰe-e   mɨ   dɛ   gɨre dai.
     you-Obl   hand-Ez   I-Obl   back-Ez   I-Obl   at   knot gave
     'You tied my hands behind me.'
     (You tied my hands in back of me.)

(29) Vɛjvɨkʰɛ nistʰan-e   ho   bɨn-e   hard   dɛ   dard wɛ.
     bride   ring-Ez   self   bottom-Ez   earth   in   hid   away
     'The bride hid her ring away in the ground.'
     (The bride hid her ring under the earth.)

(30) Manga   vɛr-e   bon   dɛr   a.
     cow   front-Ez   house   at   is
     'The cow is in front of the house.'

2 Information on the negative prefix

2.1 Means of standard negation

2.1.1 Single-word verbs

Payne (1985) notes that tense, mood, aspect, etc. can be criteria for selecting a particular negative particle in a language. He cites the use of *ne* for statements in Indo-European and *mè* for imperatives. In Zazaki the negative prefix *'ne-* and its allomorph *'ni-* negate all verbs in all tenses except the verb of existence. The imperative is negated with the prefix *'mɛ-* while the subjunctive may be negated with either the prefix *'ne-* or *'mɛ-*.

Standard negation in Zazaki is accomplished by adding the negative prefix *'ne-* to the verb stem. Stress is then displaced from the verb to the negative prefix.

(31) ɛz   'ne-zonon.
     I-Dir   Neg-know
     'I don't know.'

(32) Mɨ t͡sʰaj 'ne-sɨmɨtʰ.
      I-Obl tea Neg-drank
      'I didn't drink tea.'

(33) A t͡sʰe-e sɨma 'ne-sona.
      she-Dir house-Ez you-PLObl Neg-goes
      'She is not going to your house.'

The negative prefix *'ne-* becomes *'ni-* when the following verb stem begins with a vowel.

(34) ɛz t͡sʰaj ni-an.
      I-Dir tea Neg-bring
      'I don't bring tea.'

(35) Ma rɛsmu ni-ond͡zɛmɛ.
      we-Dir pictures Neg-pull
      'We don't take pictures.'

The negator becomes part of the stem of the verb 'to come' by deletion of the first syllable *jɛ-*.

(36) a. A jɛna.
          she-Dir comes
          'She comes.'

      b. A nina.
          she-Dir Neg-comes
          'She doesn't come.'

2.1.2 Compound verbs

Compound verbs exist in Zazaki as well as single-word verbs. A compound verb can consist of a noun + a verb or a particle + a verb. In both cases, the negative prefix comes between the two parts to attach itself to the verb stem.

(37) a. I kʰar kʰɛne.
          they-Dir work do
          'They work.'

      b. I kʰar ne-kʰɛne.
          they-Dir work Neg-do
          'They don't work.'

(38) a. Ma pʰija qɛsɛj kʰɛmɛ.
          we-Dir together words do
          'We talk together.'

b. Ma   pʰija   qɛsɛj   ne-kʰɛmɛ.
   we-Dir together   words   Neg-do
   'We don't talk together.'

The following examples show a change in word order under the influence of negation (cf. 33, 59, 60, 61). Some native speakers consider the alternate reading acceptable, but prefer the form which shows the change in word order.

(39)   a. Mɨ   kʰin͡dʐi fistʰi   ra.
          I-Obl   clothes hung   up
          'I hung the clothes.'

       b. Mɨ   kʰin͡dʐi ra   ne-fistʰi.
          I-Obl   clothes up   Neg-hung
          'I didn't hang the clothes.'

       c. Mɨ   kʰin͡dʐi ne-fistʰi ra.
          I-Obl   clothes Neg-hang   up
          'I didn't hang the clothes.'

(40)   a. Ma   nisɛmɛ ro.
          we-Dir sit   down
          'We sit down.'

       b. Ma   ro   ne-nisɛmɛ.
          we-Dir down   Neg-sit
          'We don't sit down.'

       c. Ma   ne-nisɛmɛ ro.
          we-Dir Neg-sit   down
          'We don't sit down.'

2.1.3 Copula
The negative prefix 'ne- is realized as 'ni- when added to the present and past copula. Since the present copula is a vowel, one may want to explain the negative prefix for the copula as being 'ni- because of the vowel. However, as shown in (43), the past copula has no initial vowel and the prefix remains 'ni-.

(41)   a. A   zof   rɨnd   a.
          she-Dir very   nice   is
          'She is very nice.'

       b. A   rɨnd   ni-a.
          she-Dir nice   Neg-is
          'She is not nice.'

As illustrated in (42b), the plural agreement markers are omitted when followed by the negator. Example (42c) is ungrammatical.

(42) a. Olvoz-e t^ho   rɨnd-i   e.
          friend-Ez   you-Obl   nice-NO   are
          'Your friends are nice.'

      b. Olvoz-e t^ho   rɨnd ni-e.
          friend-Ez   you-Obl   nice Neg-are
          'Your friends are not nice.'

      c. *Olvoz-e t^ho   rɨnd-i   ni-e.
          friend-Ez   you-Obl   nice-NO   Neg-are
          'Your friends are not nice.'

(43) a. O   majlɨm vio.
          he-Dir   teacher was
          'He was a teacher.'

      b. O   majlɨm ni-vio.
          he-Dir   teacher Neg-was
          'He wasn't a teacher.'

2.1.4 Verb of existence

The negative prefix $\widehat{ts}^h in(e)$- is attached to the present and past copula to form the present and past negative existential respectively. The morpheme $\widehat{ts}^h i$ by itself means 'thing'. The negative existential prefix $\widehat{ts}^h in(e)$- is most likely a combination of $\widehat{ts}^h i$ plus *ne* ('thing' + Neg). The negative prefix *ne*- is normally stressed in Zazaki, but with the negative existential, the stress is placed on $\widehat{ts}^h i$.

(44) a. $\widehat{Ts}^h$aj   εst^{h}o.
          tea   exists
          'There's tea.'

      b. $\widehat{Ts}^h$aj   'ts^hino.
          tea   Neg-exists
          'There isn't (any) tea.'

(45) a. Dεw-a   ma   dε   owa   εst^{h}a.
          village-Ez   we-Obl   in   water exists
          'There is water in our village.'

      b. Dεw-a   ma   dε   owa $\widehat{ts}^h$ina.
          village-Ez   we-Obl   in   water Neg-exists
          'There is no water in our village.'

(46) a. Mal-e   pʰi-e   mɨ   bi.
          herd-Ez father-Ez I-Obl existed
          'My father had herds.'

      b. Mal-e   pʰi-e   mɨ   ts͡ʰinevi.
          herd-Ez father-Ez I-Obl Neg-existed
          'My father had no property.'

Dimli (or 'Southern Zaza') is a dissimilar dialect of Zaza spoken in an area about 50-150 kilometers south and southeast of the Zazaki-speaking area. The Dimli prefix is t͡s:ɨ'ni- for negation of the verb of existence in the present tense and t͡s:ɨ'ne- in the preterite. Dimli has maintained stress on the usual negative prefix *ne-*, while also combining t͡s:ɨ- and *ne-* for the negation of existence.

2.2 Imperative and subjunctive

The imperative mood is always negated by using the stressed negative prefix *'mɛ-*.

(47) 'Mɛ-tʰɛrs-ɛ.
      Neg-fear-Imp
      'Don't be afraid.'

(48) Vɛng   'mɛ-kʰ-ɛ.
      sound   Neg-do-Imp
      'Be quiet.'

The subjunctive mood can be negated by using either the prefix *'ne-* or the prefix *'mɛ-*. The use of *'mɛ-* or *'ne-* with the subjunctive mood in Zazaki seems to be equally acceptable. The use of one prefix over another does not appear to make a difference in meaning. It is, however, possible that there is a very subtle difference. Native speakers judge both sentences in the following pairs as grammatical:

(49) a. ɛz wazon kʰɛ   tʰɨ   vɛng   mɛ-kʰere.
          I-Dir want that you-Dir sound   Neg-do-Subj
          'I want you not to make noise!'

      b. ɛz wazon kɛ   tʰɨ   vɛng   ne-kʰere.
          I-Dir want that you-Dir sound   Neg-do-Subj
          'I want you not to make noise!'

(50) a. Haq   kʰɛdɛr-e sɨma   mɛ-do.
          God-Dir grief-Ez you-PlObl Neg-give-Subj
          'May God not give you grief!'

b. Haq   kʰedɛr-e   sɨma   ne-do.
   God-Dir grief-Ez   you-PlObl Neg-give-Subj
   'May God not give you grief!'

(51) a. Aɛ   owa   sɨmɨtʰɛ kʰɛ rɛw tʰesan mɛ-vo.
        she-Obl water drank that early thirsty Neg-become-Subj
        'She drank water so she wouldn't soon get thirsty.'

   b. Aɛ   owa   sɨmɨtʰe kʰɛ rɛw tʰesan ne-vo.
      she-Obl water drank that early thirsty Neg-become-Subj
      'She drank water so she wouldn't soon get thirsty.'

In addition, there are frozen expressions in Zazaki employing both *mɛ-* and *ne-* in the negation of the subjunctive:

(52) Haq   sɨma   re   kʰem   ne-kʰero.
     God-Dir you-Pl Obl to:lack Neg-do-Subj
     'May God not cause you to be lacking!'
     (A blessing said after a meal that the host's hospitality
     be seen by God and his supplies replenished.)

(53) Haq   tʰo   re dɛrd pʰɛjda mɛ-kʰero.
     God-Dir you-Obl to pain seek Neg-do-Subj
     'May God not seek to trouble you!'

(54) Haq   adɨr-e   tʰo   wɛ   mɛ-daro.
     God-Dir fire-Ez   you-Obl out Neg-bury-Subj
     'May God not put out your fire!'
     (May your good fortune not turn bad.)

2.3 Influence of stress and intonation on negation

As observed by Payne (1985), some languages have special means for associating negation with focused elements. In Zazaki there is no special device to negate a focused element, The negative prefix is always bound to the verb and consequently not allowed to freely associate with just any stressed element in a sentence. A change in the scope of the negation is then accomplished by a change in the regular intonation and stress of the items in focus.

Normal intonation and stress:

(55) Hɛsɛ   'ni-amo.
     Hasan   Neg-came
     'Hasan didn't come.'

Focused intonation and stress:

(56)   ɛ'li ni-amo.
       Ali Neg-came
       '*Ali* didn't come.' (but Metin did)

2.4 Negative transport

The phenomenon of negative transport, i.e. the moving of an embedded negation into a higher clause, occurs in Zazaki. Negative transport is possible with the verbs 'believe,' 'think,' and 'want.'

Negative transport:

(57)   a. ɛz inam   ne-kʰon   kʰɛ   o   biero.
           I-Dir belief Neg-do   that   he-Dir come-Subj
           'I do not believe he is coming.'

No negative transport:

(57)   b. ɛz inam   kʰon   kʰɛ   o   nino.
           I-Dir belief do   that   he-Dir Neg-comes
           'I believe he is not coming.'

Negative transport:

(58)   a. ɛz guman   ne   kʰon   kʰɛ   a   biero.
           I-Dir think   Neg do   that   she-Dir come-Subj
           'I do not think she is coming.'

No negative transport

(58)   b. ɛz guman   kʰon   kʰɛ   a   miero.
           I-Dir think   do   that   she-Dir Neg-come-Subj
           'I think she is not coming.'

Horn (1978) notes that with French and Spanish, the main clause predicate must be a negative transporter because the subjunctive mood is obligatory in the subordinate clause. Similarly, the verb 'want' in Zazaki requires that the verb in the subordinate clause be in the subjunctive mood. Although (59b) below shows negation in the subordinate clause to be grammatical it is somewhat awkward and not generally said.

Negative transport:

(59) a. Mo-a   mɨ   ne-wast^h·
          mother-Ez   I-Obl   Neg-wanted
          k^{h}ɛ   t^{h}ɨ   biere $\widehat{ts^h}$e-e   ma.
          that   you-Dir   come-Subj   house-Ez   we-Obl
          'My mother didn't want you to come to our house.'

No negative transport:

(59) b. Mo-a   mɨ   wast^h·
          mother-Ez   I-Obl   wanted
          'My mother wanted...
          K^{h}ɛ   t^{h}ɨ $\widehat{ts^h}$e-e   ma   miere.
          that   you-Dir   house-Ez   we-Obl   Neg-come-Subj
          that you not come to our house.'

Negative transport is not allowed, however, with the verb 'to say' nor with the modal 'necessary.'

(60) a. ɛz   vaz(inɛ)   k^{h}ɛ   k^{h}ot^{h}o sar-e   t^{h}o.
          I-Dir   say-Subj   that   reached   head-Ez   you-Obl
          'I would say you (probably) grasped (the meaning of) it.'

      b. ɛz   vaz(ine)   k^{h}ɛ   sar-e   t^{h}o   ne-k^{h}ot^{h}o.
          I-Dir   say-Subj   that   head-Ez   you-Obl   Neg-reached
          'I think you (probably) didn't grasp it.'

(61) a. I   gɛrɛk^{h}ɛ   siere   k^{h}ar.
          they-Dir   necessary   go-Subj   work
          'They need to go to work.'

      b. I   gɛrɛk^{h}ɛ   k^{h}ar ne-siere.
          they-Dir   necessary   work Neg-go-Subj
          'They don't need to go to work.'

3 Other negative words

3.1 Negative one-word answer, negative coordinator

In addition to negating verbs, *ne* is employed as the negative one-word answer to a question and as the negative co-ordinator.

(62) A: T^{h}ɨ   sona   mɛk^{h}t^{h}ɛv?   B: Ne.
          you-Dir   go   school   Neg
          'Are you going to school?'   'No.'

(63)　A: O　　　qɛfɛli　　o?　　　　B: Ne.
　　　　　he-Dir　tired　　is
　　　　　'Is he tired?'

(64)　ɛz　　ne　　 ts͡ʰaj　simon　ne　　qawa.
　　　　I-Dir　Neg　tea　　drink　Neg　coffee
　　　　'I drink neither tea nor coffee.'

(65)　Ser　　ser　　o　ne　　ma　　　o　ne　　ner　o.
　　　　lion　　lion　is　Neg　female　is　Neg　male　is
　　　　'A lion is a lion; it is neither female nor male.' (a proverb)

3.2　Derivation of negative lexical items

The negative morphemes *ne-* and *be-* are used to derive other negative lexical items. Where English would use the negative prefixes 'un-', 'in-', and 'il-', Zazaki employs the prefix *ne-*. The morpheme *be-* is the equivalent of the English suffix '-less'. Participial adjectives are negated by adding *ne-*. The derived negative item can then be negated by standard negation. (cf. (66)c)

(66)　a.　O　　'wɛs　o.
　　　　　　　he　well　is
　　　　　　　'He's well.'

　　　　b.　O　　ne-'wɛs　　o.
　　　　　　　he　Neg-well　is
　　　　　　　'He's ill.'

　　　　c.　O　　ne-wɛs　　'ni-o.
　　　　　　　he　Neg-well　Neg-is
　　　　　　　'He is not ill.'

(67)　a.　Gostʰ　wɛrin　o.
　　　　　　　meat　edible　is
　　　　　　　'Meat is edible.'

　　　　b.　Gostʰ-o kʰal　ne-wɛrin　o.
　　　　　　　meat-Ez raw　Neg-edible is
　　　　　　　'Raw meat is inedible.'

　　　　c.　Gostʰ-o kʰɛ　ne-wɛrin　o mɛ-wi-ɛ.
　　　　　　　meat-Ez that　Neg-edible is Neg-eat-Imp
　　　　　　　'Don't eat meat that is inedible.'

(68)　a.　ts͡ʰaj　simin　　o.
　　　　　　　tea　　drinkable　is
　　　　　　　'Tea is drinkable.'

b. Aɣwi ne-simin o.
   poison Neg-drinkable is
   'Poison is undrinkable.'

(69) a. Na mɛkʰtʰuvɛ rind wanin a.
        this letter good readable is
        'This letter is legible.'

   b. Ne-wanin a.
      Neg-readable is
      'It's illegable.'

The negative *be-* functions as a prefixed preposition requiring the noun or pronoun that is negated to be in the oblique case.

(70) Pʰisingɛ be-hon-i ne-manɛna.
     cat without-tomcat-Obl Neg-remains
     'A female cat won't stay without a tomcat.'

(71) Tʰɨ be-mɨ ama.
     you-Dir without-I-Obl came
     'You came without me.'

When the negated noun is used as a predicative nominal/adjective, it looses the oblique marker before the copula. *Be-kʰar-i o, be-kʰes-i o,* or *be-pʰor-i o* in the examples below would be ungrammatical.

(72) Nu lazɛkʰ be-kʰar o.
     this boy without-work is
     'This boy is unemployed.'

(73) Nu mordɛmɛkʰ be-kʰes o.
     this man without-person is
     'This man has no relatives.'

(74) Sar-e mɨ be-pʰor o.
     head-Ez I-Obl without-hair is
     'I am bald.'

3.3 Negative quantifiers and adverbs

Inherently negative quantifiers such as 'nothing' and 'nobody' and inherently negative adverbs such as 'never' and 'nowhere' do not exist in Zazaki, but can be expressed by using the negator plus an indefinite pronoun, noun, or an adverb.

3.3.1 Indefinites

(75) a. Tʰo   toa   wɛrd.
          you-Obl   something/anything   ate
          'Did you eat anything?'

      b. Mɨ   toa   ne-wɛrd.
          I-Obl   something/anything   Neg-ate
          'I didn't eat anything.'

(76) a. Kʰɛs   amo.
          person   came
          'Did anyone come?'

      b. Kʰɛs   ni-amo.
          person   Neg-came
          'Nobody came.'

3.3.2 Adverbs

(77) Ma   d͡za-e   ne-simɛ.
      we-Dir   place-Ind   Neg-went
      'We didn't go anywhere.'

(78) Mɨ   qɛ   d͡zɨyara   ne-simɨtʰɛ.
      I-Obl ever   cigarette   Neg-smoked
      'I haven't ever smoked a cigarette.'

(79) Dɛstʰ-e mɨ   d͡zoru d͡zɨ ra   ne-bɛno.
      hand-Ez I-Obl   ever   it   from Neg-become
      'My hands will never leave it.'

Except for rhetorical questions, *d͡zoru* and *qɛ* are never used without the accompanying negative prefix *ne-*.

(80) Hɛr   d͡zoru   bɛno   baqɨl.
      donkey ever   become   smart
      'Does a donkey ever get smart?' (rhetorical)

(81) Dɨsmɛn qɛ   bɛno   dostʰ.
      enemy   ever   become   friend
      'Does an enemy ever become a friend?' (rhetorical)

3.4 Negative partitive

The negative partitive is also expressed by employing the negator and the indefinite pronoun.

(82) Mɨ   nu   non   ra   toa   ne-wɛrdo.
      I-Obl this bread   from some   Neg-ate
      'I didn't eat any of this bread.' (I didn't eat some from this bread.)

(83)   Sɨma   ra   toa   kʰɛs   ne-si   vɛjvɛ.
       you-Pl   Obl   from some   person   Neg-went wedding
       'None of you went to the wedding?'
       (From you some person didn't go to the wedding.)

3.5 Negation of regular quantifiers

Regular quantifiers such as 'all,' 'many,' and 'every' cannot be negated. This is supported by Payne (1985) who notes that not all languages permit negatives like 'not many' and 'not all.' He notes Persian (another Indo-Iranian language) as one of these languages. Davison (1978) quoted by Reesink (1986), also points out that SOV languages generally do not allow this kind of negation. To compensate for this lack in Zazaki the quantifier is qualified by using a subordinate clause and negated by standard negation.

(84)   I   kʰɛ   sɨlaie   goretʰa   pʰero   ni-ame.
       they-Dir that   invitation   got   all   Neg-came
       'Not all who received invitations came.'
       (Of those who received invitations, all didn't come.)

(85)   Sɛw-a   vɛjv-i   de   xɛjlɛ   kʰɛs   ni-ame   vi.
       evening-Ez wedding-Obl at   many   person   Neg-came   had
       'Not many people had come to the wedding.'
       (On the evening of the wedding, many people hadn't come.)

Although not an example of negation, another means of expressing 'not many' is simply to say 'few'.

(86)   Hɛr-e   kʰɛ   hegai   de   ts͡ʰɛrene   senikʰ-i   e.
       donkey-Ez that   field   in   graze   few-NO   are
       'Not many donkeys are grazing in the field.'
       (The donkeys that are grazing in the field are few.)

Table 2. Summary of Negators.

Negator	Used in negation of
ne- , ni-	verbs in all tenses
	verbs in subjunctive mood
	participial adjectives
	verbs beginning with vowels
ni-	copula
t͡sʰin(e)-	verb of existence
mɛ-	imperative mood
	subjunctive mood
be-	nouns

Abbreviations

Adj	adjective	NO	number (singular, plural
Dem	demonstrative		agreement marker)
Dir	direct case	Num	numeral
Ez	ezafe morpheme	Obl	oblique case
Imp	imperative	Part	particle
Ind	indefinite marker	Pl	plural
Intr	intransitive	Subj	subjunctive
Neg	negative	Trans	transitive

References

Davison, A. (1978). 'Negative scope and rules of conversation: evidence from an OV language.' In: P. Cole (ed.), *Syntax and Semantics*, Vol. 9, 23-45. New York: Academic Press.

Horn, L.R. (1978). 'Some aspects of negation.' In: J. Greenberg ed., *Universals of Human Language*, Vol. IV *(Syntax)*, 127-210. Stanford: Stanford University Press.

Institut für Entwicklungsforschung, Wirtschafts- und Sozialplanung GmbH. (1985) *Türkei – Länderkundliche Informationen.* Saarbrücken: Institut für Entwicklungsforschung, Wirtschafts- und Sozialplannung GmbH.

Pamukcu, E. (1988). 'The Dimili as People.' *Piya, journal of Dimili language and culture.* September, 7-10.

Payne, J.R. (1985). 'Negation.' In: T. Shopen ed., *Language typology and syntactic description*, Vol. I *(Clause Structure)*, 197-242. Cambridge: Cambridge University Press.

—— (1987). 'Iranian Languages.' In: Comrie ed., *The world's major languages*, 154. London: Croom Helm.

Reesink, G.P. (1986). 'Being negative can be positive.' In: G. Huttar and K. Gregerson (eds), *Pragmatics in non-Western perspective*, 115-141. Texas: Summer Institute of Linguistics.

Todd, T.L. (1985). *A grammar of Dimili (also known as Zaza).* Ann Arbor: University Microfilms International.

Hungarian

Casper de Groot

1 General typological information

Hungarian, which belongs to the family of Finno-Ugric languages[1], is spoken by about 14 million people living in Hungary and in areas which border Hungary in Czechoslovakia, Romania, and Yugoslavia. It is an agglutinative language, which marks a number of grammatical distinctions on verbs, adjectives, nouns, and adverbs. There are two tense distinctions on the verb (Past/Non-past); two aspect distinctions (Imperfective/Perfective); one mood distinction; and distinctions for 1st, 2nd, and 3rd person singular and plural. There are two paradigms of person marking suffixes on the verb. The choice which paradigm is used is determined by the quality of the object, i.e. the object being definite or indefinite (cf. 3a-b). It is possible to leave subject and object NPs unexpressed (cf. 1a in which the subject is not expressed). Hungarian does not distinguish between different genders. The order of bound morphemes is fixed. The expression of Perfective aspect is a bound morpheme when it immediately precedes the verb and a free morpheme in other cases. The distribution of the two patterns is conditioned by pragmatic factors. In (1a) there is emphasis on the perfectivity of the action and in (1b) emphasis is on 'the book'. Consider:

(1) a. El-olvas-hat-t-am   a   könyv-et.
       Pf-read-Mod-Past-1Sg   the   book-Acc
       'I could have read the book.'

    b. A   könyv-et   olvas-hat-t-am   el.
       the   book-Acc   read-Mod-Past-1Sg   Pf
       'I could have read **the book**.'

Hungarian does not have voice differences. There is just one (active) voice. Hungarian has an elaborated case system. Apart from the large number of cases, it also has a number of postpositions. Consider the following examples:

(2) a. Péter level-et   kap-ott   Mari-tól.
       Peter letter-Acc   receive-Past:3Sg   Mary-Abl
       'Peter received a letter from Mary.'

b. A   ház   mögött   van   egy   kert.
   the   house behind   Cop:Pres:3Sg a   garden
   'There is a garden behind the house.'

In typological studies Hungarian is usually classified as SOV. The neutral word order in clauses with a transitive verb and an indefinite object is indeed SOV. However, if the object is definite the most natural order is SVO. Consider the following examples and note also the different conjugations of the verb:

(3)   a. Imre level-et   ír.
          Imre letter-Acc   write:3Sg
          'Imre is writing a letter.'
       b. Imre ír-ja   a   level-et.
          Imre write-3Sg   the letter-Acc
          'Imre is writing the letter.'

Constituent order in Hungarian is relatively free (cf. É. Kiss 1981 and De Groot 1981). All twenty-four permutations of a clause such as (2a) are grammatical Hungarian sentences. For instance:

(4)   a. Péter Maritól levelet kapott.
       b. Maritól Péter kapott levelet.
       c. Levelet Maritól kapott Péter.
          etc.

The examples under (4), however, can only occur in a specific context or situation. From a pragmatic point of view word order in Hungarian can be characterized in the following way. The initial part of the clause contains topical elements, followed by a position which contains the focus, i.e the constituent which carries the most salient information. After this position the verb follows. Schematically, the Hungarian clause has the following pattern:

(5)   NP ... NP   NP   V   NP ... NP
       topic   focus   verb   neutral

Question words take the position immediately preceding the verb. Note the pragmatic value of question words, they are focal. Consider:

(6)   a. János Mari-tól   mi-t   kap-ott?
          John   Mary-Abl   what-Acc   receive-Past.3Sg
          'What did John receive from Mary?'

b. A   level-et   ki-től   kap-t-a?
    the   letter-Acc who-Abl   receive-Past-3Sg
    'From whom did he receive the letter?'

The expression of yes/no questions in Hungarian is the yes/no question intonation contour of a clause. Apart from this particular sentence intonation pattern the interrogative particle -e can be attached to the verbal or non-verbal predicate. If one wishes to stress one's curiosity or doubt, one will use the particle *vajon*. For instance:

(7) a. Vajon level-et   küld-ött-e   János-nak?
         QM   letter-Acc send-Past:3Sg-QM   John-Dat
         'Did she send a letter to John?'

Comparatives in Hungarian can be expressed in two different ways. The word order in the following examples is the unmarked or most natural ordering pattern. Consider:

(8) a. Kálmán nagy-obb   Zsolt-nál.
         Kálmán big-Comp   Zsolt-Ades
         'Kálmán is bigger than Zsolt.'

     b. Kálmán nagy-obb   mint Zsolt.
         Kálmán big-Comp   than Zsolt
         'Kálmán is bigger than Zsolt.'

The word order within nominal phrases is fixed and follows the following pattern (cf. Dezső 1969 and Kornai 1985):

(9) a. DEM ART NUM ADJ REL(non-finite) NOUN REL(finite)

     b. Az   a   két új   könyv, amely-et vett-em
         that the two new book   that-Acc bought-1Sg
         'Those two new books that I bought.'

Within embedded non-finite clauses, word order is relatively free. The position of the participle, however, is fixed: it takes the final position. If a constituent within a participle construction carries the pragmatic function of focus, it is placed in the position preceding the participle. Compare the following two examples:

(10) a. A   tegnap   könyv-et olvas-ó   fiú.
          the yesterday book-Acc read-Pres:part   boy
          lit. 'the yesterday book reading boy'
          'The boy who was reading a **book** yesterday.'

b. A   könyv-et   tegnap   olvas-ó   fiú
   the   book-Acc   yesterday read-Pres:part   boy
   lit. 'the book yesterday reading boy'
   'The boy who was reading a book **yesterday**.'

The word order pattern of participle constructions is schematically the
following:

(11)   NP ... NP   NP   PARTICIPLE
                          Focus

2 Standard negation in Hungarian[2]

Standard negation in Hungarian is expressed by means of the particle *nem*.
There are other particles, which will be discussed in section 3. In a limited
number of non-verbal clauses a negative copula is used. We shall discuss
standard sentence negation in section 2.1 (verbal and non-verbal clauses)
and local negation in section 2.2 (negation of and within constituents).[3] In
section 2.3 we will summarize the position of the negative elements in the
clause.

2.1 Sentence negation

2.1.1 Negation in verbal clauses
The following examples illustrate negation in verbal clauses. The negative
particle *nem* immediatelly precedes the verb.

(12)   a. János   nem dohányz-ik.
           John   Neg smoke-3Sg
           'John does not smoke.'

       b. Nem es-ik   az   eső.
           Neg rain-3Sg   the   rain
           'It does not rain.'

       c. Nem kap-t-am   a   pénz-t.
           Neg receive-Past-1Sg the   money-Acc
           'I did not get the money.'

       d. Mari-tól   level-et   nem kap-ott.
           Mary-Abl   letter-Acc   Neg receive-Past:3Sg
           'He did not receive a letter from Mary.'

Note that the expression of negation in constructions with either definite or indefinite NPs is the same. Compare (12c) with a definite object to (12d) with an indefinite object.

Negation in finite embedded clauses behaves the same as in main clauses, as for instance in (13a). The negative particle of the embedded clause may in some cases be placed in front of the matrix verb. An example of this so called 'negative raising' is (13b):

(13) a. Gondol-t-am,   hogy János   nem dohányz-ik.
          think-Past-1Sg   that John   Neg smoke-3Sg
          'I thought that John does not smoke.'

      b. Nem gondol-t-am,   hogy János   dohányz-ik.
          Neg think-Past-1Sg   that John   smoke-3Sg
          'I did not think that John smokes.'

There are semantic differences between the two examples similar to those which hold between the same types of constructions found in many other languages.

2.1.2 Negation in non-verbal clauses

There are two expression devices for negation in non-verbal clauses in Hungarian. There is the negative particle *nem* 'not' and there is the negative copula *nincs(en)* 'is not' or *nincsenek* 'are not'. For the description of the distribution of the two forms it is necessary to have a look at the application of the copula in non-verbal clauses in Hungarian first. Hungarian uses a copula in most but not all non-verbal clauses (cf. Kiefer 1968 and De Groot 1989). Hungarian distinguishes between a positive copula and a negative copula. There is no overt copula in clauses which meet the following four conditions at the same time:

(14) a. present tense is used;
      b. indicative mood is used;
      c. Subject is third person singular or plural;
      d. the predicate consists of an adjective, noun, or NP.

Some examples of positive non-verbal clauses in which there is no overt copula, are the following:

(15) a. Mari   okos.
          Mary   clever
          'Mary is clever.'

  b. Péter tanár.
      Peter teacher
      'Peter is a teacher.'

  c. Az a férfi a   gyilkos.
      that man the   murderer
      'That man is the murderer.'

The negative counterpart of non-verbal clauses such as those in (15) use the negative particle *nem*. Consider:

(16) a. Mari   nem okos.
          Mary   Neg clever
          'Mary is not clever.'

      b. Péter nem tanár.
          Peter Neg teacher
          'Peter is not a teacher.'

      c. Az a férfi nem a   gyilkos.
          that man Neg the   murderer
          'That man is not the murderer.'

According to the conditions formulated in (14) the following examples require a copula. Past tense is used in (17a), a conditional mood is used in (17b), the subject in (17c) is not third person, the predicate in (17d) consists of a postpostional phrase. The existential construction as examplified in (17e) behaves the same as locational constructions such as (17d). Consider:

(17) a. Mari   okos   volt.
          Mary   clever Cop:Past:3Sg
          'Mary was clever.'

      b. Az   lenne   jó.
          that Cop:Cond:3Sg good
          'That would be good.'

      c. Okos   vagy.
          clever Cop:Pres:2Sg
          'You are clever.'

      d. Fák vannak   a   ház   mögött.
          trees Cop:Pres:3Pl the house behind
          'There are trees behind the house.'

      e. Van   sör.
          Cop:Pres:3Sg beer
          'There is beer.'

A subset of the negative counterparts of the examples in (17) take the
negative copula *nincs(en)* 'is not' or *nincsenek* 'are not', the other examples
take the negative particle *nem*. In those cases in which a non-verbal clause
meets the restrictions (14) a. through c. – i.e. present tense and indicative
mood are used, and subject is third person – but does not meet the last one
– i.e. the predicate is not an adjective, noun or NP – the expression of
negation is formed by the negative copula.[4] In all other cases the particle
nem occurs. The examples in (18), which are the negative counterparts of
(17), illustrate the distribution of the two expression devices. (18d) and (18e)
take the negative copula, the other examples use the negative particle.
Consider:

(18)   a. Mari   nem volt   okos.
           Mary   Neg Cop:Past:3Sg clever
           'Mary was not clever.'

       b. Az   nem lenne   jó.
           that   Neg Cop:Cond:3Sg   good
           'That would not be good.'

       c. Nem vagy   okos.
           Neg Cop:Pres:2Sg   clever
           'You are not clever.'

       d. Fák   nincs-enek   a   ház   mögött.
           trees   NegCop:Pres:3Pl the house   behind
           'There are no trees behind the house.'

       e. Nincs   sör.
           NegCop:Pres:3Sg beer
           'There is no beer.'

Note that different subjects, one consisting of a definite NP and the other
of an indefinite NP do not result in different expressions of negation as for
instance English *not* versus *no*.
   Apart from the negative copula *nincs(en)* 'is not', *nincsenek* 'are not', there
are also the forms *sincs(en)* 'neither is', *sincsenek* 'neither are'. Consider the
use of the different copulas in the following example:

(19)   Zsuzsa nincs   itt,   és   Péter sincs.
       Zsuzsa Neg:Cop:3Sg   here   and   Peter Neg:Cop:3Sg
       'Zsuzsa is not here, and neither is Peter.'

2.2 Local negation

2.2.1 Negation of constituents

If one wishes to negate a part of a proposition and not the entire proposition as in the examples above, the particle *nem* is placed in front of the part to be negated. Together with the negative particle the constituent is placed in the position preceding the verb. Consider the following examples:[5]

(20) a. Nem Ildikó-val   találkoz-t-am.
          Neg Ildikó-Com   meet-Past-1Sg
          'It was not Ildikó whom I met.'

      b. Gábor nem úsz-ni   akar.
          Gábor Neg swim-inf   want
          'It is not swimming that Gábor wants.'

      c. Nem ki-ment,   hanem be.
          Neg out-go:Past:3Sg   but   in
          'He did not go out, he went in.'

      d. Nem kiváncsi-an   bont-ja   ki   a   csomag-ot.
          not curious-Man   unpack-3Sg   out the parcel-Acc
          'It was not in a curious way that he unpacks the parcel'.

      e. Nem a   körte   piros, hanem az   alma.
          Neg the   pear   red   but   the   apple
          'It is not the pear but the apple that is red.'

      f. Nem Péter van   itt, hanem János.
          Not Peter Cop:3Sg   here but   John
          'It is not Peter who is here, but John.'

In example (20c) there is a contrast between *ki* 'out' and *be* 'in', which is why the particle *nem* together with the element *ki* takes the position in front of the verb. In example (21d) *ki* is not in the scope of the negation, and therefore it is placed after the verb. Also note that in example (20f) the positive copula applies and not the negative copula *nincs*, because the scope of the negation is a part of the proposition and not the entire proposition. Sentence (20f) with the negative copula yields an ungrammatical sentence:

(21) *Péter nincs   itt, hanem János.
        Peter Neg.Cop.3Sg   here but   John
        'Peter is not here, but John.'

2.2.2 Negation within constituents

Adjectival modifiers of the head of an NP can be negated. For instance:

(22) a. A   nem nagy fa.
         the   Neg big   tree
         lit. 'the not tall tree'
         'The tree which is not tall.'

      b. A   nem szép nő.
         the   Neg pretty woman
         lit. 'the not pretty woman'
         'The woman who is not pretty.'

Adverbial modifiers of adjectives can also be negated, as for instance in the following examples:

(23) a. A   nem túl   kedves lány.
         the   Neg too   kind   girl
         lit. 'the not too kind girl'
         'The girl who is not too kind.'

      b. A   nem nagyon híres   író.
         the   Neg very   famous   author
         lit. 'the not very famous author'
         'The author who is not very famous.'

Within NPs numerals cannot be negated. Consider:

(24) *A   nem két   üveg.
        the   Neg two   bottle

Extensions of nominalizations can be negated as is shown by the following examples:

(25) a. Mari   nem Péter által való   megver-és-e.
         Mary   Neg Peter by   Cop:Pres:part beating up-Nom-3Sg
         lit. 'Mary's not by Peter being beating up'
         'Mary's being beaten up by someone other than Peter'

      b. A   nem a   kút-ba való   belezuhan-ás.
         the   Neg the   well-Ill Cop:Pres:part fall-Nom
         lit. 'the not into the well falling'
         'Falling somewhere else than into the well'

Participle constructions which modify the head of an NP can be negated in the same way as simple adjectives (cf. 22). For instance:

(26) a. A   nem kifizet-endő számla.
         the   Neg pay-Fut:part bill
         'The bill that is not to be paid' (Lit. 'the not to be paid bill')

b. A   nem könyv-et   olvas-ó   fiú.
the   Neg book-Acc   read-Pres:part boy
lit. 'the not book reading boy'
'The boy not reading a book'

It is, however, also possible to negate constituents within participle constructions. The negated constituents take the position immediately preceding the
participle. Recall that focal elements are placed in this position (cf. 10-11
above). Compare the following two examples with a present participle
construction:

(27) a. A   tegnap   nem könyv-et   olvas-ó   fiú.
the   yesterday Neg book-Acc   read-Pres:part boy
lit. 'the yesterday not book reading boy'
'The boy who was not reading **a book** yesterday.'

b. A   könyv-et   nem tegnap   olvas-ó   fiú.
the   book-Acc   Neg yesterday   read-Pres:part boy
lit. 'the book not yesterday reading boy'
'The boy who was not reading a book **yesterday**.'

Expressions with a negation and a participle construction may be ambiguous. Consider for instance example (28), which is ambiguous in the following way: the scope of the negation can be *a kertben* 'in the garden', or *a
kertben játszó* 'playing in the garden'.

(28) A   nem a   kert-ben   játsz-ó   gyerek.
the   Neg the   garden-Ines   play-Pres:part child
'The child which is not playing in the garden.'

The two interpretations of (28) can be paraphrased as (i) 'the child who is
playing but not in the garden', and (ii) the child who is not playing in the
garden'.

Finally consider some examples with negation in past participle constructions (29) and adverbial participle constructions (30):

(29) a. A   Péter által nem idéz-ett   példa.
the   Peter by   Neg quote-Past:part example
lit. 'the by Peter not quoted example'
'The example not quoted by Peter'

b. A   nem Péter által idéz-ett   példa.
the   Neg Peter by   quote-Past:part example
lit. 'the not by Peter quoted example'
'The example quoted by someone other than Peter'

(30) a. A   katonák   a   város-t   be   nem
          the   soldiers   the   town-Acc   in   Neg

          kerít-ve   harcol-t-ak.
          surround-Adv.part   fight-Past-3Pl

          lit. 'The soldiers the town not surrounding fought.'
          'The soldiers, while not surrounding the town, were fighting.'

      b. A   katonák   nem   a   város-t
          the   soldiers   Neg   the   town-Acc

          be-kerít-ve   harcol-t-ak.
          in-surround-Adv.part   fight-Past-3Pl

          lit. 'The soldiers not the town surrounding fought.'
          'The soldiers, while surrounding some place other than the town, were
          fighting'

2.3 The position of the negative particle

From the examples presented above we can see that the position of the
negative particle or the negated part of the clause is the one which immediately precedes the predicate, i.e. verb, copula or non-verbal predicate, or
participle in non-finite constructions. Given the general patterns (5) and
(11), we can summarize the word order in negative expressions in the
following fashion (cf. also Kenesei 1989):

I. Sentence negation

(31)   NP ... NP   *nem*   V   NP ... NP
       NP ... NP   *nem*   Cop/N/A   NP ... NP
                              nincs

II. Local negation

(a) negation of constituent in main clause

(32)   NP ... NP   *nem*   NP   V   NP ... NP
       NP ... NP   *nem*   NP   Cop N/A   NP ... NP

(b) negation of modifiers

(33)   *nem*   Adj/[Participle construction]   N
       nem   Adv   Adj

(c) negation of constituents within participle constructions

(34)   NP ... NP   *nem* NP   Participle

We have seen that in expressions with sentence negation the negative particle always immediately precedes the predicate. However, there is one case in which an element can occur in between the particle and the predicate. Consider:

(35)   a.   Nem   is   ment   haza.
            Neg   also   went   home
            'He did not indeed go home.'

       b.   Nem   is   jó   ez   a   leves.
            Neg   also   good   this   the   soup
            'Indeed, this soup is not good.'

Question words in negative sentences get more emphasis than negative particles: they seem to be more focal. However, it is quite remarkable that in these sentences the negative element still precedes the verb whereas one would expect the more focal question word to precede the verb. Consider:

(36)   János mi-t   nem   hoz-ott?
       John what-Acc   Neg   bring-Past.3Sg
       'What is it that John did not bring?'

3 Particles

In section 2 we have seen that standard negation in Hungarian is expressed by means of the particle *nem*. The particle is used in constructions which denote the negation of a proposition or a part of a proposition. There are, however, instances in which other forms than *nem* are used: these other forms are *ne*, *sem*, and *se*. The distribution of the four forms can globally be characterized as follows. There is the opposition *nem*, *ne* 'not' versus *sem*, *se* 'neither'; and there is the opposition between the forms *ne*, *se* which are used in imperative constructions versus *nem*, *sem* which are used in non-imperative constructions.

Let us first consider some examples with the application of *ne*. The form *ne* is used in constructions which express an order, a demand, a wish, an obligation or task. In these constructions the finite verb is marked for the 'imperative/adhortative' (-*j*).

(37)   a.   Ne   men-j-etek!
            Neg   go-Imp-2Pl
            'Do not go!'

b. Azért   hív-t-am,   hogy ne   jöj-j-enek   ide.
   therefore call-Past-1Sg that Neg   come-Imp-3Pl   here
   'I have called them, so that they do not come here.'

c. Az-t   akar-ja,   hogy ne   men-j-ek.
   that-Acc   want-3Sg   that Neg   go-Imp-1Sg
   'He does not want me to go.'

Let us now have a look at the negative elements which start with an *s*. In section 2 we have seen that Hungarian has two negative copulas: *nincs* 'is not' and *sincs* 'neither is' (cf. 19). The same opposition is found between the forms *ne(m)* 'not' and *se(m)* 'neither'.[6] For instance:

(38)   Mari   nem jön,   és   Péter sem.
        Mary   Neg come:3Sg   and   Peter Neg
        'Mary is not coming and neither is Peter.'

The form *se* is found in constructions similar to the ones with *ne* as given in (38) above. However, there are also other types of construction in which the particle *se* occurs. The form *sem* can sometimes optionally be reduced to *se* (see example (50b) below). The forms *sem* and *se* are also used in constructions which express an enumeration of negations, as for instance in (39a) or the elliptical utterence (39b) used in the context 'there is nothing in the shops'.

(39)   a. Nem szabad sem inni,   sem enni.
           Neg allow   Neg drink:Inf Neg eat:Inf
           'It is not allowed to drink, nor to eat.'

        b. Se   kenyér, se   tej,   se   hus.
           Neg bread   Neg milk   Neg meat
           'No bread, no milk, no meat.'

The form *se(m)* can also be used in combination with negative words. In those cases the form *se(m)* functions as a simple negative particle, i.e. it does not have the meaning 'also not', but rather 'not'. We will discuss this usage of *se(m)* in section 4 together with the negative words.

4 Negative words

Hungarian has different kinds of negative words. Apart from the negative particles and negative copulas, there are negative indefinite pronouns,

adverbs, and conjunctions. Before giving examples of these different categories, we shall briefly discuss negative concord in Hungarian.

4.1 Negative concord

If a negative pronoun or adverb is used, the clause is always marked for
sentence negation, i.e. a negative particle in front of the verb, or the application of a negative copula. We will call this negative concord.[7] For instance:

(40)   a.   Senki   nem olvas.
            nobody Neg   read:3Sg
            'Nobody is reading.'

       b.   *Senki   olvas
            Nobody   read.3Sg

(41)   a.   Sehol   nincs   sör.
            nowhere   Neg:Cop:3Sg beer
            'There is nowhere beer.'

       b.   *Sehol   van   sör
            nowhere   Pos:Cop:3Sg beer

Negative concord is not limited to just one negative word and a negative
particle or negative copula. In the case of negative concord all indefinite
pronouns and adverbs in the clause take the negative form. Some examples:

(42)   a.   Sehol   nem lát-t-am   senki-t
            nowhere   Neg see-Past-1Sg   nobody-Acc
            'I did not see anybody anywhere.'

       b.   Nem volt   soha   sehol   senki   se.
            Neg was:3Sg never   nowhere nobody   Neg
            lit. 'not was never nowhere nobody not'
            'There was absolutely nobody there.'

It is possible to use positive indefinite pronouns and adverbs together with
a negation in the clause. This is the case in for instance the following two
examples:

(43)   a.   Valaki-t   nem lát-t-am.
            somebody-Acc   Neg see-Past-1Sg
            'There was somebody I did not see.'

       b.   Nem valaki-t   lát-t-am,   hanem   valami-t.
            Neg somebody-Acc   see-Past-1Sg   but   something-Acc
            'I did not see somebody, but something.'

Negative words may precede or follow the verb. In cases in which the negative words precede the verb, the negative particle may take the form *sem* in stead of *nem*. In this usage the form *sem* does not have the meaning 'also not'; it is like *nem*. In cases in which the negative words follow the verb, the negative particle only takes the form *nem*:

(44) a. Senki   nem jön.
          nobody Neg come:3Sg
          'Nobody comes.'

      b. Senki   sem jön.
          nobody Neg come:3Sg
          'Nobody is coming.'

      c. Nem jön   senki.
          Neg come:3Sg nobody
          'Nobody comes.'

      d. *Sem jön   senki.
          Neg   come:3Sg nobody

The different applications of the negative particle seem to have to do with pragmatic differences. The form *nem* is used to express the negation more strongly, so that the contents of the proposition seem to be more exact in cases in which *nem* is used.

4.2 Negative pronouns

Hungarian has a number of negative indefinite pronouns, for instance the following:

(45) senki   'nobody'
      semmi   'nothing'
      semmilyen   'not any'
      semelyik   'none/not one of them'
      sehány   'none'
      semennyi   'nothing at all'
      semekkora   'no size at all'
      semmiféle   'no kind of'

Most negative pronouns can be used independently. In those cases they may be marked for case distinctions as is illustrated in the following examples.

(46) a. Semelyik-et sem ismer-em.
          none-Acc   Neg know-1Sg
          'I do not know any of them.'

b. Nem fél   senki-től.
   Neg fear   nobody-Abl
   'He does not fear anybody.'

Some of the pronouns can also be used attributively, as for instance *semmil-yen* 'not any'. Note the different applications of *semmilyen* in (47a), independently, and (47b), attributively:

(47) a. Milyen   hús-t   szeret? Semmilyen-t.
         which   meat-Acc   like:3Sg not any-Acc
         'Which meat does he like? Not any.'

      b. Semmilyen   eszköz-zel sem lehet   kényszerít-ni.
         not any   tool-Instr Neg possible   enforce-Inf
         'By no means can it be enforced.'

Finally consider the following example with *semmiféle* 'no kind of', which cannot be used independently.

(48) Semmiféle   szesz es   ital-t   nem iszik.
      no kind of alcoholic   drink-Acc Neg drink:3Sg
      'He does not drink any kind of alcoholic drinks.'

The form *semmiféle* consists of the negative pronoun *semmi* 'nothing' and the formative suffix *-féle* by means of which adjectives are derived from nouns. Adjectives ending in *-féle* can only be used attributively. The same holds for *semmiféle*, which is why it may rather be considered an adjective and not a pronoun.

4.3 Negative adverbs

Another class of negative words is the class of negative adverbs. Examples of this type are listed in (49). Negative adverbs are used independently as the examples (50) illustrate:

(49) soha   'never'
      semmikor   'at no time'
      semeddig   'not a moment'
      semmiképpen   'by no means'
      semmiféleképpen   'not in any shape or form
      sehogy(an)   'by no means'
      sehol   'nowhere'
      sehova   'in no direction'
      sehonnan   'from nowhere'

semerre   'in no direction'
semerről   'not from any direction'

(50)   a. Nem volt   sör   sehol.
           Neg Cop:Past.3Sg   beer   nowhere
           'There was nowhere beer'.

       b. Semeddig   se   tart.
           not a moment   Neg   keep
           'It takes no time.'

4.4 Negative conjunctions

The third kind of negative words are negative conjunctions. In Hungarian
we find the following forms:

(51)   nehogy   'so that ... not'
       semhogy   'rather than'
       semmint   'rather than'

Negative concord does not apply in constructions with this type of conjunctions. For example:

(52)   Okos-abb   volt   semhogy   bevall-ja.
       clever-Comp   Cop:Past:3Sg   rather than   admit-3Sg
       'He was too clever to admit it.'

5 Derivation

In Hungarian negative adjectives can be productively derived from verbs by
means of the privative formant -hatatlan/-hetetlen.[8] For instance:

(53)   lát   'see'   - lát-hatatlan   'invisible'
       olvas   'read   - olvas-hatatlan 'non-readable'
       tanít   'teach'   - tanít-hatatlan 'non-teachable'
       mér   'measure'   - mér-hetetlen   'non-measurable'
       fest   'dye'   - fest-hetetlen   'non-colourable'

The formative suffix -t(a)lan/-t(e)len is used to derive negative adjectives from
nouns. For example:

(54)   szív   'heart'   - szívtelen   'heartless'
       fá   'tree'   - fátlan   'treeless'
       kormány   'steering wheel'   - kormánytalan 'steerless'
       szín   'colour'   - színtelen   'colourless'
       szesz   'alcohol'   - szesztelen   'non-alcoholic'

We also find negative elements in lexicalized derivations and compounds. Some examples are:

(55)   senkiházi/semmiházi   'good-for-nothing'
       semmitmondó   'meaningless'
       semmiség   'nothingness'
       semmittevés   'idleness'

6 Conclusions

The main characteristics of negation in Hunagrian can be summarized as follows:

• The central negation device is *nem* which can be used to negate entire propositions or parts of propositions.
• Under certain conditions a negative copula is used in non-verbal clauses.
• Within clauses there is negative concord. Negative pronouns and adverbs are used in combination with the negative particle or the negative copula. When a negative pronoun or adverb is used, all indefinite pronouns and adverbs in the clause take the negative form.
• The following categories of negative words can be distinguished: particle, copula, indefinite pronoun, adverb, conjunction, and adjective.
• The position of the negative particle or the negated part of the clause is the one which immediately precedes the predicate, i.e. verb, copula or non-verbal predicate, or participle in non-finite constructions. Note that these positions are the positions in which a speaker of Hungarian place their focal elements, i.e. elements which carry the most salient information.

Abbreviations

Abl	ablative	Mod	mood
Acc	accusative	Neg	negative particle
Ades	adessive	Neg.cop	negative copula
Adv.part	adverbial participle	Nom	nominalization
Com	comitative	Past.part	past participle
Comp	comparative	Pos.cop	positive copula
Cond	conditional	Pres	present
Cop	copula	Pres.part	present participle
Dat	dative	Pf	perfective
Fut.part	future participle	QM	question marker
Ill	illative	1Sg, 2Sg, 3Sg	1st, 2nd, 3rd person
Imp	imperative/adhortative		singular
Inf	infinitive	1Pl, 2Pl, 3Pl	1st, 2nd, 3rd person
Instr	instrumental		plural
Man	manner		

Notes

1. Ruhlen (1987) classifies Hungarian as follows: Uralic-Yukaghir\Uralic\Finno-Ugric\ Ugric\Hungarian.

2. For information on negation in Hungarian we have made use of Bánhidi (1965), Bencédy (1968), Lotz (1988), and Tompa (1968). I want to thank István Kenesei for his critical comments on an earlier version of this paper.

3. We will use the terms 'sentence negation' and 'local negation' after Quirk et al. (1985).

4. The scope of the negation is the non-verbal clause. If the scope of the negation is a part of the clause, the positive copula is used. See example (20f).

5. It may be argued that these examples can at some other semantic level be analyzed as constructions in which the proposition is negated. However, for our purpose the description in terms of local negation will do.

6. *Sem* 'also not' differs semantically from *nem is* 'not even' (cf. 35).

7. Labov (1972: 234) uses the term 'negative concord'. We do not think that the term 'negative agreement' is appropriate (cf. Moravcsik 1978). We do not want to use the term 'double negation' either (cf. Hunyadi 1984), which we prefer to use for constructions such as:

(i)   Nem lehet   nem nevet-ni.
       Neg possible   Neg laugh-Inf
       'It was not possible not to laugh.' (= 'One had to laugh.')

8. The choice which form is used is determined by vowel harmony. The positive counterpart is *-ható/-hető* as in *lát-ható* 'visible'.

References

Bánhidi, Z., Z. Jókay and D. Szabó (1965)[4]. *Learn Hungarian*. Budapest: Tankönyvkiadó.

Bencédy, J., P. Fábián, E. Rácz and M. Velcsov (1968). *A mai magyar nyelv*. Budapest: Tankönyvkiadó.

Dezső, L. (1969). 'A fönévi csoport.' *Általános Nyelvészeti Tanulmányok*, 6, 25-158.

É. Kiss, K. (1981). 'Structural relations in Hungarian, a "free" word order language.' *Linguistic Inquiry* 12, 185-312.

Groot, C. de (1981) 'Sentence-intertwining in Hungarian.' In: A.M. Bolkestein et al. (eds) *Predication and expression in Functional Grammar*, 41-62. London & New York: Academic Press.

⸺ (1989) *Predicate structure in a Functional Grammar of Hungarian*. Dordrecht: Foris.

Hunyadi, L. (1984) 'A kétszeres tagadásról a magyarban.' *Általános Nyelvészeti Tanulmányok* 15, 65-73.

Kenesei, I. (1989). 'Logikus-e a magyar szórend?' *Általános Nyelvészeti Tanulmányok* 17, 105-152.

Kiefer, F. (1968). 'A transformational approach to the verb *van* 'to be' in Hungarian.' J.W.H. Verhaar (ed.) *The verb 'be' and its synonyms*, part 3, 53-85. Dordrecht: Reidel.

Kornai, A. (1985). 'The internal structure of noun phrases.' I. Kenesei (ed.) *Approaches to Hungarian. Vol I, Data and descriptions* 79-92. Szeged: JATE.

Labov, W. (1972). *Sociolinguistic patterns*. Philadelphia: University of Pennsylvania Press.

Lotz. J. (1988). *Das Ungarische Sprachsystem*. Bloomington, Indiana: Eurolingua.

Moravcsik, E. A. (1978). 'Agreement'. J.H. Greenberg (ed.) *Universals of Human Language*. Volume 4, Syntax, 331-374. Stanford: Stanford University Press.

Quirk, R., S. Greenbaum, G. Leech and J. Svartvik (1985). *A comprehensive grammar of the English language*. London & New York: Longman.

Ruhlen, M. (1987). *A guide to the world's languages*. Vol. 1: Classification. London: Edward Arnold.

Tompa, J. (1968). *Ungarische Grammatik*. Budapest: Akadémiai Kiadó.

Kresh

D. Richard Brown

0 Introduction

Kresh is a Central-Sudanic Nilo-Saharan language of Western Bahr el Ghazal Province, of the Republic of the Sudan. It has five vowels and is written with five tones. Words end with an echo vowel, which is clearly articulated before pause. The examples in what follows reflect the Kresh-Ndogo dialect, the one used for publications, and the words are spelled orthographically. The tone markings, shown here over *a*, are acute (*á*) for high, dieresis (*ä*) for mid, tilde (*ã*) for low, circumflex (*â*) for falling, and breve (*ă*) for rising. Notable consonants include the light implosives *'b* and *'d*, the flapped labiodental *'v*, the labiovelars *kp*, *gb*, and *ŋb* [ŋmgb], the retroflexed lateral flap *!*, the retroflexed alveolar affricates *j*, *nj*, and *c*, and numerous prenasalized consonants, such as *mb*, *nd*, *nj*, *nj*, *ŋg*, and *ŋb*. Note that in Western Kresh dialects, the retroflexed affricates have fused with their alveopalatal counterparts, *j* and *nj*, and the *c* has also become alveopalatal. As a result, these pairs are usually written the same, even in the Kresh-Ndogo publications, so that *j* and *nj* are usually written as *j* and *nj*.

Syntactic order is rather strictly SVO, and possessors always follow possess-ees. In the noun phrase the order is RNDetQ {RelCl/PossPh} Dem; that is, relational noun(s) (e.g., *lāgá* 'leg of'), followed by an independent noun, followed by the determiner, followed by any non-numeric quantifier (such as ones for 'all' or 'a little'), followed by any relative clauses or a possessive phrase, followed by any demonstrative. Numeric quantifiers precede the nouns, although older speakers sometimes position them after the article, as with non-numeric quantifiers. Prepositions, which are few but heavily used, precede their noun phrases. Constituent order is not adjusted to allow heavy shift of embedded clauses, even though sentences are allowed to become quite complex through recursive embedding.

A variety of lexemes exhibit verbal behavior, some serving functions that in English would typically be expressed through prepositons, predicate adjectives, conjunctions, and negatives. The language may be characterized as having multiple clause constituents with verbal behavior and phrase constituents that are relational nouns. Most of the Kresh words that one would gloss with English attributive adjectives are better analyzed as adjectival relational nouns. Their complements, when pronominal, are (inalienable) possessive in form, same as for other relational nouns. In the examples I give, such nouns are glossed along the lines of *góvó kpïkpï* 'large specimen of tree'. The word *góvó*, more briefly glossed as 'large spec of', is analyzed as an adjectival relational noun and the head of this noun phrase. Adjectival nouns exhibit singular/plural distinctions (e.g., *kprāshā* 'large specimens of'), whereas among independent nouns, only those denoting humans show number distinctions.[1] Comparatives are made as below (where *ōtō* is a frozen locative coverb 'it-pass' and *áyä* is a locativizer):

(1) Été   góvó   nî   ōtō áyä î.   or Länjä   ōtō áyä ägâ.
     he   big:spec:of one pass Loc you.   They-be:big   pass Loc us.
     'He is a bigger one than you.'   'They are bigger than we.'

This paper describes various kinds of negation in Kresh and notes a few related functions that employ negators in their expression. In section 1 sentence negation is presented. This is not meant to imply that a speaker who utilizes 'sentence negation' always means to negate a proposition with no reference to its constituent parts, but only that out of context, such a clause is pragmatically ambiguous with regard to its 'presuppositions'. In section 2 constituent negation is examined. As one might expect, the marking of constituent negation is part of the focus-marking system of the language. The use of both kinds of negation is then examined with respect to questions (section 3) and directives (section 4), with some added comments on making 'denials' (section 5). Following that is a description of ways in which negators are employed to modify predicate denotations, either to designate a more superlative property, so-called 'paradoxical negation' (section 6), or to designate a contrary property (section 7). In section 8 the interaction of negators and quantifiers is considered, after which there are some ways to just say 'No' (section 9).

Although I have striven to keep the description somehat non-theoretic, it inevitably reflects the linguistic paradigm within which I work, which is the Functional Grammar of Simon Dik (1989).

1 Sentence negation

In describing features of sentence negation in Kresh, it is convenient to distinguish between the negation of verbal predications (section 1.1), in which the main predicate is a verb, and the negation of non-verbal predications (section 1.2), in which, ignoring copulas, the main predicate is some kind of noun or pronoun.[2] Both sections include examples of negations in conditionals. Since the disjunction markers are borrowed, so to speak, from the form of a negated condition, there is a short discussion of disjunction as well (section 1.3).

1.1 Verbal predications

In Kresh, the negation of verbal predications is expressed with *'dī*, which occurs clause finally. This is the position one would expect for a sentence negator, although this is not common. Dik notes that in only 4.6% of languages examined 'does the negative particle orient itself to the sentence as a whole rather than to the predicate' (1989:327). Perhaps Kresh can do this because it has a different negator for constituent negation, presented in section 2. Meanwhile, consider the example below:

(2) Kôkó ãmbá Gõkó 'dī.
     Koko he-hit Goko not
     'Koko didn't hit Goko.'

Taken out of any context, the sentence above marks no information as given, and a Hearer[3] will not know if a particular part of it is supposed to express part of a true proposition. Within context, however, it may be clear to the Hearer that part of the sentence reflects a positive open predication; that is, the Hearer may discern that the Speaker intends to negate a constituent, but this would be determined from the context of such a sentence rather than from features of its construction.

In some contexts one is not expecting a negative statement and may interpret a clause positively until reaching the end. In fact, this feature is used to play pranks, as in *Mummy, little brother fell off the granary and broke his neck not!* By the time the Speaker gets to *'dī* 'not', Mum may have already passed out. However, Kresh has a particle *bãá* which may optionally be used clause-initially or pre-verbally to presage the negation that will follow:

(3) Bãá Kôkó ãmbá   Gõkó 'dī.
     Neg Koko he-hit Goko not
     'Koko didn't hit Goko.'

As in some other African languages, negation interacts with the aspect system in an asymmetrical way. This is exemplified in the affirmative/negative pairs in the constructions below, which may be typified as perfective, perfect, imperfective, and irrealis. (Note that the gloss 'Act' for *y*- stands for 'act' or 'process' or 'habit' in the imperfective periphrastic construction, and the gloss 'Prob' for *nd*- stands for 'prospect' or 'probability' or 'inference' in the irrealis periphrastic construction. The co-verb *ishí* is glossed 'have' to represent the perfect and telic aspects.)

(4)   Positive (P)   Negative (N)

Kôkó ãnjã   mömõ.   Kôkó   ãnjã   mömö 'dĩ.
Kôkô ˜-anjǎ mömõ   Kôkô   ˜-anjǎ mömõ 'dĩ
Koko he-go   home   Koko   he:go   home not
'Koko did (not) go home.'

In the preceding example, the negated verbal predication is expressed with a syntactic construction parallel to the positive one. In the following three examples, however, they are not parallel:

(5)   Kôkó ãnjã   mömö ĩshí.   Kôkó   ãnjã   mömö 'dĩ.
Kôkô ˜-anjǎ mömõ ˜-ishí   Kôkô   ˜-anjǎ mömõ 'dĩ
Koko he-go   home he-have   Koko   he:go   home not
'Koko has (not) gone home.'

(6)   Kôkó ǎ yãnjã   mömö.   Kôkó   ãnjã   mömö 'dĩ.
Kôkô ˜-a y˜-anjǎ   mömõ   Kôkô   ˜-anjǎ mömõ 'dĩ
Koko he-at Act:of:going home   Koko   he-go   home not
'Koko is (not) going home.' or
'Koko does (not) go home' [e.g., until dark].

(7)   Kôkó ǎ ndãnjã   mömö.   Kôkó   ǎ yãnjã mömö 'dĩ.
Kôkô ˜-a nd˜-anjǎ   mömõ   Kôkô   ˜-a y˜-anjǎ mömö 'dĩ
Koko he-at Prob:of-going home.   Koko he-at Act of-going home not
'Koko will (not) go home.'

The preceding positive irrealis construction was used to express a future likelihood; it is also used to express a non-future predication with inferential modality, as below, but in this case the negation is parallel in expression:

(8)   Kôkó ǎ ndãnjã   mömö.   Kôkó   ǎ ndãnjã   mömö 'dĩ.
Kôkô ˜-a nd˜-anjǎ   mömõ   Kôkô   ˜-a nd˜-anjǎ   mömõ 'dĩ
Koko he-at Prob of-going home.   Koko   he-at Prob of-go home not
'Koko must (not) have gone home.'

The negator *'dĩ* is used to express the negation of embedded verbal predications as well. Note that temporal and relative clauses are usually framed by *'déé* at the beginning and *kã* at the end, here glossed as '[' and ']', respectively. Verb forms between them generally have a *k-* prefix as well, here glossed as '[' as below:

(9)   'And wind when it should blow, it will carry that dust go onto various food-stuffs which they made piles of in the market'

'déé   bãá   kükü   jūjū   ëyí   'dī   kã.
[negative   [-they-cover top:of   them   not   ]
'and which they hadn't covered.'

In the preceeding clause, since the negator *'dī* is positioned before the *kã*, it clearly lies within the relative clause. If the negator belongs to the main clause, then it comes after the *kã*:

(10) Bãá   mókö   dë   'déé   róyó í   kǎ   gbõgbõ í   kã 'dī.
      neg   I-see   place-that [sore the [-it-at body:of him]   not
      'I didn't see where he had a sore on his body.'

Since the antecedent in a conditional is at the level of a propositional satellite (or higher, see Dik 1990), one would expect the negator, if any, to remain within it. This is what we find in Kresh, where the antecedent is closed by *yää* 'if so then':

(11) Ndäkpá ä'dá   ká   ŋgärūyū   'déé äwä   ūŋgú   'dī
      people   they-be at   rainy:season [they:cultivate thing   not

      yää,   gõgõ   ǎ   ndījī   áyä   ïgï.
      if:so:then,   hunger   it-at Prob of-fall-on Loc   them

      'People around during the rainy season, if they do not cultivate, then they will be hit with famine.'

1.2 Non-verbal predications

To express negated non-verbal predications, Kresh employs the negative verb *azá*, which is always trailed by the particle *ní* in a typical 'embracing' negation. (As with all verbs, the missing first tone is supplied by the subject prefix.) Two main kinds of non-verbal predication are considered: those expressed as predicate nouns and those that predicate a location.

In perfective constructions with nonlocative predicate nouns, there is no verb or copula (although a focus marker is allowed):

(12) Kôkó gẽsẽ   újū.   Kôkó   āzá   gẽsẽ   újū ní.
      Koko small:spec:of man.   Koko   he-not small:spec:of man ø.
      'Koko is a boy.'   'Koko is not a boy.'

In irrealis constructions such as those below, *a'dá* is supplied in the positive expressions. The negative employs *a ndāzá ní* in a construction parallel in form to the positive verbal irrealis in (13P) rather than to the negative verbal irrealis in (13N):

(13) (P)   Kôkó   ă   ndā'dá   góvó   nî.
            Koko   he-at Prob:of-being big:spec:of   one.
            'Koko will be big.'

      (N)   Kôkó   ă   ndāzá   góvó   nî   ní.
            Koko   he-at Prob:of-not   big:spec:of   one   ø.
            'Koko will not be big.'

This negator can also be used in embedded clauses, as in the fragment below:

(14)   ndäkpá ë   'déé käzá   yōmó   gäļä   gŏsĭ'dí
       people which [[-they-not people:of   to-do   evil:specs:of
       ūŋgú ní kä
       thing ø]
       'people who aren't doers of evil things'

In the conditional sentence below, both the protasis and apodosis have negators:

(15)   'Dé   úmü gĕsĕ   újū   'déé úfü   käzä 'dī   yää,
       [you small:of man [you-kill beast not   if:so,
       úmü ázá   újū   ní.
       you you-not man   ø
       (Long ago) 'boy, if you didn't kill a savage animal, you weren't a man.'

Some nouns in Kresh can be described as locative, while others are not. A number of verbs in Kresh require locative complements; some require non-locative complements; and some accept no nominal complements at all (i.e., stative and intransitive verbs). In the example in (4) above, *Kôkó ānjă mömō*, we saw the locative verb *anjă* 'go to' and the locative noun *mömō* 'home', (which in most other respects can distribute and be modified like a non-locative noun). However, a simple predication of location to some term is expressed using the verbal copula *a* with a locative complement. The short form *a* is unique among Kresh verbs, in that it is monosyllabic and generally present tense (that is, current time of reference), whereas *ã'dá* is used more often for past tense and always for irrealis, perfect, and imperative. The negative counterpart to *a* is the verbal copula *azá ní*, which we have seen before, only now in a locative role. This is the only verb stem in Kresh that has an accompanying particle *(ní)*. In general, this particle functions to indicate the scope of the negation. All of these are inflected for person and number.[4]

(16) Positive (P)   Negative (N)

Kôkó ǎ	mömö̃.	Kôkó	āzá	mömö̃	ní.
Kôkô ˜-a	mömö̃	Kôkô	˜-azá	mömö̃	ní
Koko he-at home.		Koko	he-not:at	home	ø.
'Koko is home.'		'Koko is not home.'			

And from a traditional story:

(17) 'And when he went inside, he saw a fire burning brightly,'

ïshíí	bǎá	ndákpã	āzá	gbö̃gbö̃	ëyí	ní.
and	Neg	person	it-not:at	side:of	it	ø

'but no one was beside it.'

Naturally, a simple predication of location has something of a durative, non-temporal aspect, so it is not surprising that the locative verb *a* was pressed into service as an auxiliary to form a periphrastic verb phrase expressing imperfective aspect. Localist analogies of this sort are not uncommon in the world's languages. And so we have the Kresh imperfective *ǎ yãnjã mömö̃* 'he-at process-of-going home' which was seen above.[5] This usage may even have reinforced the imperfective quality of *a* in its locative role. In any case, when a Kresh Speaker wants to express location with a perfective aspect, as in *Koko was at home for a short while then left*, he or she can employ *a'dá* as below. But as we saw in the negated verbal clauses, the negated locative construction exhibits no distinction between perfective and imperfective:

(18) (P)

Kôkó	ǎ'dá	mömö	ká	njónjó	ǎ.
Koko	he-be:at	home	at	night	this

'Koko was home last night.'
(but as an imperative: 'Koko must be home tonight.')

(N)

Kôkó	āzá	mömö	ká	njónjó	ã	ní.
Koko	he-not:at	home	at	night	this	ø

'Koko was not home last night.'

Note, however, that *a'dá* can have the sense of 'remain', and in that case the negative would use *'dĩ*:

(19) (N)

Kôkó	ǎ'dá	mömö	ká	njónjó	ã	'dĩ.
Koko	he-stay:at	home	at	night	this	Neg

'Koko didn't stay home last night.'

The irrealis may have been formed on analogy with the imperfective, but using a prefix that means 'place of'.[6] Earlier we saw the example *ǎndānjā mömö* 'he-at probability of-going home', perhaps diachronically derived from an earlier sense of 'he-at position of go home'. In any case, to express the irrealis for location predications, the verb *a'dá* is again employed for the positive, and the negative parallels it as below with *a ndāzá ní*:

(20) (P)   Kôkó   ǎ   ndä'dá   mömö.
           Koko   he-at Prob:of-at home.
           'Koko will (probably) be home.'

     (N)   Kôkó   ǎ   ndāzá   mömö ní.
           Koko   he-be:at Prob:of-not:at home   ø.
           'Koko will (probably) not be home.'

As in many languages, existential constructions are based on the locative. If a location can be given, then the constructions are the same, as long as the term to which existence is predicated is nonspecific:

(21) (P)   Gēḷé   glözö   ndäkpá ä   rájâ.
           Many:of good:specimens:of people they-at Raga
           'There are many good people at Raga.'

     (N)   Gēḷé   glözö   ndäkpá äzá   rájá ní.
           Many:of good:specimens:of people they-not:at Raga ø
           'There are not many good people at Raga.'

If no location is expressed, and one is simply predicating existence, then the construction is made with *ē'dē*, which in other contexts corresponds to *there* in its anaphoric (nondeictic) pronominal usage (e.g., *I was just there yesterday*). In its existential usage, however, *ē'dē* is not anaphoric, but rather refers to location within the universe of discourse. Usually this means within the limits of accessibility or knowability, similar to the usage of *there* in English.

(22) (P)   Gēḷé   glözö   ndäkpá ä   ē'dē.
           gēḷé   glözö   ndäkpá ¨-a   ē'dē
           Many:of   good:specs:of people they-at there.
           'There are many good people' (in the world).

     (N)   Gēḷé   glözö   ndäkpá äzá   ē'dē   ní.
           gēḷé   glözö   ndäkpá ¨-azá   ē'dē   ní
           Many:of   good:specs:of people they-not:at there   ø
           'There are not many good people' (in the world).

However, to express the nonexistence of something, it is not necessary to include *ẽ'dẽ* in the negation. The following excuse, given by a farmboy to his mother after she returned from a week away, illustrates both the construction without *ẽ'dẽ* and the potential narrowness of one's universe of discourse:

(23) Ũyū   lóbö   ãzá   ní.
     water:of bathing it-not ø
     'There was no water for bathing.'

As a further example of the existential nature of *ẽ'dẽ* in such constructions, note the common Kresh greeting below, which reflects their concern for survival:

(24) Úmü á   tá   ẽ'dẽ?
     úmü '-a tá   ẽ'dẽ
     you you-at still existence
     'Do you still exist?'

Kresh does not employ privative affixes such as English *in-* or *-less* or a privative preposition such as *without*, but instead employs a non-existential clause like that below:

(25) Óbö   ëté ká jájá ũyū,
     you-wash him with plain water,

     ká   kõnó ãzá   ílī   ëyí ní.
     with salt it-not:at inside:of it ø
     'Wash him with water without salt in it.' or 'Wash him with unsalted water.'

In many languages expressions of possession parallel locative expressions in construction, and Kresh is no exception. In the sentence below, note that the associative preposition *ká* functions as a locativizer for nonlocative nouns, including personal names, and by extension functions to indicate alienable possession. It is glossed here as 'Loc' but in attributive uses as 'of' and other times as 'with'. Its form before pronouns is *áyä*.

(26) Glãwã ã   ká Kôkö.   Glãwã ãzá   ká Kôkó ní.
     field it-at Loc Koko   field it-not-at Loc Koko ø
     'Koko has a garden.'   'Koko does not have a garden.'

This construction is similar to the existential one in (21) above, and it could have been glossed that way: 'There is (not) a garden associated with Koko.'

An alternative way to express nonpossession is even more nonexistential in form:

(27) Glãwã   ká   Kôkó   ãzá   (tówó)   ní.
      garden   of   Koko   it-not (further) ø
      'Koko doesn't (any longer) have a garden.'
      'There is no (longer any) garden belonging to Koko.'

If one adds one of the three specific determiners[7] to the sentence above, then its interpretation becomes solely existential:

(28) Glãwã   í   ká   Kôkó   ãzá   (tówó)   ní.
      garden the of   Koko   it-not (further) ø
      'Koko's garden doesn't exist (any longer).'

In the case of relational nouns, the 'existential' construction is the usual way to express nonpossession or nonexistence:

(29) Kópõ   Kôkó   ã   ẽ'dẽ.   Kópõ   Kôkó   ãzá   ní.
      child:of Koko   it-at there   child:of Koko   it-not   ø
      'Koko's child exists.'   'Koko's child does not exist.'
      'Koko has a child.'   'Koko has no child.'

1.3 Disjunction

Several examples have been given of conditional sentences with negated clauses. Kresh seems to have developed its expression of disjunction from such a pattern, the usual form being *'dí yää* 'if not then' as below:

(30) 'Long ago, if a person went to the home of his father-in-law,'
      kõjõ   ní   íjí   gõzõ   átá   áyá   átá   mẽné,
      in:law:of   him   he-take good:spec:of meat   it-like   flesh:of cane:rat,
      'dí   yää   íjí   ẽ̩lé̩   íshíí   rõtó   ø,
      not   if:so he-take chicken and   he-slash   it,
      'his father-in-law took good meat like that of a cane rat (guinea pig) or he took a chicken and slaughtered it,' [and he cooked it...for him.]

This form is also used to express a disjunction between noun phrases:

(31) bẽbé   ní   õjõ   50   ríní   'dí yä 40   ríní
      father:of him   he-come 50   year   not if:so 40   year
      [he lived there ... until] 'his father came to be 50 or 40 years old.'

There is another form of disjunction that employs *āzá ní* but without the conditional marker. This may be restricted to existence-type expressions:

(32)   [As for me, every year from the first day of April,]

   njïnjï ǎ   ě'dě   nïnjï āzá   ní,
   rain it-be:at there   rain it-be:not ø,
   'whether there was rain or there wasn't,' [I would prepare my fields].

2 Constituent negation

Constituent negation in Kresh is usually pragmatic in its usage. Its use in an expression usually signals that the Speaker is rejecting the validity of one proposition, while affirming that a substitute constituent could change the proposition into a valid one. The substitute constituent may or may not be provided in the context, and it might be zero. The embracing negator used for constituent negation is *azá ní*. Note, however, that unlike the verbal *azá ní* described above, this marker does not function as a main verb and only rarely does it show subject agreement.

Kresh has a morphological system for marking focus on salient information, and this system is often employed together with *āzá ní* to further delineate the scope of the denial. This leads to double marking, and in example (46) below, there is triple marking, two markers besides *āzá ní* further delimiting the scope. However, if one removes the *āzá ní* and leaves the other focus markers, one has the positive, focus-marked counterpart to the construction. This differs from predication negation, in which there are neutralizations and asymmetries between negative and positive expressions of otherwise identical underlying predications.

2.1 General patterns

In the examples to follow, the focal word is in italics, the negative marker *āzá ní* is glossed as 'Not>', the subject-focus marker *kˆ-* as '<SF', and the complement-focus marker *î* or *í* as 'CF>'. The arrow is intended to show the direction from the marker to the focal word. Negations of the subject, object, and terminus location, respectively, are shown in the three sentences below.

(33)   Gōkó kóshó ātá   nî.   Ázá Kôkó   kóshó ø   ní.
       Gōkô kˆ-oshó ātá nî   āzá Kôkô   kˆ-oshó ø   ní
       Goko <SF-eat meat the   Not> Koko   <SF-eat (it) <
       '*Goko* ate the meat.'   '*Koko* didn't eat the meat.'

(34) Kôkó ãmbá í   Gõkó.   Kôkó ãmbá ãzá í   Gõkó ní.
      Koko he-hit CF> Goko.   Koko he-hit Not> CF> Goko <
      'Koko hit *Goko*.'   'Koko didn't hit *Goko*.'

(35) Kôkó ūsú   kärá nî   ãzá ã'bã î   ūmbū   tļĭmbĭgĭ ní.
      Koko he-put pot the Not> it-on CF> underside:of eaves   <
      'Koko didn't put the pot *under the eaves*.' (but somewhere else)

When the contrast is made explicit, then there is less need for an additional
focus marker. This is shown in the text below, in which *ãzá* is also placed
after the directional co-verb rather than before it as above:

(36) 'I am not muddying the stream for you, because the water is running from
      you there towards me over here,'

      bãá   ĕshĕ ãzá ámá ãŋã   áyä î   yõ ní.
      Negative it-from Not> Loc-me it-toward Loc you there <
      'not from me to you there.'

Lack of additional focus markers is particularly common with adjuncts
which have no co-verb at all, as seen with the temporal phrase below:

(37) Kôkó õjõ   mömö ãzá ká   njónjó ã   ní.
      Koko he-come home Not> at   night   this <
      'Koko came home but (it was) not last night.' or
      'It wasn't last night when Koko came home.'

2.2 Negation of main verbs

Focus on the verb and gerund is shown with the particle *nĕ*, which follows
the verb's object, if any. Gerundial and periphrastic verb phrases seem to
have originally been formed with *nî* 'the', as in *ã lŏbö nî* 'he-at the bathing',
and the *nî* usually survives where there is no explicit complement to the verb
and also where it is followed by the verb-focus marker *nĕ*. The nî is shortened
to *í* before monosyllabic words, including *nĕ*, as will be evident in the
examples below. The focus marker *nĕ* will be glossed as '<<F', to indicate that
it usually directs focus to a word before the preceding word.

(38) Kôkó ãzá ă   rŏļö   Gõkó nĕ ní,
      Koko Not> he-at (Act:of)-bother Goko <<F <
      ă   yãná   ëté nĕ.
      he-at Act:of-help him <<F
      'Koko is not *bothering* Goko, he is *helping* him.'

Yes-no questions can include constituent negation as well. The text below is taken from a story in which some frightened boys think they have seen the night-time reflection of firelight from the eyes of a pride of lions. Their father then leads them to the spot and says,

(54) Ǎ   kã   nëë,   mókõ   ãzá î
      it-at here rheme>, you-see Not> CF>

      'dî'dí   má'bã   ãsh   kã   ní?
      firefly you-at there here <?

      'What we have here, isn't it *fireflies* that you see there?'

      Bãá   mókõ   ãzá mümü   kãzã   ní.
      Negative you-see Not> eye(s):of savage:beast <

      'It is not *the eyes of a savage beast* that you saw.'

(55) Mókõ   î   'dî'dí   'déé ókö   mbãwã ëyí kãḻã   ïgí ãkã.
      You-see CF> firefly [result fear:of it   [-it-make you]]

      'What you saw that frightened you were *fireflies*.'

Note that the two positive clauses above are marked for complement focus, whereas ãzá ní provides sufficient focus marking for the negative clause.

4 Directives

There are predications with various deontic modalities, expressed in constructions paralleling the perfective, imperfective, and irrealis, although these latter two are uncommon. Both the positive and negative directives can optionally be preceded by a deontic modal such as gõzõ nî, roughly 'it's a good idea that'. Note that if no modal operators are expressed, then the positive deontic propositions are expressed the same as the positive epistemic propositions and could be ambiguous out of context. Prohibitions, on the other hand, are expressed in constructions quite different from their positive counterparts. The two pairs below exemplify positive and negative deontic expressions for the perfective and imperfective aspects, respectively:

(56) (P) (Gõzõ nî)   Kôkó   ãgã   glãwã nî.
           (Gõzõ nî)   Kôkô   ˜-agã   glãwã nî
           (good:of it) Koko   he-dig   field the

           'Koko should/must dig up the garden.'

      (N) (Gõzõ nî)   Kôkó   ã'bã   gãgã   glãwã nî   ã'dá.
           (Gõzõ nî)   Kôkô   ˜-a'bã   g¨-agã glãwã nî   ã'dá
           (good:of it) Koko   he-forego to-dig field the ø

           'Koko should/must not dig up the garden.'

(57) (P)   (Gōzō nî)   Kôkó   ă   yăgă   glăwă   nî.
            (Gōzō nî)   Kôkô   ˜-a   y˜-agă   glăwă   nî
            (good:of it)   Koko   he-at Act:of-dig field   the
            'Koko should keep digging the garden.' or
            'Let Koko begin digging the garden.'

      (N)   (Gōzō nî)   Kôkó   ă'bă   dăgă   glăwă   nî ă'dá.
            (Gōzō nî)   Kôkô   ˜-a'bă d˜-agă   glăwă   nî ă'dá
            (good:of it)   Koko   he-forego practice:of-dig field the ø.
            'Koko shouldn't keep digging the garden.' or
            'Let Koko quit digging the garden.'

The prohibitions above utilize an embracing construction similar to the
English *Leave it alone* or *Let it be*, where *a'bă* has the literal gloss 'leave' and
ă'dá is 'it-be' or 'it-stay'. In this case, however, *ă'dá* has become an
indeclinable, discountinuous part of the verb *a'bă*, in this usage of it. (Note
that *a'bă* without *ă'dá* can be used in expressing positive exhortations such
as *Á'bä Kôkó níí ăgă glăwă* 'Allow/direct Koko so that he-dig garden'.)

Polite directives frequently employ the form of a negated question:

(58) Éné   bámä   'dĩ?   versus   Éné   bámä.
      You-give to-me   not   You-give to-me
      'Won't you give it to me?'   'Give it to me.'

One can even use the propositional attitude Q-word *kútú* and the pushy
illocutionary particle *yä*:

(59) Kútú mănjä   dĩ   löwó   ḷámbä   'dĩ   yä.
      really we-go place:of walk:of hunting   not, respond
      'Why don't we go hunting!'

One can also add a deontic tag question to the end of a directive like that
above, seeking the Addressees confirmation, not of its truth value, but of its
deontic value:

(60) Ázá   gōzō   í   nĕ   ní?
      Not> good:of one <<F   <?
      'Isn't it a good idea?'

One can use conditionals with directives, although their form is different.
A contingent clause antecedent to a directive employs the verb prefix *kˆ*,
which is identical to the subject-focus marker, but here glossed as 'whenever'. It notifies the Addressee that this is the condition, not of the truth
value of the consequent clause, but of its deontic value. The following

example, from a speech on sanitation, is marked as a negative contingent
condition to a directive, even though the consequent clause employs a
locative circumlocution to express the directive. And although the *k^* is not
marking focus in this case, a focus is nevertheless marked by the focal
determiner *í në* to emphasize that reference is to the very same entity as
before.

(61) 'Dé ïgï ūyū í në kā gī tírí kázá ní
      [they water the very this various all whenever-not ø
      yää, ā ŋgáyä ïgí dī gägá ūyū ēshē
      if:so:then it-at Loc you practice:of to-draw water it-from
      ílí gräjá tītī ūyū, 'dī yää, ...
      inside:of clean:spec:of hole:of water, not if:then, ...

'If every one of these particular aforementioned kinds of water are unavail-
able, (the necessity) is on you to draw water from a clean water hole, or' [a
running stream or ...].

If the antecedent has been realized, then the contingent prefix is not used.
The example below exemplifies that, along with a politely negated directive
with verb focus:

(62) Résé ïrí nî ïshí yää,
      you-butcher carcass the you-have if:then,
      āzá óŋbó ëté në ní yä.
      Not> you-salt it <<F < respond

'Since you have butchered the (animal's) carcass, why don't you salt it?'

5 Denials

One of the possible uses of *bāá* at the beginning of a negative statement is
to deny what someone else has claimed or assumed – this is sometimes called
'polar focus'. Bossuyt (1983) makes the point that languages like to place a
second negator at the beginning for this purpose. The Hearer can also reject
a statement or suggestion by saying *Bāá 'dī* 'Not at all', followed by a
counter-statement, whether negative or affirmative. For statements, however,
a much more common negative interjection is *kḷ̇ëzë* 'falsehood; lie'.

The text below is taken from a story in which a man has just stated, in his
brother's hearing, his intention to court a certain woman. The brother's
response is reported in semi-direct speech and exemplifies *bāá 'dī*, a negated
constituent, and a proximal/logophoric pronoun, *ëpē* 'heS':

(63)   '[When brother of Bebesheshe heard that,'
ǎ'dǎ   bǎá 'dǐ.   Ũŋgú   ǎ   nëë,   ëpë ká
he-say Neg not. thing this rheme> heS <SF-at

ndrõ'bõ   nî,   ǎzá   úmü ónjö   në   ní.
Prob:of-marry (her) ø,   Not> you brother:of himS   <

'he said, not at all! On this matter, *he* (S) is going to marry her, not *you* his (S) brother!'

Note that the particle *nëë* is an optional stage-final marker at the end of a theme, a setting, or a speech introducer. Its use always marks what follows as salient, so I usually gloss it with an arrow as 'rheme>' or 'then>' or 'quote>', respectively. One of them will commonly be used in the peak sentence of a narrative or exhortation, sometimes two of them, and exceptionally even three as below, to usher in the climax. The sentence below is the peak of a long exposition on children's need for protein foods, which has arrived at the main point, the denial of the traditional proposition that such foods should be reserved for adult men. Of interest in this sentence, besides the abundance of determiners in the theme, is that the negator is placed before the quote marker that introduces the principle to be denied. I take this unusual construction to be marking a reported denial.[9]

(64)   Ĩshíí kǎtá ǎsh kǎ   nëë,   ílǐ   ëyí ǎ'dǎ   ǎzá
       and [-it-like that]   rheme>, meaning:of it   it-say Not>

       nëë,   ïgï nõshó í   në   kǎ gǐ   kǎ   nëë,
       quote>, they food the very this various this rheme>,

       ká   ádá   göshó ká   kprǎshǎ   ndäkpá bésé ní.
       with reason:of to-eat by   big:specs:of   people only <

       'And therefore, the point is that it is not the case with these various particular aforementioned kinds of food, that they are to be eaten by adults only.'

6 Paradoxical negation

Word-meanings are generally forged and typified in everyday experience, so when there is an extraordinary state of affairs, it may exceed the normal descriptive power of the predicates in the lexicon. One recourse, rarely used in English, is to employ the best predicate, then negate it to indicate its insufficiency. Words like *invaluable* and *priceless* may have been derived in this way. Another example, cited by Horn (1989:382) from a television advertisement by Lauren Bacall, is *Around here, we don't like coffee, we love it*. Horn (1989:383) following Cormack (1980) calls this paradoxical negation.

Kresh employs a similar strategy to intensify descriptions of states-of-affairs, usually employing nominal constructions in which *azá ní* is supplied as the negative copula, as the following examples demonstrate:

(65) Ájã ë ŋgâ ãzá î gómó úgú nẽ ní.
day that it-not CF> hot:spec:of weather <<F ø
'That day it was not hot' (like you've ever seen before).

(66) Bĕdé éndé ë nëë, ë ŋgété
Certain:of woman a rheme>, which hers

ãzá gömõ ãyã nẽ ní.
it-not drink-ing alcohol <<F ø
'There was this woman, her case was not (just) *consumption* of alcohol.'
(NB: Women usually make the alcohol but don't *drink* it.)

(67) Ë kãsh ãzá yãmbá ní.
that it-not Act:of-beating ø
'That was not a beating' (like any you have seen).

Another characteristic of some such constructions is the multiple marking of focus, including the anomalous use of *nẽ* with independent nouns. In the example below I have included the arrows with *ãzá ní*, to bring out the fact that every focus marker in the language is present in this sentence:

(68) Íshíí ë kã ãzá î mbädä nẽ ká ká Ũmbũ-ádá ní.
And this it-not> CF> beauty <<F <SF-at with Umbada <
'And this was no (ordinary) beauty which Umbada had.'

7 Contrary negation

Kresh does not employ negative affixation for expanding the lexicon. In this it contrasts with the various forms of negative affixation in the English lexicon, such as *in-*, *non-*, *un-*, *dis-*, *mis-* and *-less*, used to form lexemes for various contradictories, contraries, privatives, and reversatives. In Kresh, however, there are a few gradable stative verbs which are often used with the simple negative *'dí* to refer to a contrary property rather than to the privation (contradiction) of a property. Greenberg (1966) noted that this was common in many languages, African and otherwise, and noted a universal tendency in these cases to form a term for 'bad' from 'not good' and for 'narrow' from 'not wide', rather than the reverse. This may be seen for Kresh in the examples below:

(69) ozŏ   'be good; be beautiful'   ozŏ 'dĭ   'be bad; be ugly'
      afä   'be beneficial'   afä 'dĭ   'be harmful'
      laŋá   'be difficult'   laŋá 'dĭ   'be easy'
      ogŏ   'be many/much'   ogŏ 'dĭ   'be few/little'
      olö   'be far'   olö 'dĭ   'be near'
      onjó   'be strong'   onjó 'dĭ   'be weak'
      urü   'be heavy'   urü 'dĭ   'be light'
      esé   'be wide'   esé 'dĭ   'be narrow'
      elĕ   'be pleasant'   elĕ 'dĭ   'be unpleasant'

These examples contrast with the usage of other gradable stative verbs such as *omó* 'be hot', in which *omó 'dī* does not suggest that something is cold, but only that it is not hot, most often that it is lukewarm (an intermediate property). As one might expect, there is another stative verb, *ujú* 'be cold', whose meaning is a mediate contrary to hot.[10] The following generalizations can be made made about this class of Kresh verbs:

- Among verbs, gradable stative verbs are the only ones used with a negator to refer to mediate contrary properties.[11] A negated locative verb such as *ānjā 'dī* 'he-go not' is never used to mean 'he come'. The negation of a nongradable stative verb, such as *aŋgá* 'be healthy' or *ashá* 'be alive', is used to refer to an immediate contrary property (a contradictory), but this is what one would expect, since nongradable predicates do not usually admit of intermediate interpretations.

- Stative verbs used to express concepts that lack a single, opposing, easily-conceived contrary concept do not form contraries with *'dī*. For example, phrases like *ūyú 'dī* 'it-be sweet not' are not used for a contrary flavor, although this might be expected if such phenomena were entirely lexicalized as idioms. As it is, Kresh has several contrary words like 'be sour', 'be bitter', 'be salty', and 'be unripe-tasting'. Although these flavors are somewhat contrary to sweetness, none of them has potential to be a single opposing contrary.

- For a gradable stative verb for which there is a lexeme to express the single, opposing, contrary, the negation of the verb is not generally employed alongside it to express a contrary property. For example, *õmó 'dī* 'it-be hot not' is not generally used to mean something is cold; for this the verb *ūjú* 'it-be cold' is used.[12]

My impression is that this use of a negative construction to express a mediate contrary in the absence of a suitable Kresh lexeme is fairly productive within the limits described above. These limits are strict enough that there

is little opportunity to mistake this usage for the paradoxical usage of negatives discussed in the preceeding section, most instances of which do not
involve verbs of the class in (69) above. One possible instance, however, is
taken from a traditional Kresh fable:

(70) Ë kā āzá kélē ūŋgú nĕ bï Ôzó ní.
     This it-not pleasant:spec:of thing <<F to Hare ø

The adjectival noun *kélē* is derived from the stative verb *elē* 'be pleasant', and
their negation is usually employed to express displeasure rather than indif-
ference. In the story, precious seed is leaking from Hare's seedbag, and as he
crosses a stream, he hears the sound of it plunking into the water. The sound
should have alarmed him, befitting the contrary interpretation of the
negated predicate, but in fact it pleased him so much that he began dancing
to its rythm and didn't stop until all the seed had been lost! It is the paradoxical interpretation which is intended.

8 Negation and quantifiers

In many languages, if not all, the presence of negators and quantifiers in the
same clause can give rise to ambiguity. In Kresh, however, there seems to be
less ambiguity than in English, partly because sentence and constituent
negation are usually distinguished, and also because of a distinction between
specific and non-specific indefinite reference in the determiner system as
well as in a few words.

When a universal-type quantifier is used in a clause with the external
negative *'dī*, the quantifier is usually negated:

(71) Ôjŏ ā ká úgú tírí 'dī.
     he-come here at time every not.
     'He doesn't come here every day.' (But he probably comes sometimes.)

(72) Mókö ïgï tírí 'dī.
     I-see them all not.
     'I didn't see all of them.' (But some were probably seen.)

To exclude the middle reading and express the negation of every instance,
one can negate a non-specific instance:

(73) Ôjŏ ā jéé 'dī.
     he-come here anytime not.
     'He never came here.'

(74)   Mókö 'bälä méshë áyä ïgï   'dï.
       I-see one I-from Loc them   not.
       'I didn't see any of them.' (None were seen.)

Actually, this latter construction could have the paradoxical interpretation of 'more than one' if the Speaker was in such a mood. However, it could not have the specific reading 'There was one whom I did not see.' For that one would use a word for 'specific one' as below:

(75)   Mókö bĕdé   ë méshë áyä ïgï   'dï.
       I-see certain a I-from Loc them   not.
       'I didn't see a certain one of them.' (Others may have been seen.)

The negation of every instance can be excluded and the middle reading designated by using constituent negation, as below:

(76)   Mókö ăzá ïgï   tírí   ní.
       I-see Not> them   all   <
       'I didn't see *all* of them.' (But I saw some of them.)

(77)   Ójö   ăzá ká   úgú tírí ní.
       You-come   Not> at   time every <
       'Come, but not *every* day.' (You should come sometimes but not always.)

In the example below, the focus marking is such that the 'not one' can only mean 'many':

(78)   'And the various meat-tabboos of people, they are not one, because'
       ăzá   úlú   ătá 'bälä kálä   nŏwŏ   ílï   nî bï
       Not> type:of meat one <SF-make illness:of stomach   the for

       kóshó   ïgï   gï   tírí ní.
       grandfather:of them plural all <
       'it was not one kind of meat which sickened their forefathers.'

9. Epistemic responses

To answer yes-no questions, Kresh employs the use of tonal ideophones. Since the tones can not be articulated alone (except on a whistle), the speaker employs a nasal sound, most commonly a high front nasalized vowel or a bilabial nasal. There is nothing distinctive about the vowel or nasal chosen, and normal Kresh lexemes employ neither syllabic nasals nor nasalized vowels. For 'yes', two low tones are used, written orthographically as ŋ̃ŋ̃. For 'no', there is a high-low sequence with glottal stops: 'ŋ̃'ŋ̃.

It would be incomplete to suggest that the Addressee provides epistemic responses only in answer to yes-no questions. As in English conversation, the Addressee may respond to statements as well, providing agreement *(ŋ́ŋ́)* or disagreement *('ŋ́'ŋ́)*. In addition, the Kresh Hearer may express more intermediate propositional attitudes, such as *ŋ̂ŋ́* 'I can hardly believe it!', *ŋ̄ŋ́* 'Are you serious?', *ŋ́ŋ́ŋ́* 'No way', and *ŋ̄ŋ̄* 'That's ridiculous.' This makes for interesting repartee.

Notes

1. There are also abstract relational nouns, most of which are homophonous with the adjectival ones or only slightly different. They differ syntactically in that the abstract ones lack countability and have no specific/nonspecific options. They differ semantically in that the adjectival nouns are used co-referentially with their possessors, whereas the abstract nouns are not. Sometimes there is ambiguity, as in *gómó ëyî* 'its heat' or 'a hot one', but not in *gómó ë kā* 'this hot one'.

2. In Functional Grammar, the English copula *be* would be considered a surface feature rather than the expression of an underlying verbal predicate; see especially Hengeveld (1990).

3. By Hearer I mean to include the Addressee and other Hearers.

4. Verbs conjugate for person and number as follows (in isolation):

root:		a	a'dá	anjǎ	adä
		be at	stay at	go to	call
prefix					
3s	˜-	ǎ	ǎ'dá	ǎnjǎ	ǎdä
2s	´-	á	á'dá	ánjä	ádä
1s	m˙˙-	mä	mä'dá	mánjä	mádä
3p	˙˙-	ä	ä'dá	änjä	ädǎ
2p	m´-	má	má'dá	mánjä	mádǎ
1p	m˜-	mä̌	mä'dá	mänjǎ	mä̌dä

One could argue for *á* for the auxiliary root rather than *a*, based on its 3s form *ǎ*, but in some contexts it is *ä*.

5. The *y-* prefix seems to be a recent accretion. It only occurs on vowel-initial verb stems, and even there it is optional. In one dialect there is no prefix at all; in the Boro dialect the

prefix is *n-*, the same as for verbal nouns in that dialect; in the vanishing Woro dialect the prefix is *l-*.

6. Instead of using the prefix *nd-* for the irrealis, the Boro and other western dialects employ the prefix *d-*, which is common in contractions from the locative relational noun *dī* 'place of' or 'practice of'. This prefix persists in Kresh-Ndogo in periphrastic constructions of co-verbs, both imperfective and irrealis, and in imperfective prohibitions. This suggests that the present periphrastic verb phrases arose from one that employed the locative *dī* in place of the present prefixes.

7. Actually, the number of possible determiners, including demonstratives, exceeds sixty, but only about twenty-seven are significantly distinctive. If you exclude demonstrative elements, then there are only five articles: zero is nonspecific indefinite (except with locatives and proper nouns), *í (=nî)* is unique, *ë* is selective/contrastive (specific indefinite), *í në* is focal/emphatic, and *ëté/ígï* (derived from pronouns) are anaphoric. *ëté/ígï* can combine with the other four to form four more determiners. One can also combine these nine with three basic relative distances to get 27 demonstratives, but there are numerous variations that take it all past 60, and that does not include number distinctions. Most of these forms can also be combined with possessive phrases. (And in English one can only say *a, the, this, that*.)

8. This pronoun set is also used in nonpossessive positions. There is also a set of independent focal pronouns, not used possessively. In this set '>I<' or '>me<' would be *mëŋgámä*. Corresponding to this is a focal/selective pronominal set for alienable possession and location, in which 'mine' would be *ë ŋgámä*.

9. The label 'denial' is used loosely, not neccessarily designating a speech-act. In Functional Grammar, the semantic-pragmatic representation of utterances is analyzed into four layers. Speech acts function at the outer layer, propositional attitude is embedded within the next layer, while objective modality is embedded further in yet. Most negation operates further in yet, on a predication or even a predicate. A statement like 'It is not the case that' could be taken as expressing an objective modality, but it seems to me that objective modalities are not often expressed in Kresh. See Dik, Hengeveld, Vester, and Vet (1990).

10. As I use the terms here, two predicates express contrary properties if speakers would usually describe an appropriate referent as having one or the other of those properties or neither of them, but not both. This opposition is called mediate contrariety if there are intermediate properties between the two extremes, such as warm between hot and cold. A pair of properties are immediate contraries, also called contradictories, if an appropriate referent would usually be described as necessarily having one or the other property, but not both at once and not neither. For example, mammals are usually described as being either dead and alive, healthy or ill, pregnant or nonpregnant, without intermediate possibilities. For further discussion, the reader is referred to chapters 1, 4, 5, and 6 of Horn (1989).

11. Not surprisingly, the deverbal adjectival nouns derived from these stative verbs usually designate a contrary property when used in a negated nominal sentence. An example is *Ázá gōzō ëyí nē ní* 'It-not good specimen of it', which usually means 'It's a bad one'.

12. Lyons (1977:773) said that it 'seems to be the case that the application of propositional negation to a gradable expression (e.g., 'like') will always tend to produce a contrary rather than a contradictory, whether the language-system lexicalizes the contrary (e.g., 'dislike') or not.' I doubt that this applies to Kresh in general. Horn (1989) attributes contrary negation in English to polite understatement, but this applies in Kresh only exceptionally. There is nothing polite in Kresh about 'difficult' versus 'easy', 'heavy' versus 'light', or 'far' versus 'near', and *ozō'dī* 'it-good not' can be used as a fairly serious charge.

References

Cormack, A. (1980). *Negation, ambiguity, and logical form*. Unpublished. University of London. (cited from Horn 1989)

Bossuyt, A. (1983). 'Historical functional grammar: an outline of an integrated theory of language change.' In: Simon Dik ed., *Advances in functional grammar*, 301-325. Dordrecht: Foris.

Dik, Simon C. (1989). *The theory of functional grammar; part I: the structure of the clause*. Dordrecht: Foris.

—— (1990). 'On the semantics of conditionals.' In: Nuyts, Bolkestein, Vet eds., 233-261.

Dik, Simon C., K. Hengeveld, E. Vester and C. Vet (1990). 'The hierachical structure of the clause and the typology of adverbial satellites.' In: Nuyts, Bolkestein, Vet eds., 25-70.

Greenberg, J. (1966). 'Language universals, with special reference to feature hierarchies.' The Hague: Mouton. (cited in Horn 1989)

Hengeveld, K. (1990). 'Semantic relations in non-verbal predication.' In: Nuyts, Bolkestein, Vet eds., 101-122.

Horn, L. R. (1989). *A natural history of negation*. The University of Chicago Press.

Lyons, John (1977). *Semantics*. Cambridge University Press.

Nuyts, Jan, A. M. Bolkestein, and Co Vet eds. (1990). *Layers and levels of representation in language theory*. Amsterdam/Philadelphia: John Benjamins.

Babole

Miles Leitch

0 Introduction*

0.1 Location and classification

Babole is a Bantu language spoken in the District of Epena, Likouala Region, Republic of Congo. Before the work undertaken by the author and his wife, no descriptive studies of Babole existed outside of a word-list. Although Babole may be tentatively classed in group C-10 (Guthrie's Bantu classification) on the basis of geography, no detailed comparative work has been done. Babole was long considered a dialect of the *Bomitaba* language (also Guthrie C-10) spoken in the village of Epena and elsewhere in the district of Epena. In Leitch (1989) I showed clearly that Babole is a distinct language from Bomitaba. The current study is based on data from the Babole dialect spoken in the villages of Dzeke and Impongui.

In section 1 we deal with negation in the morphological verb phrase and the special negation used with present statives. In section 2 we touch on different topics related to the negator *nàká*. We will explore in some detail the usage of *nàká* for contrastive negation of sentence constituents. We will also examine the syntax and usage of the particle *ná*, which is used to express absolute rather than contrastive negation.

0.2 Tone and orthography

Tone representation in verbal morphology

Babole has lexical high and low tone verb roots as well as grammatical high and low tones functioning in different ways in the verb phrase. Although a discussion of the tonal dynamics of the verb phrase is beyond the scope of this paper, it is necessary to have some conventions for representing tone in our examples, as below.

- tones shown in the first line of an example are as they would appear after the cyclic phonological rules and the syntax component of the grammar, but before the post-syntactic phonological rules and/or phonetic interpretation rules (Pulleyblank 1986:5-9). Unassociated or so-called 'floating' low tones that cause a following high tone to lower (downstep) are not shown. Segments that alternate between high and low tone are shown with the derived tone that they have in the context of the example.

- in the morpheme breakdown (second line of an example), lexical tone and other presumably inherent tones that do not vary *are* shown.
- in the morpheme breakdown, tone is *not* represented on inherently toneless morphemes that receive tone by leftward spreading from the final vowel. Non-initial root syllables, the aspect morpheme, -*ak*-, and all derivational suffixes (extensions) belong to this class.
- in the morpheme breakdown, by convention, tone is *not* represented on grammatical morphemes that show alternation with regard to tone. This avoids, for the time being, the question of the underlying tonal status of these morphemes. The negative morpheme -*ka*-, and other morphemes occurring before the time position in the verb phrase, belong to this class (see section 1.1 for overview).

These conventions allow the reader to appreciate some of the complexity of the material and yet not be distracted by questions not in focus in our discussion of negation.

Floating high tone
The symbol ´ at the end of the morphological verb phrase represents the so-called 'floating' high tone. This phenomenon occurs in a wide variety of verbal forms, but is always associated with the final vowel -*a*, when it does occur. The high tone is realized on the final vowel if there is any post verbal complement. Otherwise the underlying low tone on the -*a* is manifested.

Nominal forms
Nominal forms are shown with tone on each syllable except the noun-class prefix where tone is never distinctive (always low). We have not analyzed the nominal forms in our morphemic breakdown where these details are irrelevant to our discussion.

0.3 Typological sketch

In the examples (1)-(6) used in the following typological sketch, all non-essential morphological details are suppressed to highlight constituent order.

Sentence constituent order
Babole is a SVO language with obligatory pronoun prefixes in the morphological verb phrase.

192   *Myles Leitch*

(1)   Molèmbà   à-kúdí   botímbà.
        sorcerer   3sg-curse   village
        'The sorcerer cursed the village.'

Question-word position

Question words are always placed in pattern position, that is, where the
questioned constituent would be found.

(2)   Molèmbà   à-kúdí   ndè?
        sorcerer   3sg-curse   what
        'What did the sorcerer curse?'

Word Order in nominal phrase

All constituents in the nominal phrase follow the lexical head in an unmarked construction.

(3)   Nkɔ́tí   íá   bísíe   ísátò   íngàtà   íá   tò-dìngaˊ   íkèí   líosò?
        dog(s)   Rel   us   three   large   Rel   we-love   go   where
        'Where are our three big dogs that we love going?'

Adpositions

Babole has *only* prepositions.

(4)   Bohèlè   è   mú   mokíotíe.
        man   be   *in*   house
        'The man is in the house.'

Comparative constructions

Although there are several strategies for forming comparatives, the following
are typical according to our informant.

(5)   Celestin   ˊíohálòlàkaˊ   Seraphin   mú   ditélé.
        Celestin   Exceed   Seraphin   in   height
        'Celestin is taller than Seraphin.'

(6)   Seraphin   è   nkíolà   nà   Armand   mú   ditélỹ.
        Seraphin   be   same   of   Armand   in   height
        'Seraphin is the same height as Armand.'

1 Verbal negation

1.1 Sketch of verb morphology

We will first outline the morphological structure of the verb phrase to facilitate the reader's understanding of the examples. The morphological (non-conjugated) indicative verb phrase can be abstractly represented as follows:

Prfx-Neg-Time-Reflexive-RADICAL-Extensions-Aspect-Final Vowel

There are complex co-occurence relationships between verbal meaning, negation, aspect, time, final vowel and derivational extensions. These can not be treated here. We will primarily be interested in the distribution of the negation morpheme *-ka-*. A minimal affirmative verb phrase has a pronoun prefix, verb root and final vowel, as in (7).

(7) À-ø-dìh-í   nswíe.
     3sg-Tm-get-Cmpl   fish
     'He has gotten (some/a) fish.'

Negation in the morphological verb phrase involves the morpheme *-ka-* as in (8).

(8) À-ka-ø-dìh-í   nswíe.
     3sg-Neg-Tm-get-Cmpl fish
     'He hasn't gotten (some/a) fish.'

A more complex example of the verb phrase would be:

(9) À-ka-sío-á-bímb-edz-a´
     3sg-Neg-Tm-Rflx-hit-Ints-Fin
     'He would not have hit himself *really* hard ...'

In (9) the time morpheme is *-sío-*, conditional. The verbal extension *-edz-* is an intensifier.

Negative morpheme *-ka-*

With the exception of the hortative mood, *-ka-* immediately follows the pronoun prefix in the forms where *ka*-negation is allowed. Although *-ka-* appears with high tone in most contexts, this is not always the case, and so according to our conventions, we represent the *-ka-* morpheme as unspecified with regard to tone.

The existence of the verb root *-kà-*, 'to deny', may suggest that the negative morpheme was historically a negative verb. Conversely, it is possible that the negative morpheme was re-lexicalized as a verb with the negative meaning of 'deny'. When we discuss future time negation, we will touch briefly on the question of whether certain other pre-radical verbal morphemes could be derived from auxilliary verbs.

Final vowels

For the purposes of this exposition, we can posit the following meanings (following a suggestion by Morgan 1991:4) for these final vowel suffixes:

- -í   completive (-*i* is always high toned),
- -e   non-completive, (has vowel harmony variant -*ɛ*)
- -a   semantically void (required by phonology, but has no distinctive meaning).

In verbs there is vowel harmony leftward from the first syllable of the verb root. If the root has /a/, /o/, /i/, /u/, or /e/, then we see the final vowel -*a* in the constructions where final -*a* is required. If, however, the root vowel is /ɛ/ or /ɔ/, then the final vowel will be -*ɛ* or -*ɔ*, respectively, instead of final -*a*. Final -*a* and its vowel harmony variants are glossed simply as *Fin*.

Aspect morpheme -*ak*-

Comrie (1976) says: "[...] aspects are different ways of viewing the internal temporal constituency of a situation" (quoted in Morgan 1991:5). In this paper we are concerned with the distribution of a morpheme -*ak*-, which, in some contexts at least, clearly marks aspectual distinctions. We will comment on the meanings associated with -*ak*- in different contexts, but want to focus on the formal distribution of -*ak*- with regard to the -*ka*- negator and tense/mode distinctions. In cases where -*ak*- clearly marks imperfectivity, for example, it will be glossed as such. In unclear cases, -*ak*- will simply be glossed *Asp*, for 'aspect'. Our working hypothesis is that -*ak*- does mark aspect in all of its occurrences. The morpheme -*ak*- has vowel harmony variants -*ɛk*- and -*ɔk*-.

1.2 Stative negation

There is a stative verb root, -*è*, that has a unique negative form, -*ètí*-. The root -*è* is different from other verbs in that it is entirely uninflected and has a present meaning only. There are two other stative verb roots which can be inflected for tense, mode, and aspect, but these are negated with -*ka*-. Possessives, existentials, and all verbal constructions using the root -*è*, use -*ètí*- for negation. We will illustrate with possessive and existential constructions.

Possessives

The possessive construction uses the stative verb plus genitive *nà* as in (10).

(10) N-è   nà   bwátò.
      1sg-be Gen pirogue
      'I have a pirogue.'

The stative radical -*è* as in (10) is negated as in (11).

(11) N-ètí   nà   bwátò.
      1sg-be:Neg Gen pirogue
      'I don't have a pirogue.'

Existentials

Existentials use the stative with an impersonal locative subject, much like the analogous English construction. The stative is followed by the genitive preposition *nà*.

(12) Há-è   nà   mùngwà l(á) (b)otìmbá.
      loc-be Gen salt   at   village
      'There is salt in the village.'

(13) Há-ètí   nà   mùngwà lá botìmbá.
      Loc-be:Neg Gen salt   at village
      'There isn't any salt in the village.'

The other stative radicals, -*ék*-, and -*íeng*-, are described in the course of our survey of *ka*-negation in Subsection 1.3..

1.3 Survey of *ka*-negation

In this subsection we will look at the distribution of *ka*-negation with respect to several important temporal and modal categories of the morphological verb-phrase. In regard to temporality, we will examine the present, past, and future. We will then look at the deontic mode constructions, imperative and hortative. We will give special attention to the distribution of the aspect marker, -*ak*-, with respect to these categories and to *ka*-negation. Our main concern will be formal, in that we are concerned primarily with the distribution of grammatical morphemes in the verbal morphology, and only secondarily with the range of meanings associated with various verbal forms.

Pragmatic present and 'today' past

The pragmatic present construction, when unmarked with -*ak*-, has a present meaning with psychological or experiencer predicates such as -*dìng*-, 'to want', or -*έn*-, 'to see'. It has a completive meaning with action verbs. It is sometimes referred to as the 'today' tense (or hodiernal tense), where 'today' starts at nightfall last night and continues till nightfall tonight (Morgan 1992:3).

This suite of verbal constructions is characterized by:

* low-toned pronoun prefixes
* time morpheme -*ø*- (or simply absent)
* final vowel -*í*
* -*ak*- can be added with meaning difference in affirmative
* -*ak*- can be added with meaning difference in negative

Examples (14) and (15) show that an unmarked 'today' affirmative can be negated with predictable results. The completive meaning conveyed by this form is best translated in English by the present perfect. However, there is no one-to-one correspondence and it is misleading to even call this a 'present' tense. It is unmarked for tense and is concerned with pragmatic relevance to the present. Accordingly, in (15), the adverbial could have been 'since last year' and the verbal form for 'eat' would be the same.

(14)   À-dzíe-í   byèkà   yésù.
        3sg-eat-cmpl   food   all
        'He has eaten all the food!'

(15)   Swíeì mohúmá   à-ka-dzíe-í   ekɔ̀ngɔ̀.
        since morning   3sg-NEG-eat-Cmpl   manioc
        'He hasn't eaten manioc since this morning.'

Adding the morpheme -*ak*-, as in (16) and (17) below, puts the action farther in the past (although still 'today' as defined above), and de-emphasizes the importance of the result for the speaker. Native speakers often (incorrectly) translate these -*ak*- forms using a French plus-que-parfait (English past-perfect), because it gives the sense of anteriority. See gloss b) of (16).

(16)   À-dzíe-ak-í   byèkà   yésù.
        3sg-eat-Asp-Compl   food   all
        'He ate all the food.'
        'He had eaten all the food...'

(17)   Nà mohúmá   à-ka-dzíe-ak-í   ekɔ̀ngɔ́.
        at morning   3sg-NEG-eat-Asp-Compl   manioc
        'He didn't eat manioc this morning.'

The main point to notice with (14)-(17) is that all four possibilities of the formal system are exploited: affirmative without -*ak*-, affirmative with -*ak*-, negative without -*ak*-, and negative with -*ak*-.

Past time
The past is characterized by:

- low-toned pronoun prefixes
- time morpheme -*á*-
- final vowel -*á*, (-*έ*, -*ɔ́* are vowel harmony variants)
- -*ak*- possible in affirmative with meaning difference
- -*ak*- obligatory under negation

This tense deals with the time frame before 'today'. The difference between (18) and (19) is that (19) seems to have an anterior (farther in the past) meaning. Making the time of the event in the past specific also tends to require the aspect marker, -*ak*-, as in (19). Traditional grammars of a related language, Lingala, often make a distinction between past, (18), and remote past, (19), for constructions exactly parallel to these (Dzokanga 1979:233-35). The meaning and function of these forms in Babole is related, but a simple past/remote past distinction is lacking.

(18) Ngwíelíemì à-á-dzíe-á   ngámbá.
     uncle   3sg-Pst-eat-Fin   elephant
     'My uncle ate an elephant.'

(19) Ngwíelíemì à-á-dzíe-ak-á   ngámbá há   máéngέ.
     uncle   3sg-Pst-eat-Asp-Fin elephant at   two
     'My uncle ate the elephant two days ago.'

Although the pronoun prefix in (18) and (19) might seem to be high-toned on the surface, it is a low-toned pronoun fused with the high-toned past tense morpheme. In (20), the pronoun manifests its inherent low tone when the negative morpheme intervenes between it and the past tense morpheme.

(20) À-ka-á-dzíe-ak-á   ngámbá wèsù.
     3sg-Neg-Pst-eat-Asp-Fin   elephant all
     'He didn't eat the whole elephant.'

What is of interest for us is that the aspect morpheme -*ak*- is obligatory under negation, so that both (18) and (19) would be negated as in (20).

The existential paradigm in (21) to (24) serves to illustrate the past tense affirmative and negative of the stative roots *-ék-* and *-íeng-*. The root *-ék-* has a limited distribution and is found in the form 'today-past', *-ékí*, in the morphological past, as in (21) and (22), and in one other verbal form not discussed in this paper.

(21)   Há-á-ék-έ   nà   mùngwà.
        Loc-Pst-be-Fin Gen   mùngwà
        'There *was* salt.'

(22)   Há-ká-á-ék-έ   nà   mùngwà.
        Loc-Neg-Pst-be-Fin Gen   mùngwà
        'There *wasn't* salt.'

The root *-íeng-* is found in every verb tense and mode, and conjugates very much like any other verb. One difference is that, while *-ak-* is possible in the affirmative, (23), it is not obligatory under negation as with other *ka*-negated past forms. In fact, (24) is not acceptable at all with *-ak-*. The distribution and meaning of these various stative verbs in the tense/mode/aspect system needs to be clarified in further work.

(23)   Há-á-íeng-(ak)-á   nà   mùngwà.
        Loc-Pst-be-(Asp)-Fin Gen   salt
        'There *was* salt.'

(24)   Há-ka-á-íeng-(*ak)-á nà   mùngwà.
        Loc-Neg-Pst-be-(*Asp)-Fin Gen salt
        'There *wasn't* salt.'

Future
Babole has three time morphemes that express futurity:

F^1 *-pá-*   possible future
F^2 *-tá-*   possible future (same meaning as F^1)
F^3 *-sío-* conditional.

The future tenses are characterized by:

- low-toned pronoun prefixes
- time morphemes *-pá-*, *-tá-*, or *-sío*
- final vowel *-a´*
- *-ak-* prohibited
- *-ka-* negation not allowed except with F^3

The future morphemes occupy the time slot in the morphological verb phrase and never occur simultaneously. Constructions F^1 and F^2 *cannot* be negated with -*ka*- in the Dzeke dialect. The Mongouma-Bailly dialect does reportedly allow negation of F^1 and F^2 with -*ka*-. In the Dzeke dialect used for this study, only F^3 allows negation with -*ka*-. To illustrate, (25), with the -*pá*- morpheme, can only be negated periphrastically as in (26) or (27) below.

(25) Tò-pá-híet-a´.
1Pl-Fut-escape-Fin
'We will escape.'

(26) Tò-ètí tĕ tò-pá-híet-a´.
1Pl-be:Neg that 1Pl-Fut-escape-Fin
'We will not escape.'

In (26) the subject of the stative is the same as that of the negated proposition. This kind of negative paraphrase is very strong and indicates that the proposition will never happen under any cicumstances. The more casual negation of a future proposition is shown in (27).

(27) Tò-ètí mo-pá-híet-a´.
1Pl-be:Neg Comp-Fut-talk-Fin
'We will not escape.'

Example (27) shows the use of the complementizer prefix *mo-*. The morpheme *mo-* is used with same-subject complements of the verb 'to be' and other auxilliaries. In contrast, a contrary-to-fact conditional as in (28), using the -*sío*- morpheme, *is* negated using -*ka*- as in (29).

(28) Džĕngà bísíe nà muntèkú, tò-sío-là-a´ lá eàlè.
Cond 1Pl:Ob Gen fish-net 1Pl-Fut-Put-Fin in river
'If we had a fish-net, we would put it in the river.'

(29) Džĕngà bísíe nà muntèkú, tò-ka-sío-là-a´ lá eàlè.
Cond 1Pl:Ob Gen fish-net 1Pl-Neg-Fut-put-Fin in river
'If we had a fish-net, we would not put it in the river.'

Morphologically these three future constructions are parallel, characterized by the position of time morpheme and the floating high tone on the final vowel. They also share the restriction disallowing the -*ak*- aspect morpheme. However, only the 'conditional', F^3, can be negated with -*ka*-. How do we account for these facts?

Firstly, we could try to characterize the disjunction between -*pá*-/-*tá*- and -*sío*- in semantic terms. Welmer has said: "The future (in African languages) as a necessary linear component of Time is virtually absent. Such is either potential Time, ... or *No-Time*, lying beyond the conceptual horizon of the people." (Welmers 1973:352). The three Babole 'future' constructions involve possibility or potentiality, in the sense of Welmers, above. This is a more unreal kind of future than, for example, English, where the certainty of the speaker is expressed. The difference between F^1 and F^2 on the one hand, and F^3 on the other, is that with the first two, the conditions are unknown and unknowable to some extent, while with F^3, the conditions are explicit. Conditionals are thus rooted in the past and present, even though they have a future-like realization. *Ka*-negation is sensitive to this difference. It is possible that all three future morphemes are derived from auxilliary verbs historically. Under this scenario, *-sío-* alone would have later been reanalyzed as a time morpheme analogous to the past morpheme *-á-*, based on the kind of semantic criteria outlined above. Thus, *-sío-* allows *ka*-negation, but *-pá-* and *-tá-* do not.

From a logical perspective we can see that if F^1 and F^2 are used to express only possibility, then negating these runs into difficulty. Negative-possibility does not mean 'less likely', it simply means 'impossible'. The periphrastic negatives in (26) and (27) may permit utterances expressing the speaker's sense of a certain event being unlikely to happen, without getting into the logical bind of 'not-possible'. With *-sío-*, on the other hand, both the affirmative and negative are expressions of the speaker's *intent* based on past and present conditions.

Deontic negation: hortative mode
This mode is sometimes referred to as 'subjunctive' because of its semantic similarity to Indo-European subjunctive forms. It is used to request, suggest or encourage a course of action. The hortative *affirmative* is characterized by:

• pronoun prefixes with high tone
• no time morpheme
• final vowel *-è*
• *-ak-* allowed (habitual/repetitive meaning if present, see (30a))

These properties are illustrated in (30) and (30a).

(30)　a.　Á-bìs-è　　　　　mokíotíe.
　　　　　3sg-close-Incmpl　house
　　　　　'Let him close the house.'

　　　b.　Á-bìs-ak-è　　　　mokíotíe.
　　　　　3sg-close-Imp-Incmpl　house
　　　　　'Let him *regularly* close...'

The hortative *negative*, however, is characterised by:

- *ka*-negative initial and low toned
- pronoun prefix set same as hortative affirmative except for anomolous 3rd person singular -*mío*- (see example (31).)
- final vowel -*á*
- -*ak*- obligatory under negation

These properties are illustrated in (31).

(31)   Ka-mío-bìs-ak-á   mokíotíe.
       Neg-3sg-close-Asp-Fin   house
       'He should not close the house up.'
       'Let him *not* close the house up.'

Deontic negation: imperative mode

An affirmative singular command is made as in (32) or (32a). Note the clearly imperfective meaning of -*ak*- in (32a). There is no overt 2nd person pronoun in the imperative singular forms.

(32)   a.   Ø-híem-á   lòío.
             2sg-cease-Fin   noise
             'Stop making noise!'

       b.   Ø-híem-ak-á   lòío.
             2sg-cease-Imp-Fin   noise
             'Don't make noise *anymore*!'

The affirmative plural command is made as in (33). There is an overt low toned 2nd person plural pronoun.

(33)   Bò-híem-á   lòío.
       2pl-cease-Fin   noise
       'You all stop making noise!'

The negated counterparts of these commands use the 2nd person singular and plural forms of the negative hortative. Morphophonemic rules cause the bracketed segments to elide as shown. The elision is obligatory in (34) but optional in (35).

(34)   K(a)-ío-híem-ak-á   ò-tíd-í.
       Neg-2sg-cease-Asp-Fin   Comp-flee-Inf
       'Don't stop fleeing!'

(35)　Ka-(b)ío-híem-ak-á　　ò-tíd-í.
　　　Neg-2pl-cease-Asp-Fin　Comp-flee-Inf
　　　'Don't you (pl.) stop fleeing!'

The phenomena of using a hortative to negate imperatives is apparently not unusual. Palmer (1986:112) states "The way in which imperatives are negated in a number of rather different languages is interesting." He goes on to list Latin, Greek, and Syrian Arabic as languages which use a subjunctive to negate imperatives analogously to the Babole examples above. He continues: "The explanation for this is, presumably, that denial of permission (negative hortative) is equivalent to giving instructions not to act, since 'Not-possible' is equivalent to 'necessary-Not' in a logical system. [...] The imperative thus expresses 'necessity' but the negated subjunctive, jussive, etc., 'no possibility'." (Palmer 1986:113).

Summary
In this survey we have noted the irregularities of *ka*-negation across several temporal and modal categories of the morphological verb phrase and offered explanations for some of these. The distribution of -*ka*- negation and the aspect marker -*ak*- with respect to these categories is summarized in table 1.

Table 1. Distribution of -*ka*- and -*ak*-

	Affirmative	Negative
Present	-ak- possible	ka-Neg, -ak- possible
Past	-ak- possible	ka-Neg, ak- obligatory
Future $F^{1,2}$	-ak- prohibited	periphrastic negative
Future F^3	-ak- prohibited	ka-Neg
Imperative	-ak- possible	Ka-Neg, -ak- obligatory
Hortative	-ak- possible	

In the light of these data we should review our assumptions concerning the morpheme -*ak*-. While it is clearly a single element in the formal morphological system, its meaning is different in at least three contexts:

-*ak*-[1]　*V-ak-í*, today, and *V-ak-á*, past with anterior meaning.

-*ak*-[2]　*V-ak-è*, hortative, and *V-ak-á*, imperative with habitual meaning (usually considered an imperfective meaning).

-*ak*-[3]　deontic and past negatives (obligatory with no clear meaning, possibly part two of a discontinuous negative morpheme).

The characterization of -*ak*- as an aspect marker is still tenable, but we cannot espouse the stronger claim that it marks imperfectivity. The semantic status of -*ak*- is clearly an area that needs more investigation, particularly the -*ak*-[1] and -*ak*-[3] meanings. To further explore the assymetries revealed in Figure 1., we can organize the various verbal constructions along a realis-irrealis scale as in table 2.

Table 2. Time assymmetries

Today (-*i*)	Past	Contrary-to-fact Conditional F[3]	Future F[1], F[2]
	Deontic		
1	2	3	4

Realis ――――――――――――――――――――――――――――――― Irrealis

In Realis Domain 1, corresponding to the constructions with a final vowel -*i*, we find unrestricted use of the negative and aspectual morphemes, and the maximum number of semantic distinction created by their use ($2\times2=4$). In Domain 2, we note that Past and Deontic forms have exactly the same restrictions with regard to *ka*-negation and the -*ak* marker. Each permits three structural distinctions. In both cases the aspectual distinction is neutralised under negation. Continuing rightward to Domain 3, the Conditional, we have lost the aspectual distinction altogether, but retain an affirmative/negative contrast. Finally in Domain 4, it is not even possible to use the morphological negator and we only have affirmative. As we move from Realis to Irrealis we find progressive reduction in morphological marking and semantic distinctions.

A few additional points worth noting are the following:

• This schema formalizes the intuition that both the past and subjunctive are equally unreal or equally distant from a center of pragmatic relevance. This semantic similarity seems to be reflected in the parallel morphology.
• We are also able to capture the intuition concerning the conditional that it is conceptually related to both the future and the present/past. Accordingly it behaves like a present/past in allowing *ka*-negation, but like an irrealis future in is allowing the -*ak*- marker.

2 Aspects of negation beyond the verb phrase

In this section we will be exploring contrastive and absolute negation at both the sentential and phrasal/constituent levels. We will first introduce the sentential syntax of absolute negation using the particle *ná*. We will then look at the constituent-negator *nàká* and its use in contrastive phrasal negation. Finally, we will look at the interaction of *nàká* and *ná* in both phrases and sentences.

2.1 The particle *ná*

In (41) we see morphological predicate negation as in section 1.

(41) À-ka-én-í   mo-íendzà.
      3sg-Neg-see-Cmpl   Cl:Sg-buffalo
      'He didn't see a/the buffalo.'

(41) is ambiguous over several meanings, depending on context and intended contrast. (42), however, unambiguously expresses absolute negation as communicated by the English translation.

(42) À-ka-én-í   ná   mo-íendzà / N-íendzà.
      3sg-Neg-see-Compl even Cl:Sg-buffalo / Cl:Pl-buffalo
      'He didn't see a single buffalo / any buffalos.'

When used with the morphological verb negator *-ka-*, *ná* communicates absolute negation and looks, at least in (42), like the English 'any'. But this is misleading. The same *ná* in an affirmative context simply means 'even' or 'also' as in (43) and does not have the inherent negative polarity of English *any*. We will gloss *ná* simply as 'even' in negative contexts as well, with the understanding that its grammatical function is complex.

(43) À-én-í   ná   mo-íendzà.
      3sg-see-Cmpl   even Cl:Sg-buffalo
      'He also / even saw a buffalo.'

The indefinite pronominals *dzúmbá* 'a thing / something' *motò* 'a person/ someone' *lúkà* 'a place/somewhere' appear with *ná* as direct objects of negated verbs as in (44)-(45).

(44)   À-ka-én-í   ná   mo-tò   /   dz-úmbá.
      3sg-Neg-see-Cmpl   even Cl:Sg-person /   Cl:Sg-thing
      'He didn't see anybody / anything.'

(45)   À-ka-kè-í   ná   lúkà.
      3sg-Neg-go-Cmpl   even place
      'He didn't go anywhere.'

We note that as well as in object position, *ná*-phrases are quite grammatical in subject position, (46), with an appropriate negative verb.

(46)   Ná   motò   à-ka-kè-í.
      even person 3sg-Neg-go-Cmpl
      'No one has left (gone).'

We will re-examine the pair (44)/(46) later in the light of other data.

2.2 The negator *nàká*

Contrastive Negation with *nàká*

Given appropriate discourse or pragmatic context, almost any lexical item, nominal phrase, adverb, etc., can be negated with *nàká* to give contrastive or emphatic meaning in elliptical phrasal utterances. We provide the context for the first example, but leave the reader's imagination to construct appropriate contexts for the rest.

(47)   Q. bohèlè à-píomb-í?   R. Nàká bohèlè, ...
      man   3sg-arrive-Cmpl   Neg man
      Has a/the man arrived?   'Not a/the man, (rather ...).'

The response R., of (47), given normal pragmatic assumptions about gender possibilities, implies that it was a woman who arrived. We can see from this example that *nàká* selects a single semantic component of a negated lexical item. Table 3 shows different grammatical categories under negation with *nàká*.

The syntax and interpretations of these expressions follows fairly closely the analogous *not*-expressions in English. We note that indefinite pronouns are strange when negated with *nàká*. This may be because of the strangeness of negating either the [+indefinite] or [+person] components. It is possible in English, to say , 'not someone, but something', with appropriate contrastive intonation. Similarly *nàká motò* could only mean: 'not a person, but some other category of being'.

Table 3. Grammatical categories and *nàká* negation.

Category	Nàká-Phrase	Meaning
noun	nàká moíendzà	Not a buffalo.
pronoun	nàká bísè	Not us.
quantified	nàká mbíendzà yésù	Not all (the) buffalo.
quality modified NP	nàká mbíendzà íngàtà	Not (the) large buffalo
number modified NP	nàká miíendzà mítánò	Not five buffalos
adjective	nàká bolámù	Not good.
name	nàká Pierre	Not Pierre.
adverb	nàká bwâ	Not thus.
	nàká nà hátí	Not quickly.
indefinite pron.	*nàká motò	?Not someone.

Absolute phrasal negation

If we give *nàká* a *ná*-phrase complement, the result is absolute phrasal negation. In (48) we provide a possible pragmatic context for the example *nàká ná moíendzà*, 'not a single buffalo'.

(48) Q. Òéní   moíendzà?   R. Nàká ná   moíendzà.
        2sg-see buffalo   Neg even buffalo
        'Did you see a buffalo?'   'Not a single buffalo.'

Table 4 shows different grammatical categories under negation with *nàká ná*. We note that the starred nominals are at best strange, apparently because negative *ná* selects a non-referring nominal expression as complement. The *ná* transforms an N or NP which defines a class into an expression which refers to an existing real world subset of members of the class designated. The negation is a negation of the existence of this subset. The starred nominals do not work simply because they are referring expressions and cannot be construed as class definitions. The same is true of adverbs and adjectives.

We can summarise by underlining the complementarity between *nàká* and *nàká ná* phrasal negatives. *Nàká* is used with almost any complement and allows contrastive negation. *Nàká ná* is used with non-referring nominals, and expresses absolute negation.

Table 4. Grammatical categories and *nàká ná* negation.

Category	Nàká ná-Phrase	Meaning
noun	nàká ná moíendzà	No buffalo
	nàká ná mbíendzà	No buffalos
quality modified NP	nàká ná mbíendzà íngàtà	No large buffalos
indefinite pron.	nàká ná motò	Nobody/no one
	nàká ná dzúmbá	Nothing
	nàká ná lúkà	Nowhere/no place
*pronoun	*nàká ná bísè	*no us
*quantified	*nàká ná mbíendzà yésù	*no all buffalo
*name	*nàká ná Pierre	?*no Pierre
*adverb	*nàká ná bwâ	*no thus

2.3 Negative nominal expressions in the sentence

In this section we look at how these negated nominal phrases work as arguments of verbs in a sentence. By 'argument' we mean subject or direct object. We will also look at one case where a negated nominal can function as an adverbial phrase.

Nàká-Phrase as sentence constituent
We see that (49) is ungrammatical with an affirmative verb and direct object negated with *nàká*.

(49) *Tò-én-í   nàká moíendzà.
      1Pl-see-Cmpl Neg buffalo
      'We see not a/the buffalo.'

The juxtaposition of *nàká* with *moíendzà* forces the contrastive interpretation of *moíendzà*. The English translation captures well the difficulty of assigning a meaning to such a sentence. The same problem would occur with such a phrase in subject position or with a negative verb. No *nàká*-nominal expression can be used as a verbal argument. Intuitively, these *nàká* phrases seem to be full propositions with *nàká* functioning as a predicate. The ungrammaticality of sentences like (49), follows directly, since an NP is required as argument. However, such an expression *can* be used in adverbial complements of intransitive verbs, with *nàká* being interpreted as a preposition with the meaning 'without'. This is illustrated in (50).

(50)   À-búto-í   nàká   nswíe.
       3sg-return-Cmpl without fish
       'He has come back without fish'

Nàká ná-Phrase as sentence constituent

In this last section we want to look at the paradigm (51)-(54), and ask why (52) is ungrammatical and not synonomous with (51), when (53) and (54) are synonomous and grammatical.

(51)   Tò-ka-én-í   ná   mbíendzà.
       1Pl-Neg-see-Cmpl   even buffalos
       'We didn't see any buffalos.'

(52)   *Tò-én-í   nàká ná   mbíendzà.
       1Pl-see-Cmpl Neg even buffalos
       'We saw no buffalos.'

(53)   Ná dzúmbá   dí-ka-kwíe-í   lá   bwèndò.
       even thing   Agr-Neg-fall-Cmpl Loc   sky
       'Nothing fell from the sky.'

(54)   Nàká ná   dzúmbá   dí-kwíe-í   lá   bwèndò.
       Neg even thing   Agr-fall-Cmpl Loc   sky
       'Nothing fell from the sky.'

What we want to discover is why a *nàká ná*-phrase is acceptable as a subject, (54), but not as a direct object, (52). First, we examine (53) and (54), which are exactly synonomous. The *ná* does not have an inherently negative meaning, so in cases where it has negative meaning, it is in the scope of a negator somewhere in the sentence. Because both *ná* and the verb have negative meanings, we conclude that in both sentences, *ná* and the verb are within the scope of the negator. This is made explicit in the schematic representations below.

$$\underset{ná\ [X]}{\uparrow} \quad \underset{ká\ \text{-}V}{\uparrow\downarrow} \quad (53)$$

$$\underset{nàká}{\uparrow} \quad \underset{ná\ [X]}{\downarrow} \quad \underset{V}{\downarrow} \quad (54)$$

The scoping relationship of negation between the subject and verbal positions is symmetrical in (53) and (54). Let us now examine the scoping properties of (51) and (52). In (51) the verbal negator successfully scopes over both the verb and *ná* to its right as shown below.

$$\underset{ká\ \text{-}V}{\uparrow\downarrow} \quad \underset{ná\ [X]}{\downarrow} \quad (51)$$

With these scoping relationships in mind, we can now ask ourselves why (52) is ungrammatical. We suggest that it is because the verb is not within the scope of the negator in the object NP.

$$\begin{array}{ccc} \downarrow & \uparrow & \downarrow \\ \text{V} & \text{nàká} & \text{ná [X]} \end{array} \quad (52)^*$$

As a result the verb can not be interpreted negatively and the sentence fails. In fact, in attempting to interpret such a sentence, our informant tends to pause after the affirmative verb, breaking the sentence into two propositions, the first affirmative, the second negative. This supports the idea that negative scoping failure is behind the ungrammaticality of (52). Such a scope assymetry may be explicable through some notion such as C-command (Lasnik, 1988), which is characterized in terms of syntactic structural relationships. The elaboration of this suggestion is left for future work.

2.4 Summary

In general *nàká* alone simply negates a component of the meaning of its complement. This applies equally to adverbs, adjectives and referring nominal phrases, etc.. Its primary usage is for contrastive negation. Being propositions semantically, and not NPs, *nàká*-phrases cannot be used as verbal arguments, but do allow interpretation as adverbial phrases.

Nàká ná together with its non-referring nominal complement does, however, form a nominal category which can appear in subject position but not in object position. Whether used phrasally or sententially, these phrases communicate absolute rather than contrastive negation.

Conclusion

In our survey of morphological and sentential aspects of negation in the Babole language, we have seen the central role of the morpheme *ka*. We have identified the present stative negation morpheme *-ètí* and described its distribution in verbal constructions. We have noted how realis/irrealis distinctions interact with verbal negation, and with temporal and aspectual morphological marking. Two phenomena of special interest in this regard are: one, the obligatory marking with *-ak-* of the negated past and hortative forms; and two, the impossibility of negating with *-ka-* the potential future forms, F^1 and F^2.

In regards to *nàká*, *nàká nà*, and the other phenomena described in section 2.0, we have sketched how the system works in general terms and pointed out a few areas of interest for future work. These observations can form the basis for the formulation of syntactic and semantic rules in a formal treatment.

Abbreviations

Agr	Agreement prefix	pl	Plural
Asp	Aspect	Prfx	Pronominal Prefix
Cl:Pl	Plural noun-class prefix	Pst	Past time
Cl:Sg	Singular noun-class prefix	Rel	Relative pronoun
Cmpl	Completive	Rflx	Reflexive
Comp	Complementizer	sg	Singular
Cond	Condition	Tm	Time morpheme
Fin	Final vowel	1Pl:Ob	Object/Emphatic pronouns
Fut	Future time	3sg	Subject pronoun prefix
Gen	Genitive	ɛ	Open front mid vowel
Hort	Hortative	ɔ	Open back mid vowel
Imp	Imperfective aspect	´	High tone
Incmpl	Incompletive	`	Low tone
Inf	Infinitve final vowel	ˇ	Rising tone
Ints	Intensifier	ˆ	Falling tone
Loc	Locative	⁺	Floating high tone
Neg	Negative		

Notes

* The data used for this study was provided and verified by Essatole Seraphim of the village of Dzeke. Dr. Stephen Anderson, of SIL Congo, reviewed the manuscript, as did the editors, Peter Kahrel and René van den Berg. The comments and suggestions of these reviewers have resulted in considerable improvement to the paper. Any remaining errors of fact or interpretation are entirely the author's.

References

Comrie, B. (1976). *Aspect*. Cambridge: Cambridge University Press
Dzokanga, A. (1979). *Dictionnaire Lingala-Français*. Leipzig: Verlag Encyclopaedie.
Lasnik, H. and J. Uriagereka (1988). *A Course in GB Syntax*. Cambridge, Massachussetts: The MIT Press.
Leitch, M. (1989). *Langue et Dialecte au Sud du District d'Epena*. Ms. SIL. Brazzaville, Congo.
Morgan, D. (1991). *A Preliminary Outline of the Tense-Aspect System in Lobala*. Ms. SOAS, University of London.
Palmer, F.R. (1986). *Mood and Modality*. Cambridge: Cambridge University Press.
Pulleyblank, D. (1986). *Tone in Lexical Phonology*. D. Reidel Publishing Company.
Welmers, W.E. (1973). *African Language Structures*. University of California Press.

Bafut

Beban S. Chumbow and Pius N. Tamanji

0 Introduction*

This article presents a study of negation in Bafut, a Grassfield Bantu language of the Niger Congo family spoken by some 35,000 people in the North West Province of the Republic of Cameroon. Specifically, the paper sets out to examine:

- the various means employed to express negation in Bafut,
- the syntactic distribution of the negative marker and
- the various changes that the negative morpheme may cause on the morphological and syntactic structures of sentences.

In the literature, one encounters a vast range of negation types. Klima (1964), for instance, identifies the following negation types which are attested in English:

- Standard negation
- Negated quantifiers
- Inherently negative quantifiers
- Negated adverbials and
- Inherently negative adverbials.

Payne (1985) observes that, whereas all of the above are attested in English, only a few are attested in other languages of the world. In Bafut for example, the most commonly attested is standard negation to which we turn in a moment. Before that we will give some typological information. And a brief presentation of the Bafut tense/aspect system is in place as this helps the reader to better follow the discussions in subsequent sections.[1]

Some general typological information

Bafut is basically an SVO language. The subject and object positions are generally occupied by an NP which can be generated by the following PS rule:

$$NP \rightarrow \begin{array}{l} Pro \\ N \ (Adj) \ (Det) \end{array}$$

which amounts to saying that the NP can be built out of either a pronoun alone or a noun followed by two optional elements; adjective and determiner in that order. The verb position is usually occupied by the verb root as well as tense and aspect markers which are not directly attached to the verb stem since the latter can be moved to other sentence positions without the other two (aspect and tense).

Bafut makes use of prepositions but does not have any question word, for the interrogative mood is generally marked by a rise in intonation. The language however makes use of a negative one-word answer to a question which is *ŋgáŋ* 'No'. Compare the question and answer pairs below:

(11)   *Question*   *Answer*

a. Sùù kɨ túʔú ŋkɨ?   ŋgáŋ 'no'
    Suh P_2 carry water
    'Did Suh fetch water?'

b. Mɘ̀ ká zhì?   ŋgáŋ 'no'
    I F_0 come
    'Will I come?' (Should I come?)

c. Bì ká kɨ́ túʔú ŋkɨ̀ lélé?   ŋgáŋ 'no'
    Bi F_0 Impf carry water day day
    'Will Bih fetch water daily?'

The Tense system
Bafut distinguishes nine tenses:

Remote Past	(P_3)	marked by	lỳN
Yesterday Past	(P_2)		kɨ
Today Past	(P_1)		lɨ̂N~nɨ̂N
Immediate Past	(P_0)		ʟ̬
Present	(T_0)		ʟ̬
Simple future	(F_0)		ka
Today future	(F_1)		lɨ̂
Tomorrow future	(F_2)		lŏ
Remote future	(F_3)		yɨ̌

T_0 and P_0 seem to overlap with respect to their aspectual meanings as both denote the completive nature of an event/action. The major difference between the two, however, lies in the fact that in T_0 focus is on the perfective nature of the event while P_0 focuses on the immediacy of the past event. T_0 and P_0 are marked by a floating low tone. The Immediate Past (P_0) describes events that have just taken place. The Today Past (P_1) describes events that took place earlier on the day of speaking, while the Yesterday Past (P_2) describes events that took place yesterday, last week, last month or last year. It is used along with time adverbials *yŷŷ* 'adjacent day', *ŋgya* 'week', *sàŋ* 'month', *àlòò* 'year' to indicate yesterday, last week, last month and last year. The same time adverbials used with the tomorrow future indicate tomorrow, next week, next month and next year. The Remote Past (P_3) describes events that took place earlier than the time described by P_2.

The Simple Future (F_0) describes events that will soon take place and those that will take place in future but whose time of occurrence is not specified. The Today Future (F_1) describes events that will take place later on the day of speaking while the Tomorrow Future, otherwise known as Distant Future, describes events to take place the next day, next week, next month or next year. The Remote Future (F_3) describes events to take place later than the time of (F_2).

With regards to aspect, perfective and imperfective aspects are attested in the language but for the purpose of this paper, attention will be focused on the imperfective aspect. The only feature of the perfective aspect which deserves a comment is the *mɔ́* morpheme which describes a completed event. This morpheme is often positioned after the verb. The imperfective aspect has the meaning of duration and continuity. It includes in its meaning the progressive and habitual. The progressive which is more common and is of interest to us as far as this paper is concerned has different markers depending on tense. For present events, the progressive is marked by a high-low replacive tone on the subject. For past events (P_1, P_2 and P_3), it is marked by a high-low replacive tone on the tense morpheme for P_1 and by *sɨ* which occurs after the tense morpheme for P_2 and P_3. For future events, the progressive is marked by *kɨ* which also occurs after the tense morpheme. However, as will be noticed later, the insertion of a negative morpheme can change the position of occurrence and the shape of these morphemes.

1 Standard negation

Standard negation, according to Payne (1985:198), is that type of negation which can apply to the most minimal and basic sentences. Such sentences are characteristically main clauses, and consist of a single predicate with as few noun phrases and adverbial modifiers as possible. In Bafut, the form of the negative morpheme which operates within the scope of standard negation varies depending on mood as illustrated below:

1.1 The declarative mood

A discontinuous morpheme (henceforth Neg morpheme), separated by the subject is employed to negate both verbal and non-verbal clauses in the declarative mood in Bafut. This Neg morpheme consists of a presubject particle *kāā* and a postsubject particle whose phonological form varies depending on the tense and aspect.

1.1.1 The present tense (T_0) and immediate past tense (P_0)

The present tense in Bafut which corresponds to the English present perfect tense, overlaps with the immediate past tense in its aspectual meaning which shows the completed nature of an event. The difference between the two lies in the fact that whereas with the immediate past, focus is on the immediacy of the completed event, with the present tense, the nearness of the completed event to the moment of speaking is not stressed. We have thus decided to treat these two together because of the similarity in the aspectual meaning. After all, the form and meaning of a negated sentence in T_0 is identical with that in P_0. The T_0 tense marker is ø while that of P_0 is *mɔ́*. Both tenses are negated by *kāā...sî* (with an obligatory deletion of the *mɔ́* tense marker) as illustrated below:

(2) a. Mbɨŋ lòó ø.
         Rain fall T_0
         'It has rained.'

     b. Kāā mbɨŋ sɨ̀ lòò.
         Neg rain Neg fall
         'It has not rained.'

(3) a. Mbɨŋ lòò mɔ̀.
         rain fall P_0
         'It has just rained.'

b. Kāā mbìŋ sì lōò.
Neg rain Neg fall
'It has not rained.'

c. *Kāā mbìŋ sì lōò mà.
Neg rain Neg fall P_0.

(4) a. Sùù bwīī ø.
Suh sleep T_0
'Suh has slept.'

b. Kāā sùù sì bwīì.
Neg Suh Neg sleep
'Suh has not slept.'

(5) a. Sùù bwìì mà.
Suh sleep P_0
'Suh has just slept.'

b. Kāā sùù sì bwīì.
Neg Suh Neg sleep
'Suh has not slept.'

c. *Kāā sùù sì bwīì mà
Neg Suh Neg sleep P_0

(6) a. Bó tū'ū ø ŋki.
they carry T_0 water
'They have fetched water.'

b. Kāā bó sì ŋkì tū'ū.
Neg they Neg water carry
'They have not fetched water.'

(7) a. Bó tù'ù mà ŋkì.
they carry P_0 water
'They have just fetched water.'

b. Kāā bó sì ŋkì tū'ù.
Neg they Neg water carry
'They have not fetched water.'

(8) a. Ngwa bɔ̄ɔ̄ ø ndá.
Ngwa build T_0 house
'Ngwa has built a house.'

b. Kāā Ngwà sì ndá bɔ̄ɔ̄.
Neg Ngwa Neg house build
'Ngwa has not built a house.'

(9) a. Ngwà   bɔ̀ɔ̀   mɔ̄   ndá.
         Ngwa   build P_0 house
         'Ngwa has just built a house.'

     b. Kāā Ngwà sì   ndá   bɔ̀ɔ̀.
         Neg Ngwa Neg house build
         'Ngwa has not built a house.'

One notices from the identical nature of examples (2b) and (3b) that the contrast between T_0 and P_0 is neutralized in the negative.

Another striking feature of Bafut negation exhibited by the examples above is that the negative morpheme triggers movement which results in the verb occupying sentence-final position instead of preceding the object NP. We return to this in more detail much later.

It is worth noting here that the presubject negative particle is optional as its presence or not in an utterance causes no change in meaning. Thus *Ngwa sì ndá bɔ̀ɔ̀* has the same meaning as *Kāā Ngwa sì ndá bɔ̀ɔ̀* 'Ngwa has not built a house.'

1.1.2 The Today past tense (P_1)

The today past tense which is morphologically marked by either *nìN* or *lìN* is used to describe events which took place earlier in the same day, i.e. the day of speaking. The negative morpheme for this and the other past as well as future tenses is *kāā...kì'ì*. The postsubject particle *kì'ì* varies with *wā'ā*. The difference, just like that between the P_1 markers *lìN* and *nìN* is simply dialectal. In subsequent illustrations, we will consistently use *lìN* and *wā'ā* because these two are more frequent in the language. (N in *lìN* and *nìN* is a homorganic nasal which assumes the place of production features of the following consonant. Thus, N becomes *m* in front of labials, *n* in front of alveolars and *ŋ* in front of velars). The underlying tone of the postsubject Neg particle is MM which becomes ML when a low tone follows and MH when a high tone follows.

(10) a. ìdìgì   lín   lòò.
         places P_1 hot
         'It was hot today'

     b. Kāā dìgì   líŋ   wā'à lòò.
         Neg places P_1 Neg   hot
         'It was not hot (today).'

(11) a. Sùù lím   bó'ɔ́   títá.
         Suh P_1 loose   pepper
         'Suh lost pepper (today).'

b. Kāā sùù lín wā'á títá bɔ́ɔ́.
Neg Suh P₁ Neg pepper loose
'Suh did not lose pepper (today).'

(12) a. Bó lín kó mbà.
they P₁ catch animal
'They caught an animal (today).'

b. Kāā bó lín wā'ā mbà kó.
Neg they P₁ Neg meat catch.
'They did not catch an animal today.'

1.1.3 The Yesterday past tense (P₂)
The P₂ tense marked by the morpheme *kɨ̀* is used to describe events which took place yesterday, last week, last month and even last year. The negative morpheme for this tense is *kāā...wā'ā*.

(13) a. Mfɨ́'ɨ́ kɨ̀ kó yɔ́ɔ́.
cold P₂ catch yesterday
'It was cold yesterday.'

b. Kāā mfɨ́'ɨ́ kɨ̀ wā'ā yɔ́ɔ́ kó.
Neg cold P₂ Neg yesterday catch
'It was not cold yesterday.'

(14) a. Mə̀ kɨ̀ wā tì ŋgyá.
I P₂ cut tree week
'I felled a tree last week.'

b. Kāā mə̀ kɨ̀ wā'ā tí ŋgyá wā.
Neg I P₂ Neg tree week cut
'I did not fell a tree last week.'

(15) a. Bó kɨ̀ bɔ́ỹ ndá fīī sáŋ.
they P₂ build house that moon
'They built a house last month.'

b. Kāā bó kɨ̀ wā'á ndá fīī sáŋ bɔ́ỹ.
Neg they P₂ Neg house that moon build
'They did not build a house last month.'

(16) a. Sùù kɨ̀ kwérɔ̄ ŋkabɔ́ fīì lòò.
Suh P₂ take money that year
'Suh took money last year.'

b. Kāā Sùù kɨ̀ wā'á ŋkábɔ́ fīì lòò kwérɔ́.
Neg Suh P₂ Neg money that year take
'Suh did not take money last year.'

1.1.4 The Remote past tense (P_3)

The remote past tense marked by *l'ỳN* is used to describe actions that took place in the distant past. The negative marker for this tense is *kāā...wā'ā*.

(17) a. Mbìŋ   lèn   lóó.
          rain P_3 fall
          'It rained (sometime ago).'

      b. Kāā mbìŋ   léŋ   wā'á lóò.
          Neg rain P_3 Neg fall
          'It did not rain (sometime ago).'

(18) a. Bó   lén   yē'ē   ndá.
          they P_3 sweep   house
          'They swept the house.'

      b. Kāā bó   léŋ   wā'á ndá   yē'è.
          Neg they P_3 Neg house   sweep
          'They did not sweep the house.'

1.1.5 The future tenses

Four future tenses are attested in Bafut. These include the simple future (F_0), the today future (F_1), the tomorrow future (F_2) and the remote future (F_3). Generally, the future is marked by a common morpheme *kā*. However, to distinguish F_0 from F_1, F_2 and F_3, the latter cases are further marked with the morphemes *lî*, *lŏ* and *yǐ* respectively. The future negative construction behaves in the same way as we have seen for the past tenses. The negative morpheme is equally *kāā...wā'ā*.

(19) a. Nìnòò kā   tá.
          sun F_0 shine
          'The sun will shine.'

      b. Kāā nìnòò kā   wā'á tá.
          Neg sun F_0 Neg shine
          'The sun will not shine.'

(20) a. Bì   kálí   káŋ   mbwè.
          Bih F_1 fry   fish
          'Bih will fry fish (today).'

      b. Kāā Bì   kálɨ   wā'à mbwè   káŋ.
          Neg Bih F_1 Neg fish   fry
          'Bih will not fry fish today.'

(21) a. Bī'ō   kálō   ghēē   yóó.
          we(1+2) F_2 go   tomorrow
          'We will go tomorrow.'

b. Kāā bī'ō   kálō wā'ā yɔ́ɔ́   ghēē.
   Neg we(1+2) F$_2$ Neg tomorrow go
   'We will not go tomorrow.'

(22) a. Mbɨŋ   káyī lóó.
        rain   F$_3$ fall
        'It shall rain sometime in future.'

   b. Kāā mbɨŋ   káyī wā'á lóō.
      Neg rain   F$_3$ Neg fall
      'It will not rain in future or It shall never rain in future.'

Thus far, it is observed that two discontinuous morphemes; *kāā...sɨ̀* and *kāā wā'ā* are employed to mark negation in the perfective aspect. In the following paragraphs, we will realise that a similar situation obtains in the imperfective aspect. The only significant difference comes from tonal changes that occur mostly on the postsubject Neg particle and at times on the verb.

1.1.6 The present Imperfective tense (Impf T$_0$)

The Neg morpheme for the present progressive tense is *kāā...sɨ̂*. Morphologically, this is identical to the Neg morpheme of the simple present (T$_0$) and immediate past (P$_0$) tenses. However, we realise that, whereas the postsubject Neg particle of the T$_0$ and P$_0$ bears a HL tone in the UR which in most cases is realised as L in the SR, that of the Impf T$_0$ bears a HLH UR tone which in a majority of cases is realised as H in the SR.

(23) a. Mbɨŋ   lóó.
        rain   fall +Impf
        'It is raining.'

   b. Kāā mbɨŋ   sɨ́ lóó.
      Neg rain   Neg fall+Impf
      'It is not raining.'

(24) a. Sùù sàŋə̄   tìtá.
        Suh dry+Impf pepper
        'Suh is drying pepper'

   b. Kāā sùù sɨ́ tìtá   sáŋə́.
      Neg Suh Neg pepper dry+Impf
      'Suh is not drying pepper.'

(25) a. Mə́ tóŋə́   kɔ̄'ɔ̄.
        I   dig+Impf latrine
        'I am digging a latrine.'

  b. Kāā mɜ̀ sí kɔ́ɔ̀ tɔ́nɔ́.
     Neg I   Neg latrine dig+Impf
     'I am not digging a latrine.'

1.1.7 The past imperfective tenses (Impf P.)

The negative morpheme in the imperfective past tense is identical to that in the perfective past tense.

1.1.7.1 Neg Impf P₁

The Impf P_1 tense marker is *lɨN* which is very similar to that of the perfective P_1. The difference between the two forms is brought about by tone. Whereas the perfective P_1 tense marker bears a level (H) tone (cf. 1.1.2. The Today Past Tense (P_1)), that of the imperfective bears a contour (HL) tone. However, this difference has no effect on the negative morpheme for in both cases, the form and the behaviour are the same.

(26) a. Mbɨŋ   lîn   lóó.
          rain P_1+Impf fall
          'It was raining (today).'

      b. Kāā mbɨŋ   lîŋ   wā'á lóó.
          Neg rain P_1+Impf Neg   fall
          'It was not raining (today).'

      c. Kāā mbɨŋ   líŋ   wā'á lóó.
          Neg rain P_1 Neg   fall
          'It did not rain (today).'

(27) a. Sùù lîŋ   kó   nó.
          Suh P_1+Impf catch   snake
          'Suh was killing a snake (today).'

      b. Kāā sùù lîŋ   wā'á nó   kō.
          Neg Suh P_1+Impf Neg   snake catch
          'Suh was not killing a snake.'

      c. Kāā sùù líŋ   wā'á nó   kó.
          Neg Suh P_1+Impf Neg   snake catch
          'Suh did not kill a snake (today).'

1.1.7.2 Neg Impf P₂

With P_2 and P_3, the imperfective, unlike in the case of P_1, is morphologically marked. This imperfective marker is *sɨ* and is usually positioned immediately after the tense marker. It should be noted that this morpheme is different from the T_0, P_0 postsubject Neg particle *(sɨ)* which bears a low tone. These two morphemes are mutually exclusive, i.e. they never co-occur in the same utterance. The following sentences illustrate the behaviour of the Neg morpheme in imperfective P$_2$ utterances.

(28) a. Mbɨ̀ŋ   kɨ̀ sɨ́   lóó   yɔ́ɔ́.
       Rain   P$_2$ Impf fall   yesterday
       'It was raining yesterday.'

     b. Kāā mbɨ̀ŋ   kɨ̀ sɨ́   wā'á lóō.
       Neg rain   P$_2$ Impf Neg fall
       'It was not raining (yesterday).'

(29) a. Máŋká' kɨ̀ sɨ́   lɔ́   mbwē   ŋgyà.
       Manka P$_2$ Impf bait fish   week
       'Manka was fishing last week.'

     b. Kāā Máŋká' kɨ̀ sɨ́   wā'á mbwē   lɔ́.
       Neg Manka P$_2$ Impf Neg fish   bait
       'Manka was not fishing (last week).'

(30) a. Sùù   kɨ̀ sɨ́   kó   nó.
       Suh   P$_2$ Impf catch   snake
       'Suh was killing a snake (yesterday).'

     b. Kāā Sùù   kɨ̀ sɨ́   wā'á nó   kó.
       Neg Suh P$_2$ Impf Neg snake   catch
       'Suh was not killing a snake (yesterday)'

1.1.7.3 Neg Impf P$_3$

(31) a. Mbɨ̀ŋ   lé sɨ́   lōō fíí   lòò.
       Rain   P$_3$ Impf fall that year
       'It was/used to rain(ing) last year.'

     b. Kāā mbɨ̀ŋ   lé sɨ́   wā'á lóō.
       Neg rain   P$_3$ Impf Neg fall
       'It never used to/was not rain(ing).'

(32) a. Maŋká' lé sɨ́   lɔ́   mbwè.
       Manka P$_3$ Impf bait fish
       'Manka was fishing/used to fish.'

     b. Kāā Máŋká' lé sɨ́   wā'à mbwè   lɔ́.
       Neg Manka P$_1$ Impf Neg fish   bait
       'Manka was not fishing/never used to fish.'

(33) a. Sùù   lé sɨ́   kó   nó.
       Suh   P$_3$ Impf catch   snake
       'Suh was killing a snake/used to kill snakes.'

b. Kāā Sùù lɛ́ sɨ́   wā'á nó   kó.
   Neg Suh P_3 Impf Neg snake catch
   'Suh was not killing a snake/never used to...'

1.1.8 The imperfective future tenses

The imperfective future is marked by the morpheme *kɨ̂* which in the sentence structure is placed immediately after the future tense markers /kâ/ (F_0), /kálɨ̂/ (F_1), /kálŏ/ (F_2) and /káyɨ̌/ (F_3). The discontinuous morpheme *kāā... wā'ā* is employed to mark negation in the imperfective future. This morpheme is similar to that which marks negation in the perfective future. However, in the negative sentences, the imperfective marker changes from /kɨ̂/ to /kàN/. To account for this change, we postulate an underlying morpheme /kɨ̂àN/ for the negative imperfective future. This morpheme is then realised in the SR as [kàN] after the application of a vowel elision rule followed by a tone simplification rule. This morpheme is often separated from the tense marker by the Neg particle *wā'ā* as the examples below show.

1.1.8.1 The negative Impf F_0

(34) a. Mbɨ̀ŋ   ká   kɨ́   lóó.
         rain F_0 Impf fall
         'It will be raining.'

      b. Kāā mbɨ̀ŋ ká   wā'à kàn   lōō.
         Neg rain F_0 Neg   Impf+Neg   fall
         'It will not be raining.'

(35) a. Ambɛ ká   kɨ́   tá   míyáŋgō.
         Ambe F_0 Impf kick   ball
         'Ambe will be kicking the ball.'

      b. Kāā Ambɛ ká   wā'á míyáŋgó kán   tá.
         Neg Ambe F_0 Neg   ball   Impf+Neg kick
         'Ambe will not be kicking a ball.'

1.1.8.2 The negative Impf F_1

(36) a. Mfɨ́'ɨ́ kálɨ́ kɨ́   kó.
         Cold F_1 Impf catch
         'It will be cold (later today).'

      b. Kāā mfɨ́'ɨ́ kálɨ́ wā'à kàŋ   kó.
         Neg cold F_1 Neg   Impf+Neg   catch
         'It will not be cold.'

(37) a. Ngwìn kálɨ kɨ bā'ā ŋkyè.
   Ngwin F₁ Impf weave basket
   'Ngwin will be weaving a basket.'

 b. Kāā Ngwìn kálɨ wā'à ŋkyè kám bá'á.
   Neg Ngwin F₁ Neg basket Impf+Neg weave
   'Ngwin will not be weaving a basket.'

1.1.8.3 The negative Impf F₂

(38) a. Mfí'í kálō kɨ ko.
   Cold F₂ Impf catch
   'It will be cold (tomorrow/next week/next year).'

 b. Kāā mfí'í kálō wā'à kàŋ kó.
   Neg cold F₂ Neg Impf+Neg catch
   'It will not be cold.'

(39) a. Ambē kálō kɨ tá míyáŋgō.
   Ambe F₂ Impf kick ball
   'Ambe will be kicking a ball.'

 b. Kā mbē kálō wā'à míyáŋgō kán tá.
   Neg Ambe F₂ Neg ball Impf+Neg kick.
   'Ambe will not be kicking a ball.'

1.1.8.4 The negative Impf F₃

(40) a. Mfí'í káyī kɨ kó fīī ŋgú'ú.
   Cold F₃ Impf catch that decade
   'It will be cold some decades to come.'

 b. Kāā mfí'í káyī wā'à kàn kó.
   Neg cold F₃ Neg Impf+Neg catch
   'It will not be cold.'

(41) a. Àmbē káyī kɨ tá míyáŋgō.
   Ambe F₃ Impf kick ball
   'Ambe will be kicking a ball.'

 b. Kāā mbē káyī wā'á míyáŋgō kán tá.
   Neg Ambe F₃ Neg ball Impf+Neg kick
   'Ambe will not be kicking a ball.'

From the foregoing discussion on negation in the declarative mood, several phenomena have surfaced. We have noticed in the first place that the Neg marker in the declarative mood is a discontinuous morpheme separated by the subject. This morpheme behaves in a way similar to that in French. In French, the Neg particle is emphasized and reinforced by the addition of a further particle in the sentence thereby forming a pair of linked negatives. The French original Neg particle, as Payne (1985:224) observes, is the preverbal *ne* which is reinforced by the postverbal *pas*. Evidence in support of the claim that the French basic Neg particle is *ne* which has been reinforced by *pas* or *point* comes from the fact that in certain negative utterances, we have only *ne*:

(42) Je ne saurais   dire.
      I   Neg know/Imperfect tell
      'I will not be able to say.'

In Bafut, the basic Neg marker seems to be the postsubject particle *sɨ* or *sí* or *wā'ā* since one of these is obligatory in any negative utterance while the presubject particle simply reinforces the postsubject particle since its presence in a negative utterance is optional as seen in the sentences below:

(43) a. Kāā mbɨ̀ŋ   ká   wā'ā lóō.
          Neg rain F_0 Neg   fall
          'It will not rain.'
or   b. Mbɨ̀ŋ ká   wā'ā lóō.
          rain F_0 Neg   fall
          'It will not rain.'

Bafut however differs from French here in that the French discontinuous Neg morpheme is separated by the verb while that in Bafut is separated by the subject (noun or pronoun).

Segmentally, the form of the Bafut presubject Neg particle remains constant whatever the tense or aspect. On the other hand, the form of the postsubject particle varies with tense and aspect as seen in the examples above.

We also notice that in negative utterances where tense is morphologically marked such as in P_{1-3} and F_{0-3}, the postsubject Neg particle is placed immediately after the tense marker and not after the subject.

In a majority of cases, we have observed that the Neg morpheme provokes a syntactic re-ordering of the sentence elements. This is evident in sentences with an object where the verb is usually moved to sentence final position.

(44) a. Sùù kɨ̀ kó   mbà.
          Suh P_2 catch animal
          'Suh killed an animal.'
      b. Kāā Sùù kɨ̀ wā'à mbà   kō.
          Neg Suh P_2 Neg   animal catch
          'Suh did not kill an animal.'

This movement of the verb to sentence final position is very similar to what obtains in Kru (Hyman 1975:125) where the SVO order in a majority of sentences is modified to SOV. With the imperfective future in Bafut, in addition to syntactic changes, the Neg morpheme also provokes some morphological changes. The Neg morpheme in this mood usually conditions both the form and the position of the future imperfective marker. This future imperfective marker has the singular behaviour of exhibiting two forms: One for affirmative cases /kî/ and the other for negative cases /kîàN/ realised as [kàN]. The latter is usually moved along with the verb stem to sentence final position.

1.2 The imperative mood (Imp)

The imperative mood in Bafut is marked by the morpheme *káN* usually positioned at sentence initial position. This morpheme is different from *kàN* which marks the Impf future in negative sentences in two respects, namely:

- The imperative *káN* can only occur at sentence initial position while the Neg imperfective *kàN* is usually positioned sentence medially (between the object and the verb).
- The Neg imperfective *kàN* is derived from an underlying form /kîàN/ which is usually subjected to vowel elision and tone simplification to yield the SR [kàN]. On the other hand, the imperative [káN] is derived from an identical underlying form.

Utterances in the imperative mood are negated by the use of a Neg morpheme; *tsùú* which is neither discontinuous nor variable as in previous cases where one of the particles of the discontinuous morpheme varies depending on tense and aspect. Mfonyam (1988) is of the opinion that the imperfective imperative negative construction is marked by the discontinuous morpheme *tsùú...kî*. We will prefer to treat the particle *kî* as an aspectual marker thus maintaining the view that the imperative negative construction is marked by a unique morpheme: *tsùú*. The form *kî* is treated as an aspectual marker because, as earlier observed under 1.1.8, the Impf future is marked by the aspectual marker *kî* and as will be seen in the examples that follow, this morpheme is attested only in sentences that denote continuity or habituality.

(45) a. Fá   ŋkī   wá.
          give water that
          'Give that water.'

b. Tsùū ŋkī   wá   fá.
Neg water   that give
'Do not give that water.'

(46) a. Kám fá   ŋkī   wá.
Impf give water   that
'Give that water (continuously).'

b. Tsùū ŋkì   wá   kí   fá.
Neg water   that Impf give
'Do not give that water (continuously).'

(47) a. Tá   míyáŋgō   wá.
kick ball   that
'Kick that ball.'

b. Tsùū míyáŋgō   wá   tá.
Neg ball   that kick
'Do not kick that ball.'

(48) a. Kán tá   míyáŋgō   wá.
Impf kick ball   that
'Kick that ball (continuously).'

b. Tsùū míyáŋgō   wá   kí   tá.
Neg ball   that Impf kick
'Do not kick that ball (continuously).'

Similar to previous cases, the negative morpheme in imperative utterances provokes a change in the syntactic order of the sentence elements; the verb root in perfective sentences is moved to sentence final position. In imperfective future utterances, the verb stem is moved along with the aspectual (Impf) marker to this same position.

1.3 The conditional mood

Up to this point, we have noticed that with both the imperative and declarative moods, a negative particle is often sentence initial. In the case of the conditional mood, the Neg morpheme behaves rather differently. The Neg morpheme that pertains to the conditional mood is *túú* and is usually positioned after the tense marker in cases where tense is morphologically marked and after the subject in sentences where tenses is not morphologically marked.

(49) a. Mbìŋ   ká   lóó.
rain   F$_0$ fall
'It will rain.'

(61) a. Sùū ghá'sɔ́ nzhī   fāà.
      Suh often come   here
      'Suh often comes here.'

    b. Kāā Sùù sɨ́   ghá'sɔ́ nzhì   fāà.
      Neg Suh Neg often   come   here
      'Suh does not often come here.'

(62) a. Mə̀ kɨ tú'ú ŋkì   dígítsû.
      I P_2 carry water   somewhere
      'I fetched water somewhere.'

    b. Kāā mə̀ kì wā'ā ŋkì   dígítsū   tū'ū.
      Neg I P_2 Neg water   somewhere   carry
      'I did not fetch water anywhere.'
      (I fetched water nowhere.)

(63) a. Ngwín wāŋsə̀   ŋkwì.
      Ngwin quick+Impf   grow
      'Ngwin is growing very quickly.'

    b. Kāā Ngwìn sɨ́ wàŋsɔ́ ŋkwì.
      Neg Ngwin Neg quick   grow
      'Ngwin is not growing very quickly.'

A concept such as never will be expressed simply by the same discontinuous neg. morpheme followed by the action, quality or state being negated:

(64) Kāā sùù sɨ́ ŋkì   tū?ū.
     Neg Suh Neg water   carry
     Suh never fetches water.

Notice that this is identical with negation in the present imperfective tense (cf. 1.1.6. The Present Imperfective (Tense Impf T_0)). It is only the context that differentiates one from the other.

2.4 Negation and subordinate clauses (negative transport)

In many languages, as Payne (1985:240) observes, the devices which are used for negating subordinate clauses are different from those used in main clauses. In Bafut, such a distinction is not valid, for in both clause types the Neg morpheme used in standard negation could be used. One striking observation in Bafut in relation to negation in main vs subordinate clauses is neg-raising, i.e. the Neg morpheme in the subordinate clause can be raised into the main clause with the original meaning retained. The main clause verbs that permit a Neg morpheme movement from the subordinate clause are intransitive verbs that reflect a mental state. In the examples that follow, the a. sentences are unnegated, the b. sentences have the Neg morpheme in the subordinate clause while the c. sentences have it in the main clause.

(65) a. Mə̀ wā'tə́ mə́ Sùù kálō zhì.
          I   think   that Suh F_2 come
          'I think Suh will come.'

      b. Mə̀ wā'tə̄ mə́ kāā Sùù kālō wā'à zhì.
          I   think   that Neg Suh F_2 Neg come
          'I think Suh will not come.'

      c. Kāā mə̀ sí wā'tə mə́ Sùù kálό zhì.
          Neg I   Neg think that Suh F_2 come
          'I don't think Suh will come.'

(66) a. Sùù bīī mə́ Bì kálō kwō.
          Suh believe that Bih F_2 die
          'Suh believes Bih will die.'

      b. Sùù bīī mə́ kāā Bì kálō wā'ā kwō.
          Suh believe that Neg Bih F_2 Neg die
          'Suh believes Bih will not die.'

      c. Kāā Sùù Sí bīī mə́ Bì kálō kwō.
          Neg Suh Neg believe that Bih F_2 die
          'Suh does not believe Bih will die.'

(67) a. Ngwín kɔ̄ŋ mə́ Sùù kó nsə́ə́.
          Ngwin like that Suh catch elephant
          'Ngwin likes Suh to kill an elephant.'

      b. Ngwín kɔ̄ŋ mə́ kāā Sùù wā'ā nsə̄ə̄ kō.
          Ngwin like that Neg Suh Neg elephant catch
          '?Ngwin likes Suh not to kill an elephant.'

      c. Kāā Ngwìn sí kɔ̄ŋ mə́ Sùù kō nsə́ə́.
          Neg Ngwin Neg like that Suh catch elephant
          'Ngwin doesn't like Suh to kill an elephant.'

We observe that when the Neg morpheme is moved into the main clause, its form changes from *kāā...wā'ā* to *kāā...sî*. As noticed in the previous cases, the presence of the Neg morpheme also provokes a movement of the verb root from medial to sentence final position.

2.5 The negative existential

By the negative existential, we generally mean the negation of utterances
which denote the existence of something or somebody. Negation in such
phrases is in many respects similar to that in the cases discussed thus far.
Here we equally have a discontinuous Neg morpheme separated by the
subject whose existence is being refuted. The postsubject Neg particle is
usually *sì* which behaves in a way similar to the other postsubject particles
discussed so far.

(68) a. ŋkì   tsí   ghū.
        water   be   there
        'There is water.'

     b. Kāā   ŋkì   sì   ghū   tsí.
        Neg   water Neg there be
        'There is no water.'

(69) a. Sùù   tsí   ghū.
        Suh   be   there
        'Suh is there.'

     b. Kāā   Sùù   sì   ghú   tsī.
        Neg   Suh   Neg there be
        'Suh is not there.'

(70) a. Nwì   tsì   ghū.
        God   be   there
        'God exists.'

     b. Kāā   Nwì   sì   ghú   tsī.
        Neg   God   Neg there stay.
        'There is no God/God does not exist.'

Again, we notice that the Neg morpheme in the above utterances also
provokes a movement of the verb stem to sentence final position.

3 Conclusion

The aim of this paper has been to discuss the phenomenon of negation in
Bafut. It has revealed that standard negation in the language is in most cases
marked by a discontinuous Neg morpheme usually separated by the subject
of the utterance. The form of this Neg morpheme varies depending on the
aspect and mood but not tense. The presubject Neg particle is usually sen-

tence initial while the postsubject particle is normally positioned immediately after the subject or immediately after tense or aspectual markers. In a very limited number of cases, the Neg morpheme is not discontinuous. This is true of the imperative and conditional moods.

The paper also reveals that the negative morpheme usually provokes a syntactic re-ordering of sentence elements and even morphological changes in the case of the future Imperfective marker. Concerning the syntactic re-ordering of sentence elements, it is always the verb which moves to sentence final position, usually without the tense and aspect markers except in the case of the imperfective future where the imperfective marker changes its form and moves along with the verb stem to sentence final position. This syntactic re-ordering of the sentence elements however has no bearing on the semantic structure and interpretation of any sentence.

Tone-related processes in our discussion concern tonal modifications in specific environments. It was noticed that in the language, both register and contour tones are usually modified in predictable phonetic environments. However, tone per se does not play any significant role in negation in Bafut.

Finally, the paper reveals that Bafut makes use of only sentential negation. This probably explains why units like quantifiers and adverbials in Bafut can not be negated within the scope of constituent or non-sentential negation; a phenomenon which is fairly common in many languages of the world.

Table 1. Summary chart of negators and their distribution

Context	Negator	Distribution	Morphological/syntactic changes
Present and Immediate Past	*kāā...sɨ*	*kāā*: Presubject *sɨ*: Postsubject	(i) *mə* (P_0 tense marker) deletes (ii) Verb moves to sentence final position
Other Past tenses and Future tenses	*kāā...wā'ā*	*kāā*: presubject *wā'ā*: post-tense morpheme.	Verb moves to sentence final position
Present Imperfective	*kāā...sɨ́*	*kāā*: presubject *sɨ́*: postsubject	Verb moves to sentence final position
Past Imperfective	*kāā...wā'ā*	*kāā*: presubject *wā'ā*: Post Tense Aspect marker	Verb moves to sentence final position
Future Imperfective	*kāā...wā'ā*	*kāā*: Presubject *wā'ā*: Post Tense morpheme	Verb moves to sentence final position
Imperative mood	*tsùú*	sentence initial	Verb moves to sentence final position

Context	Negator	Distribution	Morphological/syntactic changes
Conditional mood	*túú*	Post Tense morpheme	(i) F_2, tense morpheme takes up N (ii) In past events, conditional morpheme is optional
Focus Constructions	*kāā...sɨ́*	*kāā*: Prefocused element (subject/object) *sɨ́*: Post focused element (subject/object)	Insertion of existential be after focused subject or object
	kāā...wā'ā	*kāā*: Presubject *wā'ā*: Post Tense Marker	None
Quantifier Negation	*kāā...wā'ā*	*kāā*: Pre-Quantifier *wā'ā*: Post Tense/Aspect	Verb moves to sentence final position
Adverbial Negation	*kāā...sɨ́*	*kāā*: Presubject *sɨ́*: Post Tense/Aspect	Verb moves to sentence final position
Main Clauses	*kāā...sɨ́*	*kāā*: Presubject *sɨ́*: Post subject	None
Subordinate Clauses	*kāā...wā'ā*	*kāā*: Presubject *wā'ā*: Post Tense/Aspect	Verb moves to sentence final position
Negative Existential	*kāā...sɨ́*	*kāā*: Presubject *sɨ́*: Post subject	Existentials *ghu* 'there' and *tsi* 'stay' switch positions

Abbreviations

Neg	Negative Particle/Negator		Sing	Singular form
T_0	Present tense		UR	Underlying representation
P_0	Immediate past tense		SR	Surface representation
P_1	Today past tense		L	Low tone
P_2	Yesterday past tense		H	High tone
P_3	Remote past tense		PR	Phonological Rule
ø	Zero morpheme		Foc	Focus
F_0	Simple future tense		Imp	Imperative
F_1	Today future tense		PS	Phrase structure
F_2	Tomorrow future tense		NP	Noun phrase
F_3	Remote future tense		Impf	Imperfective (Aspect)

Notes

* This work was sponsored in part by the University of Yaounde Research Grant No. L87001.

1. For a more detailed analysis of tense in Bafut, see Mfonyam (1988).

References

Hyman, L.M. (1975). *Phonology: theory and analysis*. Holt, Rinehard and Winston.
Klima, E.S. (1964). 'Negation in English.' In: J.J. Katz and J.A. Fodor (eds), *The structure of language*. Englewood Cliffs, N.J. Prentice-Hall, Inc.
Mfonyam, J.N. (1988). *Tone in orthography: the case of Bafut and related languages*. Doctoral Dissertation. Yaounde.
Payne, J.R. (1985). 'Negation.' In: T. Shopen (ed.), *Language typology and syntactic description*, Vol. I. (Clause Structure), 197-242. Cambridge: Cambridge University Press.

Berbice Dutch

Sylvia Kouwenberg

0 Introduction[1]

Until 1975 it was assumed that Dutch colonization of Caribbean territories had been different from English or French colonization in that it had not given rise to the development of creoles lexically based on the colonial language. Thus, while in (former) British and French colonies, English- and French-lexicon creoles are spoken, the various creole languages of Surinam (former Dutch Guiana) are lexically related to English and Portuguese, while in the Netherlands Antilles we find a creole which is lexically related to Portuguese/Spanish in the leeward islands, and an English semi-creole in the windward islands. A Dutch-lexicon creole Negerhollands, now extinct, was at one time the vernacular of St. Thomas, St. John and St. Croix (the US Virgin Islands), but this was never a Dutch colony. In 1975 however, Dr Ian Robertson discovered that Dutch-lexicon creoles had been the vernaculars of the former Dutch colonies Berbice and Essequibo. These languages, which he named Berbice Dutch and Skepi Dutch, respectively, had gone into oblivion after the Berbice and Essequibo became part of British Guiana (now Guyana), and the communities in which they were spoken became relatively isolated. Guyanese Creole (GC), a cover-term for a continuum of varieties ranging from 'deep' creole (lexically related to English) to standard Guyanese English, is now the vernacular of Guyana. Skepi Dutch is extinct, and Berbice Dutch is rapidly dying out. (For a comparative discussion of the two languages, see Robertson 1989.)

The following description of Berbice Dutch (BD) negation is based on fieldwork with ten native speakers of the language, carried out between 1986 and 1990.[2] All speakers are bilingual in BD and GC, and all are GC-dominant. Until my arrival and frequent visits, they had not spoken BD on a regular basis for some 40 years. Not surprising then, the process of language death has affected their competence to a greater or lesser extent. As a result, a description of BD negation is either a description of a theoretical construct which exists for no single speaker, or a description of a system in decay, where the extent of attrition differs for different speakers. In other words: we either describe BD negation as it may have been in its 'pure' form, i.e. its pre-English contact form, or we describe contemporary BD negation as it is used by individual speakers. The solution chosen here for this descriptive paradox is to do both: we will first describe the BD pre-English contact system of negation as it can be reconstructed from contemporary BD (section 1). Following that we will discuss the extent to which GC influence and the effects of language death have proceeded into the negation system of individual speakers (section 2). In section 3, we will briefly discuss the provenance of the items involved in BD negation.

Transcription of BD examples is phonemicized and follows IPA guidelines.[3] A free translation into standard English follows. Where relevant, the findspot is indicated in square brackets; it consists of the initials of the speaker, date of recording, and page or unit of transcription in square brackets. If the example was elicited rather than produced spontaneously, this is indicated by ! in the find-spot.

1 Berbice Dutch negation: a reconstruction

The different ways in which negation can be expressed in BD are illustrated in (1)-(4) below. In all cases, the sentence-final negator *ka(nɛ)* appears. The first example is a simple case of sentence-final negation; besides *kanɛ* no other negators appear. This type of negation will be referred to as *standard negation*.

(1)   O   habu bwa   *kanɛ*.
       3Sg   have leg   Neg
       'It doesn't have legs.' [AC 090488:34]

In addition to the sentence-final negator, BD has a preverbal negator which appears with the sentence-final negator in the resultative construction, as in (2). This construction will be referred to as the *negative resultative*.

(2)   Titi   ori   kumtɛ   en   wa   noko   la   noko   *kanɛ*.
       time   3Sg   come-PF   3Pl   Past   not:Result   reach yet   Neg
       'When he came they hadn't arrived yet.' [BB 160488:p1]

A negative verb is used in (3), and a negative adverbial appears in (4). These types of negation will be referred to as *negative verb negation*, and *adverbial negation*, respectively.

(3)   En   *kanti*   lefu.. sautu   mingi   aŋa   *ka*.
       3Pl   cannot   live salt   water   Loc   Neg
       'They cannot live in salt water.' [AC 090488:30]

(4) ɛkɛ *noiti* hor en jefi dida *ka*.
1Sg never hear 3Pl eat that Neg
'I have never heard (that) they eat that.' [AC 090488:37]

These four types of negation are discussed separately below, following a discussion of the general properties of *ka(nɛ)*; for this purpose, examples of standard negation are used as much as possible.

1.1 General properties of negation

1.1.1 The distribution of *ka* and *kan*

The sentence-final negator appears as *kanɛ* or *ka*; I will refer to the first as the full form, to the latter as the reduced form. The reduced form appears much more frequently than the full form, in agreement with a general tendency to use reduced forms of grammatical morphemes. The relative frequency of the two forms is to some extent dependent on the speaker: AC and BB, for instance, tend to use non-reduced forms of grammatical morphemes more often than other speakers, which also means that *kanɛ* is more frequent in their speech than in that of others, although occurrences of *ka* still outnumber occurrences of *kanɛ*. AK, on the other hand, tends to use reduced forms as much as possible, and hardly ever uses *kanɛ*. The distribution of the two forms is independent of the nature of the main verb; nor is it the case that in different types of negative constructions, the one is more likely to appear than the other, except that again the reduced form is more frequent than the full form; nor is the full form an emphatic form. (5) and (6) illustrate the use of the reduced form and the full form with the same main verb.

(5) ɛk *suk* mu lasan eni ka.
1Sg want go leave 3Pl Neg
'I didn't want to leave them.' [AK 290488:p4]

(6) O *suku* nati ši bwa kanɛ.
3Sg want wet 3Poss foot Neg
'He doesn't want to wet his feet.' [AC 120488:5]

The negator never bears sentential stress. It is optionally encliticized on the preceding constituent; this applies especially to *ka*, as in the example below: [boka] results from encliticization of *ka* on *boki* 'money'.

(7) Ašə pamen kɛnau dɛn ju..ju kã krik di *boka*.
if:2Sg tell:one person:now then 2Sg..2Sg can get the money:Neg
'If you tell anybody then you, you can't get the money.' [AK 050390:p18]

1.1.2 The position of *ka* and *kan*
The position of the negator is invariant. There are two cases in which something can follow the negator:
(a) Sentential tags follow the negator. This is exemplified in (8), where the tag 'you know' appears following *ka*.

(8) En   kan   sɛtɛ daŋga ka   *ju*   *ni*.
     3Pl   can   stay there Neg   you   Know
     'They can't stay there you know.' [AH210390:9]

(b) A constituent which is moved to extraposed position follows the negator. Thus, in (9), the complement clause 'such things could happen' follows the negator rather than preceding it.

(9) ɛk   wa   noiti   nikə,   solok   bɛr   kɛk di   sa   hapn.
     1Sg   Past never   Know:Neg, such   story like this Irr happen
     'I never knew such things could happen.' [AK 010390:p10]

It is possible that extraposition serves to reduce processing problems which result if the distance between the negator and the negated main verb is too large. Note however that this is optional, as shown by the following example, where the presence of a constituent of similar complexity (*fi twa di boki wanga das to*) has not resulted in extraposition:

(10) A   kriki titi fi..   twa di   boki   waŋa das to   ka.
      3Sg   get   time for   put the money where Hab put:3Sg Neg
      'He didn't get time to put the money where (he) usually puts it.'[RT280186:46]

1.1.3 Aspectual distinctions
Perfective aspect, which qualifies the event/process described by the verb as having been completed, cannot appear in the scope of negation, which serves to deny completion. There are no such constraints on the co-occurrence of negation and other tense/mood/aspect markers[4]. Compare the following examples: in the first part of (11), *nimi* 'acquire knowledge' appears with PF marking (reduced to *nin* due to suffixation), while in the second it appears without in a negative sentence (reduced to *ni*). Similarly in (12), where *nimi* appears twice: once as negated matrix verb without PF (reduced to *ni*), once as affirmative embedded verb with PF.

(11) ɛkɛ   *ni*   hoseni..   *n:ímtɛ*   dida ka.
      1Sg   Know how:3Pl   Know-PF   that Neg
      'I don't know how they knew that.' [AH210390:29]

(12) ɛkɛ *nintɛk*   atɛtɛ   batɛk   *ni*   ɛk
     1Sg Know-PF:1Sg grandmother but:1Sg Know   1Sg

     awawa   ka.
     grandfather Neg
     'I knew my grandmother, but I didn't know my grandfather.' [HA 140788:p2]

As shown in (13), negation is incompatible with the perfective verb form
nimitɛ. We will return to the incompatibility of perfective aspect and negation in the discussion below.

(13) *ɛkɛ *nimtɛ*   dida ka.
     1Sg Know-PF   that Neg

1.1.4 The distribution of negatives
Negatives are not excluded from any positions that non-negatives can appear
in. While affirmative sentences can be conjoined/disjoined, so can negative
sentences, as in (14) and (15). (14) is an instance of adverbial negation: *noiti*
'never' appears, in combination with the negator *ka*. Scope of the negative
adverbial is over all conjoined constituents.

(14) Ašu wa   noiti   bu   an   druŋgu an   mono kɛk so   ka.
     if:2Sg Past never drink and drunk and sleep like so   Neg
     'If you had never drank and gotten drunk and slept like this.' [AK 190290:14]

(15) So   bi, ku   ar ju ku   ka,   enši ma ku.
     so(:3Sg) say, catch or 2Sg catch Neg, 1Pl Irr catch
     'So (he) said, whether you catch or you don't catch, we will catch.'
     [AC 120488:9]

In the following example, a negative appears as the object of a preposition
which may be followed by a clausal complement, *tutu* 'until'.

(16) An   di   man mutɛ daŋa, tutu   am.. a   fori   ka.
     and the man go-PF there, until ehm 3Sg not-be Neg
     'And the man went there when, ehm, he wasn't in.' [RT 280186:43]

Negatives may also appear as adverbial clauses. In (17), the negative is a
conditional clause introduced by *aši* 'if'.

(17) Aš kɛnɛ   wa   noko   mu.. maŋgi gau   fu   mo..
     if person Past not:Result go, run quick for go,

     helpo   ka, ...
     help:3Sg Neg, ...
     'If somebody hadn't gone, run quickly to help him,...' [AH 210390:35]

1.2 Four types of negation

1.2.1 Standard negation

There are no constraints on standard negation related to sentence type. In the following examples, standard negation negates a verbal sentence in (18), a copular sentence in (19), a sentence with an adjectival predicate in (20).

(18) O   tambla ka.
      3Sg   answer Neg
      'He doesn't answer.' [AC 120488:10]

(19) Domni wa   jɛnda   kan.
      pastor Past be:there   Neg
      'There was no pastor.' [BB 150190:9]

(20) Didap loi   ka.
      that-PL lazy Neg
      'Those aren't lazy.' [AK 010390:p11]

Negation is not blocked by movement of any kind. Thus, in (21), the negative sentence contains a front-focussed constituent (*aši da fi boki ar wat*). The negative in (22) is a passive construction.

(21) Aši   da   fi   boki   ar   wat,   ɛkɛ   nin   kanɛ.
      if   be   for   money   or   what,   1Sg   Know   Neg
      'If it is for money or what, I don't know.' [AC 090488:26]

(22) O   mja   moi   ka.
      3Sg   make   good Neg
      'it isn't well-made' [AK 260290:p12]

1.2.2 Resulative negation

The resulative construction describes a single occasion on which an event or process takes place (the affirmative resulative), or fails to take place (the negative resulative). In the affirmative resulative, the auxiliary *kon* precedes the verb which describes the event or process; this verb appears with the PF suffix. *Kon* does not occur as a main verb, nor does it behave like a main verb on certain tests: it cannot undergo predicate-cleft and cannot appear with aspectual suffixes. Its status as an auxiliary is further confirmed by assimilation phenomena: the final nasal consonant optionally assimilates to the place of articulation of the initial consonant of the following content verb. If preverbal tense/mood markers appear, these precede *kon*. The contrast between an affirmative resulative and a non-resulative affirmative construction is illustrated below. The affirmative resulative refers to a particular occasion on

which the mother beat the child, the non-resultative construction merely
asserts that the mother, on one or more occasions, beat the child.

(23) Di   mama   *kom*   bakutɛ di   toko.
      the   mother Result beat-PF the child
      'The mother beat the child (on this particular occasion).'

(23)' Di   mama   bakutɛ di   toko.
       the   mother beat-PF the child
       'The mother beat the child (on one or more occasions).'

In the negative resultative, the sentence-final negator *ka(nɛ)* appears, while
noko precedes the content verb. I assume that *noko* consist of *no:ko* [not:
Result], which can be further reduced to *nok*. It is preceded by the tense/
mood markers. Perfective aspect cannot appear in the negative resultative,
as in any negative construction. The contrast between the negative resultative and a standard negative is illustrated below: the negative resultative
refers to a particular occasion on which the mother did not beat the child,
the standard negative asserts that the mother never beats the child, on any
occasion.

(24) Di   jɛrma   *noko*   bak   ši   toko   ka.
      the   woman   not:Result beat 3Poss child Neg
      'The woman didn't beat her child (on this particular occasion).'
      [!AK 020490:p32]

(24)' O   bak   ši   tok:a.
       3Sg   beat 3Poss child:Neg
       'She doesn't beat her child (at any time).' [!AK 020490:p32]

Stative verbs and psychological verbs do not appear in the resultative construction. With such verbs, standard negation has to be used, as shown by
the unacceptability of (25)'.

(25) ɛkɛ   nimi   di   kɛnɛ   ka.
      1Sg   Know   the   person Neg
      'I don't know the person.'

(25)' *ɛkɛ   noko   nimi   di   kɛnɛ   ka.
       1Sg   not:Result Know   the   person Neg
       attempted reading: 'I didn't get to know the person.' [!AK 250190:p34]

If a word such as *moi*, which is ambiguous between a stative interpretation
'good', and a process interpretation 'become good', appears in a negative

resultative, it is interpreted as referring to a process, as shown by the following example.

(26) O   nok   moi noka.
     3Sg not:Result good yet:Neg
     'It hasn't ripened yet.' [!AK 220290:p18]

Resultative negation is not blocked by movement of any kind. Thus, passives can be negated in this way[5], as in (27)-(28).

(27) Di   toko noko   fɛndɛ ka.
     the child not:Result find Neg
     'The child wasn't found.' [!BB 180290:29]

(28) Di   hondo bugrafto   noko   buma   ka.
     the dog   bury-PF:3Sg   not:Result throw-away Neg
     'The dog was buried, it wasn't thrown away.' [!BB 190190:p7]

Since passives tend to be interpreted as resultative states, resultative negation is more easily accepted with passives than standard negation. For instance, the standard negative in (29) refers not to a specific event, but rather to the general non-occurrence of an event: something like 'the boards are never sawn', which is judged ungrammatical. Resultative negation, as in (29)', has to be used instead.

(29) *Di plaŋgap   sagi ka.
      the board-PL   saw Neg
      attempted reading: 'The boards haven't been sawn.' [!AK 010390:p12]

(29)' Di plaŋgap   noko   sagi ka.
      the board-PL   not:Result saw Neg
      'The boards haven't been sawn.' [!AK 010390:p12]

1.2.3 Negative verb negation
BD has a negative existential/locative copula *furi* 'not be there, not exist' and a negative modal verb *kantɛ / kanti / kantimi* 'cannot, not be able'. They appear in combination with the sentence-final negator. *Furi* is the negative counterpart of *jɛn* 'be there, exist', which is neutral with respect to negation. Like it, it optionally takes a dummy complement *da* 'there', in which case it is always reduced to *furda*. (Note that *da* does not exist independent of *jɛn* or *furi*.) The dummy complement appears irrespective of the presence or absence of a 'real' complement. An example of locative use of *furi* is given in (30), where it appears with the dummy complement *da*.

(30) Namblo *forda*,   namblo mutɛ.
     horse   not-be:there, horse   go-PF
     'The horse isn't there, the horse has gone.' [HH lukuba1:p8]

Some examples of existential use of *furi* follow. It appears with a dummy complement in (31), with an adjectival complement in (32).

(31) Helpu   *forda*   ka.
     help   not-be:there Neg
     'There was no help.' [AK 220290:p14]

(32) O   *fori*   moi ka.
     3Sg not-be good Neg
     'It isn't nice.' (i.e. her hair isn't nicely done) [HA 140788:p25]

It needs to be noted that *furi* differs from *jɛn* in that it cannot appear with a verbal complement. Thus, as shown below, the negation of affirmative *en jɛnda korja* is the standard negative *eni kori ka*.

(33) a. En   jɛnda   korja.
       3Pl be:there   work-Ipf
       'They are working.' [!AK 290390:p13]

    b. *Eni furda   kori ka.
       3Pl not-be:there work Neg
       'They are not working.'

    c. Eni kori ka.
       3Pl work Neg

The neutral form *jɛn* may also appear in negative contexts, as in the examples below. Some speakers, in particular AC, use *jɛn* more frequently than *furi* in negative contexts. Also, *habu* 'have' may be used with existential meaning (both in negative and non-negative contexts), as in (35).

(34) Arnold, o   *jɛnda*   wari   kanɛ.
     Arnold, 3Sg be:there house Neg
     'Arnold, he is not at home.' [AC 230288:16]

(35) *Ha* en   kɛn:au   ka.
     have one person:now Neg
     'Nobody is there now.' [HA 140788:p27]

Kantɛ/kanti/kamtimi 'cannot, not be able' are in competition with *timi* and *kan* 'can, be able' in negative contexts. There is no obvious semantic difference between the various forms. They are all used in contexts which pertain to physical (in)ability as well as other contexts. (36) is an example of the use of *kanti*, while (37) illustrates the use of *kan* in a negative context.

(36) M:usu kɛnapu   mutɛ   daŋ   fu   brɛkɛ   an   *kanti*
     many   person-PL go-PF   there   for   break   and   cannot

     brɛkɛ   kanɛ.
     break   Neg
     'Many people went there to break (it), and (they) cannot break (it).'
     [AC 260288:1]

(37) An   pabadi   self   *kan*   mjo..   arum   ababaka.
     and   God   self   can   make:3Sg   poor   anymore:Neg
     'And even God cannot make him poor anymore.' [HA 100390:16]

The interchangeability of the various forms is illustrated below:

(38) En   kɛnɛ   alen   *kanti*   / *kan* / *kantimi*   mu   huku   daŋga ka.
     one   person alone   cannot   / can / cannot   go   angle   there Neg
     'Nobody can go fish there alone' [!BB 090488:p6]

1.2.4 Adverbial negation and other negative words

The negative temporal adverb *noiti* 'never' appears immediately following the subject, i.e. it intervenes between the subject and the verbal complex. (40) shows that *noiti* may appear in a position between the preverbal Past marker and the verb. There are no similar examples by speakers other than AK, but there are a few other adverbs which may appear in this position, viz. *alwes* 'always' and *djas* 'just'.

(39) Jə   *noiti*   mu   daŋka?
     2Sg   never   go   there:Neg?
     'Did you never go there?' [HA 050488:17]

(40) Ix   wa   *noiti*   kop..   tei   fan   di   šapap   ka.
     1Pl   Past   never   buy   tea   from the   shop-Pl   Neg
     'We never bought tea from the shops.' [AK 090388:p8]

In the resultative construction, *noiti* precedes the negative resultative auxiliary complex:

(41) Dida   nju   plɛkɛ   waŋa   en   *noiti*   noko   la   ka.
     this:be   new   place   where   3Pl   never   not:Result   reach   Neg
     'This is a new place, where they have never gone before.' [AH 210390:30]

The adverb *ababa* 'anymore' appears only in negative contexts. It appears in VP-final position, immediately followed by *ka(nɛ)*, with which it forms one phonological word.

(42) Ka:n mu   daŋašikandi *baba*ga.
      can   go   there:side:side any-more:Neg
      '(I) can't go there any more.' [BC 120286:p10]

(43) O   sukwa   danš   *ababa*ka.
      3Sg want-Ipf dance   any-more:Neg
      'She doesn't want to dance any more.' [HH lukuba1:p8]

Inherently negative words in BD are *neks* 'nothing' (refers to possession) and *nimdali* 'gratis, without charge'. They occur in NP positions. *neks* requires the sentence-final negator.

(44) ɛkɛ   habu (en)   *neks*   ka.
      1Sg   have (one)   nothing Neg
      'I have nothing.' [!BB 120488:notes]

(45) O   ma   mja   di   gutu   fi   *nimdali*.
      3Sg Irr   make   the thing for gratis
      'He will do it free of charge.' [!AK 050490:p39]

I have come across two utterances by AK in which *sondro* 'without' is used with a clausal complement, and conveys a negative interpretation to its complement; an example follows:

(46) *Sondro* ju   plagjo   mja ju en   gut   ka.
      without   2Sg   trouble:3Sg do 2Sg one thing Neg
      'As long as you don't trouble it, it won't do you anything.' [AK 050390:p17]

1.3 Scope of negation

In the following sections we will be concerned with scope of negation and possible scope ambiguities. Problems of ambiguity may arise where indefinite NPs and other indefinite quantifier phrases appear in the scope of negation. Also, there is potential ambiguity where embedding is involved. We will first discuss indefinite quantifiers, and then turn to scope of negation over complex structures, viz. embedded clauses, and serial verb constructions.

1.3.1 Scope problems related to indefinite quantifier phrases

Indefinite NPs in a negative sentence tend to get a negative interpretation, irrespective of the position in the sentence, but this is not obligatory. (47)

248 Sylvia Kouwenberg

below for instance, is ambiguous for speakers. In the a. interpretation, negation has scope over the subject NP, which is interpreted to be indefinite and non-referential; in the b. interpretation, the quantifier has higher scope, and the subject NP is interpreted as indefinite but referential. Note that emphatic stress makes no difference: informants tended to stress *en* in both the a. and the b. case. The a. interpretation is preferred, however, and attested in spontaneous usage; the b. interpretation was not used spontaneously.

(47) *En fan eni* frustan   ka.
      one of 3Pl understand   Neg
      a. 'Not one of them understands.' [!BB 090488:p1]
      b. 'One of them doesn't understand.' [!AC 090488:p1]

Similarly, informants indicated that (48) is ambiguous between negation of the referentiality of the quantifier phrase *alma*, which appears in subject position, and predicate negation, and that (49) is ambiguous between negation of the referentiality of the indefinite subject NP *en kɛnɛ*, and predicate negation. Here too, there is a preference for the a. reading. Note that (49) is a negative resultative.

(48) *Alma (di kɛnap)*   nokum   ka.
      all (the   person-PL) not:Result:come Neg
      a. 'Not all (the people) came.'
      b. 'All (of the people) did not come.' (i.e. none came)
      [!AK 250190:p36, !AK&HA 270190:p29]

(49) *En kɛnɛ*   noko   kum   ka.
      one person not:Result come Neg
      a. 'Nobody came.'
      b. 'One person didn't come.'
      [!AK 250190:p36, !BB 180290:p30]

BD has no inherently negative quantifiers such as 'nothing', 'no one', etc. Therefore, there is no way to distinguish utterances such as 'nobody knew' and 'nobody did not know'. To express the latter proposition, an affirmative of the type 'everybody knew' has to be used.

I will adopt the term 'negative attraction' to refer to the fact that an indefinite quantifier phrase tends to get a negative interpretation in a negative sentence. Some examples of negative attraction from spontaneous language use follow in (50)-(55) below. These utterances are unambiguous because the interpretation in which negation does not have scope over the indefinite NP (i.e. the NOT interpretation, in which the indefinite NP is referential) is improbable in the context of these utterances.

An indefinite NP appears in the subject position in (50) and (51); the latter contains a negative verb.

(50) *En   kɛnɛ*   kan.. kapo   ka.
     one   person can   cut:3Sg Neg
     'Nobody can cut it (i.e. a certain tree) down.' [AH 210390:41]
     NOT: 'One person cannot cut it.'

(51) *En   kɛn   mɛr*   furda   ka.
     one   person more   not-be:there Neg
     'There is nobody else.' [AK 180190:25]
     NOT: 'One other person is not there.'

An indefinite NP appears in the object position of a verb in (52) and (53). Note that the indefinite NP in (52) is of considerable complexity. (53) illustrates negative attraction in a resultative construction.

(52) ɛk ma ha *en gut*   *moi fu prusinti ju*   *fortit*   *ju*   *mu* ka.
     1Sg Irr have one thing nice for present 2Sg before 2Sg go Neg
     'I will have nothing nice to give you before you go.' [AK 120788:p5]
     NOT: 'I will not have one (particular) thing to give you before you go.'

(53) Or   nok   gui   *en* *gutu*   daŋ   noko   ka.
     3Sg   not:Result   throw one thing   there yet   Neg
     'He hasn't thrown anything down there yet.' [HH lukuba2 p.4]
     NOT: 'He hasn't thrown one (particular) thing down there yet.'

Below, negative attraction is illustrated for the object of a preposition in (54), and for the locative complement of a verb in (55), respectively.

(54) Tut ju   drai wɛrɛ   ju   drai mɛt*en*   *gutu* ka.
     until 2Sg turn again   2Sg turn with:one thing Neg
     'When you return, you return with nothing.' [RT 280186:18]
     NOT: 'You don't return with one (particular) thing'

(55) Eni kum *en* *plɛkɛ*   ka.
     3Pl come one place   Neg
     'They come nowhere/they don't come anywhere.' [BB 120488:p3]
     NOT: 'They don't come to one (particular) place'

Occasionally we find a negative utterance containing an indefinite NP or quantifier phrase in which negative attraction does not apply. Thus, in (56), the indefinite subject *en* is interpreted as being referential; this is clear from the context of this utterance. Similarly, in (57), the subject quantifier phrase is referential.

(56)   *En*   ma   karɛkɛ   ka.
        one   Irr   be-enough:1Sg   Neg
        'One will not be enough for me.' [AT 190386:p8]
        NOT: 'Not one will be enough for me.'

(57)   *Almɛk*   *aka*   moi   babnaɣa,   so ɛk   suka   nun   alma.
        all:1Sg   tooth   good any-more:Neg,   so 1Sg   want-Ipf   pull   all
        'All of my teeth are no good any more, so I want to have all extracted.'
        [AK 030688:p2]

The following elicited example shows that indefinite NPs in object position may also be interpreted referentially. There are no such examples from spontaneous language use, however.

(58)   ɛkɛ   suk   *én*   ka,   ɛk   suk   mɛrɛ.
        1Sg   want   one   Neg,   1Sg   want   more
        'I don't want just one, I want more.' [!AK 250190:p36]

In contrast, negative attraction appears to be obligatory for quantifier phrases in object position. Thus, the interpretation in which *alma* is used referentially ('I have sold none') is impossible for (59).

(59)   ɛk   nok   furkop   *alma*   noka.
        1sg   not:Result   sell   all   yet:Neg
        'I haven't sold them all yet.' (i.e. 'I have sold some, but not all') [!AK 010390:
        p12]

Negative attraction appears to apply obligatorily to the quantifiers *idri* 'every' and *musu* 'many, much'. Some examples follow. Other quantifiers (*enen* 'some, a few' - literally 'one one', and *eni* 'any'), do not appear in negative contexts.

(60)   *Idri*   kɛnɛ   nokum   ka.
        every   person   not:Result:come   Neg
        a. 'Not every person came.' (i.e. many came, but not all)
        b. *'Every person didn't come.' (i.e. nobody came) [!BB 180290:p30]

(61)   Dakta   pantɛ   bi   o   mo   jefi   *musu*   sautu   ka.
        doctor   tell-PF   say   3Sg   must   eat   much   salt   Neg
        '(The) doctor said that she mustn't eat much salt.' [BB 260288:13]

1.3.2 Scope of negation over embedded clauses

In negated utterances which contain embedded clauses, there is a potential problem in determining whether the negator is main clause negator or embedded clause negator. Is a surface string of the form *I know who drink Neg* to be analysed as a. or b. below?

(62) I know who drink Neg.
   a. [I know [who drink] Neg] 'I don't know who drank it.'
   b. [I know [who drink Neg]] 'I know who didn't drink it.'

As it turns out, surface strings of this kind are usually disambiguated by the presence/absence of perfective aspect marking: as mentioned above, a perfective verb form cannot appear in the scope of negation. Thus, in (63), the main verb *nimi* 'acquire knowledge' is not marked for perfective aspect, while the embedded verb *bu* 'drink' is. Therefore, the main verb is within the scope of negation, while the embedded verb is not.

(63) ɛkɛ   nimi   wisa   buto   fama   ka.
      1Sg   Know   who:Focus   drink-PF:3Sg finish Neg
      'I don't know who emptied it.' [BB 160488:p5]

In (64) and (65) the reverse holds: the main verb (*nimi* 'acquire knowledge', and *pama* 'tell', respectively) carries perfective aspect and is therefore outside the scope of negation. Note that in both cases, the embedded clause is introduced by the verb *bi* 'say'.

(64) ɛkɛ   nintɛ   bi   en   ma   kumorko   ka.
      1Sg   Know-PF   say   3Pl   Irr   come:tomorrow Neg
      'I know they will not come tomorrow.' [!AK 250190:p35]

(65) O   pantɛk   bi   o   kom   ababaga.
      3Sg   tell-PF:1Sg say   3Sg   come   anymore:Neg
      'He told me that he isn't coming back anymore.' [BB 86]

From the incompatibility of PF with negation, it follows that ambiguity may arise only where both the matrix verb and the embedded verb do not carry PF aspect, and can both be interpreted as either negative or affirmative. Only stative verbs comply with these conditions. Informants' judgements confirm that there is ambiguity in that case, but only with respect to the interpretation of the embedded verb. Consider AK's judgement on (66), and BB's use of (67): the locative copula *jɛn* is contained in an adverbial clause inside the complement clause of *suku* 'want'. On one occasion, *jɛn* was interpreted as being affirmative (66), whereas on another, it was interpreted as being negated (67). However, in either case, the matrix verb *suku* is within the scope of negation.

(66) ɛkɛ   suku mu tito   jɛnda   ka.
      1Sg   want go   time:3Sg   be:there   Neg
      'I don't want to go when she's there.' [!AK 250190:p35]

(67) ɛkɛ   suku mu titi.. ori   jɛndəkə.
      1Sg   want go   time 3sg   be:there:Neg
      'I don't want to go when he is not there.' [BB 110190:7]

Note that the non-negated interpretation of (66) can be unambiguously expressed by moving the adverbial clause outside the domain of negation through extraposition, as in (66)', whereas the negated interpretation (as in (67) above) is more clearly expressed by use of the negative locative copula, as in (67)' below.

(66)' ɛkɛ   suku mu ka   tito   jɛnda.
       1Sg   want go   Neg   time:3Sg be:there
       'I don't want to go when she's there.' [!AK 250190:p35]

(67)' ɛkɛ   suku mu tito   fori   ka.
       1Sg   want go   time:3Sg   not-be   Neg
       'I don't want to go when she's not there.' [!AK 250190:p35]

Additional evidence that negation, in sentences in which a matrix verb is negated, also has scope over the embedded clause, comes from the use of indefinite NPs in embedded clauses: to these, negative attraction applies, i.e. an indefinite NP in an embedded clause gets a negative interpretation, as does an indefinite NP in a main clause. Consider the following examples, in which *en plɛkɛ* [one place] is contained in the object clause of *suku* 'want'; in both cases, the referentiality of the indefinite NP is negated.

(68) ɛk   suk   stup en   plɛk   ɛkalen   ka.
      1Sg want stop one place   1Sg:alone   Neg
      'I don't want to stay anywhere by myself.'
      NOT: 'I don't want to stay in one (particular) place alone.' [!AK 050490:p39]

(69) O   dasuk   iç   mu   en   plɛka.
      3Sg Hab:want   1Pl go   one place:Neg
      'He doesn't want us to go anywhere.' [HA 140788:p25]
      NOT: 'He doesn't want us to go to one (particular) place.'

Lastly, there is the following example of an embedded conjoined clause, where negation has scope both over the main clause and over one part of the conjoined constituent:

(70) Wɛl ɛkɛ ni aš ju ma laki ar ju ma laki ka.
well 1Sg Know if 2Sg Irr laugh or 2Sg Irr laugh Neg
'Well I don't know if you will laugh or you will not laugh.' [HH lukuba2:p5]

Example (70) must be assumed to contain two negators underlyingly:

(70)' əkə nimi [aši [ju ma laki] ar [ju ma laki ka]] ka]
1Sg Know if 2Sg Irr laugh or 2Sg Irr laugh Neg Neg

Additional evidence that negative operators appear in the embedded clause comes from the co-occurrence of standard negation in the main clause with resultative negation in the embedded clause in the following example:

(71) ɛkɛ ni hosiši noko kjant ka.
1Sg Know how:1Pl not:Result topple Neg
'I don't know how we didn't turn over.' (i.e. how this was prevented from happening) [BB 110788:11]

Still, only one negator surfaces. As shown below, two negators cannot surface adjacent to each other, as in (71)'; neither can extraposition of an embedded negated clause result in the surface realization of two negators, as in (67)":

(71)' *ɛkɛ ni hosiši noko kjant ka(nɛ) ka(nɛ).
1Sg Know how:1Pl not:Result topple Neg Neg

(67)" *ɛkɛ suku mu *ka* tito jɛnda ka.
1Sg want go Neg time:3Sg be:there Neg [!AK 250190:p35]

We may conclude that although there is evidence that an embedded clause is within the scope of negation, there is no evidence that it can be within the scope of negation to the exclusion of the main clause, unless the embedded clause is a tensed, subject-containing clause; this was illustrated in (64) and (65) above, where *bi* 'say', which subcategorizes for a tensed subject-containing clause, appears. An additional example follows: in (72) below, the embedded clause is introduced by *dati* 'that'.

(72) En bi dat ju mu jef.. aboko ka.
3Pl say that 2Sg must eat fowl Neg
'They say that you mustn't eat chicken.' [AK 220290:p9]
NOT: 'They don't say...'

1.3.3 Scope of negation over serial verb constructions

In serial verb constructions (SVCs) two or more verbs appear which are not separated by a conjunction or complementizer; they usually – but not always – share one or more arguments and there is usually – but not always – a close semantic relation between the verbs. The structure of SVCs is a much debated issue, and far from being resolved. (See for instance Jansen et. al. 1978, Sebba 1987, Byrne 1987, Muysken 1989, Baker 1989.) We will limit the discussion below to constructions which are unequivocally accepted as SVCs. The serial verbs are underlined.

There are very few negative SVCs in my spontaneous language data. They follow as examples (73), (75), and (77) below. In (73), a completive serialization appears, i.e. a serialization in which the last verb is *fama* 'finish', which serves to signal the completion of the event/process described by the preceding verb, *furkopu* 'sell' in this case. Note that it is the completedness which is negated, not the event described by the first verb. This is corroborated by informants' judgements, as illustrated in (74).

(73)   Eni   masi noko   *furkop*   eni   stiljap   *fama*   ka.
       3Pl   must not:Result sell   3Pl   post-PL   finish   Neg
       'They probably haven't sold all their posts.' [BB 030390:p12]

(74)   Di   kumbuši   nok   *brɛk*   *fama*   ka.
       the   kitchen   not:Result break   finish   Neg
       'The kitchen has not been broken down completely.' [!AK 100390:p28]

In the dative SVC, the transfer of an object is descibed. The last verb is *pi* 'give', and it is followed by a NP which is the recipient of the transferred object. The following example shows that the dative construction may be negative. In (75), *eni* [3Pl] is the recipient of *gutu* 'thing'. In this case, negation has scope over the entire construction. In other words, if we assume that this SVC describes an event which consists of at least two stages, one the motion stage denoted by *deki..mu* 'take..go', the other the transfer stage denoted by *pi* 'give', then it is so interpreted that none of these stages was realized. Attempts to get exclusive scope over the transfer stage failed; thus, (76), where I tried to force an interpretation of the motion stage as having been realized by suffixing PF on *tiri* 'send', was rejected.

(75)   Eni   bi   kɛkɛ   o   suku jefi   ka,   mja   en   kɛnɛ   *deki*
       3Pl   say   like   3Sg   want eat   Neg,   make   one   person   take
       gutu   *mu*   *pj*eni   ka.
       thing   go   give:3Pl Neg
       'They say (it is) as if he doesn't want to eat, which is why nobody brings them anything.' [BB 100788:p5]

(76) εkε   *tirto*   *pi*   εkε   mama   ka.
      1Sg   send-PF:3Sg   give   1sg   mother Neg
      attempted reading: 'I sent it (but) not to my mother.' [!BB 230488:p9]

(77) is an example of a negative action-result construction. In the action-result construction, the second verb (*lasan* 'leave') denotes the result of the preceding event. This construction patterns with the completive construction, in that only the referentiality of the last verb is negated, whereas the referentiality of the event described by the first verb (*doko* 'paddle') is not negated.

(77) Ju   kant   fə   *dok*   *lasan* ka.
      2Sg   cannot   for   paddle   leave   Neg
      'You cannot outpaddle it.' (because it is faster than you are) [AK 290488:p2]

In the directional SVC, the first verb is a motion verb, followed by a verb which specifies the direction of motion; the latter is either *mu* 'go', or *kumu* 'come'. Informants' judgements on negative directional SVCs show a great deal of variation, as illustrated below. Thus, AK's initial judgement of the negative directional SVC in (78) suggests that *mangi mu* 'run go' is interpreted as one negatable constituent. However, compare his later judgements of similar constructions in (79)-(80), which suggest that negation has scope over the first verb only. Similar variation is found in BB's judgements of negative directional SVCs.

(78) SK: O   noko   *mangi*   *mu*   šapaŋga   ka.
            3Sg   not:Result run   go   shop:Loc Neg
      AK: 'He ain't go to the shop at all.' [!AK 050490:p40]

(79) O   nok   *mangi*   *mu*   šapwaŋka,   o   weŋgitε.
      3Sg   not:Result run   go   shop:Loc:Neg, 3Sg   walk-PF
      'He didn't run to the shop, he walked.' [!AK 050490:p40]

(80) εk   ma   *doko*   *kum*   ka,   εk   ma   *weŋgi*   *kum*.
      1Sg   Irr   paddle   come   Neg, 1Sg   Irr   walk   come
      'I won't come paddling, I will come on foot.' [!AK 050490:p41]

1.4 Other issues in BD negation

1.4.1 Constituent negation

Constituent negation does not exist in BD, although, as we have seen in the section on indefinite NPs above, negation has scope over NPs. Nevertheless, utterances such as (81)-(82) below, where a constituent appears independently with the negator, seem to suggest that BD does have constituent negation.

(81)   Duŋgru, bidaka   kanɛ.
        night,   daylight   Neg
        'At night, not during the day.' [AC 090488:33]

(82)   Da gugujap   ju   nintɛ,   kalkal   tau   ka.
        be big:big-Nom-PL   2Sg   Know-PF,   small:small   snake   Neg
        'Big ones you know, not small snakes.' [AK 260290:p4]

These utterances are however more appropriately described as sentence
fragments or elliptical forms, rather than negated constituents. This can be
seen in utterances such as (83)-(85) below. Thus, in (83), the statement 'my
ID card doesn't have the date' is followed by a further specification of the
NP 'the date' as referring to the date of birth of the speaker. This part of the
utterance consists only of a complex NP and the negator (*di det wanɛr ɛk
bantɛ ga*), whereas the NP is not interpreted as being negated; clearly the
negation of the preceding 'full' utterance is carried over into the sentence
fragment.

(83)   ɛk   'ID card'   hab di,   di   det ka,   di   det   wanɛr   ɛk
        1Sg   ID card   have the, the   date Neg, the   date when   1Sg

        bantɛ   ga.
        born-PF Neg
        'My ID card doesn't have the date, my date of birth.' [HA 140788:p.26]
        NOT: 'not the date of my birth'

Similarly, the clause introduced by *fi* 'for' in (84) is an elliptical form which
specifies the NP *oli* 'oil', and contains a negator, whereas the clause is not
interpreted as a negative clause. Also, in (85), the fragments *di fɛnsrɛ ka, di
doro ka*, expand on the request in the first part of the utterance.

(84)   In   ha   oli   ka,   fi   twa   in   lampwaŋ   ka.
        3Pl   have   oil   Neg, for   put   3Pl   lamp:Loc   Neg
        'They didn't have oil, to put in their lamp.' [HA 140788:p12]
        NOT: 'not to put in their lamp'

(85)   Ju   mu   kaši di   en   'window'   ka,   di   fɛnsrɛ   ka,   wɛl
        2Sg   must shut the   one   window   Neg, the   window   Neg, well

        di..   di   doro ka.
        the.. the   door Neg.
        'You mustn't shut the one window, the window, well, the door'
        [BB 260288:p1]

The only somewhat problematic cases are those of *en gutu ka* [one thing Neg] 'nothing' and *fi en gutu ka* [for one thing Neg] 'for no reason'. The latter is often used to answer questions pertaining to the reason of events. These expressions are probably best treated as idioms. Thus, in the following example, the verb appears with perfective aspect, which is normally incompatible with negation. It is clear therefore, that the negator does not have scope over the verb.

(86) Di   mantoko   bilatɛkɛ   kujara fi   en   gutu   ka.
      the man:child sink-PF:3Sg   canoe   for   one   thing Neg
      'The boy sank my canoe for no reason at all.' [!BB 230290:p13,
      !AK 270190:p28]

1.4.2 Other uses of negation

Negative interrogatives can be used as confirmative or rhetorical questions, which prompt the hearer to agree with the assumption contained in the question. They then serve a discourse purpose rather than the normal function of asking a question. Confirmative questions are formed as negative yes/no questions. Some examples follow. Note that a perfective verb form appears in (87) (*kutɛ*); since the referentiality of the event is not negated, the restrictions on the occurrence of PF in the scope of negation do not hold in confirmative questions.

(87) O   noko..   tɛ   en   toko daŋka?
      3Sg not:Result   catch-PF   one   child there:Neg
      'Didn't it catch a child overthere?' [BB 090488:p3]

(88) Ju   kiki hosɛkɛ   habu..   musu   ka?
      2Sg see   how:1Sg   have   many   Neg
      'Don't you see how I have many?' [BB 150190:37]

In (89) below, the assumption is that getting rich, is the inevitable result of whatever is happening, viz. getting pain. (90) again illustrates the use of a perfective verb form in a confirmative question.

(89) ɛkjok   ma   kriki riki ka   bikɛkjɛ   krikja   pín.
      1Sg:Nom:too   Irr   get   rich Neg   because:1Sg:Nom   get-Ipf pain
      'Mustn't I be getting rich too, because I am getting so much pain!'
      [EK 080688:138]

(90) O   noko   bilatɛ   ofriši   duŋgru ka?
      3Sg not:Result sink-PF   over:side   night Neg?
      'Didn't he sink on the other side at night?' [BB 050488:p9]

258   *Sylvia Kouwenberg*

1.4.3 Prohibitives/negative imperatives

There is no special verb morphology to convey a request or command in BD. Requests, commands, etc. are formed as declaratives ('you must tell her...') or as imperatives ('tell her...'). Both types can appear as negatives. However, whereas the imperative type is dominant in affirmative commands, the type which contains an overt subject pronoun is dominant in prohibitives. The overt pronoun is *ju* [2Sg] for singular reference, *jɛndɛ* [2Pl] for plural reference; the absence of examples of prohibitives with a plural subject is due to lower frequence of *jɛndɛ* in discourse.

(91) Ju   ma   landa bu   kɛkɛ juɲu   kɛnap   ka.
      2Sg   Irr   follow drink like young   person-PL Neg
      'You shouldn't continue to drink like young people.' [BB 050488:p9]

(92) ɛkɛ   pantɛ ju   bu   sofɛlɛ   ka.
      1Sg   tell-PF 2Sg drink so:much   Neg
      'I told you not to drink so much.' [HH lukuba1:9]

(93) Šima fan daŋga ka!
      move from there   Neg
      'Don't move away from there!' [BB 86]

2 Language death and negation

The effects of language death and the ever increasing pressure of the GC model have had some impact on the negation system of all speakers. One of the most obvious examples is the disuse into which the BD independent negator *nɛnɛ* has fallen. Although all speakers know it, they prefer to use the GC negator *no*. Note that the same holds for *ja*, which has been replaced by GC *jɛs* 'yes'. Attrition in the negation system takes the following forms:

- GC forms are introduced; these may be used in alternation with or in combination with original BD negation. This is done by all speakers.
- GC distinctions are introduced; this pertains to the introduction of constituent negation.
- BD forms of negation are lost, either because speakers lose the ability to distinguish different kinds of negation which are not distinguished in GC (HA and BC), or because BD negators are no longer used (all speakers, but especially prominent in BC's speech).

Among those who I consider to be fluent speakers of BD in the sense that they speak with confidence, express themselves without hesitation, and are able to discuss any normal topic in BD, the speech of BC shows evidence of the most extreme attrition. We will first discuss the strategies of negation which he employs, and then turn to evidence for attrition in the negation system of other speakers.

2.1 Language death and negation in the speech of BC

BC employs the following strategies of negation, listed in descending order of frequency:

- Negation is marked by use of a GC morpheme. Below follow illustrations of various types of GC-derived negation used by BC, viz. *no/na* for constituent negation and for sentential negation, and negative *kjaan* 'cannot'.

(94)   If en, *no*   kɛnap   fu   futɛlɛ   mɛtɛkɛ,...
     if one, no   person-PL for   speak   with:1Sg
     'If no one, nobody to talk with me,...' [BC 120286:p13]

(95)   ɛhɛ *kjan*   pama   ju   bikas   ɛkɛ *na* ni.
     1Sg cannot   tell   2Sg because 1Sg not know
     'I cannot tell you because I don't know.' [BC 160190:3]

- Negation is marked by the sentence-final negator *ka(nɛ)*. (96) is an instance of BD sentence-final negation in combination with GC preverbal negation. (97) is an example of 'pure' BD sentence-final negation.

(96)   ɛkɛ *na:..* mja: kori tun ababəkə.
     2Sg not   do   work field anymore:Neg
     'I don't work in the field anymore.' [BC160190:33]

(97)   E:n   mali kumtɛ   an   ɛkə ki   ababaga.
     one   time come-PF   and 1Sg see anymore:Neg
     '(He) came once and I haven't seen him anymore.' [BC 080286:p3]

- Negation is left unmarked. Note that there are no other devices such as intonation to compensate for the absence of overt marking of negation; thus, the negative interpretation of (98) and (99) below is totally dependent upon context.

(98)   ɛk   ha   en   kɛnɛ.
     1Sg have one person
     'I have nobody.' [BC 120286:p21]

(99)   If en   kɛnɛ bifi   mɛtɛkɛ, ...
     if one person speak with:1Sg
     'If nobody speaks with me, ...' [BC 120286:p12]

As shown above, BC uses GC devices to mark constituent negation, which is not an original feature of BD. Resultative negation is absent from BC's speech, although he uses the affirmative resultative construction occasionally. He has no intuitions on (negative or affirmative) resultative constructions. Nor does he have intuitions pertaining to the constraints on the cooccurrence of perfective aspect and negation. In spontaneous speech he does not usually use perfective aspect with negation, as in the correctly used forms of *nimi* 'acquire knowledge' in (100) (appearing as *ni* and *ninte*), but there are mistakes, as in (101) below.

(100) Wateke   na   ni,   ju   ninte.
      what:1Sg   not Know,   2Sg   Know-PF
      'What I don't know, yóu know.' [BC 160190:44]

(101) I   se   na   ninte?
      3Sg   say   not Know-PF?
      'she said (he) doesn't know?' [BC 160190:45]

The negative copula *furi* 'not be there, not exist' is never used by BC. He uses the neutral form *jɛn* in all cases.

(102) Pote   kɛnap   na   jɛn.
      old   person-PL   not be
      'There are no old people.' [BC 160190:63]

But note that he still follows BD in extending sentential scope of negation over indefinite NPs, even when negation is marked by GC preverbal *na/no*, as in the following examples; if he had followed the GC system of negation wholly, he would have used a GC form of constituent negation.

(103) *En   gutu*   na   jɛnda   fi   jefi.
      one   thing   not be:there   for eat
      'There is nothing to eat.' [BC 160190:15]

(104) *én   kɛ*na   futel   mɛtɛkɛ.
      one   person:not   speak   with:1Sg
      'Nobody speaks (this language) with me.' [BC 160190:62]

2.2 Language death and negation in the speech of other speakers

Now let us turn to evidence of attrition in the negation system of other speakers. We note two seemingly contradictory tendencies: on the one hand, 'redundant' marking of negation is reduced; this is done by making the appearance of the negator *ka(nɛ)* optional with the negative existential copula *furi* 'not be there, not exist', with the negative auxiliary verbs *kantɛ/kanti/kantimi* 'cannot', and with the negative adverbial *noiti* 'never'. On the other hand, 'redundancy' is introduced by the use of 'double' negation, i.e. the use of GC-derived negators in combination with the BD sentence-final negator.

The first tendency is illustrated in examples (105) and (106): the negative locative/existential copula appears in (105), a negative adverbial in (106); in both cases, the sentence-final negator is omitted. This is by no means incidental.

(105) En   gut   *for*   fi   ɛk jefi.
       one   thing   not-be   for   1Sg eat
       'There is nothing for me to eat.' [EK lukuba2]

(106) ɛk   *noiti*   kik   bili   kori bai   ši   self.
       1Sg   never   see   axe   work by   3Poss   self
       'I have never seen an axe working by itself.' [EK lukuba2:p6]

Besides the very frequent omission of the sentence-final negator in combination with a negative verb or adverbial, speakers' intuitions indicate that the appearance of the sentence-final negator has become optional in these cases: they find the a. and b. versions of (107) equally acceptable.

(107) a. Ori   furi   wari.   b. Ori   furi   wari   kanɛ.
          3Sg   not-be   house   3Sg   not-be   house   Neg
          'She is not at home.'

Evidence for the second tendency comes from frequent use of GC sentential negation (marked by *na/no*), negative verbs, and negative adverbials, in combination with the BD sentence-final negator *ka(nɛ)*. Thus, in (108) and (109), the GC preverbal negator *na/no* appears; also in (109), the GC negative quantifier *nan* 'none' appears.

(108) ɛk   *na*   lur.. waŋgɛ   goja   bwa *ka*.
       1Sg   not   look where:1Sg   throw-Ipf   foot Neg
       'I wasn't paying attention to where I was putting my feet.' [AK 040488:p6]

(109) ɛkɛ   noiti   *no*   kiki *nan*.. wiruni krɛkɛ   ben   *ka*.
       1Sg   never   not   see   none   Wiruni creek   inside   Neg
       'I have never seen any, in the Wiruni creek.' [AH 210390:21]

A step further, GC negation appears to have replaced that of BD altogether. Examples of this kind can also be found in the spontaneous speech of all speakers. In the following examples, a GC form of negation appears without BD negation.

(110) ɛk   *na*   kiki di   kɛnɛ.
       1Sg   not   see   the person
       'I didn't see the person.' [RT 280186:38]

(111) En   kɛ*na*   mu.
       one person:not   go
       'Nobody went.' [AK 080390:p9]

There are also utterances where negation seems to have been 'forgotten' altogether. For instance, there are a few cases where EK omits negation with the main verb *bionto* 'believe', as in (112). Another curious example is (113), where AC uses resultative negation, but omits the sentence-final negator. Although omitting negation altogether is a regular feature of BC's negation system, it is too infrequent in the speech of others to think of it as a 'strategy' for negation.

(112) ɛkan   rili   bionto   nau bikaš,   iš   wa   juŋgu   an   so.
       1Sg:can really   remember now because,   1Pl   Past young   and so
       'I can't really remember now because, we were young and so on.'
       [EK 050688:2,14]

(113) O   noko   tiri   fi   X.
       3Sg not:Result send   for X
       'He didn't send for X.' [AC 090488:19]

Besides obvious intrusions into the BD negation system in the form of GC negators, there is also evidence for the loss of distinctions and restrictions which are part of the BD negation system but not of that of GC. Thus, AC has suffixed perfective aspect on a verb which is negated in the following example, and like BC, he does not have clear intuitions on the incompatibility of negation and perfective aspect; this is a feature characteristic of BD but not of GC.

(114) ɛke nintɛ   husen   das mjori ka.
       1Sg Know-PF   how:3Pl Hab do:3Sg Neg
       'I don't know how they do it.' [AC 090488:5]

We have noted earlier that BC does not know resultative negation. This is part of the general decay which can be noted in his negation system. HA is much more of a 'real' fluent speaker,[6] but lacks the resultative construction altogether. This also means that she lacks the negative resultative. Whenever

I asked her opinion on resultative constructions (whether negative or not), she accepted them, but would not repeat them. In situations where the non-negative resultative construction would have been appropriate, she used a simple affirmative construction. In situations where the negative resultative would have been appropriate, she tended to use a combination of GC preverbal negation with BD sentence-final negation. This may point to an awareness of the existence of a negative resultative. Below an example of such an utterance, followed by the appropriate negative resultative. Note however that HA uses GC preverbal negators quite often, and that it may be chance that they occur also in cases where other speakers would have used a BD negative resultative.

(115) Ina   pamɛk hoso   sɛt:ɛ ka.
       3Pl:not   tell:1Sg how(:3Sg) stay Neg
       'They didn't tell me what it looks like.' (lit: how it stays) [HA 100390:29]

(115)′ Inoko   pamɛk hoso   sɛt:ɛ ka.
       3Pl:not:Result tell:1Sg how(:3Sg) stay Neg

3 The provenance of BD negation

BD is unique among the Caribbean creole languages in the extent to which its vocabulary is not related to its European lexifier language Dutch. This holds for content vocabulary as well as for function words: many BD words derive from its substrate language Eastern-Ịjọ (EI; a Nigerian language), as was discovered by Smith et.al. (1987). In BD basic vocabulary we find a seemingly free mixture of words related to Dutch and to EI. This is illustrated below: near-synonyms of D(utch) and EI derivation are listed in (116) and (117).

(116) 'old': potɛ (EI) [±human] / hau (D) [-human] 'ancient' / pakra (EI) [-human] 'worn' / groto (D) '[+human]

(117) 'fall' (v.): falu (D) (uncontrolled) / koro (EI) (controlled or of rain) / sara (EI) 'drop'

Some etymologically contrastive pairs are given in (118).

(118) jɛrma (EI) 'woman/wife' - man   (D) 'man/husband'
       mu   (EI) 'go'   - kumu (D) 'come'
       kali (EI) 'small'   - gu   (D) 'big'

264   *Sylvia Kouwenberg*

EI has contributed to BD vocabulary, as well as morphology and syntax. Thus, the sentence-final negation pattern of BD is related to the negation system of EI. EI *-ka appears sentence-finally, as does BD ka(nɛ). This is illustrated in (119) below.

(119) Árị   ọ   bẹlẹma-áa.
       she   him   love-not
       'She doesn't love him.' [Jenewari 1977:251]

The form of the BD negator ka(nɛ) itself reflects the history of the language: it derives from a combination of the EI negator *-ka and the Dutch independent negator *nee*. The short form *ka* (which is the original EI form) may have been retained alongside the long form, or developed in a later stage, as the result of reduction, which frequently applies to grammatical morphemes. Unfortunately, there is no obvious etymological source for the preverbal negation that BD developed in the resultative construction. The negative verbs again reflect the mixed history of BD, while other negative words are mostly Dutch derived.

Table 1. Etymology of BD negative words

Berbice Dutch	etymon
nɛnɛ 'no'	D nee nee 'no no'
ka(nɛ) Neg	EI *-ka / D nee 'no'
no (resultative negation)	?
furi 'not be, not exist'	EI *ofori 'not exist'
kanti 'cannot'	D kan niet [can Neg] 'cannot'
noiti 'never'	D nooit 'never'
neks 'nothing'	D niks 'nothing'
nimdali 'nothing'	D niemendal 'nothing'
sondro 'without'	D zonder 'without'

Notes

1. The data presented here were gathered in fieldwork carried out between 1986 and 1990. This fieldwork was financially supported by grant number W39-116 of the Netherlands Foundation for the Advancement of Tropical Research (WOTRO). It is a pleasure to acknowledge this, as well as the supervision by Prof. Pieter Muysken and Dr. Norval Smith of the University of Amsterdam. The data were provided by native speakers of Berbice Dutch Creole.

2. Examples have been selected from recordings of spontaneous speech of almost all speakers. Elicited examples and judgements by speakers other than AK and BB are not used, since other speakers' judgements are often inconsistent, and may not be reliable.

3. The BD vowel system consists of /u, o, a, ɛ, e, i/. Allophones of /u/ are [u] and [o], while other vowels do not display this kind of variation. Unaccented vowels may reduce to [ə]. /ŋ/ represents the velar nasal consonant.

4. Berbice Dutch marks past tense and irrealis mood preverbally, while perfective and imperfective aspect are marked by the use of suffixes:

Tense	Mood	Aspect
wa Past	*ma* Irrealis	*-tɛ* Perfective
	sa Unlikely	*-arɛ* Imperfective

In addition, iterative aspect is marked by reduplication of the verb, and GC preverbal habitual markers *das* and *justu* have found their way into the BD aspectual system. Note that the overt marking of past tense is discourse-dependent; hence the many examples with a past tense translation but lacking overt past tense marking. See Kouwenberg & Robertson (1988) and Bruyn & Veenstra (in press) for a discussion of the tense/mood/aspect system of Berbice Dutch, and Kouwenberg (1990) for a discussion of reduplication in BD.

5. Note however that passives are a fairly marginal phenomenon in BD, and that all examples of negative resultative passives are elicited examples.

6. I judge HA to be more of a 'real' fluent speaker than BC because (a) her vocabulary is larger, (b) there are less GC intrusions in vital parts of her speech such as tense-marking and the pronominal system, (c) her responses to questions about grammaticality of test sentences are much more consistent.

Abbreviations

1, 2, 3	grammatical person	NegHab	negative habitual aspect
Sg	singular	Nom	nominalizer
Pl	plural	Past	past tense
Poss	possessive	PF	perfective
Focus	focus marker,	PL	plural
Hab	habitual aspect	Result	resultative auxiliary
Ipf	imperfective	Come	the 'connective' verb *kumu*
Irr	irrealis		'come'
Loc	locative postposition	Go	the 'connective' verb *mu* 'go'
Neg	negation	Know	*nimi* 'acquire knowledge'.

References

Baker, M.C. (1989). 'Object sharing and projection in serial verb constructions.' *Linguistic Inquiry* 40:4, 513-553.

Bruyn, A. & T. Veenstra. (1993). 'The creolization of Dutch.' *Journal of Pidgin and Creole Languages* 8, 29-80.

Byrne, F. (1987). *Grammatical relations in a radical creole.* Amsterdam: John Benjamins.

Dance, Rev. Ch.D. (1881). *Chapters from a Guianese log-book.* Georgetown, Demerara: The Royal Gazette Establishment.

De Goeje, C.H. (1928). *The Arawak language of Guiana.* Amsterdam: Koninklijke Akademie van Wetenschappen te Amsterdam.

Holm, J. (1988). *Pidgins and Creoles. Volume I. Theory and Structure.* Cambridge: Cambridge Language Surveys.

Jenewari, Ch. E. (1977). *Studies in Kalaḅarị Syntax.* University of Ibadan dissertation.

Jansen, B., H. Koopman & P.C. Muysken. (1978). *Serial verbs in the creole languages.* Amsterdam Creole Studies II, p.125-159.

Kouwenberg, S. (1990). 'Reduplication in Berbice Dutch Creole.' Boretzky et al. (eds) *Beiträge zum 6. Essener Kolloquium.* Bochum: Brockmeyer.

—— forthc. 'From OV to VO in the development of Berbice Dutch Creole.' To appear in *Lingua.*

Kouwenberg, Silvia & Ian E. Robertson. (1988). 'The marking of tense, mood and aspect in the Berbice Dutch Creole language.' Boretzky et al. (eds) *Beiträge zum 4. Essener Kolloquium.* 151-174. Bochum: Brockmeyer.

Muysken, Pieter. (1989). 'Parameters for serial verbs.' Victor Manfredi & K. Demuth (eds) *Studies in Niger-Congo Syntax and Semantics II.* 65-76. Indiana University Linguistics Club.

Robertson, Ian E. (1982). 'Redefining the post-creole continuum – Evidence from Berbice Dutch.' *Amsterdam Creole Studies IV,* 62-77.

—— (1989). 'Berbice and Skepi Dutch. A lexical comparison.' *Tijdschrift voor Nederlandse Taal- en Letterkunde.* 105:1, 3-21.

Romaine, Suzanne. (1988). *Pidgin & Creole languages.* London and New York. Longman.

Sebba, M. (1987). *The syntax of serial verbs.* Amsterdam: John Benjamins.

Smith, Norval S.H., Ian E. Robertson & Kay Williamson. (1987). 'The Ịjọ element in Berbice Dutch.' *Language in Society* 16, 49-90.

Waorani

C. Peeke

0 Introduction

The Waorani language is spoken by approximately 1000 Waorani in the upper Amazonian rainforest, east of the Andes and just south of the equator in Ecuador, South America. The people and the language have been variously called 'Ssabela' or 'Auka', by Tessman (1930:298-303); 'Huarani', by Saint and Pike (1959); 'Auca', by Saint and Pike (1959, 1962) and by Peeke (1973); 'Huao', by Peeke (1979); 'Huaorani', by Peeke (1991); 'Waodani', by Kelley (1988); and 'Waorani', by Pike and Saint (1988). In addition, apparently due to confusion with a Zaparoan group which Tessman (ibid) calls 'Aushiri', the Waorani have mistakenly been called 'Aushiri'. Both the local name, 'Auca' and the misnomer, 'Aushiri' are terms which denote, 'savage, enemy' in local languages.

The autochthonous name for the people is /waodãdi/ [wao'dani], and the name for the language is /waodãdi tededõ/ [wao'dani ti'didõ] 'the people's speech' or /wao tededõ/ [wao tididõ] 'person speech', as explained by Peeke (1979:05). The language is listed by Ruhlen (1987) as Amerind of the Andean substock, family Urarina. However, having had extensive contact with various other Amazonian languages, and having found no apparent cognates with Urarina in wordlists compiled by Manus and Manus (1971) nor in lists of other Amazonian languages, I consider Waorani to be an unclassified language.[1]

Phonologically, each of the five oral vowels in Waorani has a nasal counterpart, whereas there are no phonemically nasal consonants. Subject to certain conditions which are stated in Peeke (1979:9-13), each of the consonants has a nasal or a prenasalized actualization contiguous to nasal vowels. Table 1 below lists the 18 phonemes with a rough representation of the phonetic character of each and an indication of orthographic symbols as they appear in this article. The phonemes are indicated by slashes (/ /); the phonetic characters are indicated by brackets ([ ]); and the orthographic symbols are the third item in each cell.

Stress is penultimate in words of more than one syllable. Thus, in a sequence of two vowels at the end of a word, stress falls on the first in the sequence. For further phonological discussion see Saint and Pike (1959), Saint and Pike (1962), Pike (1964), Peeke (1979), and Kelley (ibid). For a more precise phonetic transcription, see these and Peeke (1991).

Table 1. Waorani phonemes

Consonants	Labial	Alveolar/alveopltl	Velar
Voiceless stops	/p/ [p/^{m}p] p	/t/ [t/^{n}t] t	/k/ [k/^{ŋ}k] k
Voiced stops	/b/ [b/m] b	/d/ [d/d̆/n] d	/g/ [g/ŋ] g
Semivowels	/w/ [w/ẉ] w	/y/ [y/ñ/^{d}y] y	
Vowels	Oral	Nasal	
	/i/ [i] i	/ḭ/ [ḭ] ḭ̄	
	/ı/ [ı] e	/ı̣/ [ı̣] ẽ	
	/æ/ [æ] æ	/æ̣/ [æ̣] æ̃	
	/a/ [a] a	/ạ/ [ạ] ã	
	/ɨ/ [ɨ/u/o/ʋ] o	/ɨ̣/ [ɨ̣/ʉ/ǫ/ʋ̣] õ	

A few typological generalizations can be made as an introduction to Waorani syntax. In general, word order is SOV, while OSV also occurs, be it less frequently. However, clauses tend to contain no more than one clause element in addition to the verb.

In content questions, the question word, marked by *-dõ* 'content', is pattern positioned, replacing the head word in the place where the latter functions.

(1)   Bitõ   gĩta   æ-dõ-dõ   go-te   dææ   ã-gã?
      your   dog   which-way-Cntnt   go-ing   none   be-3S
      'Where did your dog go that it is not here?'

Yes-no questions are not necessarily marked, other than by rising intonation. When they are marked in the past tense, as in example (2), *-wo* 'dubitative' occurs as a final or prefinal suffix, following the past tense marker *-ta*, and potentially followed by an irrealis suffix, as described in section 4.1 below. Yes-no questions in present or future are optionally marked by reduplication of the otherwise-final vowel of the final verb in the clause, as illustrated in example (5).

(2)   Põ-bi?   Doo   kæ̃-bi-ta-wo?
      come-2S   already   eat-2S-Past-Dubit
      'You have come? Have you already eaten?'

Nominal phrases optionally include an initial demonstrative or a qualifying adjective. It is not natural for both to occur but, if elicited, the demonstrative precedes the qualifying adjective. Since most nouns are represented by a classifying suffix which compounds with qualifying stems (as well as with demonstrative, locational, verb, and relative-interrogative stems), the resulting qualifying compound often replaces the head noun. Otherwise, it follows the head noun in an appositional relationship or occurs as predicate complement.

(3) Ĩ̃ dooyæ̃ weo-koo bæ̃æ̃ õyõ-pa.
this long cloth-mass existent lie-Assert
'This long dress is lying (here).'

(4) Bãdĩ-koo dooyæ̃-koo bæ̃æ̃ õyõ-pa.
that-mass long-mass existent lie-Assert
'That long cloth is lying (here).'

A noun or a pronoun which functions as possessor precedes the possessed noun. The head noun is optionally preceded by a short quantifier. However, longer quantifying phrases and even the one-word quantifiers tend to follow the head noun. Postpositions which function as relationals occur final in the noun phrase to which they pertain. The same is true of object markers or, more precisely, 'affective' markers, as explained in Peeke (1973:100). These are forms of the stative participle *ĩ-te* 'be-ing', normally inflected for person and number in agreement with the noun head. In example (5), the participle *ĩ-da-te*, glossed 'be-3Dual-ing', marks the head as third person dual object.

(5) Bitõ tõdĩya-da ĩ-da-te a pe-bi-i?
your sibling-3Dual be-3Dual-ing shout call-2S-Past-Ig
'Are you calling out to your two brothers?'

Nonperson head nouns are generally unmarked for object or affectant, although reference to domestic animals and, rarely, reference to other large animals, is marked for object, with or without indication of person and number.

(6) Bẽye tæ̃dõ-te bõdõ õta baga æ̃æ̃-gæ̃-ĩ-pa.
jaguar spear-ing we:N claw tooth get-should-Infer-Assert
'Spearing the jaguar, let's take (its) claws and teeth.'

The equivalent of a relative clause in Waorani is most often headless. The head noun, when it occurs, may either precede or follow the relative clause. When the head is a noun denoting a person, the clause begins with the relative pronoun *dẽ* '(the one) who(m), which' and the verb is nominalized by a relative tense marker and/or by a person-number marker. In addition, when the head person-noun functions as object, an object marker follows the final constituent. In example (7), *-gaĩ* 'Far past nominalizer' is the relative tense marker which nominalizes the verb, and the participle *ĩ-gã-te*, glossed as 'be-3S-ing', marks the person-noun object.

(7)   Dĕ   waa   kæ-gaĩ-gã   bǽbǽ   ĩ-gã-te
       who   well   do-FarpNz-3S   grandfather   be-3S-ing

       wĩwa   kæ-gaĩ-da-ĩ-pa.
       wickedly   do-Farp-3Dual-Infer-Assert

       'They two mistreated grandfather, who was one who did well.'

When the head noun occurs in a relative clause marked as object, the same object marker is frequently repeated following the relative clause. Thus both the head noun and the relative clause, which are interpreted as being in apposition to one another, are marked as objects.

(8)   Dĕ   waa   kæ-gaĩ-gã   ĩ-gã-te   bǽbǽ   ĩ-gã-te
       who   well   do-FarpNz-3S   be-3S-ing   grandfather   be-3S-ing

       wĩwa   kæ-ga-da-ĩ-pa.
       wickedly   do-Farp-3Dual-Infer-Assert

       'They two mistreated grandfather, the one who did well.'

On the other hand, when the head noun denotes a nonperson object, the relative pronoun does not occur and the verb is nominalized by a relative tense marker and/or by a noun classifier, as in example (9).

(9)   (Dika)   bãdĩ-yõbõ   õgõ-ka   ǽǽ-te   wo-todõ*-gã-pa.
       (rock)   that-place   sit-rock   take-ing   fly-propel-3S-Assert

       'He takes (the rock,) the rock that was sitting there and throws (it).'

Most areas of comparison are stated in absolute terms, either juxtaposed in separate sentences or conjoined in the same sentence by a form of the object marker in which the switch-referent suffix *-yõ* 'while, whereas' occurs. The particle *wæætē* 'rather, on the other hand, in turn', is commonly employed initially in the second statement or after its subject.

(10)   Bitõ   okaa-bi   ĩ-yõ-bi-te   bitõ   wĕ-gã   wæætē
       you   short-3S   be-while-2S-ing   your   child-3S   in:turn

       dooyǽ-gã   ĩ-gã-pa.
       long-3S   be-3S-Assert

       'Whereas you are short, your child, on the other hand, is tall.'

There are two comparative adjective stems which indicate relative size in Waorani, *wædā* 'large' and *oga* 'larger'. However, since the status of the first element in the comparison is generally implicit in the context, it is unusual for both elements to be expressed in a given statement.

(11) Îî-kade   giyã-kade   ĩ-pa.
      this-vessel small-vessel   be-Assert

      Bõditõ   oga-ĩ-kade   ã-ta-bõdi-pa.
      we:X   larger-Nz-vessel   say-Past-1X-Assert

      'This vessel is a small vessel. We (exclusive) wanted a larger vessel.'

With regard to relative distance or to relative value in trading, the quantitative terms *godõbĕke* 'further, more' and/or *põdõbĕke* 'nearer, lesser' occur. More rarely, the same terms occur preceding a qualifier in a statement of comparative quality.

(12) Yõwo go-dõbĕke edõke   ba.
      now go-further clear become
      'Now it becomes clearer.'

The Waorani verb phrase comprises an optional initial adverb, an optional motion stem, the obligatory head, and an optional performative. The head itself may be a close-knit, compound verbal construction expressing motion-motion, motion-action, cause-action, action-reaction, action-observation, or a combination involving three or more of these categories (motion, cause, action, reaction, observation) or a sequence of two reactions. Except in the case of motion-verb components, these compound verb phrases function as switch-reference mechanisms. The causal or the action verb in such a construction is potentially complex, consisting of a qualifying particle plus the verb.

Finally, the restricted set of performatives which optionally terminate the verb phrase are themselves verbs or verb phrases in first or second-person, although they are not formally marked for person. In example (13), the series of verbs in the verb phrase are the motion stem *põ* 'go', the qualifying particle *õõ* 'grab' + action verb *ǽǽ* 'take', the reaction verb stem *a* 'see', and a second-person performative *-pa kĕwēedãdi* '-Assert live-Impv-Pl'.

(13) Kĩgǽ põ   õõ   ǽǽ-gã a-pa   kĕwĕ-e-dãdi.
      fast come grab take-3S see-Assert live-Impv-Pl
      'See how he's coming fast to grab it; get a move on!' (Literally, 'Live!')

An important feature of the compound verbal head is that only the final verb of the phrase is fully inflected; the other verbs, such as the causal verb *odõbõ* 'show' in (14, 15), indicate only person and number. Contrast the full inflection (14) of the action verb, *ēyē* 'hear' with its truncated inflection when it is followed by the reaction verb *a* 'see', in example (15).

(14)   Wẽyǽ-dãdi   ĩ-dãdi-te   odõbõ-gã   ẽyẽ-dãdi-pa.
        child-3Pl   be-3Pl-ing   show-3S   hear-3Pl-Assert
        'He teaches the children.'

(15)   Wẽyǽ-dãdi   ĩ-dãdi-te   odõbõ-gã   ẽyẽ-dãdi   a-ta-bo-pa.
        child-3Pl   be-3Pl-ing   show-3S   hear-3Pl   see-Past-1S-Assert
        'I saw him teaching the children.'

Example (16) illustrates a compound verb phrase of action-reaction-reaction.

(16)   Wǽto   o-bi   wæ-kã   to-kǽ-ĩ.
        nettle switch-2S cry-3S   laugh-should-Infer
        'Switch him with nettles so he will cry, and let's laugh!'

Examples of compound phrases where negation is involved are presented in sections 1.1 and 1.2. For further explication and for examples of clause, sentence, and discourse structure in Waorani, see Peeke (1973), Peeke (1979), and Pike and Saint (1988).

Negation in Waorani takes a variety of forms. Clauses (section 1) are negated either by a deverbalizing negative suffix on the verb or by a negating particle in the verb phrase. The same negating particle is widely used in negation of constituent phrases (section 2). Negative words (section 3) include one-word responses, a negative existential particle, negative conjoining words, and some few nouns and qualifiers with a negative semantic component. In addition, there are fairly complex irrealis constructions (section 4). Combinations of negation within a clause are treated in section 5.

1 Clause negation

There are two forms of standard negation in Waorani verbal clauses: negation of the head verb by the negative deverbalizing suffix *-dãbaĩ* (section 1.1); and negation of the predicate by the negative particle *wĩĩ* 'not' preceding the verb phrase (section 1.2). When *-dãbaĩ* is used, the clause as a whole is equative, and the copula may be omitted, especially in conversation. Certain negative particles also function as nonverbal clauses (see section 2).

1.1 Deverbalizer *-dãbaĩ*

The most common way to negate the clause is by the deverbalizer *-dãbaĩ* 'non-...-er'. The deverbalized element functions as predicate complement with the copula *ĩ-* 'to be', which is inflected for tense, mode, person, number, and the like. The copula is frequently omitted, especially in conversation, leaving inflectional information to be understood only by clues from the verbal or nonverbal context. The deverbalized element itself normally has no further inflection (17). However, the future suffix, *-kĩ ~ -gĩ* occasionally occurs following the verb stem and preceding the negative deverbalizer (18).

The deverbalizer *-dãbaĩ* negates assertive clauses, whether personal (17, 18), nonpersonal (animal, vegetable, mineral) (19, 20), or impersonal (21).

(17) Apæde-dãbaĩ   ĩ-kæ-bo-ĩ-pa.
      speak-Neg   be-Incept-1S-Infer-Assert
      'I shall not speak.'

(18) Kĕwĕ-gĩ-dãbaĩ   (ĩ-gã-pa).
      live-Fut-Neg   (is-3S-Assert)
      'He/she is not one who will live.'

(19) Gatã   pokǽ-dãbaĩ   ĩ-ta-pa.
      woolly:monkey bite-Neg   be-Past-Assert
      'The woolly-monkey did not bite.'

(20) Bodo-pã-a   ĩ-te   ǽǽ-te   go-dãbaĩ.
      little-liquid-Qty be-ing get-ing go-Neg
      'The water, being low, does not take (driftwood) away .'

(21) Kõõdæ   kæ-dãbaĩ   (ĩ).
      rain   do-Neg   (be)
      'It is not raining.'

Negation of the interrogative of any verb class is normally expressed by the verb stem plus the deverbalizer *-dãbaĩ* 'negative', followed by one of the interrogative forms of *ĩ*'be'. In examples (22, 23), the interrogative elements are *-wo* 'dubitative' and interrogative intonation, indicated by the question mark *?*.

(22) Éyĕ-dãbaĩ   ĩ-bĩdi-ta-wo?
      hear-Neg   be-2Pl-Past-Dubit
      'Did you (plural) not hear?'

(23) Æpǽ ayǽ iyǽ-te   põ-dãbaĩ   ĩ-bĩda-ta-wo?
      water yet draw-ing   come-Neg   be-2D-Past-Dubit
      'Have you two not yet drawn water and brought it?'

The interrogative markers in example (24) are *-dõ* 'content', reduplication of the final vowel of the final verb (*ã*, in this case), and *?* 'interrogative intonation'.

274   *Catherine Peeke*

(24)   Æ-po-ga-dŏ   ĭ-yŏ-te   kæ-dãbaĭ   ĭ-gĭ-gã-ã
        which-many-Qty-Cntnt   be-while-ing   do-Neg   be-Fut-3S-Ig
        'During how long a time is he not going to do it?'

The normal negative response to yes-no questions with regard to an action
is formed by negating the verb stem of the question with the deverbalizer
-dãbaĭ. The inflected copula optionally follows. Examples (25, 26) illustrate
conversations between two speakers.

(25)   "Bitŏ   badã   pŏ-dã-ta-wo?"
        your   mother come-3Hon-Past-Dubit

        "Pŏ-dãbaĭ (ĭ-dã-ta-pa.)"
        come-Neg (be-3Hon-Past-Assert)
        "'Did your mother come?' '(She did) not come.'"

(26)   "Ŏbæ-dĕ   go-te   pŏ-bi-i?"   "Go-dãbaĭ (ĭ-ta-bo-pa)."
        empty-in   go-ing   come-2S-Ig   go-Neg   (be-Past-1S-Assert)
        "'Did you come from going to the forest?' '(I did) not go.'"

Other negative responses to yes-no questions are described in sections 1.2,
2 and 3.1, below.
    Negation of the imperative of any verb class is expressed exclusively by the
verb stem plus *-dãbaĭ*, optionally followed by one of the imperative forms
of *ĭ* 'be'.

(27)   Gãpo-dãbaĭ (ĭ-e).
        touch-Neg (be-Impv)
        'Don't touch!'

(28)   Æpæ-dĕ   go   gii-dãbaĭ   (ĭ-e-da).
        water-in go   enter-Neg   (be-Impv-Dual)
        'Don't (you two) go and enter the water!'

In compound verb phrases, negation of the various elements is accomplished
in different ways. In a motion-motion or a motion-action verb phrase, the
uninflected initial motion verb participates in the deverbalizing negation
of the immediately following verb.

(29)   Bitŏ   pŏ   kæ-dãbaĭ   ĭ-bi-ta-pa.
        you   come   eat-Neg   be-2S-Past-Assert
        'You did not come eat.'

(30)   Go   gii-dãbaĭ   ĭ-dãdi   awædŏ.
        go   enter-Neg   be-3Pl   1:Neg:React
        'I'm concerned because they do not go enter.'

To negate a compound verb phrase of action-observation, only the observation verb *a* 'see' is deverbalized. In this case the range of the negation is ambiguous; it is not clear whether the action did not take place or whether it did take place and was not observed.

(31) Tõbẽgã wodii wĩdõ-gã a-dãbaĩ ĩ-ta-bo-pa.
he/she away flee-3S see-Neg be-Past-1S-Assert
'I did not see him/her flee away.'

The observation of an action is negated by subordinating the action verb in a positive clause while negating the observation verb. In example (32), the conjunction *ĩkæte* 'although' (see section 3.2) subordinates the causal verb in a concessive relationship.

(32) Wodii wĩdõ-gã ĩkæte botõ a-dãbaĩ ĩ-ta-bo-pa.
away flee-3S although I see-Neg be-Past-1S-Assert
'Although he/she fled away, I did not see (him/her flee).'

The deverbalizer is used to negate the cause of what would be, if positive, a cause-action construction, but the action is then omitted as being nonexistent. Example (33) represents the negation of cause in the positive cause-action construction presented in example (14).

(33) Wẽyæ̃-dãdi ĩ-dãdi-te tõbẽgã odõbõ-dãbaĩ ĩ-gã-pa.
child-3Pl be-3Pl-ing he/she show-Neg be-3S-Assert
'He/she is not teaching the children.'

On the other hand, negation of the action verb in a cause-action construction is accomplished by subordination of the causal verb, leaving only the action verb to be negated. In example (34) the causal verb is subordinated by the switch-referent marker *-yõ* 'whereas, while'.

(34) Tõbẽga odõbõ-yõ-gã ẽyẽ-dãbaĩ ĩ-dãdi-pa.
he/she show-while-3S hear-Neg be-3Pl-Assert
'Although he/she teaches, they do not listen.'

In other compound verb phrases, similar subordination allows for negation of the head verb, alone. Example (35) illustrates negation of the reaction verb in the action-reaction verb phrase *o-bi wæ* 'switch-2.S cry', found in example (16). Here the conjunction *ĩkæte* 'although' (see section 3.2) subordinates the action verb in a concessive relationship.

(35) Wǽto   o-bi   ǐkæte   wẽyǽ-gǎ   wæ-dǎbaǐ   ǐ-gǎ-pa.
      nettle   switch-2S   although   child-3S   cry-Neg   be-3S-Assert
      'Although you switch the child with nettles, he/she does not cry.'

For negation of both elements in motion-action or cause-action verb phrases, an irrealis construction is employed, as described in section 4.4.

The deverbalizer *-dǎbaǐ* is used to negate subordinate clauses, whether their subject is the same as (36) or different from (37) that of the main clause.

(36) Okabo   ǐyǽ   ǽ-ka-dǎbaǐ   gagǐbǽ-koo-dě   go-kǎ-ǐ-pa.
      head   upward   raise-head-Neg   grass-bunch-in   go-3S-Infer-Assert
      'It (snake) goes inside the grass cover without lifting its head.'

(37) Tǒběgǎ   bǽgǎ   a-dǎbaǐ   ǐ-yǒ-gǎ   wẽyǽ-gǎ
      his   older:sister   look-Neg   be-while-3S   child-3S

      edæ   æpǽ-dě   doo   gii-kǎ-ǐ-pa.
      climactic   water-in   already   enter-3S-Infer-Assert
      'While his older sister was not watching, the child entered right into the water.'

Embedded clauses are normally negated by the deverbalizer *-dǎbaǐ*. Note example (38), where the equivalent of a relative clause in apposition to the subject is negated.

(38) Dě   ěyě-dǎbaǐ   ǐ-gǎ   ǐ-yǒbǒ   tǒběgǎ   wæ-kæ-kǎ-ǐ-pa.
      one.who   hear-Neg   be-3S   this-place   he/she   cry-Incept-3S-Infer-Assert
      'He (in focus) who is one who does not listen, he will surely be sorry.'

When the predicate of the protasis in a contrary-to-fact conditional sentence is negated by *-dǎbaǐ*, it serves to express a semantically positive condition; the apodosis, however, remains contrary to fact (39). The converse is true when the apodosis is negated by the deverbalizer (40).

(39) Botǒ   pǒ-dǎbaǐ   ǐ-bo   baǐ   badǎ-bǐ   doo
      I   come-Neg   be-1S   if   mother-2Hon   already
      wæ-kædǒ-bǐ-pa.
      die-would-2Hon-Assert
      'If I had not come, mother, you would already have died.'

(40) Ǒkǒ-dě   owo-te   baǐ   wæ-dǎbaǐ   ǐ-kædǒ-gǎ-ǐ-pa.
      house-in   swing-ing   if   die-Neg   be-would-3S-Infer-Assert
      'If he/she had stayed at home, he/she would not have died.'

The deverbalizer *-dābaĩ* is used in conjunction with an indefinite relative pronoun to express the concept of 'no one', often with the quantifying pronoun *tõbā-dādi* 'all-3Pl'. In example (41), the indefinite relative pronoun is *æ-kā-bĕ-ke* 'which-3S-ever-Rstr'.

(41) Æ-kā-bĕ-ke   ĩkæ (tõbā-dādi)   põ-dābaĩ   ĩ-dādi-ta-pa.
      which-3S-ever-Rstr even (all-3Pl)   come-Neg   be-3Pl-Past-Assert
      'Even whoever he might be they (all) did not come.'
      I.e., 'No one whatsoever came.'

1.2 The particle *wĩĩ*

The second means of negating the clause in Waorani is by negation of the main verb phrase by the particle, *wĩĩ* 'not', which likewise negates constituent phrases (see section 2). The negating particle ordinarily occurs initial in the verb phrase to which it pertains, whether that verb occurs in a subordinate, coordinate, participial, or main clause. The verb used in a negated verb phrase carries no modification.

Negation of the main verb phrase by the particle *wĩĩ* 'not' occurs less commonly than does the negative deverbalizer in assertive clauses. When it does occur, it gives special emphasis to the negated action, such as in the rebuttal of a positive statement.

(42) "Ĩĩbõ   kõõdæ kæ-ta(-pa)."   "Wĩĩ kæ-ta(-pa)."
      yesterday rain   do-Past(-Assert) not do-Past(-Assert)
      "'It rained yesterday." "It did not."'

The particle *wĩĩ* sometimes approaches the strength of the adverb 'never', indicating that a negative habitual state prevails (43, 44). It occurs with personal (43) and nonpersonal (44) verbs more frequently than with impersonal verbs (42).

(43) Wĕyæ-gā ĩ-te   tõbĕgā (õõĩgā) wĩĩ kæ-gā-pa.
      child-3S be-ing he/she (meat) not eat-3S-Assert
      'He/she, being a child, does not eat (meat).'

(44) Gatā   ĩ-yõbõ   wĩĩ pokæ-pa.
      woolly:monkey this-place not bite-Assert
      'The woolly monkey (in focus) does not bite.'

Use of the negative particle rather than the negative deverbalizer in yes-no (45) or content (46) questions gives some (often disapproving) emphasis to the negated action.

(45)   Wĩ   ẽyĕ-bi?
       not   hear-2:S
       '(Why) do you not hear/listen/obey?'

(46)   Æ-po-ga-dõ   ĩ-yõ-te   tõbĕgã wĩ   ǽdõ-gã-ã?
       which-many-Qty-Cntnt   be-while-ing   she   not   cook-2S-Ig
       'During how long a time does she not cook?'
       I.e. 'How long will it be until she cooks?'

The action questioned in a yes-no question is sometimes negated in the response by the particle *wĩ* in the verb phrase, although this occurs less commonly than negation of the whole clause by the deverbalizer *dãbaĩ*. When *wĩ* does occur, the contradiction is more emphatic.

(47)   "Bitõ badã   põ-dã-ta-wo?"   "Wĩ   põ-dã-ta-pa."
       your   mother   come-3Hon-Past-Dubit   not come-3Hon-Past-Assert
       '"Did your mother come?" "She did not come."'

(48)   "Õbæ-dẽ   go-te   põ-bi-i?"   "Wĩ   go-ta-bo-pa."
       empty-in   go-ing   come-2S-Ig   not go-Past-1S-Assert
       '"Are you coming from having gone to the forest?" "I did not go."'

Negative potentiality is sometimes expressed by a simple statement utilizing the negative particle in the verb phrase, with the strong implication of inability to perform (49). However, the more common way to express negative potential is by a type of irrealis, as described in section 4.3.

(49)   Wĩ   pi-bo-pa.
       not   net:hammocks-1S-Assert
       'I do not net hammocks.'
       I.e., 'I can't...' or 'I don't know how to...'

As noted in section 1.1, negation in compound verb phrases varies according to the construction. In motion-action or motion-motion verb phrases, negation applies both to the initial, uninflected motion verb and to the action (50) or concomitant motion (51) verb.

(50)   Bitõ wĩ   põ   kǽ-bi-ta-pa.
       you   not   come   eat-2S-Past-Assert
       'You did not come eat.'

(51)   Wĩ   go   gii-dãdi   awædõ.
       not   go   enter-3Pl   1:Neg:React
       'It concerns me that they do not go enter.'

The particle *wii*, like the deverbalizer, is used to negate the cause of what would be, in the positive case, a cause-action verb phrase.

(52) Wĕyǽ-dãdi ĩ-dãdi-te   wĩĩ odõbõ-gã-pa.
      child-3Pl   be-3Pl-ing not teach-3S-Assert
      'He/she does not teach the children.'

In an action-reaction or an action-observation verb phrase, the particle *wĩĩ* precedes and negates the action verb which, being the first verb in the phrase, is inflected only for person and number. In this case, the semantic import is a positive reaction to a nonoccurring action. The reaction or observation verb, fully inflected, is not negated by the noncontiguous negative particle, nor can it be immediately preceded by the negative particle.

(53) Wĩĩ kǽ-gã   a-bi-ta-wo?
      not eat-3S   see-2S-Past-Dubit
      'Did you see that he/she did not eat?'

Negation of the reaction verb or of the observation verb is expressed, rather, by the negative deverbalizer (see section 1.1). However, by subordinating the action, the reaction or the observation verb is disengaged from the action verb and may be negated either by the deverbalizer *-dãbaĩ* or by the particle *wĩĩ*, as in example (54). As a response, the subordinated phrase (in parentheses) would normally be lacking.

(54) (Tõbĕgã kǽ-yõ-gã)   botõ wĩĩ a-ta-bo-pa.
      he/she eat-while-3S I   not see-Past-1S-Assert
      'I did not see (him eat).'
      Literally, '(While he was eating,) I was not looking.'

As is the case when a subordinate clause is negated by the deverbalizer *-dãbaĩ*, the particle *wĩĩ* is likewise used to negate subordinate clauses, whether their subject is the same as that of the main clause, as in example (55), or different from it (56).

(55) Wĩĩ ĕyĕ-te   (beyǽ-ke)   wæ-kæ-kã-ĩ-pa.
      not hear-ing   (because-Rstr)   cry-Incept-3S-Infer-Assert
      'He's going to be sorry (simply because of) not listening.'

(56) Tõbĕgã bǽgã   wĩĩ a-yõ-gã   wĕyǽ-gã edæ
      his   older:sister not look-while-3S child-3S climactic
      æpǽ-dĕ doo   gii-kã-ĩ-pa.
      water-in already enter-3S-Infer-Assert
      'While his older sister was not watching, the child entered right into the water.'

When the negative particle *wĩ* occurs in the predicate of the protasis in a contrary-to-fact conditional sentence, it serves to express a semantically positive condition; the apodosis, however, remains contrary to fact (57). The converse is true when the apodosis is negated by the negative particle *wĩ* (58).

(57) Botõ wĩ   põ   a-bo   baĩ badã-bĩ   doo
      I   not come   see-1S if   mother-2Hon   already
      wǽ-kædõ-bĩ-pa.
      die-would-2Hon-Assert
      'If I had not come and seen (you), mother, you would already have died.'

(58) Õkõ-dę̃   owo-te   baĩ wĩ   wǽ-kædõ-gã-ĩ-pa.
      house-in swing-ing   if   not   die-would-3S-Infer-Assert
      'If he/she had stayed at home, he/she would not have died.'

2 Negation of other constituent phrases

The particle *wĩ* 'not' which, because it negates the verb phrase, is included in the description of standard clause negation (see section 1.2), negates other constituent phrases, as well. It occurs initial in the phrase which it negates.

When negating either the verb phrase or other constituents, the negative particle *wĩ* has a strong element of contrast with an opposite condition, stated or unstated. Example (59) is here included for comparison of its contrastive potential in negating the verb phrase with its same function in a subject noun phrase (60), and in a location phrase (61).

(59) Botõ bǽpo   wĩ   yi-kã-pa.   (Õkõ   bǽdõ-gã-pa.)
      my   father not   chop-3S-Assert   (house   build-3S-Assert)
      'My father is not chopping. (He is building a house.)'

(60) Wĩ   botõ bǽpo   yi-kã-pa.   (Wa-kã   yi-kã-pa.)
      not   my   father chop-3S-Assert   (other-3S   chop-3S-Assert)
      'It is not my father who is chopping. (It is another who is chopping.)'

(61) Wĩ   ĩ-yõbõ   yi-kã-pa.   (Wa-yõbõ   yi-kã-pa.)
      not   this-place   chop-3S-Assert   (other-place   chop-3S-Assert)
      'It is not here that he is chopping. (It is elsewhere that he is chopping).'

The particle *wĩ* 'not' also negates qualifying phrases:

(62) Wẽyǽ-gã   wĩ   tõĩgã   yewǽbõ-gã-pa.
      child-3S   not   straight write-3S-Assert
      'The child does not write straight.'

(63)   Wĩĩ   wa-ĕ-bŏ   awædŏ.
       not   good-appear-face   1:Neg:React
       'I don't like (it).'
       Literally, 'It concerns me (that it is) not good-appearing.'

(64)   Wĩĩ   kĩgæ̃ kægŏ-gã.
       not   fast   walk-3S
       'He/she doesn't walk fast.'

The negative response to a yes-no question regarding a constituent phrase normally repeats the questioned phrase, beginning with the particle *wĩĩ* 'not'.

(65)   "Go-dĩ-ke   bĩdatŏ   wãtæpiyæ̃ kẽwẽ-gĩ-bĩda?"
       go-Pfnz-Rstr   you:two   long:time live-Fut-2D
       "Wĩĩ   wãtæpiyæ̃ kẽwẽ-gĩ-bŏda."
       not   long:time live-Fut-1D
       "'When you two go, will you stay a long time?" "Not for long shall we two stay.'"

(66)   "Kæ̃guĩwæ̃   picæ̃   ĩ-ta-wo?"   "Wĩĩ   picæ̃   ĩ-ta-pa."
       hawk   old   be-Past-Dubit   not   old   be-Past-Assert
       "'Was the hawk old?" "It was not old.'"

3 Negative words

Negative words are of such divergent usage and syntactic function that categorization does not seem to be useful. However, a subclassification is here made on the basis of cooccurrence restrictions. Presented in section 3.1 are negative one-word responses; section 3.2 is reserved for those negative words which function in the conjoining of clauses; the function of three diverse qualifiers is described in section 3.3.

3.1 Negative one-word responses

Negative one-word responses are particles which occur in isolation. Each of them, with the exception of *dikæ*, 'No way' (section 3.1) is normally followed by an abrupt glottal closure. The glottal stop is optionally present even when another word follows, and it is particularly likely to be present in case of exaggerated emphasis.

Of the negative particles which occur as one-word responses, the two considered in this section are limited to that function. These are the particle of disinvolvement *wa* 'Don't ask me!' or 'How should I know?' (67); and the particle of noncommittal *'m* 'Maybe!', whose phonetic realization lies outside the phonemic system (68).

Both of these one-word responses constitute a subtle noncommittal to fulfil a request or to assume responsibility to supply information; thus, whereas they are not definitely negative statements, the implication is strongly negative. They may likewise be used as negative responses to a yes-no question.

(67) "Bitõ   wĕ-gã   botõ   õkõ-dĕ   gii-kã-ta-wo?"
     your   child-3S   my   house-in   enter-3S-Past-Dubit
     "Wa!"
     disinvolvement
     "'Did your child enter my house?" "How should I know?"'

(68) "Bitõ   botõ tõdõ gĕa   kæ-kĩ-bi?" "'m!"
     you   me   with together do-Fut-2S   noncommittal
     "'Will you help me?" "Maybe!"' I.e., "'Probably not!"'

The negative words which function either as a one-word response or as a semantically determinate particle closely bound to a head verb in a verb phrase are the response particle of refusal *baa* 'No; I refuse!' (69, 70) and the negative existential particle *dæœ* 'none, nonexistent' (71).

The particle of refusal *baa* 'No; I refuse!' contrasts with the acquiescence particle *Ao* 'O.K.; agreed.' Both are limited to occurrence without a verb or with the verb *ã* 'say'. The particle *baa*, either in isolation or with the first-person form of *ã* 'say', constitutes the normal refusal in response to a yes-no question of request.

(69) "Botõ   bĩyæ   õbæ-dĕ   go-kĩ-bi?" "Baa   (ã-bo-pa)."
     me   following   empty-in   go-Fut-2S   no   (say-1S-Assert)
     "'Will you go with me to the forest?" "(I say,) No!"'

So tight is the intonational linkage of each of these two particles with the verb *ã* 'say' that the sequence is not interpreted as a normal quotation plus verb of speech, but rather as a complex verb phrase corresponding to those illustrated in example (13) in the introductory material above.

(70) Baa   ã-dãdi(-pa).
     no   say-3Pl(-Assert)
     'They refuse.' Literally, 'They say, "No!"'

Nonverbal indications of refusal occur as well: viz., an emphatic ingressive bilabial click or implosive, which is often accompanied by a rapid jerk of the head to one side; or a profound silence with no change of facial expression (in contrast to raising of the eyebrows or blinking, which would indicate agreement).

The negative existential particle *dæœ* 'none, nonexistent' contrasts with the positive existential particle *bǽǽ* 'existent, there is (some)'. These existential particles often occur as one-word responses. Otherwise, like the refusal and acquiescence particles just described, they likewise occur in a complex verb phrase with the verb *ã* which is normally glossed, 'say'. However, in this and other cases, the verb *ã* carries a semantic load 'be in existence' or 'be (here)'.

(71) Dæœ (ã-gã-ta-pa).   Bǽǽ   (ã-gã-ta-pa).
     none exist-3S-Past-Assert there:be   exist-3S-Past-Assert
     '(He/she was) nonexistent (here/there).' '(He/she was) existent (here/there).'

The particle *dæœ* is frequently used as a negative response to a yes-no question.

(72) "Bõdõ wǽpo doo   põ-gã?"   "Dæœ   (ã-gã)."
     our:N father already come-3S   none   (exist-3S)
     "'Has our (inclusive) father already come?'" "'(He is) nonexistent (here).'"

The negative words which function either as a one-word response or as a constituent morpheme in the clause are the particle of denial *dikœ* 'No way!' and the negator *wĩ* 'not' (see sections 1.2 and 2). However, the distribution of the two as constituents in no way coincides.

The denial particle, *dikœ* 'No way!' or 'You can search me!' functions as a negative adverb (see section 4.1) or stands alone as a one-word response. The following example represents a question and a reply which shuns responsibility.

(73) "Badã   æ-dõ-dõ   go-dã?"
     mother which-way-Cntnt   go-3Hon
     "Dikæ.   (Éyĕ-dãbaĩ ĩ-bo-pa.)"
     denial (hear-Neg be-1S-Assert)
     "'Where is Mother going?' 'You can search me! (I haven't heard.)'"

(74) "Botõ yaĕbĕ   õõ   ǽǽ-bi-ta-pa."
     my   machete grab get-2S-Past-Assert
     "Dikæ.   (Ǽǽ-dãbaĩ ĩ-bo-pa.)"
     denial (get-Neg be-1S-Assert)
     "'You stole my machete.' 'No way! (I am not a taker.)'"

The particle *dikæ* also functions as a noncommittal response to a yes-no question, with or without further explanation.

(75) "Botõ gĩta ĩ-gã-te   wæ̃dõ-dãdi-ta-wo?"
      my   dog   be-3S-ing   kill-3Pl-Past-Dubit

      "Dikæ.   (Botõ   a-dãbaĩ ĩ-ta-bo-pa)."
      denial   (I   see-Neg be-Past-1S-Assert)

      "'Did they kill my dog?" "You can search me! (I didn't see (it).)"'

3.2 Negative words in conjoii:ed clauses

While there are no intrinsically negative conjunctions in Waorani, three means of conjoining clauses have negative overtones: the concessive conjunction *ĩkæte* 'yet, although', the conjoining particle of rebuttal *ĩyæ̃pa* 'but why not', and the conjoining particle of alternation *gikẽdẽ* 'on the other hand'.

Concessive *ĩkæte* 'although' occurs final in the initial concessive clause.

(76) Bæ̃po-kã   pã-gã   ĩkæte   wẽyæ̃-gã   go-dõbẽke
      father-3S punish-3S   although child-3S   go-further

      wẽdæ wẽdæ   kæ-kã-ta-pa.

      bad bad   do-3S-Past-Assert
      'Although the father punished him, the child acted even worse.'

The conjoining particle of rebuttal *ĩyæ̃pa* 'but why not' or 'but in fact' occurs initial in a rebuttal or following the initial subject which becomes the focus of accusation or defense.

(77) "Go-dõ-bi   æ̃æ̃-gã-e."
      go-way-2S   get-3S-Impv

      "Bitõ tõbẽ-bi   ĩyæ̃pa   go-dõ-bi   æ̃æ̃-gã-e."
      you   person-2S rebuttal go-way-2S   get-3S-Impv

      "'Give it to him." "But why don't you give it to him yourself!"'

The alternation particle *gikẽdẽ* 'on the other hand', follows a noun phrase or a pronoun that is being brought into alternative focus.

(78) Badã   tẽdẽwæ̃   æ̃æ̃-kæ   go-dã-pa.
      mother firewood   get-Incept go-3Hon-Assert

      Bæ̃po   gikẽdẽ   õkõ-dẽ   aa   õgõ-gã-pa.
      father alternation   house-in openly sit/stand-3S-Assert

      'Mother is going to get firewood. Father, on the other hand, is there at home.'

3.3 Negative qualifiers

Three diverse qualifiers have negative components: the adverb *wĩwa* 'badly, wickedly', the adverb *ǽbǽwo* 'for the last time', and the qualifying stem *õbœ-/õba-* 'empty'.

The adverb *wĩwa* 'badly, wickedly' appears to be a litotes derived from the constituent phrase particle *wĩĩ* 'not' (sections 1.2, 2, 3.1) compounded (in an atypical fashion) with the qualifier *waa* 'good, well', negating that quality in an exaggerated manner.

(79) Wĩwa kæ-kǎ awædõ.
     not:well do-3S 1:Neg:React
     'It seems to me that he is acting wickedly.'

In certain contexts the adverb *ǽbǽwo* 'for the last time' yields the negative meaning, 'Never again'.

(80) Ǽbǽwo põdĩ wẽdæ wẽdæ kæ-bo-pa.
     for:the:last:time very bad bad do-1S-Assert
     'For the very last time I do badly.'
     I.e., 'Never again will I do badly!'

The qualifying stem *õbœ-/õba-* 'empty', forms a qualifying compound with any of a number of relational classifying suffixes (such as *-dẽ* 'inside', *-ga* 'on surface', *-po* 'in hand', *-dœca* 'top of head'). It affirms the absence or nonexistence of a specified substance that would be expected to stand in the expressed relationship to the noun represented by the classifier.

(81) Kǽ-gĩ õbæ-po-bõdi ĩ-bõdi-pa.
     eat-Fut:Nz empty-hand-1X be-1X-Assert
     'We (exclusive) are without food.'

(82) Ocai õbæ-dæka-bi ĩ-bi-pǽǽ.
     brain empty-head:top-2S be-2S-Derisive
     'You are brainless – ha ha!'

4 Irrealis

4.1 Simple irrealis

The simple irrealis suffix *-a/-gaa/-yaa* varies phonologically according to the quality of the preceding vowel: *-a* follows the vowels *a* and *ã*, *-gaa* follows the vowels *o* and *õ*, and *-yaa* follows the vowels *i* and *ĩ*. The suffix is restricted in occurrence to final position following person-number suffixes and, optionally, the verb suffix string *-ta-wo* 'past-dubitative'. Irrealis clauses likewise potentially include the normal negative markers (see section 5).

(83)   A-bo-gaa.
       see-1s-Irreal
       'I see – not so!'
       I.e., 'I do/did not see (it).'

The particle *dikæ* (section 3.1) commonly occurs somewhere in the irrealis frustrative clause with the meaning 'indeed not, scarcely', apparently insuring that the unreal import be clearly understood. In response to a positive statement or a yes-no question, the particle *dikæ* frequently occurs as a nonverbal clause replacing the entire frustrative clause.

(84)   "Wǽdõ-dãdi-ta-wo?""Dikæ   (wǽdõ-dãdi-yaa)."
       kill-3Pl-Past-Dubit   denial   kill-3Pl-Irreal
       "'Did they kill (it)?" "Indeed not! (they kill (it) – not so!)"'

(85)   (Dikæ)   põ-dõ-gã-a.
       (denial)   come-way-3S-Irreal
       'Indeed not! he gives (it to me) – not so!'
       I.e. 'Indeed not! So he gives (it to me), does he? He certainly does not!'

4.2 Complex irrealis

A complex irrealis construction is also fairly common. It consists of a protasis in which the only markers on the verb are optional person-number and the assertive suffix *-pa*, followed by an apodosis whose verb carries an obligatory future *-kĩ/-gĩ* suffix plus an optional person-number suffix plus an obligatory interrogative-marking reduplication of the final vowel of the verb itself. Since both the protasis and the apodosis express semantically unreal situations, transport of negation from the negated apodosis to the protasis seems to occur. I am not aware that negative transport occurs elsewhere.

(86)   A-bo-pa   go-kĩ-bo-o.
       see-1S-Assert   go-Fut-1S-Ig
       'I see; shall I go?'
       I.e., 'Am I able to see, that I should go? (No!)'

4.3 Negative potential

Negative potential, with a few exceptions (see section 1.2), is based on the question *æ-dõ kœ-te* (which-Cntnt do-ing) 'how could?' The verb is often marked for future, and the otherwise final vowel is often reduplicated. The intended import is an irrealis, 'No way!'

(87)   Pikǽ-gã   ĩ   ĩ-dĩ-ke   æ-dõ   kæ-te   ẽbǽ-gĩ-gã?
       mature-3S   be   be-Pf:Nz-Rstr   which-Cntnt   do-ing   tame-Fut-3S
       'Since he (peccary) is mature, how could he become tame?'
       I.e., 'He cannot be tamed because he is too old.'

4.4. Compound verb phrases

Irrealis constructions serve to negate the totality of certain compound verb phrases, especially motion-action, cause-action, and motion-cause-action (88). To a lesser extent, irrealis constructions may negate compound verb phrases involving reaction or observation (89).

(88)   Tõbẽgã   gii   odõbõ-gã   ẽyẽ-dãdi-yaa.
       he/she   enter   show-3S   hear-3Pl-Irreal
       'He/she enters and teaches and they learn – not so!'
       I.e., 'He/she doesn't enter and teach and therefore they do not learn.'

(89)   Cowodẽ   põ-gã   a-bo-gaa.
       outsider   come-3S   see-1S-Irreal
       'I see an outsider come – not so!'
       I.e. 'I don't see the outsider coming because he/she does not come.'

5 Combinations of negation within a clause

5.1 Negative deverbalizer plus negative particle

When the deverbalizer *-dãbaĩ* 'negative' (section 1.1) and the negative particle *wĩĩ* 'not' (section 1.2) occur in a single clause, there are three possible effects, which are now discussed.

When the particle *wĩĩ* negates a nonpredicate phrase, the verb phrase in the predicate may likewise be negated by the deverbalizer *-dãbaĩ*, resulting in two independent negations. For example, in (90), *wĩĩ* negates the adverbial phrase of time, whereas *-dãbaĩ* negates the clause as a whole.

(90) Wĩĩ   yõwo   kǽ-dãbaĩ   ĩ-gǽ-ĩ-pa.
      not   now   eat-Neg   be-should-Infer-Assert
      (Beĩbõ be-te   a-te   bõdõ kǽ-dãbaĩ   ĩ-gǽ-ĩ-pa.)
      pill   drink-ing see-ing we:N eat-Neg   be-should-Infer-Assert
      'It is not now that we (inclusive) are not to eat. (We are not to eat after having
      taken a pill.)'

When *wĩĩ* negates the verb which is marked by the negative deverbalizer, the
double negative yields a positive.

(91) Bõdõ   wĩĩ   kǽ-dãbaĩ   ĩ-gǽ-ĩ-pa.
      we:N   not   eat-Neg   be-should-Infer-Assert
      'We are not to refrain from eating.'

There is, however, a situation in which the negative particle reinforces the
effect of the negative deverbalizer. In this case the initial negative particle
is usually followed by a pause and/or a high-level glottal stop (see section
3.1) which apparently is a phonological signal that the negative particle is
functioning as a one-word response, leaving the full negative situation to
be explained by the following deverbalized verb.

(92) Wĩĩ,.   botõ   kǽ-dãbaĩ   ĩ-ta-bo-pa.
      not   I   eat-Neg   be-Past-1S-Assert
      'Not so; I did not eat (it).'

5.2 Negative deverbalizer plus irrealis

When the clause is negated by the negative deverbalizer plus an irrealis
marker, the result is generally positive.

(93) Wǽ-dãbaĩ   ĩ-bi-ta-wo-gaa.
      cry-Neg   be-2S-Past-Dubit-Irreal
      'So you didn't cry, eh? You certainly did!' Literally, 'It is not true that you
      weren't crying.'

(94) Ǽ-dõ   kæ-te   kǽ-dãbaĩ   ĩ-gĩ-dãdi-i?
      which-Cntnt do-ing   eat-Neg   be-Fut-3Pl-Ig
      'How could they not eat?' I.e., 'They are not to refrain from eating.' Or 'They
      are to eat.'

5.3 Quotations

In clauses which include a quotation, either the quotation (95) or the margin
(96), or both (97), may be negated, but negative transport evidently does not
occur.

(95) Botõ,"Wæ-dãbaĩ ĩ-kæ-kã-ĩ-pa,"   ã-te   põdĕ-bo-pa.
    I   cry-Neg   be-Incept-3S-Infer-Assert say-ing think-1S-Assert
    'I think he will (surely) not cry.'

(96) "Pĩĩ-gĩ-gã,"   ã-te   botõ ĕyĕ-dãbaĩ ĩ-ta-bo-pa.
    be:angry-Fut-3S   say-ing I   hear-Neg be-Past-1S-Assert
    'I did not know he/it would be angry.'

(97) "Wæ-dãbaĩ ĩ-kæ-kã-ĩ-pa,"
    cry-Neg   be-Incept-3S-Infer-Assert
    ã-te   botõ dikæ   ã-ta-wo-gaa.
    say-ing I   denial say-Past-Dubit-Irreal
    'No way did I say, "He will not cry."'

Notes

1. Data for this paper have been collected and analysis made during some thirty years of contact with the Waorani. Some illustrations are drawn from texts collected by Elizabeth Elliot Gren and Rachel Saint, to whom I am indebted for original materials which facilitated my introduction into the Waorani language. I am indebted to Stephen Levinsohn for advice at critical points and for substantial help in the organization of this article.

Abbreviations

Assert	assertive	Noncom	noncommittal
Cntnt	content (question)	Nz	nominalizer
Dubit	dubitative	Pf	perfect
Farp	farpast	Pl	plural
Fut	future	Qty	quantity
Hon	honorific	React	reaction performative
Ig	interrogative	Rstr	restrictive
Impv	imperative	X	exclusive
Incept	inceptive	1	firstperson
Infer	inferential	2	second person
ing	participle, same subject	3	third person
Irreal	irrealis	!	exclamatory intonation
N	inclusive	?	interrogative intonation
Neg	negative		

References

Kelley, Patricia M. (1988). *Issues for literacy materials development in a monolingual Amazonian culture: the Waodani of Ecuador.* Vancouver: University of British Columbia.

Manus, Ronald Raker and Phyllis Wright de Manus (1971). 'Urarina.' In: Jakway, Martha Todd (ed). 1975. *Listas comparativas; idiomas vernáculas de la Selva*, Datos Etno-Lingüísticos, No. 4. Microfiche. Lima: Instituto Lingüístico de Verano.

Peeke, M. Catherine (1973). 'Preliminary Grammar of Auca.' *Summer Institute of Linguistics Publications in linguistics and related fields*, Publication 39. Norman: Summer Institute of Linguistics.

——— (1979). *El idioma Huao: gramática pedagógica. Tomo 1. Cuadernos etnolingüísticos*, No. 3. Quito: Instituto Lingüístico de Verano.

——— (1991). 'Vocabulario huaorani'. In: *Listas comparativas de palabras en diez idiomas autóctonos ecuatorianos. Cuadernos Etnolingüísticos*, No. 13. Quito: Instituto Lingüístico de Verano.

Pike, Evelyn G. and Rachel Saint (1988). *Workpapers concerning Waorani discourse features. Language data Amerindian series*, Publication Number 10. Dallas: The Summer Institute of Linguistics.

Pike, Kenneth L. (1964). 'Stress Trains in Auca'. In: David Abercrombie and others (eds), *In honour of Daniel Jones: papers contributed on the occasion of his eightieth birthday, September 12, 1961*, 425-31. London: Longmans.

Ruhlen, M. (1987). *A guide to the world's languages*, Vol.I. Stanford: Stanford University Press.

Saint, Rachel, and Kenneth L. Pike. (1959). 'Notas Sobre Fonémica Huarani (Auca)'. In: *Estudios acerca de las lenguas Huarani (Auca), Shimigae y Záparo*, 4-17. Quito: Publicaciones Científicos del Ministerio de Educación del Ecuador.

Saint, Rachel, and Kenneth L. Pike (1962). 'Auca Phonemics.' In: *Studies in Ecuadorian Indian languages*, Vol. I, 2-30. Norman: Summer Institute of Linguistics.

Tessman, Günter (1930). *Die Indianer nordost-Perus*. Hamburg: Friedrichsen, de Gruyter & Co.

Nadëb

E.M. Helen Weir

1 Introduction

Nadëb is a Brazilian indigenous language spoken by a few hundred people in north-west Amazonas state. It has been classified as belonging to the Makú or Makú-Puináve family (see, for example, Rivet and Tastevin 1920, Mason 1950:257-258, Tovar 1961:156-157, Loukotka 1968:190-193). Ruhlen (1987) classifies it as Amerind\Equatorial-Tucanoan\Macro-Tucanoan\ Puinave-Maku\Maku. To date, little comparative work has been done on this family, but preliminary findings suggest that Nadëb seems to be only distantly related to other languages in the family. There are at least two dialects of Nadëb. The data on which the present analysis is based are from the upper Uneiuxi dialect.[1]

The study of negation in Nadëb reveals some very unusual features. The negation of any non-imperative verbal main clause requires a radical change in the structure of the clause, resulting in a non-verbal equative clause (section 2). There are a number of other negative constructions which have no direct affirmative equivalent. These include the grammaticalized negated relative clause (GNRC) construction (section 2.2),[2] negative existential clauses (section 5), and the functional equivalent of an agentive negative passive construction (section 17.1). In fact, the only negative constructions which have direct affirmative equivalents seem to be dependent or embedded clauses (sections 8 and 17.2) and imperatives (section 9). There appears to be no sentence negation in the sense of Klima (1964) (section 8), but there are two alternative ways of performing standard negation of intransitive and certain transitive clauses. There are three negative morphemes in Nadëb: *dooh*, *na-*, and *manih*. The first, *dooh*, is a syntactic negative, a nominal which functions as predicate complement NP, or as a constituent of the predicate complement, in an equative clause. It is used to negate non-imperative main clauses (sections 2.1 and 3) and as the negative one-word answer to a question (section 7). The second negative morpheme, *na-*, is a morphological negative, a verb prefix. It is used to negate dependent clauses (section 8) and in GNRC constructions. A GNRC may be used to negate intransitive and certain transitive non-imperative main clauses, as an alternative to the syntactic negative *dooh* (section 2.2). The syntactic negative *dooh* and the morphological negative *na-* may in certain circumstances be used in the same clause to produce a positive result (see section 14). The third negative morpheme, *manih*, is used to negate imperative clauses (section 9).

Among the other unusual features presented by Nadëb is the OSV basic word order in non-imperative verbal main clauses (see, for example, 5a below). The alternative order SVO is also found. OSV is reportedly very rare as a basic word order (see, for example, Derbyshire and Pullum 1986:16-18). For arguments in support of the claim that this is the basic order in Nadëb, see Weir (1980; 1984:270-284).

There are two true question words, *yaah* 'who' and *niih* 'which'. Both occur only as predicate complement, or as a constituent of the predicate complement, in an equative clause. As such, they are normally in clause initial position. A third question word, *hxuúd* 'what', is a nominalized form of the root of a very generic verb *a-hxuút*, which can substitute any verb in the language. In addition to its interrogative use, *hxuúd* is also used with a variety of other meanings, and has more freedom of position than the true question words. Polar questions are distinguished from statements by intonation. There are no question particles as such, although there are certain particles which may occur in questions to indicate contra-expectation, etc.

There is no copula in the surface form of a basic equative main clause. The two equated phrases appear in juxtaposition, with the predicate complement preceding the subject in the basic order, as in (1).[3]

(1)   Suuw   ta   ib.
       shaman 3Sg   father
       'His father is a shaman.'

The structure of the nominal phrase is basically very simple, although embedding can make a particular NP appear quite complex. A NP may consist of (i) a head nominal only; (ii) a head nominal preceded by a dependent NP in genitive relationship; (iii) a relative or other nominalized clause; or (iv) two NPs in apposition or juxtaposition. Two appositive NPs are often separated by other clause constituents. There is no class of adjectives as such in Nadëb. Demonstratives and numerals, when they function as nominals, occur only as the sole constituent of a NP, although they may be used in apposition to other NPs or as dependent NPs in a genitive construction. In relative clauses, the head immediately follows the verb. There are only two possible heads for a relative clause: *doo* 'referential' and *péh* 'non-referential'.

In some contexts, headless relative clauses are found.[4] Another NP may occur in apposition to a relative clause, further identifying the domain of the head. For examples of relative clauses, see (5c,d), (21a,b), (23a,b) below.

Nadëb is a postpositional language, but there is an obligatory rule which moves a first person singular possessive pronoun to the position immediately following its head noun or postposition (see, for example, 2 and 59a below). This obligatory post-posing of a pronoun for one person only is another unusual feature of Nadëb. Comparatives are generally expressed by means of a postpositional phrase which contains the standard of comparison, as in (2).

(2) Txaah   ii   a-eeh-dúk   a   txaah   bahinh.
     son   1Sg:Poss Form-be:big-Cmpl   2Sg:Poss   son   beyond
     'My son is bigger than your son.'

Comparison may also be expressed by juxtaposed clauses of the type 'A is big; B is small'. Nadëb verb roots have several forms: indicative/non-indicative, unitary/multiple, simple/extended. Suffixes also have indicative and non-indicative forms. A verb may have more than one root. Second roots and some suffixes may have arisen from auxiliary verbs. A non-indicative root form has a certain nominal quality. Any verb root or suffix requires any preceding root or suffix to be in the non-indicative form. A non-indicative form also occurs in non-finite clauses, such as conditional clauses, in nouns formed from verb roots, and in imperatives. Thus, the non-indicative form bears some resemblance to the English infinitive.

Nadëb verb prefixes are classified in six types:

1. the formative prefix, *a-*, which is usually attached to the main verb root in the absence of other prefixes, elements incorporated into the verb, or proclitic pronouns;
2. the multi-function 'aspect' prefix, *i-*, which occurs obligatorily in all contexts with some verbs and only in certain contexts with others (the aspect prefix, when present, always occurs immediately preceding the main verb root);
3. derivational prefixes, which add a further dimension of meaning;
4. thematic prefixes, which occur obligatorily with certain verb roots, but not at all with others, and whose meaning is often difficult or impossible to isolate from that of the root (a verb may have more than one thematic prefix);

5. relational prefixes, which change grammatical relations within the clause (sometimes called 'applicative'; see, for example, Baker 1988:230);
6. subordination prefixes, which occur only in certain dependent clauses, such as relative clauses and clausal complements.

Nadëb has an unusual prefix ordering rule. When more than one prefix occurs with the same verb root, their relative order is determined by surface form rather than by type or meaning. For example, the derivational negative prefix *na-* precedes the thematic, derivational, and relational prefixes *da-*, *ha-*, *la-*, *ta-*, and *ya-*, and follows the thematic, derivational, and relational prefixes *ba-*, *ga-*, *ja-*, *ka-*, *ma-*, *pa-*, *sa-*, *wa-*. The negative prefix *na-* may also co-occur with another *na-* prefix (derivational or thematic). However, it is not possible to determine which *na-* precedes the other, since they are identical in form and never separated by any other prefix. Any prefix (Ca-) which occurs immediately preceding the aspect prefix *i-* combines with it to form Ci-. For more details on Nadëb verb prefixes, see Weir (1986).

2 Standard negation

Standard negation, i.e. the negation of a simple verbal intransitive clause, may be expressed in one of two ways: (i) by use of the syntactic negative *dooh* (see section 2.1); or (ii) by use of a grammaticalized negated relative clause (GNRC) construction which contains the morphological negative *na-* (see section 2.2). In each case, the resulting negative expression is a non-verbal equative clause.

2.1 Negation of verbal main clauses using the syntactic negative *dooh*

Non-imperative verbal main clauses (intransitive or transitive) may be negated using the negative nominal *dooh* which could be translated 'something non-existent' but is glossed here simply as 'Neg'. It appears to be a nominalization of the root of the verb *ba-doh* 'be non-existent'. Payne (1985:228) states that 'standard negation [...] realized by means of a negative morpheme which has nominal properties' is rare. He cites as the only example of this known to him the Evenki *ācin*, with similar forms in related languages. For discussion of Evenki *ācin* see Nedyalkov's article in this volume; for discussion of the interpretation of the Nadëb *dooh* as a nominal morpheme, see Weir (1984:193-211).

Dooh usually functions as the predicate complement NP of a non-verbal equative clause, but is occasionally found as a constituent of the predicate complement of such a clause (see sections 6, 14). The sentence being negated becomes a non-finite nominalized clause which is often marked by the postposition *bú* 'ablative' (see 3b), although *bú* is optional in many contexts (see 3c).[5] The form of the verb root changes from indicative in the affirmative main clause to non-indicative in the negative, i.e. to the form required in all non-finite nominalized clauses. It is not completely clear at this stage whether the non-finite clause should be understood as subject of the equative clause or as a subordinate clause with the equative subject empty. A literal translation in English is difficult to give, but might be something like: 'The child crying is something non-existent' or 'It is something non-existent, the child crying'. The nominalization is over the whole embedded clause, and not just the verb as the literal translation in English might suggest.

(3)   a. Kalapéé a-óót.
          child   Form-cry+Indic
          'The child is crying.'
    b. Dooh   kalapéé a-ód.   bú.
          Neg   child   Form-cry+NonInd Abl
          'The child isn't crying.'
    c. Dooh kalapéé a-ód.
          'The child isn't crying.'

The same non-finite nominalized clause may be used with other meanings, for example as a conditional or universal temporal clause, as in (4). In this case, however, the postposition *bú* is obligatory. For other uses of non-finite nominalized clauses, see Weir (1984:80-83).

(4)   Kalapéé a-ód   bú   ta   inh   a-tón.
    child   Form-cry+NonInd Abl 3Sg sister Form-hold:in:hand+Indic
    'If/Whenever the child is crying, his sister carries him.'
    (Lit., 'The child crying his sister carries (him).')

2.2 Negation of verbal main clauses using a grammaticalized negated relative clause (GNRC) construction

The second way of negating non-imperative verbal main clauses is by forming a GNRC from the predicate of the clause. The result is a non-verbal equative clause in which the GNRC is the predicate complement NP. The negative prefix *na-* appears in the nominalized form of the verb, which is always non-indicative. A prefixal negative is contrary to the tendency for OV languages to have suffixes rather than prefixes. Givón (1984:337), however, notes that for affixes which have arisen from negative intensifiers (usually nouns) a prefixal negative marker would be expected in an OV language. The origin of the negative prefix *na-* in Nadëb is unclear.

(3a) above negated in this manner results in (3d), where the subject is *kalapéé* 'child', while the predicate complement is *na-ód* 'a non-crier'. The state of 'non-crying' applies to the time to which the statement refers, and is not to be regarded as indicating any permanent or semi-permanent characteristic, as the English literal translation might imply (see section 4).

(3)   d.   Na-ód   kalapéé.
           Neg-cry:NonInd child
           'The child isn't crying.'
           (Lit., 'The child is a non-crier.')

One complement of the affirmative verb, direct object or adverbial, may be included in a GNRC, as in (5b). There are, however, restrictions on the referentiality of the nominal which may be included (see below).

(5)   a.   Tóóh   dab kad   a-wuh.
           wild:pig   meat uncle   Form-eat+Indic
           'Uncle is eating wild pig meat.'

      b.   Tóóh   dab na-wuuh   kad.
           wild:pig   meat Neg-eat+NonInd   uncle
           'Uncle isn't eating wild pig meat.'
           (Lit., 'Uncle is a non-wild-pig-meat-eater.')

As with intransitive verbs, the GNRC does not indicate a permanent characteristic. Thus, in (5b) the non-eating of wild pig meat applies to the time to which the statement refers, leaving open the possibility that uncle may eat wild pig meat on other occasions.

The derivation of the GNRC in (5b) is explained in more detail by considering (5c-e): (5c) is the relative clause formed from (5a) by relativization of the subject (the prefix *ha-* marks the fact that it is the subject which is relativized, while *doo* is the head of the relative clause); (5d) is the negation of the relative clause in (5c); (5e) is the grammaticalization (formation of a word) of the negated relative clause in (5d).

(5) c. tóóh   dab ha-wʉh   doo.
         wild:pig   meat RS-eat+Indic Ref
         'one who is eating wild pig meat.'

     d. tóóh   dab na-wʉh   doo.
         wild:pig   meat Neg-eat+Indic Ref
         'one who isn't eating wild pig meat.'

     e. tóóh   dab na-wʉʉh.
         wild:pig   meat Neg-eat+NonInd
         'a non-wild-pig-meat-eater.'

The direct object, or other complement, of an embedded verb in a GNRC may be specified in the equative clause other than as part of the GNRC (see 5f). However, it must then be marked with the postposition *hã* 'dative', indicating that it is an explicitation of an implicit embedded nominal.[6, 7] So far as I am aware, there is no difference in meaning between (5b) and (5f).

(5) f. Na-wʉʉh   kad   tóóh   dab hã.
         Neg-eat+NonInd   uncle   wild:pig   meat Dat
         'Uncle isn't eating wild pig meat.'
         (Lit., 'Uncle is a non-eater with respect to wild pig meat.')

Grammaticalizations of relative clauses such as in this example are normally permitted only with negated relative clauses. Thus, **tóóh dab ha-wʉʉh*, which would be the equivalent grammaticalization of (5c), is ungrammatical.[8] Inherently negative verbs, however, may occur in a grammaticalized relative clause construction with no overt marker of negation (see section 10).

It appears that referential nominals cannot normally be included in GNRCs.[9] In (6) below the speaker is making a general statement to the effect that he does not tell (something to) any members of the class of children, and in (8a) that he does not offer medical treatment to anyone who is dirty. In neither case does he have specific individuals in mind, i.e. the nominals included in the GNRCs are non-referential. Both these structures are grammatical. In (7) and (8b), however, the nominals included in the GNRCs (*ɨ̃m ɨ̃* 'my wife' and *ha-sus doo* 'the one(s) who is/are dirty', respectively) necessarily refer to specific individuals, i.e. they are referential. Both these structures are ungrammatical.

(6) Kalapé ma   na-hi-lxood   ɨ̃h.
     children Ben Neg-Dat+Asp-speak+NonInd   1Sg
     'I don't tell children.' (Lit., 'I am a non-children-teller.')

(7)   *iim   ii   ma   na-hi-lxood   iih.
       wife   1Sg+Poss   Ben   Neg-Dat+Asp-speak+NonInd   1Sg
       'I don't tell my wife.'

(8)   a. Ha-sus   péh   ni-biin   iih.
           Theme-be:dirty+Indic   NonRef   Neg+Asp-treat+NonInd   1Sg
           'I don't treat (medically) anyone who is dirty.'
           (Lit., 'I am a non-treater-of-one(non-referential)-who-is-dirty.')

       b. *Ha-sus   doo   ni-biin   iih.
           Theme-be:dirty+Indic   Ref   Neg+Asp-treat+NonInd   1Sg
           'I don't treat (medically) the dirty one(s).'

Similarly, a referential nominal (*uun* '(my) mother' in 9 below) may not
occur in any other position in the same clause as a GNRC to specify the
identity of an implicit embedded nominal.

(9)   *Ni-biin   iih   uun   hă.
       Neg+Asp-treat+NonInd   1Sg   mother   Dat
       'I don't treat my mother.'

2.3 Factors which influence the choice of method of standard negation

There is no evidence to suggest that either method of performing standard
negation is to be regarded as more forceful than the other. The choice
between the two methods is partly a question of style, but there are also
certain lexical and contextual factors which influence it. With descriptive
verbs and intransitive composite verbs which contain an incorporated
element,[10] the preferred method of negation is by use of a GNRC. With all
other verbs, the syntactic negative morpheme *dooh* is preferred, although
aspectual modification of the negation (see section 11) increases the tendency to use a GNRC. Perhaps the question of negative scope also influences
the choice, but this is not clear at this stage. In the case of repetition of the
negative expression, the tendency is to use the preferred form first, followed
by the non-preferred form.

3 Negation of non-verbal clauses

Basic equative main clauses in their surface form are non-verbal. The underlying form of the clause, however, contains the verb *a-doo* 'be'. This verb
is never realized in its basic form, although its non-indicative form occurs

in all negated equative clauses. It also appears in many affirmative contexts, such as relative clauses formed from equatives, conditional equative clauses, and in certain incorporation constructions (for details, see Weir 1984:26-28).

Equative clauses may be negated by either of the methods of standard negation described above. The postulated underlying form of the equative clause in (10a) would be something like (10b). The alternative forms of the equivalent negative are shown in (10c,d).

(10) a. Ta   txaah ïïh.
          3Sg son   1Sg
          'I am his son.'

      b. *Ta txaah ïïh a-doo.
          3Sg son   1Sg Form-be+Indic

      c. Dooh ta   txaah   ïïh a-do   bú.
          Neg   3Sg son   1Sg Form-be+NonInd Abl
          'I am not his son.'
          (Lit., 'I-being-his-son is something non-existent.')

      d. Ta   txaah na-do   ïïh.
          3Sg son   Neg-be+NonInd 1Sg
          'I am not his son.'
          (Lit., 'I am a non-his-son-be-er.')

There is a homophonous transitive verb *a-doo* 'take'. Thus, (10b) is in fact grammatical, but with the reading 'I take his son', while (10c,d) are ambiguous, with the alternative reading 'I don't take his son'.[11]

When the subject of an equative clause is a full NP, rather than a pronoun as in (10a-d), this NP subject cannot occur in its expected position immediately preceding the embedded copula in the negative (see 11b). The full NP subject must be moved to post-verbal (see 11c) or pre-complement (see 11d) position in the embedded clause, the normal subject position being filled by the appropriate third person proclitic pronoun. My impression is that there may be a difference in scope of the negative between the two forms (11c) and (11d), but this is not completely clear at this stage.

(11) a. Ta   txaah Sil.
          3Sg son   Sil
          'Sil is his son.'

      b. *Dooh ta txaah Sil a-do bú.

      c. Dooh ta   txaah ta-do   bú Sil.
          Neg   3Sg son   3Sg-be+NonInd Abl Sil
          'Sil isn't his son.'

d. Dooh Sil ta txaah ta-do bú.

The reason for this obligatory movement of a full NP subject is not immediately obvious. There seems to be a strong link between the copula and its predicate complement. The predicate complement cannot occupy the immediately preverbal position, since the subject must appear in this position, at least in pronominal form, in any dependent clause. The most that can be done to bring the copula and its predicate complement together is to move any full NP subject to another position, leaving only a pronominal subject in its place. This positioning of the predicate complement as close to the verb as possible is also observed in all other types of dependent equative clause.[12] Another factor in the positioning of the predicate complement might perhaps be the avoidance of confusion with the homophonous transitive verb *a-doo* 'take'. Thus, (11b) above is in fact grammatical, but with the reading 'Sil doesn't take his son'.

4 Negative habitual/iterative constructions

The concepts indicated by adverbs such as 'seldom' or 'never' in other languages are expressed in Nadëb by use of a negative habitual/iterative construction. The habitual/iterative construction uses the verbal aspect prefix *i-* or the habitual+aspect prefixes *hi-* in conjunction with the extended verb root. It may be negated by either of the methods of standard negation. Compare the negative habitual/iterative constructions in (5h-k) with the simple negative constructions in (5g,b).

(5) g. Dooh   kad   a-wųųh   bú   tóóh   dab.
         Neg   uncle Form-eat+NonInd   Abl wild:pig meat
         'Uncle isn't eating wild pig meat.'

     b. Tóóh   dab na-wųųh   kad.
         wild:pig   meat Neg-eat+NonInd uncle
         'Uncle isn't eating wild pig meat.'

     h. Dooh   kad   i-wųųh   bú   tóóh   dab.
         Neg   uncle Asp-eat+NonInd   Abl wild:pig meat
         'Uncle seldom/never eats wild pig meat.'

     i. Tóóh   dab ni-wųųh   kad.
         wild:pig   meat Neg+Asp-eat+NonInd uncle
         'Uncle seldom/never eats wild pig meat.'

     j. Dooh   kad   hi-wųh   bú   tóóh   dab.
         Neg   uncle Hab+Asp-eat+Ext+NonInd   Abl wild:pig meat
         'Uncle seldom/never eats wild pig meat.'

k. Tóóh   dab na-hi-wɨh   kad.
wild:pig   meat Neg-Hab+Asp-eat+Ext+NonInd uncle
'Uncle seldom/never eats wild pig meat.'

5 Negative existential clauses

As with all other negative main clauses, negative existential clauses are non-verbal equative clauses. They often include the qualifier *péh* which in the affirmative indicates non-referentiality. In a negative existential, the use of *péh* is preferred in most cases of NPs which would normally be considered referential, such as many possessed nouns (see 13 below), but is optional in most other cases (see 12a,b below). It is not used with proper names (see 14 below), and is obligatorily present with relative clauses (see 15, 16 below).

Semantically, negative existentials may be subdivided into the following types: basic (see 12a,b), possessive (see 13), locative (see 14), and indefinite (see 15, 16). In indefinite negative existentials, the subject of the existential clause is a relative clause.

(12) a. Dooh   bóóg   kxɨɨ péh.
           Neg   manioc stalk NonRef
           'There are no manioc stalks.'
           (Lit., 'Manioc stalks (non-referential) are something non-existent.')

      b. Dooh bóóg kxɨɨ
           'There are no manioc stalks.'

(13) Dooh ta   waa péh.
       Neg 3Sg   food NonRef
       'He has no food.'
       (Lit., 'His food (non-referential) is something non-existent.')

(14) Dooh Subih tii   bɨ́.
       Neg Subih Dem Abl
       'Subih isn't there.'
       (Lit., 'Subih is something non-existent there.')

(15) Dooh ha-wɨh   péh.
       Neg RS-eat+Indic NonRef
       'No one is eating.' (or, 'There is no one who is eating.')
       (Lit., 'One who is eating (non-referential) is something non-existent.')

(16) Dooh Subih a-wɨh   péh.
       Neg Subih Form-eat+Indic NonRef
       'Subih has nothing to eat.' (or, 'Subih isn't eating anything.')
       (Lit., 'What Subih is eating (non-referential) is something non-existent.')

There is no directly equivalent affirmative form corresponding to negative existentials. In each case the affirmative must contain some appropriate verb. For example, a possible affirmative equivalent to (14) would be:

(17) Subih a-guut   tii bú.
      Subih Form-be:standing+Indic Dem Abl
      'Subih is standing there.'

6 Distributional possibilities for dooh and grammaticalized negated relative clauses (GNRCs)

As seen in section 2.1, the syntactic negative *dooh* usually functions as predicate complement NP in an equative clause. However, it occasionally occurs as dependent of a postposition, i.e. as a constituent of the predicate complement PP, in such a clause (see 18a). The equivalent paraphrase in which the postposition is incorporated into the verb is more frequently used (see 18b). So far as I am aware, there is no difference in meaning between the incorporated and non-incorporated forms.

(18) a. Dooh   sii ma-ba-hing   péh.
          Neg   with 2Sg-RA-go:downriver+Indic NonRef
          'There is no one for you to go downriver with.'
          (Lit., 'The circumstances of your going downriver (non-referential) are with someone non-existent.')

      b. Dooh   ma-sii   hing   péh.
          Neg   2Sg-with   go:downriver+Indic NonRef
          'There is no one for you to go downriver with.'
          (Lit., 'The one you with-go-downriver (non-referential) is something non-existent.')

GNRCs usually function as predicate complement NPs in equative clauses. They do not seem to occur as subject, direct object, or dependent of a postposition, although negated relative clauses may function in any of these ways.

Both the syntactic negative *dooh* and GNRCs may also occur as a constituent of a GNRC formed from an equative clause, resulting in the double negative *dooh na-do* or GNRC *na-do* (see section 14).

7 Use of dooh as a one-word answer

The syntactic negative *dooh* is used as a one-word answer to polar (see 19) and non-polar (see 20) questions, the latter sometimes, perhaps with ironical overtones, to make light of a situation once the danger has passed.

(19) A. Õm   li-yóóh   nadɨp   hã?
          2Sg   3Pl+Asp-pierce+Indic   wild:indians   Dat
          'Did wild indians stab you?'

      B. Dooh. Yahuun.
          Neg   anteater
          'No. It was an anteater.'

(20) A. Hxɨɨd   ma-ha-ɨɨnh   óów?
          what   2Sg-motive-call+Indic   grandfather
          'Why did you call, grandfather?'

      B. Dooh. Ĩih   awad   a-wɨɨh-yɨɨh-paawɨ́.
          Neg   1Sg   jaguar   Form-eat+NonInd-Cmpl+NonInd-Frust
          'Nothing. A jaguar nearly ate me up.'

Dooh is also used in conversation as a negative answer to an imperative or suggestion, or to refute a statement made by someone else. In texts, it may additionally be used to indicate the absence of expected or desired results.

8 Sentence and constituent negation

Klima (1964) distinguished between sentence and constituent negation, and devised a set of three diagnostic tests for determining whether or not a particular negative construction is to be regarded as sentential negation. Klima's tests are specific to English, but similar tests have been found for a variety of other languages. Payne (1985:198-201), however, points out that, even in so-called sentence negation, the actual scope of the negative is usually something less than the whole sentence. He proposes as a further diagnostic test for Klima's sentence negation the existence of a performative paraphrase of the type *I say of X that it is not true that Y*, where X contains the contextually bound elements (i.e. those outside the scope of negation), Y contains the contextually free elements (i.e. those within the scope of negation), and the negative relates the two. The notion of sentence negation does not seem to be a particularly relevant one for Nadëb. I have not been able to find equivalents in Nadëb for any of Klima's diagnostic tests, nor does there appear to be an equivalent to Payne's performative paraphrase. A restricted scope for the negation seems to be the norm in Nadëb.[13]

In the rest of this section, I deal with the negation of dependent clauses, viz relative, pseudorelative, clausal complement, resultative, and non-finite nominalized clauses. All these clause types are negated by use of the morphological negative *na-* attached to the verb. The form of the verb remains unchanged, i.e. a verb which was indicative in the affirmative clause remains indicative in the negative, while one which was non-indicative in the afirmative remains non-indicative in the negative. This is illustrated in (21a,b) and (22a,b) for a relative clause and a non-finite conditional clause, respectively.

(21) a. Óów   a-wuh   doo.
          grandfather Form-eat+Indic Ref
          'What grandfather eats.'

      b. Óów   na-wuh   doo.
          grandfather Neg-eat+Indic Ref
          'What grandfather doesn't eat.'

(22) a. Kalapéé i-ug   bú.
          child   Asp-drink+NonInd Abl
          'If the child drinks (it).'

      b. Kalapéé ni-ug   bú.
          child   Neg+Asp-drink+NonInd Abl
          'If the child doesn't drink (it).'

The presence of the morphological negative blocks the realization of any subordination prefix which would occur in the corresponding affirmative clause, as illustrated in the relative clause in (23a,b) with the prefix *ha-* 'relativized subject'.

(23) a. Ha-wuh   doo.
          RS-eat+Indic   Ref
          'One who is eating.'

      b. Na-wuh   doo.
          Neg-eat+Indic   Ref
          'One who isn't eating.'

In certain contexts, this blocking of a subordination prefix can lead to ambiguity. For details, see Weir (1984:219).

9 Negation of imperative clauses

There are two basic types of imperative in Nadëb: simple and embedded. The latter present four sub-types: hortatory, factive, permissive, and performative. All types of imperative normally use a non-indicative form of the verb. Simple imperatives are negated by use of the negative morpheme *manɨh*, as in (24b).

(24) a. Mi-ug.
          2Sg+Asp-drink+NonInd
          'Drink (it)!'

      b. Mi-ug   manɨh.
          2Sg+Asp-drink+NonInd   Neg
          'Don't drink (it)!'

At this stage, it is not completely clear exactly how the negative morpheme *manɨh* should be interpreted. In the verb morphology, it follows the verb root(s) and precedes most suffixes and particles. However, aspectual modifications of the negative, viz. the suffix *-wɨd* 'completive' and the particle *nɨh* 'still', generally occur before *manɨh*. For further discussion, see Weir (1984: 250-257).

All embedded imperatives, except intransitive permissive and performative imperatives, may be negated, when semantically acceptable, in the same way as simple imperatives, i.e. by use of *manɨh*. This is illustrated in (25a,b) and (26a,b) for an intransitive factive imperative and a transitive permissive imperative, respectively.

(25) a. Nxoo   a   txaah   i-hob.
          Fact   2Sg+Poss son   Asp-take:a:bath+NonInd
          'Make your son take a bath!'

      b. Nxoo   a   txaah   i-hob   manɨh.
          Fact   2Sg+Poss son   Asp-take:a:bath+NonInd Neg
          'Make your son not take a bath!'

(26) a. Na   a   txaah   i-ug   ta   biin.
          Perm   2Sg+Poss son   Asp-drink+NonInd   3Sg   medicine
          'Let your son drink the medicine!'

      b. Na   a   txaah   i-ug   manɨh ta   biin.
          Perm   2Sg+Poss son   Asp-drink+NonInd Neg 3Sg medicine
          'Let your son not drink the medicine!'

Intransitive permissive and performative imperatives are negated by use of the morphological negative *na-* (see 27a,b and 28a,b, respectively). Transitive performative imperatives may also be negated in this manner, as an alternative to the use of *manih*.

(27) a. Na   mi-hoob   a   txaah.
          Perm   Caus+Asp-take:a:bath+Ext+NonInd   2Sg+Poss   son
          'Let your son take a bath.'

      b. Na   ma-ni-hoob   a   txaah.
          Perm   Caus-Neg+Asp-take:a:bath+Ext+NonInd 2Sg+Poss   son
          'Let your son not take a bath.'

(28) a. Hapaleeh   ta-da-yʉb.
          Perf   3Sg-Theme-die+NonInd
          'May he die!'

      b. Hapaleeh   ta-na-da-yʉb.
          Perf   3Sg-Neg-Theme-die+NonInd
          'May he not die!'[14]

Although an embedded imperative may be negated as described above, the matrix word (*nxoo, na,* and *hapaleeh* in the above examples) cannot. In English, the situation is almost the opposite for factive and permissive imperatives: negation in the matrix clause is acceptable, while negation of the embedded clause is at best rare. Semantically, 'Don't make your son take a bath' is equivalent to 'Let your son not take a bath' (see 27b), and 'Don't let your son take a bath' is equivalent to 'Make your son not take a bath' (see 25b). Thus, negation of the matrix clause of a factive/permissive imperative in English would be substituted by negation of the corresponding embedded permissive/factive imperative in Nadëb.

10 Inherently negative lexical items

There are a few inherently negative verbs in Nadëb. They are not derived from existing affirmative forms and may have no overt marker of negation. However, syntactically they behave in the same way as negated verbs and semantically they have a negative component of meaning. In main clauses, they appear only in non-indicative form, i.e. in the equivalent of a GNRC construction. Only in dependent clauses which require an indicative verb can they occur in an indicative form. Examples of inherently negative verbs are *sa-kook* 'be light (weight)', *ga-na-pok* 'be short (length)', *na-saa* 'be ugly',

N *ta-mah* 'be without N', which occurs only with an incorporated noun, and *ba-doh* 'be non-existent'. As stated in section 2.1, the syntactic negative morpheme *dooh* is a non-indicative form of the root of this last verb. (29) illustrates the use of the inherently negative verb *sa-kook* in the indicative form in a relative clause. In (30), the same inherently negative verb occurs in the equivalent of a GNRC construction which functions as predicate complement NP in an equative clause.

(29) sa-kook   doo
      Theme-be:light+Indic Ref
      'one which is light (weight)'

(30) Sa-kog-ij   a   txõom.
      Theme-be:light+NonInd-Dim+NonInd 2Sg+Poss panacu
      'Your panacu (type of basket) is light.'
      (Lit., 'Your panacu is a light-one.')

There are a few adverbs which are classed as inherently negative on semantic grounds. Examples are *halɨ* 'in vain', *daap* 'for no reason' (see 31).

(31) Daap   ta-bi-ɨɨk   ta   biin.
      for:ńo:reason 3Sg-RA+Asp-drink+Indic 3Sg medicine
      'It's for no reason that he drinks the medicine.' (i.e., he isn't ill.)

There is one inherently negative suffix, *-paawú* 'frustrative', which indicates an unrealized event or state (see 32).

(32) Kad   a-hɨɨh-paawú.
      uncle Form-go:downriver+NonInd-Frust
      'Uncle was going (or wanted) to go downriver (but didn't go).'

11 Aspectual modifications with negation

There are two semantically mutually exclusive aspectual modifications which can occur with negation: 'no longer' and 'not yet'. The first, 'no longer', is expressed by use of the completive suffix *-wút* in one of its forms. In the affirmative, this suffix indicates cessation of an action or state (see 33).

(33) Kalapéé a-ód-wút.
      child   Form-cry+NonInd-Cmpl+Indic
      'The child cried (and stopped crying).'

In a negative clause, the completive suffix, when present, is usually attached to an embedded verb, if there is one (see 34). Otherwise it may be attached to the negative morpheme *dooh* (see 35), to a NP, or to more than one constituent in the clause.

(34) Dooh kalapéé a-ód-wúd   bú.
      Neg child   Form-cry+NonInd-Cmpl+NonInd Abl
      'The child is no longer crying.'

(35) A. Da-tés?   B. Dooh-wúd.
         Theme-hurt+Indic   Neg-Cmpl+NonInd
         'Does it hurt?'   'No longer.'

The affirmative and negative forms (33) and (34) appear to be very close in meaning, since both state that the child cried and stopped crying. The difference is a question of focus. In the affirmative, the focus is on the specific terminated action, while in the negative it is on the non-continuation of the action.

The ingressive suffix in its non-indicative form *-kú* may co-occur with, or occasionally replace, the completive suffix in a negative clause, emphasizing the change in the situation:

(36) Dooh-kú iih hiih-kú.
      Neg-Ingr 1Sg Dem-Ingr
      'I will no longer be here.'

The second aspectual modification, 'not yet', is expressed by use of the particle *nih*. In the affirmative, this particle indicates continuation of an action or state.

(37) Ba-da-yung   nih.
      Theme-Theme-be:dark+Indic   still
      'It's still dark.'

In a negative clause, the particle *nih* usually follows an embedded verb, when there is one (see 38). Otherwise it may follow the negative morpheme *dooh* (see 39), a NP, or may occur more than once in the clause.

(38) Dooh ta-yuuh   nih bú.
      Neg 3Sg-return+NonInd   still Abl
      'He hasn't returned yet.'

(39) Dooh nih miim.
      Neg still axe
      'There were no axes yet.'

In some contexts, the particle *dó* may replace *nih* to indicate 'not yet'.

(40) Pxóóyub   dooh   nadub   dó.
      long:ago   Neg   Nadëb   still
      'Long ago there were no Nadëb yet.'

As in affirmative clauses, evidential and emphatic particles may be used in a negated clause to introduce degrees of certainty or emphasis.

12 Scope of negation

Givón defines neutral negation – the least-marked variety – to be one which:

- Takes under its scope only the assertions but not the presupposition(s) associated with the corresponding affirmative;
- Leaves the subject of the corresponding affirmative outside the scope of negation; and
- Otherwise does not specify the exact grounds for denying the corresponding affirmative.

Neutral negation denies the occurrence of an event or state. The scope of the negation may be narrowed 'depending on a variety of discourse-pragmatic and real-world pragmatic assumptions that the speaker makes about the beliefs and communicative intent of the hearer' (Givón 1984:335-336).

At this stage in the analysis of the language, any discussion of scope of negation in Nadëb is necessarily tentative. It is difficult to obtain reliable native speaker reaction on questions of scope and ambiguity from people who have not previously thought formally about their language. My intuition about the language, although based on several periods of living with the Nadëb since 1975, is not native speaker intuition.

With the syntactic negative *dooh*, syntactic coding of wider or narrower scope seems to be effected by differences in word order. *Dooh* is usually the first constituent in the clause. Although both OSV and SVO orders are permitted in the embedded non-finite clause (see 41b,c), the latter (SVO) seems to be the more common order in texts, and my impression is that this appears to be the more neutral form of negation.

(41) a. Awad   kalapéé ha-púh.
          jaguar child   Theme-see+Indic
          'The child sees the jaguar.'

      b. Dooh   awad   kalapéé ha-púúh   bú.
          Neg   jaguar child   Theme-see+NonInd Abl
          'The child doesn't see the jaguar.'

c. Dooh kalapéé ha-púúh bú awad.

In texts, when a direct object or adverbial appears in second position in the clause, i.e. immediately following *dooh*, that constituent often seems to be the real scope of the negation. (42) is from a text which describes the habits of insects. Here the speaker is emphasizing that mosquitos appear at night and not in the daytime. In the second sentence, the real scope of the negation is the temporal *adub* 'by day', which immediately follows *dooh*.

(42) Ajum   ta-ba-bong   tii giiy   ajum.
      at:night 3Sg-RA-be:in:movement+Mult+Indic   Dem mosquito at:night
      'It's at night that those mosquitos come out.'

      Dooh adub   ta-booh   bú.
      Neg by:day 3Sg-be:in:movement+Mult+NonInd Abl
      'They don't come out in the daytime.'

A constituent may appear to the left of *dooh,* often to highlight a contrast with something previously mentioned or implicit in the discourse and/or to indicate a change in local topic. The following example comes from a text which begins by describing what someone used to do when he visited the village. In (43), *hiih-kú* 'nowadays' is fronted to indicate that it is the new local topic and is in contrast with the time when the said person used to come to the village. (43) is a topic-comment construction, in the sense of Li and Thompson (1976:459).

(43) Hiih-kú   dooh ta-na-wúd   bú.
      Dem-Ingr Neg   3Sg-come+NonInd-Cmpl+NonInd Abl
      'Nowadays he doesn't come any more.'

I understand constituents which are fronted in this way to be removed from the scope of negation.[15] Some occurrences of constituents to the left of *dooh* represent simple removal from the scope of negation rather than topic-comment constructions (see 46f, 49c below).

In the GNRC construction, the scope of the negation usually seems to be the whole GNRC as a unit. Thus, in (5b) above I understand the scope of the negation to be wild-pig-meat-eater as an indivisible whole, rather than one or other of its components. This is similar to the English expression *a non-church-goer*, where the scope of negation is the composite noun *church-goer* rather than one or other of its components. So far as I am aware, there is no difference in meaning or scope of the negation in a GNRC construction when the complement of the embedded verb is specified in another position in the clause, i.e. between (5b) and (5f) above (see section 2.2). The scope of negation with GNRCs may be further illustrated by comparing (44a) and (45a), the former of which contains a GNRC.

(44) a. Awad   hʉbnxaa   na-wúd   ɨɨh   húúy   bʉ́.
          jaguar   cause   Neg-be:in:movement+NonInd 1Sg   jungle Abl
          'I don't walk in the jungle because of jaguars.'
          (Lit., 'I am a non-because-of-jaguars-walker in the jungle.')
          (i.e. 'I walk in the jungle, but not because of jaguars (e.g. to kill them for
          their meat or skin).')

      b. [awad hʉbnxaa na-wúd]   [ɨɨh]   [húúy bʉ́]
          NP   NP   PP

(45) a. Awad   hʉbnxaa   ɨɨh   na-wʉ́t   húúy   bʉ́.
          jaguar   cause   1Sg   Neg-be:in:moviment+Indic   jungle Abl
          'It's because of jaguars that I don't walk in the jungle.'
          (Lit., 'The circumstances of my not walking in the jungle are because of
          jaguars'.) (e.g. because I'm afraid of them)

      b. [awad hʉbnxaa] [[ɨɨh] [na-wʉ́t]   [húúy bʉ́]]
          PP   NP   NP   V   PP

(44a) is an equative clause whose predicate complement is the grammatical-ization of the relative clause *awad hʉbnxaa na-wʉ́t doo* 'one who doesn't walk because of jaguars', whose subject is *ɨɨh* 'I', and which contains the locative PP *húúy bʉ́* 'in the jungle' as adjunct. Its structure is represented in (44b). The reason adverbial *awad hʉbnxaa* 'because of jaguars' is included in the GNRC, and is therefore included within the scope of the negation. By way of con-trast, (45a) does not contain any GNRC. It is an equative clause whose subject is the negated adverbial subordinate clause *ɨɨh na-wʉ́t húúy bʉ́* 'the circumstances of my not walking in the jungle',[16] and whose predicate complement is the PP *awad hʉbnxaa* 'because of jaguars'. Its structure is represented in (45b). Thus, (44a) implies that I do walk in the jungle, while (45a) implies that I do not walk in the jungle.

It has often been noted that negation tends to be associated with a focused constituent (see, for example, Payne 1985:232). In Nadëb at least, certain constituents, notably certain adverbials and quantifiers, require limited scope of negation. This is illustrated with the inherently negative adverb *daap* 'for no reason' in (46a-f). When a clause such as (46a) is negated, semantically either the event of going downriver or the adverbial, but not both, may be within the scope of negation. So far as I can tell, in all the alternatives (46b-e), the adverbial *daap* is within the scope of negation, while the event of going downriver is outside its scope, i.e., in each case, uncle went downriver and had a reason for doing so. That is, (46b-e) appear all to have essentially the same meaning.[17]

(46)   a.   Kad   a-hing   daap-hĕ.
            uncle   Form-go:downriver+Indic   for:no:reason-Adv
            'Uncle is going downriver for no reason.'

       b.   Dooh   kad   a-hiih   bú   daap-hĕ.
            Neg   uncle   Form-go:downriver+NonInd   Abl   for:no:reason-Adv
            'Uncle isn't going downriver for no reason.'
            (i.e. he has a reason for going.)

       c.   Dooh daap kad a-hiih bú.

       d.   Na-hiih   kad   daap-hĕ.
            Neg-go:downriver+NonInd   uncle   for:no:reason-Adv
            (Lit., 'Uncle is a non-goer-downriver with respect to "for no reason".')

       e.   Daap na-hiih kad.
            (Lit., 'Uncle is a non-for-no-reason-goer-downriver.')

The inherently negative adverb *daap* may be removed from the scope of the negation by placing it to the left of the syntactic negative *dooh*. In (46f), the event of going downriver is within the scope of negation, while the adverbial is not, i.e., uncle did not go downriver, and it was for no reason that he did not go. Thus, (46f) seems to be regarded as roughly equivalent to (47).

(46)   f.   Daap-hĕ dooh kad a-hiih bú.
            'For no reason uncle isn't going down river.'

(47)   Daap-hĕ   kad   ba-iiw   gú.
       for:no:reason-Adv   uncle   RA-stay+NonInd   lie:in:hammock+Indic
       'It is for no reason that uncle is staying.'

13 Quantifiers and negation

There are several quantifier verbs in Nadëb, most of which mean 'be many'. These may be negated by either of the methods of performing standard negation, as illustrated in (48b,c) with the quantifier verb *ha-yõng* 'be many'. (48b,c) appear to have essentially the same meaning.

(48)   a.   Ha-yõng   ta   taah.
            Theme-be:many+Indic   3Sg   sons
            'He has many sons.'
            (Lit., 'His sons are many')

b. Dooh   ta   taah ha-yõoh   bú.
   Neg   3Sg sons Theme-be:many+NonInd   Abl
   'He doesn't have many sons.'
   (Lit., 'His sons being many is something non-existent.')

c. Na-ha-yõoh   ta   taah.
   Neg-Theme-be:many+NonInd 3Sg sons
   'He doesn't have many sons.'
   (Lit., 'His sons are a non-many thing.')

The universal quantifier *sahõnh* may occur in negative constructions. It requires limited scope of negation, as described in section 12 for certain adverbials. In (49b) *sahõnh* appears immediately following the negative *dooh*, and is the real scope of the negation, while the verb is outside the scope of negation. In (49c), however, *sahõnh* is removed from the scope of negation by being placed to the left of *dooh*, and it is the verb which is negated. The only examples I have of GNRCs which include the universal quantifier *sahõnh* are those formed from equative clauses. Thus, while (49d) is not acceptable, (49e) is, with essentially the same meaning as (49b).

(49) a. Sahõnh-hĕ   ɨɨh   nooh ki-nxaak.
      all-Adv   1Sg mouth Theme+Asp-like+Indic
      'I like them all.'

    b. Dooh sahõnh ɨɨh   nooh ki-naag   bú.
      Neg   all   1Sg mouth Theme+Asp-like+NonInd Abl
      'I don't like them all.' (i.e. I like some but not all.)

    c. Sahõnh dooh ɨɨh   nooh   ki-naag bú.
      'All   of   them I   don't like.' (i.e. I like none.)

    d. *Sahõnh nooh ka-ni-naag   ɨɨh.
      all   mouth Theme-Neg+Asp-like+NonInd 1Sg

    e. Sahõnh na-do   ɨɨh   nooh ki-nxaak.
      all   Neg-be+NonInd 1Sg mouth Theme+Asp-like+Indic
      'It's not all of them that I like.' (i.e. I like some but not all.)

Partitives may occur in negative constructions. In the affirmative, the partitive *dinaa* is found only in adverbial expressions (at least, in the available data), as in *pxééj dinaa-hẽ* 'fairly near'. In negative expressions, the partitive *dinaa* may follow the negated verb when there is one (see 50), or the syntactic negative *dooh* (see 51).

(50) Dooh ta-da-tééy   dinaa.
      Neg 3Sg-Theme-hurt+NonInd Part
      'It doesn't hurt much.'

(51) A. Da-tés?   B. Dooh   dinaa-hĕ.
          Theme-hurt+Indic   Neg   Part-Adv
          'Does it hurt?'   'Not much.'

The incorporated partitive *hãd* also may occur in a negative construction with certain verbs, as in:

(52) Hãd   na-nag   yahuun   dab.
      Part   Neg-be:tasty+NonInd   anteater meat
      'Anteater meat isn't very tasty.'

The affirmative form of this verb, *hãd naak* 'be fairly tasty', also exists with a similar, if not identical, meaning to the negative. The negative form, however, seems to be preferred.

14 Multiple negative elements in a clause

In general, any main or subordinate clause can be negated independently of other sentence constituents. Except in the case of Neg-transport (see section 15), the negation applies only to the clause in which the negative morpheme occurs. GNRCs and other independently negated constituents may co-occur in the same clause, as in (53). The GNRC *na-ɨh* 'a non-sleeper' functions as predicate complement NP in an equative clause whose subject is the negated relative clause *ta biin ni-ʉʉk doo* 'one who didn't drink the medicine'.

(53) Na-ɨh   ta   biin   ni-ʉʉk   doo.
      Neg-sleep+NonInd   3Sg   medicine Neg+Asp-drink+Indic Ref
      'The one who didn't drink the medicine isn't sleeping.'

Negated relative clauses, but not GNRCs (see section 6), may function as subject, object, or dependent of a postposition in a clause which is negated by the syntactic negative. In all these cases, the negatives are independent of each other, so the question as to whether the result is positive or negative does not arise.

There are, however, some instances in which a clause may contain two negative elements, one of which acts upon the other to produce a positive result. An example of the syntactic and morphological negatives acting upon an inherently negative adverb to produce a positive result was seen in section 12 above (see 46b-e). In indefinite negative existential clauses, the relative clause functioning as subject may itself be negative, again with an overall positive result (see 54).

(54)   Dooh na-wɨh   péh.
       Neg Neg-eat+Indic   NonRef
       'There is no one who isn't eating.' (i.e. 'Everyone is eating.')

The syntactic negative *dooh*, GNRCs, and inherently negative verbs may themselves be negated by use of a GNRC construction formed from an equative clause (see 55-57, respectively).[18] Such constructions are used only in very restricted contexts, such as to deny a negative statement made by someone else or sometimes to give a negative answer to a negative question. The result of this double negative is positive.

(55)   A.   A-saah   mɨh Yóy txaah.
            Form-be:hungry+Indic   Rlt Yóy son

            Dooh   ta   waa péh.
            Neg   3Sg   food NonRef

            'Yóy's son is hungry. He has no food.'

       B.   Dooh   na-do.
            Neg   Neg-be+NonInd

            Mooh   na-hũuy   ta   ɨɨn.
            hand   Neg-be:industrious+NonInd 3Sg   mother

            'It's not that there is none. His mother is lazy.'

(56)   A.   Na-ɨh   a   txaah.
            Neg-sleep+NonInd 2Sg+Poss son
            'Your son isn't sleeping.'

       B.   Na-ɨh   na-do;   a-ɨɨh.
            Neg-sleep+NonInd Neg-be+NonInd Form-sleep+Indic
            'He isn't not sleeping; he's sleeping.'

(57)   A.   Sa-kog-ij   a   txõom.
            Theme-be:light+NonInd-Dim+NonInd 2Sg+Poss   panacu
            'Your panacu (type of basket) is light.'

       B.   Sa-kog   na-do;   ya-wɨk.
            Theme-be:light+NonInd Neg-be+NonInd Theme-be:heavy+Indic
            'It isn't light; it's heavy.'

In the same very restricted contexts cited above, the non-finite nominalized clause in a negative equative whose predicate complement is *dooh* may be negated by the morphological negative *na-* or may contain an inherently negative verb (see 58B first clause). Inherently negative verbs are not generally negated with *na-*, although I do have one example of this, viz. the verb *ba-doh* 'be non-existent' (see 58B second clause).

(58)   A. Dooh-wúd   a   nahúúh?
Neg-Cmpl+NonInd 2Sg+Poss illness
'Has your illness completely gone?'

B. Dooh   ta-ba-dooh   bú;
Neg   3Sg-Theme-be:non:existent+NonInd Abl
ba-na-dooh.
Theme-Neg-be:non:existent+NonInd
'It's not gone; it's not gone.' (Lit., 'It-being-non-existent is something
non-existent; it is a non-non-exister.')

15 Neg-transport

Horn (1978:183-191) notes that mid-strength verbs on his scale of subjective
certainty (e.g. 'think') or manipulation (e.g. 'want') or adverbial epistemic
operators (e.g. 'be likely') are some of the most likely candidates for Neg-
transport.[19] However, most of these concepts are generally expressed in
Nadëb by evidential particles or by other constructions, such as
postpositional phrases, as in (59a).

(59)   a. Hã   ii   da-yup.
Dat 1Sg+Poss Theme-die+Indic
'To me he died.' (i.e. 'I think he died.')

The only way of negating such a sentence is by negating the predicate (see
59b,c). Neg-transport is not applicable in such a construction since there is
no embedded clause.

(59)   b. Hã   ii   dooh ta-da-yub   bú.
Dat 1Sg+Poss Neg   3Sg-Theme-die+NonInd Abl
'To me he didn't die.' (i.e. 'I don't think he died.')
(Lit., 'To me he-dying is something non-existent .')

c. Hã   ii   na-da-yub.
Dat 1Sg+Poss Neg-Theme-die+NonInd
'To me he didn't die.' (i.e. 'I don't think he died.')
(Lit., 'To me he is a non-dier.')

The only construction I am aware of which seems to allow Neg-transport is
the mid-strength manipulative or modality verb *ka-lẽn* 'want'.

(60)   a. Óów   ka-lẽn   Subih   ba-hing.
grandfather   Theme-want+Indic Subih   ClComp-go:downriver+Indic
'Grandfather wants Subih to go downriver.'

b. Óów   ka-lĕn   Subih   na-hïng.
   grandfather   Theme-want+Indic   Subih   Neg-go:downriver+Indic
   'Grandfather wants Subih not to go downriver.'

c. Dooh   óów   ka-lĕn   bú
   Neg   grandfather   Theme-want+NonInd   Abl

   Subih   a-hïïh   bú.
   Subih   Form-go:downriver+NonInd   Abl

   'Grandfather doesn't want Subih to go downriver.'

However, some speakers express uncertainty as to whether (60b,c) are
semantically equivalent. The latter can also have the reading 'Grandfather
doesn't want it (something unspecified) if Subih goes downriver'. In English
also, these two sentences do not always have the same meaning. 'Grandfather doesn't want Subih to go downriver' can be understood to mean either
something similar to (60b) or 'It is not true that grandfather wants Subih to
go downriver'. It has been pointed out that even with the first reading there
is a difference in force between sentences which have the Neg marker in the
embedded clause and those which have it in the matrix clause (see, for
example, Givón 1984:342).

16 Use of the morphological negative *na-* in the deri-
vation of lexical items

The prefix *na-* occurs in a few apparently derived lexical items, such as the
adverb *naïïw* 'soon'. This adverb has probably arisen from the morphologically negated from of the verb *a-ïm* 'stop, stay'. It has become lexicalized as
an adverb in its own right, and does not obey the distribution constraints
on GNRCs. For example, in (61) it occurs as a constituent of another GNRC
which is not formed from an equative clause.

(61) Naïïw   na-yuuh   kaat.
      soon   Neg-return+NonInd   aunt
      'Aunt will not soon return.'

The use of the morphological negative in the derivation of lexical items,
however, is not a productive process in Nadëb.

17 Other negative constructions

Two other negative constructions are worthy of mention. Further studies are necessary to determine the best interpretation of the data, but the constructions are mentioned here for completeness. The first appears to be a functional equivalent of an agentive passive, while the second seems to be an adverbial construction.

17.1 Functional equivalent of agentive negative passive

In this construction, the negative element is the morphological negative *na-*, and the form of verb used is always a non-indicative 'extended' root.[20] The aspect prefix *i-* is always present. (62) illustrates the form of this construction.

(62) Wúng buuh   ni-uug   kad   hã.
      patauá juice Neg+Asp-drink+Ext+NonInd uncle Dat
      'The patauá juice isn't drunk by uncle.'

The underlying subject/agent (in this case, *kad* 'uncle') is obligatorily present in post-verbal position as dependent of the postposition *hã* 'dative'. On the other hand, the underlying object (in this case, *wúng buuh* 'patauá juice') is usually deleted when its reference is clear from the context. When present, it may occur before or after the verbal constituent.

This construction may be used to refer to a specific situation, as in (62) above. In this case, the underlying object must be referential. Sometimes there seems to be an implication that the action specified as not having occurred ought to have occurred. Alternatively, the construction may be a general statement conveying information about the underlying object, as in (63). In this case, the underlying object is non-referential.

(63) Dooh yi   a-wuuh   bú   tii lakakuuw;
      Neg Indef Form-eat+NonInd   Abl Dem lakakuuw

      ni-wuh   yi   hã.
      Neg+Asp-eat+Ext+NonInd   Indef Dat

      'People don't eat those lakakuuw (sp. of frog); they are not
      eaten by people.'

The difference between a GNRC construction and the construction under consideration in relation to referentiality of the underlying object is illustrated by comparing the unacceptability of the referential NP *ɨ̃m ɨ̃* 'my wife' in the GNRC in (7) (repeated here) with its acceptability as underlying object of the functional equivalent of the agentive negative passive (see 64).

(7)   *Ɨ̃m   ɨ̃   ma   na-hi-lxood   ɨ̃h.
        wife   1Sg+Poss   Ben   Neg-Dat+Asp-speak+NonInd   1Sg
        'I didn't tell my wife.'

(64)   Ɨ̃m   ɨ̃   ma   na-hi-lod   hã   ɨ̃.
        wife   1Sg+Poss   Ben   Neg-Dat+Asp-speak+Ext+NonInd   Dat   1Sg+Poss
        'My wife wasn't told by me.'

I have no clear evidence for the existence of an agentive passive construction in Nadëb. The form of the verb used in this functional equivalent suggests that the construction should be interpreted as an equative clause with a literal translation for (62) something like 'The pataué juice is a not-drunk-thing to uncle'. I have no examples of this construction used with an underlying intransitive verb.[21]

17.2 Adverbial negative construction

Unlike most other negative constructions in Nadëb, the adverbial negative construction has a direct affirmative equivalent. Both affirmative and negative forms are marked by the adverbial suffix *-hẽ* attached to the verb which is always non-indicative. In the negative, the morphological negative *na-* is used. (65a,b) illustrate the afirmative and negative forms of this construction, respectively.

(65)   a.   Ɨ̃h   i-ug-hẽ   wúng   buuh.
             1Sg   Asp-drink+NonInd-Adv   pataué   juice
             'I'm just drinking pataué juice.'

            b.   Ɨ̃h   ni-ug-hẽ   wúng   buuh.
             1Sg   Neg+Asp-drink+NonInd-Adv   pataué   juice
             'I'm just not drinking pataué juice.'

This construction appears to be an adverbialized nominalized clause, and is more commonly found without an explicit direct object (in this case, without *wúng buuh* 'pataué juice'). It may be used as a way to avoid giving a direct answer to a question of the form 'Why are you drinking/not drinking pataué juice?' It could also be an answer to the question 'Are you drinking/not drinking pataué juice?', but not to the question 'What are you drinking?'

18 Conclusion

The present study of negation in Nadëb is far from exhaustive. It does, however, reveal that Nadëb presents some very unusual features in comparison with the languages of the world which have received more linguistic attention to date. Several aspects of this little-known language merit further consideration and could make valuable contributions to linguistic theory in general.

Notes

1. I wish to thank the Fundação Nacional do Índio and the Conselho Nacional de Desenvolvimento Científico e Tecnológico for authorization to live and work in the Nadëb area. I am grateful to R.M.W. Dixon and Carl H. Harrison for helpful discussion and comments on a previous version of this paper. My special thanks go to the Nadëb community, without whose patient cooperation this study would have been totally impossible.

2. I use the term 'grammaticalized negated relative clause' (GNRC) to refer to a construction which behaves like a noun word and is derived from a negated relative clause. Its structure may be quite complex. This term is not meant to imply that these structures exist as entries in the lexicon. The process of GNRC formation is very productive in the language, although there are restrictions on referentiality of included nominals.

3. In vernacular text, x represents laryngealization of the following vowel, ˜ represents nasalization of the vowel, and a double vowel letter (e.g. *aa*) represents a long vowel. For abbreviations used, see appendix.

4. An alternative analysis would be to regard all relative clauses as headless, and interpret *doo* and *péh* as types of relative pronouns. *Péh* is found in other contexts marking non-referentiality of a noun. See footnote 9 on referentiality.

5. The postposition *bú*, together with its correspoding relational verb prefix *ba-*, is for convenience glossed as 'ablative' (Abl). In many contexts, it is a non-contrastive locative marker. Its use, however, is very much wider than the term 'ablative' would imply. Here it functions as a general subordinator.

6. Some speakers accept (5f) without the postposition *hã*, but regard this as less grammatical than (5f). The same speakers allow *hã* to be dropped in other contexts, but only in clause final position.

7. The postposition *hã*, together with its correspoding relational verb prefix *ha-*, is for convenience glossed as 'dative' (Dat). In some contexts, it functions much like a dative case marker. Its use, however, is very much wider than the term 'dative' would imply.

8. Apparently similar affirmative constructions, such as *salool suung* 'instrument for sewing' (from *salool* 'clothes' and a nominalized form of the verb *a-suuh* 'sew') are genitive constructions rather than grammaticalized affirmative relative clauses. The form of the verb root used is different from that which would be expected in a grammaticalized relative clause. The form *tahawɨɨh* exists, with the meaning 'one who eats everything'. However, such a construction occurs with an extremely limited number of verbs (I have only two examples). The distributional possibilities of all these constructions are quite different from those of GNRCs.

9. By 'referential nominals' I mean those nominal arguments which the speaker intends to refer to specific entities in the real world or in the discourse context. This follows closely Givón's (1978:293) definition of referentiality. Referential nominals may occur in GNRCs formed from equative clauses. Thus, *Subih na-do* 'not Subih' is acceptable.

10. Head nouns of a genitive construction, postpositions, and a few other morphemes may be incorporated into the verb. For details, see Weir (1990).

11. Certain intransitive verbs, including the copula *a-doo*, permit the non-realization of the formative prefix *a-* in some non-finite nominalized clauses. Thus, the following alternative to (10c) is unambiguous, with 'I am not his son' as the only possible reading.

(i)   Dooh ta txaah ɨɨh do bɨ́.
    'I am not his son.'

12. Compare this hypothesis with Kuno's (1980:157) statement that 'the copula in Japanese forms an extremely tight unit with the preceding constituent. Nothing can be inserted into this unit. The precopulative constituent cannot be moved around, either.'

13. Kuno (1980) argues for the limited scope of negation in Japanese, Korean and Turkish.

14. Performative imperatives are more than just a wish. They are backed up by special powers to bring about the expressed result. Normally they could only be used by certain spirit beings and individuals believed to possess these special powers.

15. Kuno (1980:166) argues that contrasted constituents in Turkish are outside the scope of negation.

16. Negation here is constituent negation of the adverbial subordinate clause (which functions as a NP) *ɨɨh ba-wɨ́t hɨ́ɨ́y bɨ́* 'the circumstances of my walking in the jungle' (see section 8).

17. I suspect that (46b) might be ambiguous, with an alternative reading similar to (46f), but have not yet been able to confirm or refute this.

18. *Dooh*, GNRCs, and inherently negative verbs do not occur as constituents in GNRC constructions formed from verbal clauses.

19. See also section 9 on negation of factive and permissive imperatives.

20. An extended verb root is used in a variety of other contexts, such as some causatives, continuation of action, pretence, etc.

21. The only passive construction I am aware of in Nadëb is non-agentive. It uses the lexical reflexive/reciprocal verb prefix *ka-*, as illustrated in negative form below. The agent/underlying subject is obligatorily deleted.

(ii) a. Miïm   ka-na-wiïd.
          axe   Refl/Rec-Neg-find+NonInd
          'The axe wasn't found.'

      b. *Miïm ka-na-wiïd hã ï.

Compare the functional equivalent of the agentive negative passive construction below, where the agent/underlying subject is obligatorily present.

(iii) a. Miïm   ni-wïd   hã   ï.
           axe   Neg+Asp-find+Ext+NonInd   Dat   1Sg+Poss
           'The axe wasn't found by me.'

       b.*Miïm ni-wïd.

Abbreviations

Abl	'ablative' postposition or verb prefix (see footn. 5)	Ingr	ingressive suffix
Adv	adverbial suffix	Mult	multiple form of verb root
Asp	'aspect' verb prefix	Neg	negative morpheme
Ben	benefactive	NonInd	non-indicative form of verb root or suffix
Caus	causative		
ClComp	clausal complement verb prefix	NonRef	non-referential (see footn. 9)
		Part	partitive
Cmpl	completive suffix	Perf	performative
Dat	'dative' postposition or verb prefix (see footn. 7)	Perm	permissive
		Poss	possessive
		RA	relativized adverb
Dem	demonstrative pronoun	Ref	referential (see footn. 9)
Dim	diminutive	Refl/Rec	reflexive/reciprocal verb prefix
Ext	extended form of verb root		
Fact	factive	Rlt	related particle
Form	formative verb prefix	RS	relativized subject
Frust	frustrative	Theme	thematic verb prefix
GNRC	grammaticalized negated relative clause (see footn. 2)	3Pl	third person plural pronoun
		1Sg	first person sing. pronoun
Hab	habitual	2Sg	second person sing. pronoun
Indef	indefinite pronoun		
Indic	indicative form of verb root or suffix	3Sg	third person sing. pronoun

References

Baker, Mark C. (1988). *Incorporation. A theory of grammatical function changing.* Chicago/ London: University of Chicago Press.

Derbyshire, Desmond C. and Geoffrey K. Pullum (1986). *Handbook of Amazonian languages*, Vol. 1. Berlin/New York/Amsterdam: Mouton de Gruyter.

Givón, T. (1978). 'Definiteness and referentiality.' In: J. Greenberg, C. Ferguson, and E. Moravcsik (eds., 1978), 291-330.

—— (1984). *Syntax. A functional-typological introduction*, Vol. 1. Amsterdam/Philadelphia: John Benjamins.

Greenberg, J., C. Ferguson, and E. Moravcsik (eds., 1978). *Universals of human language*, Vol.4 (Syntax). Stanford: Stanford University Press.

Horn, L. (1978). 'Some aspects of negation.' In: J. Greenberg, C. Ferguson, and E. Moravcsik (eds), 127-210.

Klima, Edward S. (1964). 'Negation in English.' In: Jerry A. Fodor and Jerrold J. Katz (eds), *The structure of language. Readings in the philosophy of language*, 246-323. Englewood Cliffs, New Jersey: Prentice Hall.

Kuno, Susumu. (1980). 'The scope of the question and negation in some verb-final languages.' In *Papers from the sixteenth regional meeting of the Chicago Linguistics Society*, 155-169. Chicago: CLS.

Li, Charles N. and Sandra A. Thompson. (1976). 'Subject and Topic: A New Typology of Language.' In: C.N. Li (ed.), *Subject and Topic*. New York: Academic Press.

Loukotka, Cestmir (1968). In: J. Wilbert (ed.) *Classification of South American indian languages*. Los Angeles: University of California/Centro Latinoamericano de Venezuela.

Mason, J. Alden (1950). 'The Languages of South American Indians.' In: J.H. Steward (ed.), *Handbook of South American indians*, Vol. 6, 157-317. Washington, DC: Smithsonian Institution, U.S. Bureau of American Ethnology.

Payne, John R. (1985). 'Negation.' In: Timothy Shopen (ed.), *Language typology and syntactic description*, Vol. I (Clause structure), 197-242. Cambridge: Cambridge University Press.

Rivet, P. and C. Tastevin (1920). 'Affinités du Makú et du Puináve.' *Journal de la Société des Américanistes de Paris* 12.69-82.

Ruhlen, M. (1987). *A guide to the world's languages*. Stanford: Stanford University Press

Tovar, Antonio (1961). *Catálogo de las lenguas de América del Sur.* Buenos Aires: Editoral Sudamericana.

Weir, E.M. Helen. (1980). 'Um caso de OSV: a língua Nadëb.' Paper presented at the XII Reunião brasileira de antropologia. Rio de Janeiro.

—— (1984). *A negação e outros tópicos da gramática nadëb.* Universidade Estadual de Campinas. Unpublished master's thesis.

—— (1986). 'Footprints of yesterday's syntax: diachronic development of certain verb prefixes in an OSV language (Nadëb).' *Lingua* 68.291-316.

—— (1990) 'Incorporation in Nadëb.' In: Doris L. Payne ed., *Amazonian Linguistics. Studies in Lowland South American Languages*, 321-363. Austin: University of Texas Press.

Tuyuca

Janet Barnes

0 Introduction

The Tuyuca language is the native language of some 200 to 300 people in the Vaupés region of south-eastern Colombia, and of some 500 to 600 people on the same rivers in Brazil. Since Tuyuca men never marry Tuyuca women, but rather obtain wives from one of the other language groups in the area, each child grows up speaking at least two languages, and even more, if the other women in the village speak languages that are not the same as that of his/her mother. In general, each person speaks his own language, even when in conversation with someone from a different language. Thus, in a conversation between five people of five different languages, it is not unusual to hear all five languages being spoken.

Tuyuca is a Tucanoan language of the Macro-Tucanoan stock (see Ruhlen 1987:239). Cognate lists show a high degree of correspondence between the Tucanoan languages, and the grammars are also quite similar. Nevertheless, significant differences do exist. Thus, though in general the description of negation in Tuyuca is representative of negation in Tucanoan languages, one should not expect to find exact parallels between Tuyuca negation and negation in the other Tucanoan languages.

Nasalization in Tuyuca spreads from left to right and can spread through more than one morpheme in a word. Phonologically, the only morphemes that allow nasal spreading are those that begin with /g, r, w, y, h/ or that consist of a single vowel. However, not all morphemes which begin with one of these phonemes accept nasal spreading; each morpheme in the lexicon is specified for accepting or rejecting nasal spreading.

1 General typological information

1.1 Morphology

This section presents morphological information that is relevant to an understanding of the examples throughout the paper. For a fuller description of Tuyuca morphology, see Barnes and Malone (in press). Tuyuca is an agglutinative language and it is not too unusual to see four or more suffixes (or other roots) attached to a stem, as in the following examples[1].

(1)   Ñéé-bia-to-hã-yigɨ.
       grab-close-trap-Emph-Ev
       'He grabbed (the flea) and trapped it (in his mouth).'

(2)   Sãí-bosá-dɨga-ri-wi[2].
       buy-Benefactive-Desid-Neg-Ev
       'He did not want to buy it for another.'

(3)   Díayi-a-ye-mãkẽ-rẽ.
       dog-Pl.Anim-Poss.Pl-things-Sp
       'The dogs' things (as object of the verb)'

Table 1. Declarative evidentials

		Visual	Nonvisual	Apparent	Second-hand	Assumed
Past	other	-wɨ	-ti	-yu	-yiro	-hĩyu
	3.M.Sg	-wi	-ti	-yi	-yigɨ	-hĩyi
	3.F.Sg	-wo	-to	-yo	-yigo	-hĩyo
	3.Pl	-wa	-ta	-ya	-yira	-hĩya
Present	other	-a/-ã	-ga	–	–	-ku
	3.M.Sg	-i/-ĩ	-gi	-hĩĩ	–	-ki
	3.F.Sg	-yo	-go	-hĩõ	–	-ko
	3.Pl	-ya	-ga	-hĩrã	–	-kua

The future tense suffixes are all glossed Fut in the examples of this paper.

Table 2. Future tense suffixes

	Indefinite	Definite
Person	Future	Intention
1,2.M.Sg	-ɨdaku	-ɨda
1,2.F.Sg	-odaku	-oda
1,2.Pl,Inan	-adaku	-ada
3.M.Sg	-ɨdaki	
3.F.Sg	-odako	
3.Pl	-adakua	

Table 1 presents the declarative evidentials, all of which are glossed as EV in the examples of this paper. Note that the designation 'other' in table 1 refers to first and second persons singular and plural as well as inanimate. For a more complete explanation of Tuyuca evidentials see Barnes (1984). The interrogative evidentials are all glossed Interr.

Table 3. Interrogative evidentials

		Visual	Nonvisual	Other
Present		-i/-ĩ	-gari	-gari
Past		-ri/-rĩ	-tari	-yiri
Future	M.Sg			-idari
	F.Sg			-odari
	Pl,Inan			-adari

The nominalizing suffixes are glossed Nom, and their tense, person, gender and animacy is also specified (explicitly or by default), since the negative suffix used depends on the tense of the nominalizer.

Table 4. Nominalizers

	Animate			Inanimate			
	Sg		Pl	Countable		Non-count.	Place
	M	F		Sg	Pl		
Pres	-gi/-ŋĩ	-go/-ŋõ	-ra/-rã	-ri+CL	-re+CL	-re	-ro/-rõ
Past	-rigi	-rigo	-rira	(not specified		-rige	-riro
Fut	-idi	-odo	-adara	for time)		-adare	-adaro

1.2 Constituent order

The constituent order in Tuyuca sentences varies depending on discourse considerations. However, the unmarked order is SOV. Non-adjunct grammatical functions such as object, time and location are marked by the suffix *-re/-rẽ* 'specificity marker' (SP) when referring to a specific person, object, time or location. Subject is unmarked.

(4) Pakí   yái   sĩã-yígi.
     father jaguar   kill-Ev
     'Father killed a jaguar.'

(5)   Pakí   yái-re   sĩã-yígɨ.
       father   jaguar-Sp   kill-Ev
       'Father killed the jaguar (that had been killing the chickens).'

1.3 Questions

In content questions, the question phrase precedes the verb, and an interrogative evidential (see table 3, section 1.1) is suffixed to the verb in the position that the declarative evidential (see table 1, section 1.1) occupies in declarative verbs. The subject may occur in any position, though final position is normal. Putting the subject in initial position sets it in contrast to other participants in the context.

(6)   Nõã-rẽ́   Ĩñã́-rɨ̃   mɨ̃í.
       who-Sp   see-Interr   2.Sg
       'Whom did you see?'

(7)   Nõõ̃-pí   wáa-hõã-rɨ̃   pakí.
       where-Loc   go-Completely-Interr   father
       'Where did father go?'

In polar questions, an interrogative evidential is suffixed to the verb word as in the content questions above.

(8)   Wese-pí   heá-ri.
       field-Loc   arrive-Interr
       'Did you go to the field?'

(9)   Mɨ̃í   pakí   wĩmã́ɲɨ̃   nɨ̃í-ɲɨ̃   wií   sóe-yiri.
       2.SG   father   child.M   be-CC.M.Sg   house   burn-Interr
       'When your father was a child, did he burn down the house?'

1.4 Noun phrases

Noun phrases of more than one word are rare, possibly due to the use of classifier suffixes.[3] However, a few noun phrases of more than one word are found in both oral and written texts:

(10)   Sĩã-rí-dɨka   ñãñã-rí-dɨka
        illuminate-Nom.Inan.Sg-Cl:stick   be.bad-Nom.Inan.Sg-Cl:stick
        bɨkí-dɨka.
        old.object-Cl:stick
        'A terrible, old flashlight'

(11) Wekí-ya-bu   kitá-bu   bikí-bu.
      tapir-Poss.Sg-Cl:heap   excrement-Cl:heap   old.object-Cl:heap
      'An old pile of tapir excrement'

(12) Ti-bú   kitá-bu   õmế   busé-ri-bu.
      that-CL:heap   excrement-Cl:heap   steam   rise-Nom.Inan.Sg-Cl:heap
      'That heap of fresh excrement'

1.5 Modifiers

In Tuyuca there exist demonstrative, possessive and numerical adjectives. There are no qualifying adjectives as such, since concepts such as size, color, etc., are verb roots, and 'old' and 'new' are nouns. Demonstrative, possessive and numerical adjectives generally occur first in a noun phrase (see examples 12 and 17), although they may occur in second position as well.

(13) Koó-ya-gi   díayi yii-re   tutí-wi.
      3.F.Sg-Poss.Sg-Nom.M.Sg   dog   1.Sg-Sp   scold-Ev
      'Her dog barked at me.'

(14) Ĩmĩ-ấ   pia-rấ   heá-wa.
      man-Pl.Anim   two-Pl.Anim.Quantity   arrive-Ev
      'Two men arrived.'

1.6 Postpositions

Adjunct grammatical functions are indicated by postpositions. The postpositions function phonologically as suffixes. In noun phrases of more than one word, the postposition is suffixed to the final word of the noun phrase.

(15) Día-wesa.
      river-beside
      'Beside the river'

(16) Wese-pí.
      field-LOC
      'To the field/at the field'

(17) Kĩí-ya-wi   yukusóro mãmã-wí-pi
      3.M.Sg-Poss.Sg-Cl:hollow   canoe   new.object-Cl:hollow-Loc
      hoó-re   sấã-ñã.
      bananas-Sp   put.in-Imperative
      'Put the bananas in his new canoe.'

1.7 Comparison

When comparing items, the main item appears first in the sentence, and the standard of comparison immediately follows it, followed in turn by the comparative.

(18) Kɨ́ɨ́-ya-gɨ   mɨ́ɨ́-ya-gɨ   nẽmõ-rṍ
      3MSg-PossSg-NomMSg 2Sg-PossSg-NomMSg more-Adv
      pai-gɨ́   nɨ́ɨ́-ɨ̃.
      be:big-NomMSg be-Ev
      'His animal is bigger than your animal.'

When the two items being compared are identical in some respect, the suffix -kõrõ is added to the standard of comparison.

(19) Koó-ya-gɨ   kɨ́ɨ́-ya-gɨ-kõrõ   nɨ́ɨ́-ɨ̃.
      3FSg-PossSg-NomMSg 3MSg-PossSg-NomMSg-alike be-Ev
      'Her animal is the same as his animal.'

2 Negation

Standard negation in Tuyuca is expressed by the suffix -ri. In addition to the suffix of standard negation, there is another negative suffix, an enclitic and two negative verbs. The negative suffixes are -ri, which negates verbs and past and future tense nominalized verbs; and -e, which negates present tense nominalized verbs, the dependent verb of condition-consequence clauses, and adverbialized verbs. The enclitic mẽ́ẽ́ negates both nominal and adverbial constituents. The negative verbs are mãnĩ- 'to not be' and mõõ- 'to not have'.

2.1 Negative morphemes

2.1.1 The suffix -ri
The morpheme -ri is used without morphophonemic alternation on declarative verbs and on past and future tense nominalized verbs.

2.1.1.1 The suffix -ri on declarative verbs
The suffix -ri occurs between the verb stem and the evidential ending in declarative verbs. (See table 1 for the evidential endings.) The morpheme -ri is compatible with all the evidentials.

(20) Kɨ́ã-mẽnã   yaá-ri-wo.
     3Pl-Accompaniment   eat-Neg-Ev
     'She did not eat with them.'

(21) Ãñṹ-rõ   basá-ri-ya.
     good-Adv   sing-Neg-Ev
     'They do not sing well.'

(22) Díayi yɨ́ɨ-re   baka-rí-ti.
     dog 1Sg-Sp bite-Neg-Ev
     'The dog did not bite me.' (I did not feel his teeth in my flesh.)

A large number of mood and aspect suffixes also appear between the verb stem and the evidential ending, though it is most common to see just one or two in any one verb word.

(23) Ñãñã-ŋɨ́   nɨ́ɨ́-ri-hɨ̃ɨ̃   kãmẽ-rí-a-yi.
     be:bad-NomMSg be-Neg-Ev reciprocate-Neg-Recent-Ev
     'Apparently he is not bad, apparently he did not reciprocate (wound for wound).' (Said after viewing the wounds and evidence of a fight and seeing that the subject apparently did not fight back.)

(24) Kɨ́ã-rẽ   ĩñã́-dɨga-ri-yigo.
     3Pl-Sp   see-Desid-Neg-Ev
     'She did not want to see them.'

(25) Yaa-ré   kṹũ-bosa-ri-a-hɨ̃ya.
     eat-NomInan place-Benefactive-Neg-Recent-Ev
     'Apparently they didn't put out any food (for us).'

Some of the mood and aspect suffixes can have their order relative to the negative suffix reversed, with a resultant difference in the meaning of the word. In particular, *-ri* negates only the information which occurs to its left. A formal study of the order and cooccurrence restrictions of verb suffixes has yet to be undertaken.

(26) Bué-ruku-ri-wɨ.
     study-constantly-Neg-Ev
     'I did not study constantly (i.e., I studied, but not constantly).'

(27) Bué-ri-ruku-wɨ.
     study-Neg-constantly-Ev
     'I constantly did not study (i.e., I was constant in not studying.)'

2.1.1.2 The suffix -ri *on interrogatives*

In negative questions *-ri* occurs in the same position in the order of suffixes as in the corresponding negated declarative verb.

(28)   Sĩnĩ-dɨgá-ri-ri.
        drink-Desid-Neg-Interr
        'Didn't (whoever) want to drink?'

2.1.1.3 The suffix -ri *on imperatives*

In negative imperatives, *-ri* is always followed by the emphasis marker *-hã*, which in turn is followed by the imperative suffix *-ya/-ñã*.

(29)   Wáa-ri-hã-ñã.
        go-Neg-Emph-Imperative
        'Don't go!'

2.1.1.4 The suffix -ri *on verb stems in serial sentences*

To associate together a series of related actions performed by the same participant, a serial sentence is used, consisting of one or more dependent clauses followed by an independent clause. Each dependent clause ends with a verb stem (generally unsuffixed), and often the independent clause does not describe the final action in the series, but is the summary statement 'The participant(s) did'. If a dependent clause is negative, the verb stem of that clause is followed by the negative suffix *-ri*. In the following example, the verbs of the dependent clauses relate the actions that did not take place, and the independent verb provides a summary statement.

(30)   Kɨ́ã-rẽ   yaa-ré   eka-rí,   kɨ́ã-rẽ
        3Pl-Sp   eat-NomInan   give:food-Neg   3Pl-Sp

        tɨ́ã-ri,   tii-hã́-yira.
        serve:drink-Neg   do-Emph-Ev

        'They did not give them anything to eat or drink.'
        Literally: 'Not giving them food, not giving them drink, they did.'

Transporting the negative suffix *-ri* from the dependent verb(s) to the independent verb produces a sentence that the native speaker considers to be understandable but unnatural.

2.1.1.5 The suffix -ri *in concessive clauses*

The morpheme *-ri* may occur on dependent verbs suffixed with one of the following morphemes meaning 'although'.

Same subject in independent clause

M.Sg   -pakɨ
F.Sg   -pako
Pl   -pakara
Inan   -pakaro

Different subject in independent clause

DS   -pakari

(31) Yaá-ri-pakɨ   kãnɨ̃-hṍã-wi.
      eat-Neg-ConcessiveMSg   sleep-completely-Ev
      'Although he did not eat, he fell asleep.'

2.1.1.6 The suffix -ri *in reason-result clauses*

The morpheme -*ri* may occur on dependent verbs suffixed with one of the
following morphemes meaning 'since'. In these sentences, the subject of the
reason clause is always the same as the subject of the result clause[4].

M.Sg   -hĩŋɨ̃
F.Sg   -hĩŋṍ
Pl   -hĩrã

(32) Atí-ri-hĩŋɨ̃   mũmí ñẽé-ri-yigɨ.
      come-Neg-sinceMSg sweet receive-Neg-Ev
      'Since he did not come, he did not receive any candy.'

2.1.1.7 The suffix -ri *on past and future tense nominalized verbs*

The morpheme -*ri* appears on past and future tense nominalized verbs, but not
on present tense nominalized verbs (see section 2.1.2.1). Although all the
other occurrences of -*ri* are with verbs, in this instance the constituent with
which it occurs has been nominalized and is the head of a relative clause.

(33) Padé-ri-a-rigo   yɨ́ɨ mãkṍ nɨ̃í-yo.
      work-Neg-Recent-NomPastFSg 1Sg daughter be-Ev
      'The one who did not work is my daughter.'
(34) Ãnṍ heá-ri-rigɨ   Bogotá-pɨ wáa-hṍã-yigɨ.
      here arrive-Neg-NomPastMSg Bogotá-Loc go-Completive-Ev
      'The one who did not arrive here went to Bogotá.'
(35) Dokapúara-ye   bué-ri-odo   ñãmɨ́ɲã heá-odako.
      Tuyuca-language study-Neg-NomFutFSg tomorrow arrive-Fut
      'The woman who will not be studying the Tuyuca language will arrive tomor-
      row.'

When the past tense nominalized verb is followed by a declarative verb whose root is *nĩĩ́*- 'to be', this indicates that the assertion made by the speaker about what the person in question did or did not do is deduced from evidence.

(36)   Yaá-ri-a-rigɨ   nĩĩ́-ã-wɨ̃.
        eat-Neg-Recent-NomPastMSg   be-Recent-Ev
        'Evidently he did not eat (the food is still here).'
        Literally: 'Evidently he was a non-eating one.'

2.1.2 The suffix -e

The morpheme -*e* is used with present tense nominalized verbs, the dependent verb of condition-consequence clauses, and other adverbialized verbs. This morpheme can be penetrated by nasalization, and thus has the morphophonemic variant -*ẽ*.

2.1.2.1 The suffix -e *on present tense nominalized verbs*

(See table 4 for the chart of nominalizers and section 2.1.1.7 for examples of past and future tense nominalized verbs.) The suffix -*e* occurs between the verb stem and the nominalizer. The context indicates whether or not the meaning of the nominalized verb, be it negated or not, is to be understood as temporarily or habitually the case.

(37)   Waí   yaá-e-gɨ   nãĩ́-rõ   diá-ki.
        fish   eat-Neg-NomMSg   be:frequent-Adv   be:sick-Ev
        'The one who is not eating/does not eat fish is frequently sick.'
(38)   Wati-é-ri-wɨ-re   nẽẽ́-wa-ya.
        break-Neg-NomInanSg-CL:hollow-Sp   take-go-Imperative
        'Take the canoe which is not broken.'

2.1.2.2 The suffix -e *in condition-consequence clauses*

Dependent verbs in condition-consequence clauses, regardless of the tense of the verb of the independent clause, terminate with one of the following condition-consequence suffixes. Although these suffixes are composed of the same segments as four of the present tense nominalizers, the present tense nominalizers are stress attracting suffixes whereas these are not. The suffix -*e* occurs between the verb stem and the condition-consequence suffixes.

Same subject in independent clause

M.Sg	-gɨ/-ŋɨ̃	Pl-ra/-rã
F.Sg	-go/-ŋõ	Inan-ro/-rõ

Different subject in independent clause

DS   -ri/-rĩ

(39) Kĩ́ĩ   sĩnĩ-ŋĩ́   kúa-hõã-wi.
      3MSg drink-CCMSg be:angry-completely-Ev

      sĩnĩ-é-ŋĩ́   ãñṹ   nĩ́ĩ-wi.
      drink-Neg-CCMSg be:good be -Ev
      'When he drank, he became really angry; when he did not drink, he was fine.'

(40) Mĩ́ĩ boo-rí,   wáa-oda; mĩ́ĩ boo-é-ri,   ãnṍ pitiá-oda.
      2Sg want-DS go-Fut   2Sg want-Neg-DS here remain-Fut
      'If you want, I will go; if you do not, I will stay.'

2.1.2.3 The suffix -e on *adverbialized verbs*

Adverbialized verbs terminate with one of the following suffixes. The suffix
-*e* occurs between the verb stem and the adverbializer.

-*ro*/-*rõ* adverbializer (general)
-*ri*/-*rĩ* adverbializer of time

(41) Ãñṹ-ĕ-rõ   wedé-hã-wi.
      be:good-Neg-Adv explain-Emph-Ev
      'He explained (it) in a disorganized (i.e., not good) manner.'

(42) Yoá-e-ri   nĩ́ĩ wáa-hõã-wi.
      be:long-Neg-Adv.of.time be   go-completely-Ev
      'Being (there) a short (i.e., not long) time, I left.'

2.1.3 The enclitic *mēe*

The enclitic *mēe* negates the previous constituent, which may be nominal,
verbal or adverbial. Phonologically this morpheme is an enclitic, as it depends
on the previous word for its pitch-accent. Only two noun suffixes may be
attached to this morpheme: -*re*/*rē* 'specificity marker' and -*ra*/-*rā* 'precisely'.
The negated constituents in the following examples are in square brackets.

(43) [Wekĩ   mēē] nĩ́ĩ-ĩ.
      tapir   Neg be-Ev
      'He is not a tapir.'

(44) [Wekĩ-a   mēé-rē] ĩñã́-wĩ.
      tapir-PlAnim Neg-Sp see-Ev
      'I did not see tapirs.'
      Literally: 'I saw non-tapirs (i.e., I saw animals, but they were not tapirs).'

(45) [Wáa-gĩ   tií-a   hĩ́ĩ-ŋĩ́   mēē] wáa-hõã-wi.
      go-CCMSg do-Ev say-CCMSg Neg go-completely-Ev
      'Without saying 'I'm going', he left.'

(46) Kɨ́   basí [yaá-adara   mɛ̃ɛ̃] tii-yíra.
      3.Pl self eat-NomFutPl   Neg do-Ev
      'They did it intending to not eat by themselves.'
      Literally: 'They set up elaborate traps intending to share their catch with others, and not be ones who eat by themselves.'

(47) Tii-bú   kɨtá-bu
      that-Cl:heap excrement-Cl:heap

      [ɔ̃mɛ̃   busé-ri-bu   mɛ̃ɛ̃] nɨ́ɨ́-ã.
      steam rise-NomInanSg-Cl:heap Neg be-Ev
      'That heap of excrement is a not fresh heap.'

(48) [Nɔ̃kɔ́rɔ̃ yoá-ri   mɛ̃ɛ̃] nɛ́ɛ́-toa-yira.
      this:much be:long-Adv.of.time   Neg take-already-Ev
      'In this much short (not long) time they had already taken (them) out.'

In the following three examples the negative morphemes are substituted for one another in otherwise identical sentences. In the first example, the sentence is negated. In the second the positive subject is negated, indicating that she was not what she was thought to have been. In the third example, the subject is negated, indicating the character of the subject.

(49) Ati-gó   nɨ́ɨ́-ri-a-wɔ̃.
      come-NomFSg be-Neg-Recent-Ev
      'She did not come.'
      Literally: 'She was not a coming one.'

(50) [Ati-gó   mɛ̃ɛ̃] nɨ́ɨ́-ã-wɔ̃.
      come-NomFSg Neg be-Recent-Ev
      'She did not come.'
      Literally: 'She was (on that occasion) a not-coming one.'

(51) Atí-e-go   nɨ́ɨ́-ã-wɔ̃.
      come-Neg-NomFSg be-Recent-Ev
      'She never came.' (Lit: 'She is (habitually) a not-coming one.')

2.2 Negative verbs

There are two negative verbs in Tuyuca: *mãnĩ-* 'to not be', and *mõõ-* 'to not have'.

2.2.1 The negative verb mãnĩ- 'to not be'

The verb *mãnĩ-* 'to not be' or '(there) not to be' is the negative existential verb. It is not equivalent to the negative of the verb *nĩĩ-* 'to be, exist, live', as can be seen in the examples below.

(52) Yaa-ré   mãnî́-ã.
      eat-Nom:Inan   not:be-Ev
      'There isn't any food.'

(53) Yaa-ré   nĩí́-ri-a.
      eat-NomInan   be-Neg-Ev
      'That is not food.'

(54) Mãnĩ-á́-wĩ.
      not:be-Recent-Ev
      'He wasn't (there).'

(55) Nĩí́-ri-a-wĩ.
      be-Neg-Recent-Ev
      'That was not he.'

2.2.2 The negative verb mõõ- 'to not have'

The verb *mõõ-* 'to not have' is used interchangeably with the negative of the verb *kɨo-* 'to have'.

(56) Nĩyéru   mṍő-ã.
      money   not:have-Ev
      'I do not have any money.'

(57) Nĩyéru   kɨo-rí-a.
      money   have-Neg-Ev
      'I do not have any money.'

(58) Waí   kɨó-yo   koó-ha;   ĩsá-pe   mõő-ã.
      fish   have-Ev   3FSg-Contrast   1PlExclusive-Focus nothave-Ev
      'She has fish, but we don't (have).'

The negative verbs *mãnĩ-* and *mõõ-* have been found to cooccur with only two modal/aspectual suffixes (the negative *-ri* and the emphasis suffix *-hã*), and these always appear together in an idiomatic expression of strong affirmation (see section 3.3).

3 Other negative concepts

3.1 Negative emphases

The negative aspect of a statement may be intensified by adding the suffixes *-do* 'absolutely' and *-hã* 'Emphasis' to the negative suffix *-ri*. (The suffix *-do* never occurs apart from the negative suffix *-ri*.)

(59) Wáa-ri-do-hã-ĭdaku.
      go-Neg-absolutely-Emph-Fut
      'I will never go.'

(60) Tĭo-rí-do-hã-ã.
      hear-Neg-absolutely-Emph-Ev
      'You never listen/pay attention.'

(61) Bĭa-rí-do-hã-ã-tĭ.
      find-Neg-absolutely-Emph-Recent-Ev
      'I did not find a thing.'

The following three examples illustrate how suffixes are added to a stem to arrive at the concept 'absolutely nothing'.

(62) Pée-ro.
      be:small-Adv
      'A few/a little'

(63) Pée-ro-ŋã.
      be:small-Adv-Dim
      'A little bit'

(64) Pée-ro-nõ[5]-ŋã.
      be:small-Adv-Unspecified-Dim
      'Absolutely nothing (of that kind)'

Quantifiers such as 'everybody', 'some', 'others', etc., are not negativized in Tuyuca; rather, the accompanying verb is a negative verb or a negativized verb.

(65) Basoká   mãnĭ-ã́-wã.
      people   not:be-Recent-Ev
      'There was nobody (there).' (Literally: 'People were not.')

(66) Ãpĕ-rã́   kĭo-rí-kua.
      other-PlAnimQuantity have-Neg-Ev
      'No one else has (one of these).'
      (Literally: 'Others do not have (one of these).')

(67) Sĭkĭ́-nõ   mãnĭ-ã́-wĭ.
      one-Unspecified   not:be-Recent-Ev
      'There was not even one (alligator).' (Lit: 'One of that kind was not.')

(68) Kĭĭ́-nõ-hã   kĕmĭ-ñã́   mãnĭ-kí.
      he-Unspecified-Emph catch:up-Impersonal   not:be-Ev
      'No one can catch up with one of his kind.'
      (Literally: 'One of his kind can not be caught up with.')

(69) Sĩkí-nõ   waí   yaá-ri-a-ya.
      one-Unspecified fish   eat-Neg-Recent-Ev
      'Not even one ate fish./Nobody ate fish.'
      (Literally: 'One of them did not eat fish.')

If the subject or complement of the verb is understood from context, it is left unexpressed. (Note the ideas of 'nobody' and 'anywhere' in the following examples.)

(70) Heá-ri-a-wã.
      arrive-Neg-Recent-Ev
      'Nobody arrived.' (In answer to: Who arrived?)

(71) Wáa-ri-a-wĩ.
      go-Neg-Recent-Ev
      'I didn't go (anywhere)' (In answer to: Where did you go?)

In the following example, the context determines whether the combination of -*nẽmõ* 'repeat' and the negative suffix -*ri* indicates 'not again' or 'never'. The context for the first gloss may be that the speaker has decided not to sing again in the present setting. The context for the second gloss would be one so serious that the speaker vows never to sing again.

(72) Basá-nẽmõ-ri-ku.
      sing-repeat-Neg-Ev
      'I won't sing again./I'll never sing again.'

3.2 Negative responses

Whereas a Tuyuca can respond positively by saying *ĩhĩ* 'Uh-huh/yes', there is no short form for responding in the negative. To give a negative response, one negates the very same verb that was used in the question.

(73) Yaá-ĩdari.   Yaá-ri-a.
      eat-Interr   eat-Neg-Ev
      'Will you eat?'   'I will not eat.'

(74) Wáa-hõã-rĩ.   Wáa-ri-wi.
      go-Completely-Interr   go-Neg-Ev
      'Did he go away?'   'He did not go.'

(75) Basá-diga-gari   Basá-diga-ri-ga.
      sing-Desid-Interr   sing-Desid-Neg-Ev
      'Do you want to sing?'   'I do not want to sing.'

If a question is asked in the negative, such as *Is he not coming?*, the positive response *íhĩ* means, 'Yes, he is not coming.'

(76)   Atí-ri-gari.   íhĩ.
       come-Neg-Interr   uh-huh
       'Is he not coming?'   'Yes, (he is not coming).'

3.3 Double negatives

Two double negative constructions occur, one resulting in a semantically strong positive statement, the other in a contrafactual comparison. The double negative that results in a strong positive statement is formed by negating with *-ri* both a main verb and a following auxiliary verb *tii* 'do'. The emphasis morpheme *-hã* is always added to the main verb.

(77)   Tikóko-ri-hã   tii-rí-hã-ñã.
       send-Neg-Emph   do-Neg-Emph-Imperative
       'Send it!/Be sure to send it!'

(78)   Nĩyéru kĩo-rí-hã   tii-rí-a.
       money have-Neg-Emph   do-Neg-Ev
       'I certainly do have money!'

Although the main verb in this construction may itself be negative, the introduction of the third negative does not change the polarity; rather, the semantic impact remains positive.

(79)   Nĩyéru   mõõ-rí-hã   tii-rí-a.
       money   not:have-Neg-Emph   do-Neg-Ev
       'I certainly do have money!'

(80)   Mãnĩ-rí-hã   tii-rí-wi.
       not:be-Neg-Emph   do-Neg-Ev
       'I assure you that he really was (here)!'

A contrafactual comparison is formed when the enclitic *mẽẽ́* follows either a negative dependent verb or a negativized dependent verb.

(81)   [mãrí   mãnĩ-rí   mẽẽ] ati-mãkã́
       1PlInclusive   not:be-DS   Neg this-Cl:town
       witisã́-rõ   tií-a.
       be:overgrown-CCInan do-Ev
       'This town is growing with weeds as though we were not (here).'

(82) Mɨ̃́ɨ́ [mõõ̃-ŋɨ̃́   mẽẽ̃]
2Sg nothave-CCMSg Neg

pée-ri-ga-ŋã̃   wapa-tí-a-wɨ̃.
be:small-NomInanSg-Cl:3:Dimensional-Dim pay-do-Recent-Ev
'You bought a tiny outboard motor as though you did not have (any money)!'

(83) Kɨ̃́ɨ́ [kuí-e-gɨ   mẽẽ̃] mɨ̃́ã̃-wa-i.
3MSg fear-Neg-CCMSg Neg go:up-go-Ev
'He is going up the tree as though he were not afraid.'

4 Additional comments

The following comments are intended to answer questions that might arise regarding negatives in Tuyuca. Negated constituents can occur in negated clauses.

(84) Tɨo-é-ra   kuí-ri-wa.
hear-Neg-Nom.Pl fear-Neg-Ev
'Those who did not hear (it) were not afraid.'

Negative transport does not occur (see section 2.1.1.4). The scope of negation is not affected by stress or intonation differences. There are no negative auxiliary verbs (and only one positive auxiliary verb: *tii* 'do', which is used in progressive constructions (see examples 45 and 81). There are no derivational restrictions on negated constructions.

Notes

1. Examples are written morphophonemically with one exception. To facilitate reading, /b, d, g, y/ are written *m, n, ŋ ,ñ* when followed by a nasal vowel. For example, /dã/ is written *nã*. /r/ is an alveolar flap, /y/ varies between being a palatal semivowel and an alveopalatal affricate, and /h/ is a voiceless semivowel that assumes the quality of the following vowel. The accent mark over the vowels indicates a combination of high pitch and intensity. For a phonological analysis of Tuyuca, see Barnes and Takagi (1976).

2. The negative morpheme *-ri* differs from the other *-ri* morphemes which occur in this paper in one or both of the following ways: (1) whether the morpheme accepts or rejects nasal spreading, and (2) whether the morpheme is stress attracting or stress accepting. The negative *-ri* rejects nasal spreading, whereas some of the other morphemes do not; and it accepts stress, whereas one of the other morphemes attracts it.

3. Classifiers in Tuyuca are suffixes which denote some salient characteristic of their referent. For example, they indicate shape, collection (i.e., the type of grouping), arrangement (i.e., the present configuration), container, etc. At this writing, more than one

342   *Janet Barnes*

hundred classifiers have been identified. For more information on Tuyuca classifiers see Barnes (1990).

4. If the subject of the result clause is different from the subject of the reason clause, the dependent verb is suffixed with *-ri* 'Different Subject' and the negative suffix employed is *-e*; see section 2.1.2.2.

5. The morpheme *-nõ*, which occurs in several of the above examples, refers to any entity that might fit in the context. In example (67), which is part of a text about alligator hunting, the morpheme *-nõ* indicates that the speaker did not find any alligators of any shape or description. The morpheme *-nõ* also occurs in positive statements. To illustrate, if example (68) referred to turtles rather that armadillos, the sentence would be changed to say, 'One can catch up with one of his kind'.

Abbreviations

Adv	adverbializer		Loc	locative
Anim	animate		M	masculine
Cl	classifier		Neg	negative
Cc	condition=consequence		Nom	nominalizer
Desid	desiderative		Pl	plural
Dim	diminutive		Poss	possessive
DS	different subject		Pres	present
Emph	emphasis		Sg	singular
Ev	evidential		Sp	specificity marker
F	feminine		1	first person
Fut	future tense		2	second person
Inan	inanimate		3	third person
Interr	interrogative			

References

Barnes, Janet. (1984). 'Evidentials in Tuyuca.' *International Journal of American Linguistics*, Vol. 50, No. 3, 255-271. Chicago: The University of Chicago Press.
———— (1990). 'Classifiers in Tuyuca.' In: Doris L. Payne (ed.) *Amazonian Linguistics*: Studies in Lowland South American Languages, 273-292. Austin: University of Texas Press.
Barnes, Janet and Sheryl Takagi (de Silzer). 1976. 'Fonología del tuyuca', *Sistemas fonologicos de idiomas Colombianos*, III: 123-137. Traducción de Jorge Arbeláez G. y Hno. Bernardo Montes U. Colombia: Instituto Lingüístico de Verano.
Barnes, Janet and Terrell Malone (in press). 'El tuyuca.' *Estudio preliminar para el atlas etnolingüístico Colombiano*. Bogotá: Instituto Caro y Cuervo.
Ruhlen, Merritt. (1987). *A guide to the world's languages*, Vol 1. Stanford: Stanford University Press.

Wayampi

Allen A. Jensen

1 Introduction[1]

In Wayampi[2], a Tupi-Guarani language spoken in northern Brazil, there are four morphological negation constructions used in modifying the word, phrase or clause, each of which has constructions directed toward a particular function. There is an additional independent morpheme meaning 'no' (see table 1). These five morphemes have cognates in common usage throughout the Tupi-Guarani language family (see Appendix), although their range of usage isn't necessarily the same.

Table 1. Occurrence of negation morphemes in Wayampi

Morpheme	Verb	Noun
n-...-i[3]	main clause verbs, stative verbs, predicated nouns, some subordinate conditional temporal verbs	
-e'ỹ	nominalized verbs, subordinate purpose, some subordinate temporal, and non-initiating serial verbs	on nouns it means: 'without/lacking'
-ruã	adverbials including postpositional phrases and stative verbs functioning as adverbials	on nouns it means: 'not' or 'it is not'
ne	imperatives	
ani	free-form response	

In addition there are three semi-negative morphemes, two *(tite, panẽ)* which indicate frustration (lack of success) on the part of the agent of the sentence, and, *sõ*, which occurs in direct quotes and indicates disapproval on the part of the speaker.

Wayampi is best classified as a free word order language (C. Jensen 1980). Although there are five word order variations in main clauses (SOV, SVO, VSO, OVS, & OSV), word position depends upon focus, old/new information and definiteness/indefiniteness (C. Jensen 1980, A. Jensen 1982.) Non-initiating serial verbs, when they occur, always follow the main verb. In temporal subordinate clauses the verb generally occurs in word final position. Like other Tupi-Guarani languages, Wayampi has the syntactic orders Genitive + Noun and Noun + Postposition. Nouns in Wayampi are either grammatically possessible (e.g., body parts) or non-possessible (e.g. 'rain'). Possessible nouns require a prefix or a noun to indicate the possessor whereas non-possessible ones do not. Modificational suffixes may denote size (large vs small), performance (devolved and anticipatory), or quality (genuine or imitation relative to some norm). There are also two patterns for complex noun formation: N + N, where the first noun may modify the second or where the second noun indicates some distinguishing feature of the first noun; N + V, where the verb is a stative or intransitive verb and in composition with the noun acts as an adjective (modifier).

The position of interrogative morphemes in content question sentences is invariably clause initial. In yes-no question sentences the question morpheme *po* occurs immediately after the initial phrase, which is the element in question.

In main intransitive verbs, and in main transitive verbs where the subject is hierarchically superior to the object, a nominative-accusative system of prefixes is employed. However, in some of its subordinate verbs, all of its stative verbs, and those main transitive verbs in which the object is hierarchically superior to the subject, it employs an ergative-absolutive system (C. Jensen 1990).

2 Presentation of data

2.1 The split affix negation morpheme, *n-...-i*

2.1.1 Independent verb phrase

Negation of the independent verb phrase in Wayampi is indicated by a split affix or double particle (term used by Dahl 1979:88-89) *(n-...-i)* on the verb: *n-* occurs as the initial prefix and *-i* as a suffix. Both parts of the split affix are obligatory. Any element which functions as the verb in a main clause will be negated by the *n-...-i* affix.

2.1.1.1 Transitive verbs

(1)   N-a-'u-i.
       Neg-1sA-eat-Neg
       'I didn't eat it.'

(2) N-o-juka-i.
Neg-3A-kill-Neg
'He didn't kill it.'

2.1.1.2 Intransitive verbs
(3) Aja-ire   n-ere-vaĕ-i.[4]
Dem-after   Neg-2S-arrive-Neg
'Afterwards you didn't arrive.'

(4) Yvytu   remĕ,   n-o-ata-i   kupa.
windy   when   Neg-3S-hunt-Neg   SPl
'When it's windy they don't hunt.'

2.1.1.3 Stative verbs
(5) Ani,   n-i-katu-i,   e'i.
no   Neg-3S-good-Neg   3-say
'"No, it's not good," he said.'

(6) N-e-karay-i   ky'y.
Neg-1S-fever-Neg   finally
I don't have a fever any longer.

2.1.1.4 Predicated Nouns
When predicated nouns are negated they express lack of the item, or of a
quality innate of that item.

(7) N-i-paje-i.
Neg-3S-shaman-Neg
'He doesn't have the quality of a shaman.'

(8) N-i-kamisa-i   kupa.
Neg-3S-cloth-Neg   SPl
They didn't wear clothes (because it wasn't their custom.)

2.1.1.5 Predicated adverbs
(9) N-awĩ-vo-i   jypy remĕ,   e'i.
Neg-Dem-like-Neg   past when   3-say
'It wasn't like this in the past, he said.'

(10) Moma'e   kwer n-i-manyvo-'ãi.
something Col Neg-3S-how-Fut:Neg
'There was no way they could get things.'

See also section 2.2.3 for negation of unmarked nouns giving the meaning
'without'.

2.1.1.6 Existential verbs

Although the existential verb *iko* may be conjugated in its non-negative form like any intransitive verb, it has a single frozen form in the negative: *naikoi*. This is derived from the first person singular form *(a-iko)* but may refer to any person. Some negative indefinites *(nothing, no one)* may sometimes be expressed using this frozen-form existential verb.

(11) Aja-ire   naikoi   kamisa   ky'y,   e'i.
     Dem-after not:exist cloth   finally   3:say
     'Afterwards I had (there was) no more cloth, he said.'

(12) Maevo   akyky   naikoi   ky'y,   e'i.
     perhaps monkey (sp) not:exist anymore   3:say
     'Perhaps there are no howler monkeys anymore, he said.'

(13) Naikoi   jane   a'e pe   ky'y,   e'i.
     not:exist people Dem at   anymore 3:say
     'There is no one there anymore (no one lives there anymore).'

2.1.2 Allomorphic variations

There are three allomorphs of the prefix, n-, of the split morpheme:
         n-   / __ V
         ni-   / __ j /y/
         na-   / __ C

(14) N-a-'u-i.
     Neg-1sA-eat-Neg
     'I didn't eat it.'

(15) Ni-ja-'u-i.
     Neg-1genA-eat-Neg
     'We (in general) don't eat it (Nobody eats it).'

(16) Na-pe   'u-i.
     Neg-2PlA   eat-Neg
     'You (Pl) didn't eat it.'

Certain variations in the choice of allopmorphs occur, which are best explained diachronically. In (17) the 3rd person subject is indicated with a zero morpheme *(ø)*. The protoform of this zero morpheme was the consonant *c-* [ts-]. Although this class II[5] prefix has since become a zero morpheme in the Wayampi language, it is still preceded by the *na-* allomorph appropriate to consonants (see C. Jensen 1989:84-87).

(17) Na-ø-ory-i.
     Neg-3S-happy-Neg
     'He's not happy.'

In (18) the first person inclusive agent prefix, *si-*, co-occurs with the *ni-* allomorph rather than with *na-*. This occurrence with the allomorph which characteristically precedes the semivowel *j* /y/ reflects the historical derivation of the prefix *si-* from the prefix *ja-*, in fusion with two other prefixes *(t+ja+i > si)* (C. Jensen 1987:50-52.)

(18) Ni-si-'u-i.
      Neg-1inA-eat-Neg
      'We (inc) didn't eat.'

In examples (19) and (20), it may superficially appear that the negation suffix is *-ri* rather than *-i*. However, it has been demonstrated through language reconstruction (C. Jensen 1989:25-27) that the *r* is in fact the final consonant of the stem (**potar* and **ker*, respectively) which remained untouched by the process of elimination of final consonants when suffixed.

(19) Kara   n-o-potar-i   yvy-pijõ. Ysig te   o-pota.
      sweet:potato Neg-3A-like-Neg soil-dark sand Emp 3A-like
      'Sweet potato doesn't like (grow well in) dark soil. It likes (grows well in) sandy soil.'

(20) N-a-ker-i.
      Neg-1sS-sleep-Neg
      'I didn't sleep.'

2.1.3 Constituents of the negated main verb phrase
There are several affixes which may modify the negated verb phrase, most of which occur within the split affix negation morpheme. The relative order of these constituents are fixed, as outlined in this paper. Although in theory it is possible to attach many affixes to a verb stem, in practice the Wayampi prefer not to overload the verb in this way. Instead, they prefer to spread out the information load among several sentences. Three or four modifiers (prefixes and suffixes combined) would normally be maximum for each sentence. The presence of suffixes on a verb is generally recognized in everyday speech through stress change on the verb stem from the penultimate to the final syllable and through the stressing on all but the final suffixes (A. Jensen 1979).

2.1.3.1 Prefixes
a. Person Marker: Obligatorily following the negation prefix, *n-*, is the person marker prefix. On main transitive verbs, the prefix refers to either the subject

(21) or the object (22), depending on which of these is superior on an agency hierarchy (1 > 2 > 3) (C. Jensen 1990).

(21)   N-a-nupã-i.
        Neg-1sA-hit-Neg
        'I didn't hit him (it/her).'

(22)   N-ore-nupã-i.
        Neg-1exP-hit-Neg
        'He didn't hit us (excl.)'

b. Reflexive: The reflexive prefix, *ji-*, optionally follows the person marker on transitive verbs, thereby detransitivizing them.

(23)   N-a-ji-mo'e-i.
        Neg-1sS-Refl-teach-Neg
        'I didn't teach myself.'

(24)   N-oro-ji-mony(i)-i.
        Neg-1exS-Refl-frighten-Neg
        'We (exc) weren't frightened.'

(25)   N-o-ji-po-kusu-i.[6]
        Neg-3S-Refl-hand-wash-Neg
        'He didn't wash his (own).'

c. Causative: The simple causative morpheme *mo-* may occur immediately preceding the verb stem and transitivizes any intransitive or stative verb. The causative-commitative morpheme *ero-* may also occur in this position.

(26)   N-o-mo-jau-i
        Neg-3A-Caus-bath-Neg
        'He didn't bathe it.'

(27)   N-o-ero-jivy-i
        Neg-3A-CC-return-Neg
        'He didn't return it (personally).'

(28)   N-o-ero-'ar-i
        Neg-3A-CC-fall-Neg
        'He didn't fall with it.'

2.1.3.2 Post verb stem morphemes

a. Second element of compound verbs: The transitive verb *kua*, 'to know', may serve as the second element of a compound verb and immediately follows the nuclear verb. The transitive verb *pota(r)*, 'to want', is reduced to the morpheme *-ta(r)* when used as the second element in negated compound verbs.

(29) N-o-jiporaka-kua-i   kupa.
     Neg-3S-hunt-know-Neg   SPl
     'They don't know how to hunt.'

(30) N-o-me'ẽ-tar-i   i-jupe.
     Neg-3A-give-want-Neg   3P-to
     'He didn't want to give it to him.'

b. Completive: The suffix *-pa/-ma* occurs within the bounds of the split affix immediately following the verb and indicates the completion of an activity. On negated verbs it indicates a partial (incomplete) activity, see (31). Allomorphic variation of this suffix depends upon whether or not the preceding verb stem is nasalized.

(31) N-o-me'ẽ-ma-i   ajama'ẽ.
     Neg-3A-give-Cmp-Neg   Cntr:Exp
     'But (counter to expectation) he didn't give everything.'

c. Causative: When the suffix *-oka(r)* co-occurs on transitive verbs with the negative affix, it indicates that the agent prevents the action from taking place, see (32). The suffix *-yty* co-occurs only on non-transitive negated verbs and seems to direct the hearers attention to the innate quality of an obstacle, see (33) and (34). This suffix appears to occur only on negated verbs in the third person.

(32) Na-poro-mo-kasi-okar-i.
     Neg-people-Caus-strong-Caus-Neg
     'It does not allow people to be strong. (It weakens people.)'

(33) N-o-ji-upi-yty-i   pino-'y   i-jãmai   te   remẽ.
     Neg-3S-Refl-raise-Caus-Neg   bacaba:tree   3S-slippery   Emp when
     'The bacaba palm tree is unclimbable when it is slippery.'

(34) Tare'yr   jarõ   poro-su'u-ve   ipi.
     Traira:fish   mad   people-bite-also   Hab
     Aja-wyi   yy   rupi   n-o-'y-asa-yty-i.
     Dem-because   river   through   Neg-3S-river-cross-Caus-Neg
     'For this reason the river is uncrossable (through the water). When the traira fish are mad they also bite people.'

d. Future tense: The suffix *-ta*, which indicates future tense on non-negated verbs, does not co-occur with the negative. Another morpheme, *-'ã*, fuses with the negative suffix to indicate that the action will not be realized (35)-(36) or would not have been realized, see (37).

(35)   N-a-me'ẽ-'ãi   i-(j)upe.   [a-me'ẽ-ta]
       Neg-1sA-give-Fut-Neg   3-to
       'I will not give it to him.'

(36)   Rapar korijõ   te   n-o-ereko-'ãi.   [o-ereko-ta]
       arrow only   Emp   Neg-3A-have-Fut-Neg
       'It's only arrows that they won't have.'

(37)   N-o-posiko-'ãi   mijã.
       Neg-3S-work-Fut-Neg   Unr
       'He wasn't going to work.' Or: 'He wouldn't have worked.'

As seen in (38), the negation affix may occur on subordinate conditional-temporal clauses as well as the main clause.

(38)   N-o-ji-nami-mo-mu-i   tamõ   kõ   remẽ,
       Neg-3A-Refl-ear-Caus-pierce-Neg   grandfather   Pl   if

       n-o-kyje-'ãi   apã   kõ   i-wyi kõ   amẽ mijã.
       Neg-3A-fear-Fut-Neg   enemy   Pl   3-of Pl   then Unr
       'If our grandfathers hadn't pierced their (own) ears, their enemies wouldn't
       have been afraid of them.'

e. Augmentatives/diminutives: When the augmentative suffix, *-wete*, is used on non-negated verbs, it means 'a lot'. On the negated verb, however, *-wete* becomes *-we'e* and means 'not very much'. The diminutive suffix, *-miti*, on the non-negated verb means 'a little'. On the negated verb, however, it indicates 'not at all' or 'not even a little'.

(39)   Ni-ja-kua-we'e-i   ajama'ẽ.
       Neg-1genA-know-Aug-Neg   Cont-Exp
       'But nobody knows very much.'

(40)   N-a-ke-miti-(i).
       Neg-1S-sleep-Dim-Neg
       'I didn't sleep at all OR I didn't sleep even a little.'

2.1.3.3 Post-verb stem morphemes occuring outside the split affix morpheme
a. Another diminutive suffix, which only occurs outside the negative split affix morpheme, is *-'ete*. It gives the same meaning as with the suffix *-miti* on negated verb phrases.

(41)   N-a-ma'ẽ-i-'ete   ø-ee.
       Neg-1sS-see-Neg-Aug   3P-at
       'I didn't see it at all.'

b. Incompletive: The suffix -ve is another morpheme which only attaches to a verb phrase outside the split affix unit and is always the last item in the phrase. The two morphemes mean 'not yet'.

(42) N-i-men-i-ve   ma'ẽ.[7]
      Neg-3S-husband-Neg-yet   Nom
      'One who is not yet married.'

(43) N-e-kamisa-i-ve.
      Neg-1S-cloth-Neg-yet
      'I didn't yet wear clothes.'

2.1.4 Summary of aspects of the negated verb phrase
Table 2 on the following page summarizes the differential meaning of one negative verb using the various affixes described above.

Table 2. Summary of negative verb usage.

N-o-juka-pa-i	He didn't kill them all.
N-o-juka-miti-(i)	He didn't kill any at all.
N-o-juka-i-'ete	He didn't kill any at all.
N-o-juka-we'e-i	He almost killed nothing. He (it) didn't kill much.
N-o-juka-i-ve	He didn't kill it yet.
N-o-juka-'ãi	He won't kill it
N-o-juka-tar-i	He doesn't want to kill it.
N-o-juka-okar-i	He didn't allow it to be killed.

2.2 The negative morpheme e'ỹ

In Wayampi the morpheme -e'ỹ negates the subordinate purpose clause and certain subordinate temporal clauses. It also negates nouns and nominalized verbs.

2.2.1 Subordinate clauses
2.2.1.1 Subordinate purpose clause
Subordinate purpose clauses are most often used when the subject of the purposed action is other than the subject of the initial action. They can be recognized by the obligatory purpose prefix, t-, on the dependent verb. When this prefix co- occurs with the negation suffix, -e'ỹ, they mean 'in order for ... to not'.

(44) Tyvija   rupi te   o-mo-ĕ   i-mono,
      hiddenly   Mns Emp 3A-Caus-leave   3P-send:away
      amõ kõ   t-o-juka-e'ỹ.
      other Pl   Purp-3A-kill-Neg
      'He sent him away undercover, in order that others wouldn't kill him.'

(45) Potopotori o-mo-katu,   ja'yr-er
      nails   3A-Caus-put:away   child-Col
      t-o-posiko-e'ỹ   ø-ee.
      Purp-3S-mess:with-Neg   3-with:respect:to
      'He put the nails away in order that the children wouldn't mess with them.'

The same prefix *t-* may also communicate the idea of permission and is
negated in the same way as subordinate purpose verb clauses. It may be
translated 'shouldn't'.

(46) T-ere-mome'u-e'ỹ,   e'i.
      Perm-2A-tell-Neg   3-say
      'You shouldn't (may not) tell about it, he said.'

2.2.1.2 Temporal subordinate clause

Three temporal subordinate clause types indicate action taking place before,
during or after the action indicated in the main clause. When the action of
the main clause takes place before the action of the subordinate clause, the
conjunction which is most easily translated in English as 'before' is actually
derived from the negative morpheme, *-e'ỹ: -e'ỹ-ve* 'Neg-yet' meaning, 'before
it had taken place'. The same meaning is communicated by *-e'ỹ remẽ -ve*.

(47) Jyy r-eko-e'ỹ-ve,   i-koo-siri-te.
      axe Rel-be-Neg-yet   3-garden-small-Emp
      'Before there were axes, gardens were very small.' (Or: 'When there were not
      yet axes, gardens were very small').

(48) Punai vaĕ-e'ỹ-ve,   oro-o.
      Funai arrive-Neg-yet   1exA-go
      'Before FUNAI's arrival, we went (there).'

(49) N-a-a   'aĩ   e-men-e'ỹ   remẽ-ve, e'i.
      Neg-1S-go Neg:Fut 1S-husband-Neg   when-yet 3:say
      'I will not go husbandless (before I have a husband), she said.'

Another temporal application uses the conjunction, *-me* 'when' (*-me* is a
contraction of the morpheme, *remẽ* 'when'.)

(50) Ne-ykyrỹ   remẽ   e-pary   kõ   re   karamõ,
2S-child   when   1S-grandchild   Opl about future

ne-ji-mo-akwã'ã-tae-reko-e'ỹ-me,   e'i   tamõ.
2S-Refl-Caus-comfort-Fut-1S-be-Neg-when he-said grandfather.

'In the future when you have children, my grandchildren, you will be comforted in my absence (after I am dead), grandfather said.'

2.2.1.3 Non-initiating serial verb

Serial verbs are used when two or more verbs are perceived to express part of a single action, with the subject of both verbs being the same. The second verb may be negated by -*e'ỹ*. Non-initiating serial verbs take absolutive pronominal prefixes.

(51) "Ja'yr-er o-ekyi   ø-ena   pe   wyi,"
child-Col   3A-remove   3-house at   from

oro-'e   tite   i-kua-e'ỹ.
1exS-say falsely   3P-know-Neg

'"Children took (stole) them from the house," we said mistakenly unknowingly.'

(52) O-ji-monyi   i-kua-e'ỹ   amẽ.
3S-Refl-afraid 3P-know-Neg so:then
'He was afraid because he didn't know (it).'

(53) "N-a-pytyvõ-'ãi,"   e'i   i-tekokua-e'ỹ.
Neg-3A-help-Fut:Neg   3:say 3-wisdom-Neg
'"I won't help him," he said unknowingly (not having wisdom).'

2.2.2 Nominalized verbs

There are various types of nominalizations which co-occur with *e'ỹ*. In (54) the transitive verb, *kua*, is detransitivized by the reflexive *ji-*, then nominalized by the suffix *e'ỹ* and occurs in apposition to another noun, *tekorãn*, 'sickness':

(54) Tekorãn ji-kua-e'ỹ   oro-mogy a'e pe.
sickness Refl-know-Neg   1ex-catch Dem at
'We caught a sickness, an unknown one, at that place.'

In a somewhat parallel situation, see (55), the transitive verb *(e)sa(g)* is prefixed by the object nominalizer, *emi-*, and is negated with *e'ỹ*.

(55) Ka'a   t-emi-sag-e'ỹ   pupe   o-jarõ-ai-te   mijar   ipi.
jungle 3-Nom-encounter-Neg in   3-wild-bad-Emp game:animal Hb
'In (the places of) the jungle that we haven't seen, game animals are wild (easily angered).'

(56)   E-r-emi-kua-e'ỹ   n-a-movy-'ãi.
        1s-Rel-Nom-know-Neg Neg-1sA-tell-Fut:Neg
        'I won't tell about the ones I don't know.'

(57)   Gasi-e'ỹ   o-juka.
        strength-Neg 3A-kill
        'He died of hunger (lack of strength killed him).[8]

E'ỹ co-occurs with the nominalizer of 'place' (**e'ym* + *ab — *e'ỹ-ma*) to indicate 'a place characterized by the absence of...'

(58)   Oro-o   oro-posiko gasi   e'ỹ-ma   r-upi.
        3exS-go 3exS-work strength Neg-place Rel-around
        'We (excl) worked at a place where there was hunger (strengthless place.)'

(59)   Teko   e'ỹ-ma   kyty wyi o-eraa   kupa.
        People Neg-place at   from 3A-bring Pl
        'They brought it from an uninhabited (peopleless) place (teko is from the verb, eko 'to be').'

2.2.3 Nouns

Unmarked (uninflected) nouns are negated with *-e'ỹ* and mean 'without ...'

(60)   Yvyra-'a-e'ỹ-te.   N-i-'a-'ãi.
        tree-fruit-Neg-Emp-Neg   3S-fruit-Fut:Neg
        'It's a fruitless tree. It won't give fruit.'

(61)   Tepy-e'ỹ   te   n-o-potar-i   kõ.
        payment-Neg Emp Neg-3A-want-Neg Pl
        'They don't want to give it free (without payment).'

2.3 The negation morpheme *ruã*

The morpheme *-ruã* negates nouns and adverbials, including postpositions; occurs in frozen form with certain adjectives; and occurs in some rhetorical questions.

2.3.1 Contrastive negation

When the purpose of the sentence is to make an assertion, the noun (62)-(64) or adverbial (65)-(66) in focus in the sentence is fronted. When the assertion is negated, the morpheme *ruã* immediately follows that first element. Negative assertions are usually preceded or followed by another assertion in opposition to it. Frequently, the noun or adverbial of the assertion in opposition includes the morpheme *-te* emphasizing the contrast, as in (63) and (64).

(62) Ja'yr-er-ruã   amẽ tamõ   kõ.   O-ji-movija-pa.
child-Col-Neg then grandfather   Pl   3S-Refl-grow:up-Cmp
'So then our grandfathers were NOT children. They had grown up.'

(63) Tamõ   kõ-ruã   jẽ   e'i.   Ajã-te-jẽ   e'i.
grandfather   Pl-Neg   Vrf   3:say   spirit-Emp-Vrf   3:say
'It was NOT (our) grandfathers who said it. It was an evil spirit that said it.
(Context: how a river got its name.)'

(64) Poro-moripe   ma'ẽ ruã   ene,   e'i.
people-deceive   Nom Neg   you(s) 3-say

Ivo   katu ne-poregeta   ma'ẽ-te   ene,   e'i.
just   good 2A-speak   Nom-Emp you(s) 3:say

'You are NOT a people deceiver, he said. You are an honest speaker, he said.'

In (65) and (66), stative verbs are treated as adverbials preceding an intransitive verb. If they had been negated independent stative verbs, they would have taken the contrasting forms with *n...i.*

(65) E-wari-ruã a-poregeta.   N-e-war(i)-i.
1s-lie-Neg 1S-speak   Neg-1s-lie-Neg
'I speak unlyingly. I don't lie.'

(66) a. E-piryvypy-ruã   a-iko.
1s-feel-at-ease-Neg 1S-be
'I am living uneasily (not at peace).'

b. N-e-piryvypy-i.
Neg-1s-feel:at:ease-Neg
'I am ill at ease.'

2.3.2 Frozen forms
Certain adjectives and adverbs are negated with *ruã* but have become frozen forms. They are distinguished from negative assertions in that they are not usually accompanied by an apposing statement as in (62)-(64). Also, they are not necessarily fronted. The best translation of such frozen forms is simply the opposite meaning of the non-negated adjective. Table 3 (see next page) contains a list of the frozen forms.

(67) Aja-ire   oro-ity   koo   ta'yruã.
Dem-after   3exA-fell garden large
'Afterwards we (exc.) felled (trees for a) large garden.'

Table 3. Frozen forms on -ruã

Ke'ĩ-ruã here-Neg	'far away'
Ta'y-ruã small-Neg	'large'
Miti-ruã small-Neg	'large'
Pe'ĩ-ruã one-Neg	'many'
Mua'ã-ruã ?[9]-Neg	'many'

(68) Ke'ĩruã paranã-wasu   popy,   e'i.[10]
      far:away river:sea-large   edge   3:say
      'The opposite shore of the sea/river is a long ways away, he said.' (Context:
      He's talking about the opposite shore of the Amazon River, which it took
      several days to cross.)

(69) E-ja'yr   me   keve   aja-ire   pe'ĩruã mamã   kõ o-ji-mo-eko-a.
      1S-child when there   Dem-after   many   mother Pl 3A-Refl-Caus-live-Nom
      'When I was a child many of my mothers made their home there (that is, my
      mother, her sisters, and my father's brothers' wives).'

2.3.3 Rhetorical questions

The affix *-ruã* also occurs in rhetorical questions when the speaker expects
confirmation about his impressions, as illustrated in the left-hand column
of Table 4 on the following page. By contrast, the absence of *-ruã* in rhetorical questions indicates that the speaker suspects that his original impression
was wrong, as illustrated in the right-hand column.

Table 4. Different uses of negation in rhetorical questions

	Observation confirms orig- inal impression	Observation contradicts original impression
Positive expectation	o-manõ-ruã sipõkõ 3A die Neg Rhet-Q He died, didn't he?[11] (I think he did)	o-manõ sipõkõ 3A die Rhet-Q Can it be that he died? (I didn't think so)
Negative expectation	n-o-manõ-i ruã sipõkõ Neg 3A die Neg Rhet-Q He didn't die, did he? (I didn't think so)	n-o-manõ-i sipõkõ Neg 3A die Neg Rhet-Q He didn't die? (I thought he did)

(70) "E-ji-syry,"   a'e ruã sipõkõ ene.
2Imp-Refl-leave 1:say Neg Rhet-Q 2sP
'Did I not say to you, "leave!"' (Meaning: 'I already told you to leave!')

(71) Jane moju   o-'u,   e'i amõ   kõ.
an   snake 3A-eat 3:say someone Pl

Amẽ e'i   taivĩgwer: A'e-te   sipõkõ a-esa, e'i.
so:then 3:say ancestor Dem-Emp Rhet-Q 1A-see   3:say

A-ma'ẽ ø-ee, e'i.   Arara teipo, a'e,   e'i.
1S-look 3-at 3:say Macaw must:be 1S:say 3:say

'"The snake ate the man," others said. So then an ancestor said, "So that (a person) is what I saw?" he said.' (Meaning: 'I didn't think it was a person.')
"I saw it," he said. "It must be a macaw," I said (to myself), he said.

(72) Manyvore põkõ   ne-mome'u, e'i   erekwar i-jupe
why   Rhet-Q 2sA-tell   3:say wife   3-to

A-mome'u põkõ,   e'i i-men   amẽ
1sA-tell   Rhet-Q 3:say 3-husband then

Ne-mome'u ruã sipõkõ, e'i.
2A-tell   Neg Rhet-Q 3:say

"Why did you tell," his wife said to him. (So her husband replied), "Did I tell?" (Meaning: "I didn't know I did."). "You did tell them, didn't you?" she said (Meaning: "You did.").

(73) Awĩ-te   ruã sipõkõ e-mokatu,   e'i. E-tekorã reme, e'i.
Dem-Emp Neg Rhet-Q 1sP-make:well 3:say 1P-sick   when   3:say
"Was it not he that made me well," he said.
"When I was sick," he said. (Meaning: 'I am sure it was he.')

(74) N-a-vaẽ-'ãi   ruã sipõkõ mijã, e'i. A-manõ mijã, e'i.
Neg-1sS-arrive-Neg:fut Neg Rhet-Q Unr   3:say 1sA-die Unr 3:say
'"I wouldn't have arrived, would I?" he said. "I was dead," he said.'

2.4 The negation morpheme *ne*

The morpheme *ne* is used to negate imperative clauses and occurs as the last element of the clause quote margin.

(75) Ne-ji-ko'õ   karamõ ne-iko ne, e'i papa   ije.
2sS-Refl-anger future 2sS-be Neg 3:say father 1P

Aja-wyi   ije   age'e n-a-jiko'õ-i   a-iko.
Dem-because 1P   now   Neg-1sS-be:angry-Neg 1sS-be

'Don't be getting angry (control your anger) in the future, father said (counseled) me. For this reason I don't go around angry.'

In negative imperatives, the normal second person prefixes *ne-* and *pe-* are used rather than the prefixes *(e-* and *pe-)* used in positive imperative sentences (although the second person plural prefixes are identical): *e-ji-ko'õ* 'be angry!' and *pe-ja'o* 'cry!' When the object of a transitive verb is first person the prefix on the verb stem refers to the object rather than to the agent. Since the first person singular prefix, *-e*, is identical to the second person singular imperative prefix used in positive commands, it may appear superficially that the prefix in (76) is the latter.

(76) E-mome'u   papa   retarãgwer pe   ne,   e'i.
      1sP-tell   father   relative   to   Neg   3:say
      'Don't tell about me to father's relative, she said (Don't let him know I was here).'

However, it is clear contextually by comparison with (77), (the sequential sentence of the text) that the prefix on (76) refers to the first person object:

(77) N-ore-mome'u-i   aja-ire.
      Neg-1exP-tell-Neg   Dem-after
      'They didn't tell about us afterwards.'

2.5 The free-form negation morpheme *ani*

The morpheme *ani* 'no!' occurs as a negative free response to a question or as a rebuttal to a perceived false statement.

(78) A-a-ta   ne-rupi, e'i tite.   Ani, aku-vay   e-rata, e'i kwaray.
      1sA-go-Fut 2s-with 3:say in:vain No   hot-very 1-fire   3:say sun
      'I'm going to go with you, he said in vain. No! (you're not). My fire is very hot, said the sun.'

(79) Amẽ   e-muu   t-a-'u,   e'i ajã.
      then Imp-bring Purp-1sA-eat 3:say spirit

      Ani, e'i   taivĩgwer   i-jupe.
      No!   3-say ancestor   3-to

      'So then bring me some (of it) to eat, said the spirit. No, our ancestor said to him.'

2.6 Semi-negative morphemes

2.6.1 The morpheme *sõ*

The morpheme *sõ* is used in a clause to indicate undesirability or disapproval on the part of the speaker.

(80) Manyvo re   põ   e-py'a-mo-pirai   sõ   ne-iko,   e'i.
      why   Rfr   Q   1sP-spirit-Caus-agitate disapproval 2sS-go:about 3:say
      'Why are you going about agitating me (disapproval), he said.'

(81) Ne-posiko   sõ.
      2sS-mess:around disapproval
      'You are messing around (which I disapprove of).'

2.6.2 The morpheme *tite*

The morpheme *tite* is a frustrative, and may indicate that some activity is done 'without success' (82, 83) or 'mistakenly' (82) and (84).

(82) Oro-eka-eka   tite   mutu.
      1exA-search-search   Frs   motor

      Ni-ja-esa-'ãi,   oro-'e   tite.
      Neg-2genA-search-Neg:Fut   1exA-say   Frs

      'We (exc) searched repeatedly in vain for the motor. "Nobody will find it, we (exc) said mistakenly (not knowing we would later find it).'

(83) Jypy remẽ   a-a   tite   ka'a   r-upi   a-iko.
      past when   1A-go   Frs   jungle   Rel-by   1A-go:about

      Mijar n-a-juka-i   ajama'ẽ.
      game Neg-1A-kill-Neg   but

      'In the past I went (hunting) without success in the jungle. But I didn't kill any game.'

(84) Mani'o-ja-'u   ipo,   a-'e   tite   mani'o-e'e   pe,   e'i-jẽ.
      mandioca-1genA-eat   Vfr   1A-say Frs   mandioca-true to   3:say-Vrf
      'This is edible manioc, I said mistakenly about true (poisonous) manioc, he said. (He ate it without processing it and nearly died.)'

Tite also occurs in the idiom, *maevo so tite*, meaning 'giving the false appearance of'.

(85) Pira r-eka   o-jau   maevo:so:tite kupa.
      fish Rel-search   3A-bath FI   Pl
      'It looked like they were bathing but they were really fishing.'

(86) Amẽ a'e o-ẽ   kuise'ẽ. ø-ory   maevo:so:tite ajama'ẽ.
      then DET 3S-sprout   fast   3S-happy   falsely   but

      Kwaray aja-ire   o-juka,   n-apo-i   rewaramõ.
      sun   DET-after 3A-kill   Neg-root-Neg   because

      'So then afterwards it sprouts quickly. It looks healthy (deceivingly), but afterwards the sun kills it because it has no roots.'

2.6.3 The morpheme *panē*

The morpheme *panē* occurs on rare occasions in free form after the verb (usually in hunting narratives) and is a frustrative, indicating that the activity was unfruitful.

(87) Oro-o   panē ka'a   rupi. Naikoi mijar.
      1exA-go Frs forest by   not:be game
      'We (exc) went (hunting) in the jungle without success. There was no game.'

(88) Yy-panē.
      river-Frs
      'The river which is fruitless (to fish in). (Name of a specific river and village.)'

3 Conclusions

Negation in Wayampi is moderately complex. There are four negation morphemes which modify the word, phrase, and/or clause. Which morpheme is used depends upon several choices: mood (imperative vs non-imperative), tense (future vs non-future), clause type (main vs subordinate), and phrase type (verbials vs nominals; see Table 1). The morpheme *ne* negates imperative clauses only. Although the morphemes *-e'ȳ* and *-ruā* both may negate nominals and occur in the same position with respect to the noun in the phrase, they function different semantically: *-e'ȳ* declares that there is an absence of the item being negated, whereas *-ruā* is used to declare that 'A is not B', or 'it is not A'. In addition to nominals, *e'ȳ* also negates nominalized verbs, subordinate purpose clauses, non-initiating serial verbs, and some subordinate temporal clauses, whereas *-ruā* negates adverbials (including post-positional phrases and stative verbs acting as adverbials.)

The split affix *n...i* and its allomorphs negate predicates in main verb clauses and predicated nouns. It also negates subordinate conditional-temporal verbs. A number of inflections occur on the verb within this split affix which may modify the valence or aspect. The suffix *'āi* is a combination negative suffix and tense marker. A change in morphology occurred so as not to confuse *-ta* 'future' in non-negated verbs with *-ta* 'desiderative' in negated verbs. Table 5 on the following page shows the various uses of the negation morphemes on a typical verb and noun. Three morphemes operate on the clause level and indicate frustrated effort *(tite, panē)* or disapproval *(sō)* on the part of the speaker.

There are two suffixes which occur only on negated verbs within the split affix morpheme, the other outside. Although they are not negative morphemes in themselves, they coordinate only with the negative morpheme:

-yty refers to the innate quality of the subject in intransitive clauses, and *-ve* 'yet' refers to an action not yet having taken place.

Most Wayampi negation morphemes are suffixes. This is in accord with Dahl's (1979) observation that morphological negation and, in particular, suffix negation, tends to be significantly more common in free word order languages, of which Wayampi is one.

All five morphemes used in Wayampi negation have cognates in common use throughout the Tupi-Guarani language family (see Appendix). Cognates of the split affix morpheme, *n...i*, which negates main verbs, and *e'ỹ* which negates subordinate verbs, are the most widely used throughout the language family.

**Table 5. Contrasts of the various negation morphemes
in their usage on a typical verb and a typical noun.**

Verb	
O-kua	He knows.
N-o-kua-i	He doesn't know.
I-kua-e'ỹ	Ignorance.
Ji-kua-e'ỹ	The one which we don't know.
Temi-kua-e'ỹ	Something which is not known.
T-o-kua-e'ỹ	For him not to know.
N-o-kua-i-ruã sipõkõ	He doesn't know,does he! (I didn't think so.)
N-o-kua-i sipõkõ	Doesn't he know! (I thought he knew.)
Ne-kua ne	Don't know!
Ene-ruã n-ere-kua-i	It's not you that doesn't know.
Ani, n-o-kua-i	No, he doesn't know.
Noun	
I-men	Her husband.
N-i-men-i-ve	She is not yet married (husbanded).
I-men e'ỹ	She is without a husband (husbandless).
I-men-ruã	He's not her husband.
I-men-ruã sipõkõ	He's her husband, isn't he? (I thought so.)

4 Appendix

Distribution of negation morpheme cognates among Tupi-Guarani language subgroups (according to Rodrigues 1984-85) and possible re-construction of morpheme: Gi(O) = Old Guarani, Gi(M) = Mbya Guarani, Kw = Kaiwa, Gu = Guaraju, Tb = Tupinambá, Gj = Guajajara, As = Assurini, Pn = Parintintin, Kb = Kayabi, Km = Kamajurá, Ur = Urubu-Kaapor, *PTG = Proto-Tupi-Guarani, and W = Wayampi.

*PTG Tupi-Guarani Language Subgroups

	I	II	III	IV	V	VI	VII	VIII
*n..i	Gi(O) n..i	Gu n..i	Tb n..i	Gj n...i	Kb n...i	Pn n..i	Km	W n..i
	na-		na-	As n-..-ihi	na-		n..ite	na-
na-	ni-				ni-			ni-
ni-	n-				n-			n-
*e'ym	Gi(M)	Gu e'ỹ	Tb e'ym	Gj 'ym	Kb e'ém	Pn e'ym	Km e'ym	W e'ỹ
	Kw e'ỹ			As y'ym				Ur 'ym
*ruã	Gi(O)		Tb ruã			Pn ruĩ	Km roĩn	W ruã
ruĩ	ruwãi						roen	
*eme	Gi(O/M) eme	Gu rẽnẽ	Tb ume	As eme			Km em	W ne
*ani	Gi(O) ani	Gu ĩnĩ	Tb ani	As ahãn		Pn ahãn	Km anite	W ani

Abbreviations

A	subject of transitive verb	Mns	means
Aug	augmentative	Neg	negative
Caus	causative	Nom	nominalizer
CC	commitative causative	P	object of transitive verb
Col	collective	Pl	plural
Cmp	completive	Perm	permissive
Cntr-Exp	counter expectation	Purp	purpose
Dem	demonstrative	Q	question
Dim	diminutive	Refl	reflexive
Emp	emphatic	Rel	relator
ex	exclusive	Rfr	referent
FI	false impression	Rhet-Q	rhetorical question
Frs	frustrative	S	subject of intransitive or
Fut	future		stative verb
gen	generic	s	singular
Hab	habitual	Unr	unrealized
Imp	imperative	Vfr	verification particle
in	inclusive	1, 2, 3	first, second, third person

Notes

1. This work is made possible through a contract between the Summer Institute of Linguistics and FUNAI (National Indian Foundation of Brazil). I am indebted to several Wayampi for their language help: Mo'yrupir and Mikutu provided a wealth of texts and Mikutu and Matapi provided regular informant help over several years. I am also indebted to my wife, Cheryl, for her insights and criticism throughout this manuscript.

2. Wayampi is a member of the Tupi-Guarani language family. This study is based on speakers of the Amapari dialect of Wayampi. Members of this dialect live in the state of Amapa, Brazil, along tributaries of the Amapari River. There are about 320 speakers. In addition to the Amapari dialect, there are about 300 speakers of the Oiapoque dialect. These people live along the north side of the Oiapoque River which divides Brazil and French Guiana. Four other speakers of that dialect live in northern Para state.

3. Wayampi has the following phonemes; vowels: front *i, ĩ, e, ẽ*; central *y /ɨ/, ỹ/ɨ̃/, a, ã*; back *u, o, õ*; consonants: stops *p, t, k, ' /ʔ/*; fricatives *v /β/, s*; nasals *m, n, g /ŋ/*; liquids *r /r/*; semivowels *j /y/* and *w*.

4. In the Amapari dialect of Wayampi, the original prefix **ere-* was substituted by *ne-* when occurring initially in the word. *Ere-* is maintained when preceded by another prefix.

5. All inflectable stems are subdivided in Tupi-Guarani languages according to their behavior in relation to 2 basic morphemes. Class I stems combine with **i-* (third person) and a **ø-* (linking morpheme), and Class II stems combine with **c-* (third person) and with **r-* (linking morpheme).

6. When an obligatorily possessed noun is incorporated in a verb, the verb continues to be transitive. It can therefore receive the reflexive prefix.

7. Diachronic phonological changes have resulted in various homologous suffixes; *ve-* 'yet', *ve-* 'almost', and *ve-* 'also'. The suffix *ve-* 'yet', occurs only with negatives.

8. *Gasi* is from *kasi* 'to be strong'. The nasalization of the initial consonant indicates the generic or unmarked form of the word.

9. This apparent adjective stem seems to occur only in this frozen form. Unlike the other adjectives having frozen forms it occurs only in combination with *-ruã*.

10. The frozen forms may all be emphasized by stretching out the last vowel of the nuclear adjective or adverb.

11. The translation such as 'didn't he?' is meant to create a clearer understanding of the spirit of the question. However it does not require a response by the hearer.

References

Barbosa, Pe A. Lemos (1970). *Pequeno vocabulário Português-Tupi*. Livraria São José. Rio de Janeiro, Brazil.

Bender-Samuel, David (1972). *Hierarchical structures in Guajajara*. Norman, Oklahoma: Summer Institute of Linguistics.

Betts, Lavera (1981). *Dicionário Parintintín-Português*. Summer Institute of Linguistics, Brasilia, Brazil.

Dahl, Östen (1979). 'Typology of sentence negation.' *Linguistics* 17:79-106.

Dietrich, Wolf (1990). 'Chiriguano e Guarayo word formation.' In: Doris L. Payne (ed.), *Amazonian Linguistics*, 293-320. University of Texas Press, Austin.

Dooley, Robert A. (1982). *Vocabulário do Guarani*. Summer Institute of Linguistics, Brasilia, Brazil.

Dobson, Rose (1988). 'Aspectos da língua Kayabí.' *Série Lingüística* 12. Summer Institute of Linguistics, Brasilia, Brazil.

Grenand, Francoise (1975). *La langue wayãpi: phonologie et grammaire*. Paris: École des Hautes Études en Sciences Sociales.

Jensen, Allen A. (1979). 'Análise preliminar do grupo de acentuaçâo e do grupo rítmico em Oiampí.' Ms, Universidade Estadual de Campinas, SP, Brazil.

—— (1982). 'Análise formal do discurso de dois textos didáticos na língua Wayampí (Oiampí).' Ms, Summer Institute of Linguistics, Brasilia, Brazil.

Jensen, Cheryl (1980). 'Word order in Wayampi'. Ms, Summer Institute of Linguistics, Brasilia, Brazil.

—— (1987). 'Object-prefix incorporation in proto Tupi-Guarani verbs.' *Language Sciences*, 9, 1, 45-55.

—— (1989). *O desenvolvimento histórico da língua Wayampi*. Editora da UNICAMP, Campinas, SP, Brazil.

—— (1990). 'Cross-referencing changes in some Tupí-Guaraní languages.' In: Doris L. Payne (ed.), *Amazonian Linguistics*, 117-160. University of Texas press, Austin.

Kakumasu, James (1986). 'Urubu-Kaapor.' *Handbook of Amazonian languages*, Vol.1:326-403. Mouton de Gruyter, NY.

Newton, Dennis (1978). 'Guarayu Discourse.' *Work papers of the Summer Institute of Linguistics*. Ed. by Ursula Wiesemann et al., 252-268. Riberalta, Bolivia.

Nicholson, Velda (1978). *Aspectos da língua Assurini*. Summer Institute of Linguistics, Brasilia, DF, Brazil.

Rodrigues, Aryon Dall'Igna (1953). 'Morfologia do verbo Tupi.' *Letras* 1:121-152. Universidade de Parana, Curitiba, Brazil.

—— (1984/1985). 'Relações internas na família linguística Tupí-Guaraní.' *Revista e Antropologia* 27/28, 33-53.

Ruiz de Montoya, Antonio (1892). *Arte de la lengua Guaraní* [with commentaries by Paulo Restivo (ed)], Stuttgart: Guiglielmo Kohlhammer.

Seki, Lucy (1976). 'Negação em Kamaiurá.' Ms, Universidade Estadual de Campinas, Campinas, Brazil.

Weiss, Helga (1972). 'Kayabi Verbs.' Ms, Summer Institute of Linguistics, Brasilia, DF, Brazil.

Maya-Mam

Wesley M. Collins

1 Introduction

Mam is a Mayan language spoken in Western Guatemala and parts of Chiapas, Mexico by perhaps 600,000 people. There are three major dialect divisions: Northern, Southern and Western (Godfrey and Collins: 1987). Western Mam, though quite conservative linguistically and distinct from the other two dialects, is rapidly falling into disuse. Data for this article were gathered in Comitancillo, a major town in the Central Mam area, closely related to other Southern dialects.

Mam uses a basic VSO word order. Both object and subject are marked grammatically before the main verb, but occur lexically after the verb:

(1) N-chi   ok   t-tzyu'n   tata tx'yan.
     Prog-3Pl.A Dir.enter 3Sg.E-grab man dog
     'The man is grabbing the dogs.'

Nevertheless, either the subject or object can be fronted lexically for emphasis (see section 2.6 on antipassives below). Word order in the noun phrase is demonstrative, numeral, adjective(s) noun:

(2) Aye   kab'a matij-xix   b'etin   xjal.
     Those two   big-Emph   walking people
     'Those two very large foreigners.'

Mam questions are formed in one of three ways: with question words, by using question suffixation, or by making a declaration with rising final intonation. Question words always occur first in the question phrase.

(3) Ankye-qe-taq jni' xnaq'tzil?
     who-Pl-Prp   all   teachers
     'Who were all the teachers?'

(4) Ja'   ma' txa'y?
     where Rec 2Sg.go
     'Where did you go (just now)?'

(5) Ti-tzin   t-echil   ø-kub   t-yek'in?
     what-Int 3Sg.Poss-sign Rem-Dir.down 3Sg-demonstrate
     'What sign did he demonstrate?'

Question words occur even before negatives, which would otherwise occur first in the sentence:

(6) Mi'   ø-kub   t-yek'in   jun t-echil.
     Neg   Rem-Dir.down   3Sg-show   one 3Sg.Poss-sign
     'He did not demonstrate a sign.'

(7) Tiqu'n mi'   ø-kub   t-yek'in   jun t-echil?
     why   Neg   Rem-Dir.down   3Sg-show   one 3Sg.Poss-sign
     'Why didn't he demonstrate a sign?'

Mam does not have simple prepositions to describe grammatical relations between sentence elements. Rather, these are expressed through a set of possessed relational nouns:

    twi'   'its head' or 'on top of'
    ttxlaj   'its side' or 'beside'
    ttxa'n   'its nose' or 'at the edge of'
    ttzi   'its mouth' or 'at the entrance to'

These occur before the elements they relate to:

    twi' ja   'on the house'
    ttxa'n tnam 'at the edge of town'

Mam is an ergative language. Objects (patients) of transitive verbs are inflected with the same set of person markers as the subjects (agents) of intransitive verbs (table 1 on the next page gives an overview of the markers):

(8) N-chi   rinin.
     Prog-3Pl.A run
     'They are running.'

(9) N-chi   tzaj   t-limo'n   Pegr.
     Prog-3Pl.A Dir.come 3Sg.E-push Peter
     'Peter is pushing them. '

Notice that in (8) *chi* is the subject or actor ('they'), whereas in (9) *chi* is the patient ('them'). This set of person markers is called the absolutive set. The complete paradigm is given in table 1 (to distinguish similar forms, see the note following (15)).

Absolutives mark the subject of intransitive sentences as well as the object of transitive sentences. In dependent clauses, absolutive person marking is rescinded – even in intransitive sentences. All person markers (for all agents, patients and actors) conflate to the ergative set and are kept separate by grammatical constraints on word order. Compare the dependent clause in (10) with (8) and the dependent clause in (11) with (9).

Table 1. Absolutive person markers.

chin	1Sg	*qoy*	1Pl exclusive
		qo	1Pl inclusive
ø	2Sg	*chi*	2Pl
ø	3Sg	*chi*	3Pl

(10) T-aj   tata tu'n ky-rinin.
      3Sg.E-want man   that 3Pl.A.Dep-run
      'The man wants them to run.'

(11) N-yolin-taq   tata, tej   ky-tzaj   t-limo'n   Pegr.
      Prog-talk-Prp man   when 3Pl.A.Dep-Dir.come   3Sg.E-push   Peter
      'The man was talking when Peter pushed them.'

Table 2. Ergative person markers.

w/n-...-y/a	1Sg	*q-...-y/a*	1Pl exclusive
		q-...	1Pl inclusive
t-...-y/a	2Sg	*ky-...-y/a*	2Pl
t-...	3Sg	*ky-...*	3Pl

The suffix alternation between *w* and *n* and *y* and *a* above depends on the root marked '...' above; W precedes vowels; *n* precedes consonants, while y follows vowels and *a* follows consonants.

Ergative markers indicate the subject of transitive verbs and also dependent absolutive marking as in (10) and (11) above.

Mam also boasts an extremely complex aspectual system. Based on six 'simple aspects', these are further inflected to produce at least twenty different complex aspects, most of which are in past time. The simple aspects are:

Progressive:
(12) Tzun   n-chin   yolin.
      Prog   Prog-1Sg.A   talk
      'I am talking.'

Recent completive:
(13) Ma'   chin   yolin   qlixje.
      Rec   1Sg.A   talk   morning
      'I talked this morning.'

Recent completive demoted:

(14) Xh-in   yolin   qlixje.
      Rec.Dem-1Sg.A   talk   morning
      'I talked this morning (demoted verb).'

In Northern Mam, the *x* aspect is used only in Recent Completive dependent clauses (England 1983:58). In the Central dialect, used as a basis for data in this paper, the x aspect includes Recent Completive dependency, but is expanded to independent clauses as well, where the verb is thereby demoted in focus. In the present example, the *x* plus the *ch* of *chin* 'first person singular absolutive' conflate to form *xh* (fronted *x*). Unmarked Mam sentences focus on the action of the verb, as in (13) above. The use of the *x* aspect (Recent Completive Demoted) takes emphasis off of the verb and makes it semantically, if not grammatically, dependent.

Remote completive:

(15) ø-In   yolin   ewa.
      Rem-1Sg.A   talk   yesterday
      'I talked yesterday.'

Actually, remote completive aspect is unmarked. Zero-marked aspect plus the *ch* of *chin* conflate to form in. The complete paradigm is:

```
ø + chin  = in yolín   'I spoke'
ø + ø     = ø yolín    'you spoke'
ø + ø     = ø yólin    'he/she/it spoke'
ø + qo    = o yolín    'we exclusive spoke
ø + qo    = o yólin    'we inclusive spoke'
ø + chi   = i yolín    'you all spoke'
ø + chi   = i yólin    'they spoke'
```

Compare this paradigm with that for absolutive person marking in table 1. Note here that the syllable stress shifts, which otherwise keeps separate identical forms: 2Sg from 3Sg, 1Pl exclusive from 1Pl inclusive; and 2Pl from 3Pl. Interestingly, in other Mam dialects, these forms are differentiated by a final vowel suffix that appends to the main verb. For example: *yolina* 'you spoke', *yolin* 'he spoke', always with penultimate stress. Comitancillo has lost the final vowel, yet the stressed syllable usually remains as a residue of the earlier form. In this paper, only significant ultimate stress is marked.

Perfective:

(16) O   chin   yolin.
      Perf 1Sg.A   talk
      'I have talked.'

Potential:

(17)   Ok   chin   yoli-la   nchi'j.
        Pot   1Sg.A   talk-Fut   tomorrow
        'I will talk tomorrow.'

2 Negation

Mam sentences are negated by using negative particles which occur first in the sentence and are directly followed by the element(s) being negated. This by definition emphasizes negative particles, since they occur in the preverbal focus slot. There are many negative particles used in Mam, which will be discussed in the following sections.

2.1 Existentials

Existence is specified in Mam by the use of *at*, 'singular existence' and *ite'* 'plural existence'. The singular is negated by *nti'* and the plural by *nti'qe'*.

(18)   At   jun   ichin.
        Sg.exist   one   man
        'There exists a man.'

(19)   Nti'   jun   ichin.
        Neg.exist   one   man
        'There does not exist a man.'

(20)   Ite'   junjun   tx'yan.
        Pl.exist   several   dog
        'There exist several dogs.'

(21)   Nti'-qe'   junjun   tx'yan.
        Neg.exist-Pl   several   dog
        'There do not exist several dogs.'

(22)   At   jun   u'j   twi'   watb'il.
        Sg.exist   one   book   on   bed
        'There is a book on the bed.'

(23)   Nti'   jun   u'j   twi'   watb'il.
        Neg.exist   one   book   on   bed
        'There is not a book on the bed.'

(24)   Ite'   kyaja   xjal   tuja.
        Pl.exist   four   people   in.house
        'There are four people in the house.'

(25) Nti'-qe'   kyaja   xjal   tuja.
      Neg.exist-Pl four   people   in.house
      'There are not four people in the house.'

2.2 Locatives

Location is negated by the particle *nya'*. Looking at (22) and (24) above, the location is negated as follows:

(26) Nya' twi' watb'il (ate)(ta'ye)   u'j.
      Neg   on   bed   Loc.Sg.exist   book
      'Not on the bed is the book.'

In (26), either *ate* or *ta'ye* may be used. The choice is speaker specific.

(27) Nya' tuja   ite'ya   kab'a   xjal.
      Neg   in.house Loc.Pl.exist two   people
      'Not in the house are the two people.'

In (22) and (24), the existence of the book and the people is in focus, whereas in (26) and (27), their existence is assumed; the location is in focus. Notice that the existence words are different. *At* and *ite'* denote simple existence, whereas *ate* and *ta'* (singular) and *ite'ya* (plural) denote existence in a specific location.

2.3 Statives

Mam statives are non-verbal.

(28) Ichin qi'n.
      man   I
      'I am a man.'

(29) Nim-xix   ky-alil   ab'j.
      much-Emph 3Pl.Poss-heavy   rock
      'The rocks are very heavy.'

(30) Aj   Txolja te   q'a.
      from Txolja Sg.the boy
      'The boy is from Txolja.'

All statives, like locatives, are negated with the particle *nya'*:

(31) Nya' ichin qi'n.
      Neg   man   I
      'I am not a man.'

(32) Nya' nim-xix ky-alil ab'j.
Neg much-Emph 3Pl.Poss-heavy rock
'The rocks are not very heavy.'

(33) Nya' aj Txolja te q'a.
Neg from Txolja Sg.the boy
'The boy is not from Txolja.'

2.4 Verbal predicates

Mam does not have one single way to say 'yes' to a question, since the answer is aspect specific. Negation of sentences is also aspect specific, although not nearly as complex as saying 'yes'. Below we discuss negation of simple (2.4.1) and complex aspects (2.4.2).

2.4.1 Simple aspects
Among the simple aspects are those negated by *mi'* or *mina*.

Progressive

(34) Tzun-tzin n-chin yoli'n? Tzun.
Prog-Int Prog-1Sg.A talk yes
'Am I talking?'

(35) Mi'/Mina n-chin yoli'n.
Neg Prog-1Sg.A talk
'I am not talking.'

In (35) (also 39 and 41), *mi'* or *mina* can be used interchangeably. For the two progressive aspects: present, as in (35), and past, some speakers (though not all) freely alternate *nya'* and *mi'*:

(36) Nya' n-chin yoli'n.
Neg Prog-1S.A talk
'I am not talking.'

(37) Nya' n-yolin-taq tata.
Neg Prog-talk-Prp man
'The man was not talking.'

Recent completive

(38) Ma'-n chin yoli'n qlixje? Ma'y.
Rec-Int 1Sg.A talk morning yes
'Did I talk this morning?'

(39) Mi'/Mina xh-in yoli'n qlixje.
Neg Rec.Dem-1Sg.A talk morning
'I did not talk this morning.'

Notice here in (39) that the negated sentence calls for demoted verb aspect.
See note with (14).

Potential

(40) O-n   k-chin   yoli-la   nchi'j?   Ok.
      Pot-Int   Pot-1Sg.A   talk-Fut   tomorrow   yes
      'Will I talk tomorrow?'

(41) Mi'/Mina chin   yoli'n   nchi'j.
      Neg   1Sg.A   talk   tomorrow
      'I will not talk tomorrow.'

Potential aspect or future tense are not marked in the negative. They are
understood by their contrast with all other aspects, which are marked in
negative constructions.

Remote completive negated by *mix*:

(42) Ø-In   yolin-tzi'n ewa?   In yoli'n.
      Rem-1Sg.A   talk-Int   yesterday   I talked
      'Did I talk yesterday?'

(43) Mix   ø-in   yolin-i'y   ewa.
      Neg   Rem-1Sg.A   talk-Rem   yesterday
      'I did not talk yesterday.'

Perfective negated by *na'm*

(44) O-n   chin   yoli'n?   Oja.
      Perf-Int   1Sg.A   talk   yes
      'Have I talked?'

(45) Na'm   n-yoli'n.
      Neg   1Sg.A.Dep-talk
      'I have not talked.'

In these examples of the simple aspects, *mina* (or *mi'*) negates four of them:
Progressive, Recent Completive, Recent Completive Demoted, and Potential.
Mi' can substitute freely for *mina* in negating any of these four aspects.
Recent Completive Demoted aspect cannot be used in an interrogative
sentence. However, when Recent Completive aspect is negated, it takes
Recent Completive Demoted aspect. *Mix* negates Remote Completive aspect.
Na'm negates Perfective, which takes dependent person marking. *Mina* is also
the simple one word negation. *Mi'* cannot be used in this way.

(46) At-tzin   jun t-tx'yan?   Mina.
     Sg.exist-Int one 3Sg.Poss-dog no
     'Does he have a dog?'

Mina can also serve as the one word answer for any question based on the six simple aspects, except for perfect past. For example, a good answer to the question posed in (42) would be:

(47) Mina.   Mix ø-in   yolin-i'y   ewa.
     Neg   Neg Rem-1Sg.A talk-Rem   yesterday
     'No, I did not talk this morning.'

2.4.2 Complex aspects

In order to show some of the derivational possibilities related to the simple aspects discussed above and in the introduction, let us look at just one aspect, Perfective.

(48) O   chin   uk'tzi'n t-i'j   n-ja'-y.
     Perf 1Sg.A paint   3Sg-against 1Sg.Poss-house-1Sg.Poss
     'I have painted my house.'

Here the *o* marks Perfective aspect, or: 'At some point in the past, I painted my house, the results of which are still relevant as of this moment.' The *o* aspect can be further refined with the following suffixes: *taq* 'preceding past', *tla* 'frustrated volition' and *la* 'dubitative' to form the following complex aspects. Also listed are their negations:

Pluperfect

Pluperfect aspect (marked by *otaq*) is composed of the simple aspect Perfective plus the suffix 'preceding past.'

(49) O-taq chin   yolin t-u'k-iy,   tej
     Pl   1Sg.A talk   2Sg-with-2Sg   when

     t-ul   kanin' n-xu'jil-a.
     3Sg.E-Dir.come   arrive 1Sg.Poss-wife.1Sg.Poss

     'I had already spoken to you when my wife arrived'.

(50) Na'm-taq n-yolin   t-uk'-iy,   tej
     Neg-Prp   1Sg.A.Dep-talk 2Sg-with-2Sg   when

     't-ul   kanin n-xu'jil-a.
     3Sg.E.-Dir.come   arrive 1Sg.Poss-wife.1Sg.Poss

     'I had not (yet) spoken to you when my wife arrived.'

Note that in (50) the verb *yolin* takes dependent person marking (as in (45) above). See also (77) and the note preceding (10) and (11). Similarly, the following three aspects are complex:

Perfective of frustrated volition

(51)   O-tla   chin   kanin,   noqit   b'a'n.
        Perf-Fv   1Sg.A   arrive   IR   good
        'I would have arrived, if it would have been good.'

(52)   Mi'xa-tla   ø-in   kanin,   noqit   nya' b'a'n.
        Neg-Fv   Rem-1Sg.A arrive   IR   Neg good
        'I would not have arrived, had it not been good.'

Dubitative perfective

(53)   O-taq-la   b'aj   oxa   xjaw.
        Pl-Dub   finish   three   months
        'Perhaps three months would already have passed.'

(54)   Na'm-taq-la   t-b'aj   oxa   xjaw.
        Neg-Prp-Dub   3Sg.A.Dep-finish   three   months
        'Perhaps three months would not have already passed.'

Pluperfect of frustrated volition

(55)   O-taq-tla   chin   meltz'aja,   aj   t-ul.
        Pl-Fv   1Sg.A   return   when   3Sg.A.Dep-come
        'I would have already returned when he came.'

(56)   Na'm-taq-tla   n-meltz'aja,   aj   t-ul.
        Neg-Prp-Fv   1Sg.A.Dep-return   when   3Sg.A.Dep-come
        'I would not have already returned when he came.'

2.5 Negating imperatives

There are two basic ways to form Mam imperatives for either transitive or intransitive verbs, both using directionals. Mam directionals are a set of twelve auxiliary verbs derived from intransitives; they are used to further specify the action of a verb by attaching a direction to it, as in the following examples:

(57)   Ø-ø-Kub'   t-b'isin   Juan.
        Rem-3Sg.A-Dir.down   3Sg.E-think   John
        'John thought.'

(58)   N-chi   jaw   t-iqin   Pegr   t-iqitz
        Prog-3Pl.A   Dir.up   3Sg.E-carry   Peter   3Sg.Poss-load
        'Peter is carrying his loads.'

In (57) *kub'* 'down' helps further specify the action of 'think;' in (58), *jaw* 'up' further specifies the action of 'carry.' The directional in (58) emphasizes that the load had to be lifted in order to be carried. In (57), the directional adds the concept of bowing one's head while thinking. Directionals are rarely used with intransitives (except in imperative constructions), and rarely not used with transitives.

(59) and (60) show an imperative construction with an intransitive verb, and (61) and (62), with a transitive verb. In (59) and (61) the directional precedes the verb. In (60) and (62) it follows the verb.

(59) Ku-x chi b'itzín!
Dir.down-away 2Pl.A sing
'You (all) sing!'

(60) Chi b'itzin-ku-y!
2Pl.A sing-Dir.down-2Pl
'You (all) sing!'

(61) Ku-x chi kub' t-b'inchín!
Dir.down-away 3Pl.A Dir.down 12Sg.E-make
'You make them!'

(62) T-b'inchin-ku-y!
2Sg.E-make-Dir.down.2Sg
'You make it.'

Despite the two ways of forming an imperative construction, there is only one way to negate them:

(63) Mi' ø-b'itzín.
Neg 2Sg.A-sing
'Don't you sing!'

(64) Mi' chi rinín.
Neg 2Pl.A run
'Don't you (all) run.'

(65) Mi' chi kub' t-b'inchín.
Neg 3Pl.A Dir.down 2Sg.E-make
'Don't you make them!'

(66) Mi' chin xi t-limo'n.
Neg 1Sg.A Dir.away 2Sg.E-push
'Don't you push me!'

Unlike (35), (39) and (41), mina cannot be used interchangeably with *mi'* in negating imperatives.

2.6 Antipassives

For purposes of focus, Mam speakers can front either the agent or patient. The antipassive construction is used for this purpose, which basically entails the use of a transitive verb in an intransitive construction. (67) shows a nonfocused transitive, (68) focuses the agent, while (69) focuses the patient. (67) and (68) show an intransitive construction with an intransitive verb

(67) N-chi   el   t-xilin   k'wal   lob'j.
      Prog-3Pl.A   Dir.out   3Sg.E-pick   child   fruit
      'The child is picking the fruits (unfocused).'

(68) A   k'wal   n-ø-xilin   lob'j.
      That child   Prog-3Sg.A-pick fruit
      'It is the child that is picking fruits.'

(69) Ky-i'j   lob'j, n-ø-xilin   k'wal.
      3Pl-against fruit Prog-3Sg.A-pick   child
      'It is the fruits that the child is picking.'

In the antipassive, in order to front either the agent (68) or the patient (69), ergative person marking on the verb is replaced by absolutive marking. This fronting can also be negated. Antipassive agents and patients are negated with *nya'*, as with statives above:

(70) Nya' k'wal   n-ø-xilin   ky-i'j   lob'j.
      Neg   child   Prog.3Sg.A pick   Pl-against fruit
      'It is not the child that is picking fruits.'

(71) Nya' ky-i'j   lob'j, n-ø-xilin   k'wal.
      Neg   3Pl-against   fruit Prog.3Sg.A child
      'It is not the fruits that the child is picking.'

The antipasive operates in all aspects and its verbs are negated in the same way as their non-antipassive counterparts:

(72) A   k'wal   ø-ø-xilin   ky-i'j   lob'j.
      that child   Rem-3Sg.A-pick   Pl-against   fruit
      'The child picked the fruits.'

(73) A   k'wal   mi'   ø-ø-xilin   ky-i'j   lob'j.
      that child   Neg Rem-3Sg.A-pick   Pl-against   fruit
      'The child did not pick the fruits.'

(74) Nya' k'wal,   ø-ø-xilin   ky-i'j   lob'j.
      Neg   child   Rem-3Sg.A-pick   Pl-against   fruit
      'It was not the child that picked the fruits.'

(75) Nya' ky-i'j   lob'j,   ø-ø-xilin   k'wal.
     Neg 3Pl-against fruit   Rem-3Sg.A-pick child
     'It was not fruits that the child picked.'

(76) Aye   k'wal otaq chi   xilin ky-i'j   lob'j.
     those child   Pl   3Pl.A pick Pl-against fruit
     'Those children had picked the fruits.'

(77) Aye   k'wal   na'm-taq   ky-xilin   ky-i'j   lob'j.
     those children Neg-Prp 3Pl.A.Dep-pick Pl-against fruit
     'Those children did not (yet) pick the fruits.'

(70-77) are antipassive constructions. (72) is in the Remote Completive – or unmarked – aspect. Compare with (68) above. (73) negates the verb of (72); (74) negates the subject; (75) negates the object. (76) and (77) are in Pluperfect aspect. (77) is negated with *na'm*, just as in (45) and (50) above. Note that the verb takes dependent person marking when negated.

3 Rhetorical questions

Rhetorical questions and declarations are used in Mam for emphasis. Commonly, they are constructed with the particle *ma* and imply the opposite of that which is expressed.

(78) Ichin-qo   qe.
     man-1Pl.IN Pl
     'We are men.'

(79) Ma   qya-qo-tzin   qe-tz?
     Rhet woman-1Pl.IN-Int Pl-well
     'Well, are we women? (Of course not!)'

(80) Ma   nya' ichin-qo   qe-tz.
     Rhet Neg man-1Pl.IN   Pl-well
     'So, we're not really men then. (Of course we are!)'

(79) is a rhetorical question, while 80 is a rhetorical statement. Note the interrogative suffix in 79 which is missing from 80.

(81) ø-In   rini'n   ewa.
     Rem-1S.A run   yesterday
     'I ran yesterday.'

(82) Ma   ø-in   rinin-tzin-tza ewa?
     Rhet Rem-1S.A   run-Int-well   yesterday
     'Could it possibly be that I ran yesterday?' (I in fact didn't!)

(83)   Ma   mix   ø-in   rinin-tzin-tza ewa?
         Rhet   Neg   Rem-1S.A   run-Int-well   yesterday
         'Could it possibly be that I did not run yesterday?' (I obviously did.)

Note that rhetorical sentences employ the same negative particles as their non-rhetorical counterparts.

4 Other particles

Mam has several other negative particles. These also occur first in the sentence, assuring that negation, when employed, is always in focus.

Nlay 'unable'
(84)   Nlay   b'ant   tata   tu'n   t-xi'   nchi'j.
         Neg   be.able man   that   3Sg.A.Dep-go   tomorrow
         'The man cannot go tomorrow.'

(85)   Nlay   chi   u'jin   qu'n nti'   tzaj.
         Neg   3Pl.A   read   since Neg   light
         'They can't read since there's no light.'

Mib'in 'impossible'
(86)   Ite'   nim   xjal   mib'in   u'j   ky-u'n
         Pl.exist many   people   Neg   read   3Pl-by
         'There are many people who cannot read.'

Nlay differs from *mib'in* in that *mib'in* is clear impossibility. In (86), the people can't read because they never learned how, whereas in (85), they might know how to read, but can't because there's no light.

4.1 *Mix* 'non-specific negative'

Although not used in isolation, *mix* is used with several words to render the following meanings:

Mix a'l 'no one', 'not anyone'
(87)   Mix   a'l   jun   yab'? (with rising intonation)
         Neg   anyone   one   sick
         'No one is sick? (Is anyone sick?)'

Mix ti' 'nothing'
(88)   Ti'-n   tzaj   t-q'o'n   te'y? Mix   ti'!
         thing-Int   Dir.come   3Sg.E-give   you Neg   thing
         'What did he give you? (What was given to you?) Nothing!'

Mix jtojx 'never ever'

(89) Mix   jtoj-x   tu'n n-b'inchin   ikyjo.
      Neg   when-Emph   that 1Sg.A.Dep-do like.that
      'I would never ever do that.'

4.2 M-, a negative affix

Very occasionally, the prefix *m-* is used for negation.

(90) Ikytzi'n.   M-ikytzi'n.
      That's right! Neg-that's right!
      'That's not right'

A probable reason for its rare usage is the ambiguity between similar forms. *Mikytzi'n* also represents the contracted form of me *ikytzi'n*, 'but that's right.' Other occurrences of this prefix are equally ambiguous.

4.3 A negative verb

Mam has one verb, *ky'e* 'to not want', which is always negative, and defective as to aspect. It is unmarked for aspect and occurs only in the progressive aspects (present and past). In addition, the verb is inflected as a transitive (using ergative agent person markers), yet it never occurs with a directional, which is very rare for transitives; neither can it be recast into an antipassive construction. These same constraints hold true for *aj* 'want,' the opposite of *ky'e*.

(91) T-aj   Lexh   tu'n t-xi'   toj tnam nchi'j.
      3Sg.E-want   Andrew that 3Sg.A.Dep-go to   town tomorrow
      'Andrew wants to go to town tomorrow.'

(92) T-ky'e   Lexh   tu'n t-xi'   toj tnam nchi'j.
      3Sg.E-not want Andrew that 3Sg.A.Dep-go to   town tomorrow
      Andrew does not want to go to town tomorrow.

(93) Ky-aj-taq   qya   tu'n ky-xi'   ewa.
      3Pl.E-want-Prp woman that 3Pl.A.Dep-go yesterday
      'The women wanted to go yesterday.'

(94) Ky-ky'e-taq   qya   tu'n ky-xi'   ewa.
      3Pl.E-not.want-Prp women that 3Pl.A.Dep-go yesterday
      'The women did not want to go yesterday.'

5 Conclusion

In summary, Mam uses various strategies for negation. Several negative particles are used in nonverbal predicates dependent upon whether the element to be negated is an existential, a locative or a stative. In verbal predications, negation is aspect specific. Additional negative particles are used for emphasis (as in 84-89). Mam also employs very occasionally the use of a negative prefix *m-*. These particles and the negative prefix all begin with a nasal consonant. Finally, Mam employs a negative verb 'not to want', which, together with its positive counterpart, is an unusual and defective transitive verb. Table 3 summarizes the use of all negative morphemes discussed in this article.

Table 3. Summary of negative morphemes.

Particle	Negates
nya'	Locatives and Statives and related Rhetoricals; Progressive aspects (for some speakers), Antipassive agents and patients
nti'	Existentials and related Rhetoricals
mi'	Imperatives
mi'/mina	Aspects: Progressive, Recent Completive, Recent Completive Demoted, Potential and related Antipassives and Rhetoricals
mina	All sentences (used as one-word answer), including all aspects except Perfective, and those complex aspects built upon the Perfective
mix	Aspects: Remote Completive, Perfective of Frustrated Volition and related Antipassives and Rhetoricals
na'm	Aspects: Perfective, Pluperfect, and those complex aspects built upon the Pluperfect and related Antipassives and Rhetoricals

Table 4. Lexical negative elements

Morpheme	Meaning
nlay	unable
mib'in	impossible
mix	non-specific negative
m-	not
ky'e	to not want

Abbreviations

A	absolutive	Neg	negative
Dem	demoted	Perf	perfective
Dep	dependent	Pl	plural
Dir	directional	Pl	pluperfect
Dub	dubitative	Poss	possessive
E	ergative	Pot	potential
Emph	emphatic	Prog	progressive
Fut	future	Prp	preceding past
Fv	frustrated volition	Rec	recent completive (today)
IN	inclusive	Rem	remote completive (before
Int	interrogative		today)
IR	irrealis	Rhet	rhetorical marker
Loc	locational	Sg	singular

References

England, Nora C. (1983). *A grammar of Mam, a Mayan language.* Austin: University of Texas Press.

Godfrey, Thomas James and Collins, Wesley M. (1987). *Una encuesta dialectal en el área Mam de Guatemala. (A dialect survey of the Mam area of Guatemala.)* Guatemala City: Summer Institute of Linguistics.

Genetic affiliations

Evenki	Altaic
Turkish	Altaic
Waorani	Andean
Tuyuca	Macro-Tucanoan
Wayampi	Equatorial
Nadëb	Macro-Tucanoan
Mam	Penutian
Lewo	Austronesian
Zazaki	Indo-Iranian
Sentani	Indo-Pacific
Bafut	Niger-Kordofanian
Babole	Niger-Kordofanian
Kresh	Nilo-Saharan
Berbice	Creoles
Mandarin	Sino-Tibetan
Hungarian	Uralic-Yukaghir

Language	Region/Country	No. of speakers
Tuyuca	Columbia	200-300
Kresh	Sudan	?
Bafut	Cameroon	35,000
Mam	Guatemala	600,000
Zazaki	Anatolia	1-3m
Hungarian	Hungary	14m
Lewo	Epi (Oceania)	1,000
Sentani	New Guinea	25,000
Wayampi	N. Brazil	?
Berbice	Berbice	<10
Babole	Congo	?
Evenki	Siberia	29,000
Waodani	Ecuador	1,000
Turkish	Turkey	60m
Nadëb	Amazonas (Brazil)	400
Mandarin	China, Singapore, Taiwan	750m

Janet Barnes
Instituto Lingüístico de Verano
Apartado Aéreo 100602
Bogotá, Colombia

René van den Berg
Kotak Pos 2
Raha 93601, Indonesia

Richard Brown
Box 1724
Limassol, Cyprus

Beban S. Chumbow
University of Buea
P.O. Box 63
Buea
Cameroon

Wes Collins
Central America Branch
Apartado Postal 1949
01901 Guatemala

Marie Crandall
Emil von Behringstrasse 8
D-6085 Nauheim, Germany

Casper de Groot
Dept. for General Linguistics
University of Amsterdam
Spuistraat 210
1012 VT Amsterdam
The Netherlands

Robert Early
Linguistics, RSPacS
Australian National University
GPO Box 4
Canberra, ACT 2601
Australia

Margaret Hartzler
P.O. Box 54
Jayapura, Irian Jaya
Indonesia

Cheryl Jensen
Ag. Guanabara
C. P. 381
67013-970 Belém, PA
Brazil

Peter Kahrel
Dept. for General Linguistics
University of Amsterdam
Spuistraat 210
1012 VT Amsterdam
The Netherlands

Sylvia Kouwenberg
Dept. of Linguistics
University of the West Indies
Mona, Kingston 7
Jamaica

Myles Leitch
B. P. 12
Impfondo
République Populaire de Congo

Igor Nedyalkov
Institut Jazykoznanija AN SSSR
Tuchkov pereulok 9
199053 St Petersburg
Russia

Catherine Peeke
270 Ollie Weaver Road
Weaverville NC 28787
USA

Gerjan van Schaaik
Kampstraat 12
3714 AR Baarn
The Netherlands

Pius N. Tamanji
Dept. of African Languages and Linguistics
University of Yaounde
P.O. Box 8029
Yaounde
Cameroon

Helen Weir
SAI/NO, Lote D, Bloco 3
70770-730 Brasilia - DF
Brazil

Jeroen Wiedenhof
Sinological Institute
Leiden University
P.O. Box 9515
2300 RA Leiden
The Netherlands

In the TYPOLOGICAL STUDIES IN LANGUAGE (TSL) series the following volumes have been published thus far and will be published during 1994:

1. HOPPER, Paul (ed.): *TENSE-ASPECT: BETWEEN SEMANTICS & PRAGMATICS*. Amsterdam/Philadelphia, 1982.
2. HAIMAN, John & Pam MUNRO (eds): *PROCEEDINGS OF A SYMPOSIUM ON SWITCH REFERENCE, Winnipeg, May 1981*. Amsterdam/Philadelphia, 1983.
3. GIVÓN, T. (ed.): *TOPIC CONTINUITY IN DISCOURSE: A QUANTITATIVE CROSS-LANGUAGE STUDY*. Amsterdam/Philadelphia, 1983.
4. CHISHOLM, William, Louis T. MILIC & John GREPPIN (eds): *INTERROGATIVITY: A COLLOQUIUM ON THE GRAMMAR, TYPOLOGY AND PRAGMATICS OF QUESTIONS IN SEVEN DIVERSE LANGUAGES, Cleveland, Ohio, October 5th 1981 - May 3rd 1982*. Amsterdam/Philadelphia, 1984.
5. RUTHERFORD, William E. (ed.): *LANGUAGE UNIVERSALS AND SECOND LANGUAGE ACQUISITION*. Amsterdam/Philadelphia, 1984. 2nd edition 1987.
6 HAIMAN, John (ed.): *ICONICITY IN SYNTAX. Proceedings of a Symposium on Iconicity in Syntax, Stanford, June 24-6, 1983*. Amsterdam/Philadelphia, 1985.
7. CRAIG, Colette (ed.): *NOUN CLASSES AND CATEGORIZATION. Proceedings of a Symposium on Categorization and Noun Classification, Eugene, Ore. October 1983*. Amsterdam/Philadelphia, 1986.
8. SLOBIN, Dan I. & Karl ZIMMER (eds): *STUDIES IN TURKISH LINGUISTICS*. Amsterdam/Philadelphia, 1986.
9. BYBEE, Joan L.: *Morphology. A Study of the Relation between Meaning and Form*. Amsterdam/Philadelphia, 1985.
10. RANSOM, Evelyn: *Complementation: its Meanings and Forms*. Amsterdam/Philadelphia, 1986.
11. TOMLIN, Russ (ed.): *COHERENCE AND GROUNDING IN DISCOURSE*. Outcome of a Symposium on -, Eugene, Ore, June 1984. Amsterdam/Philadelphia, 1987.
12. NEDJALKOV, Vladimir P. (ed.): *TYPOLOGY OF RESULTATIVE CONSTRUCTIONS*. Translated from the original Russian edition publ. by "Nauka", Leningrad, 1983, English translation edited by Bernard Comrie. Amsterdam/Philadelphia, 1988.
14. HINDS, John, Senko MAYNARD & Shoichi IWASAKI (eds): *PERSPECTIVES ON TOPICALIZATION: The Case of Japanese 'WA'*. Amsterdam/Philadelphia, 1987.
15. AUSTIN, Peter (ed.): *COMPLEX SENTENCE CONSTRUCTIONS IN AUSTRALIAN LANGUAGES*. Amsterdam/Philadelphia, 1987.
16. SHIBATANI, Masayoshi (ed.): *PASSIVE AND VOICE*. Amsterdam/Philadelphia, 1988.
17. HAMMOND, Michael, Edith A. MORAVCSIK & Jessica R. WIRTH (eds): *STUDIES IN SYNTACTIC TYPOLOGY*. Amsterdam/Philadelphia, 1988.
18. HAIMAN, John & Sandra A. THOMPSON (eds): *CLAUSE COMBINING IN GRAMMAR AND DISCOURSE*. Amsterdam/Philadelphia, 1988.
19. TRAUGOTT, Elizabeth C. & Bernd HEINE (eds): *APPROACHES TO GRAMMATICALIZATION. 2 volumes*. Amsterdam/Philadelphia, 1991.
20. CROFT, William, Keith DENNING & Suzanne KEMMER (eds): *STUDIES IN TYPOLOGY AND DIACHRONY. Papers presented to Joseph H. Greenberg on his 75th birthday*. Amsterdam/Philadelphia, 1990.
21. DOWNING, Pamela, Susan D. LIMA & Michael NOONAN (eds): *THE LINGUISTICS OF LITERACY*. Amsterdam/Philadelphia, 1992.
22. PAYNE, Doris (ed.): *PRAGMATICS OF WORD ORDER FLEXIBILITY*. Amsterdam/Philadelphia, 1992.

23. KEMMER, Suzanne: *THE MIDDLE VOICE*. Amsterdam/Philadelphia, 1993.
24. PERKINS, Revere D.: *DEIXIS, GRAMMAR, AND CULTURE*. Amsterdam/ Philadelphia, 1992.
25. SVOROU, Soteria: *THE GRAMMAR OF SPACE*. Amsterdam/Philadelphia, 1994.
26. LORD, Carol: *HISTORICAL CHANGE IN SERIAL VERB CONSTRUCTIONS*. Amsterdam/Philadelphia, 1993.
27. FOX, Barbara & Paul J. HOPPER (eds): *VOICE: FORM AND FUNCTION*. Amsterdam/Philadelphia, 1994.
28. GIVÓN, T. (ed.): *VOICE AND INVERSION*. Amsterdam/Philadelphia, n.y.p.
29. KAHREL, Peter & René van den BERG (eds): *TYPOLOGICAL STUDIES IN NEGATION*. Amsterdam/Philadelphia, 1994.